T0384379

CHAIN OF FIRE

CHAIN OF FIRE

CAMPAIGNING IN EGYPT
AND THE SUDAN, 1882–98

PETER HART

Profile Books

First published in Great Britain in 2025 by
Profile Books Ltd
29 Cloth Fair
London
ECIA 7JQ
www.profilebooks.com

1 3 5 7 9 10 8 6 4 2

Typeset in Dante by MacGuru Ltd
Printed and bound in Great Britain by
CPI Group (UK) Ltd, Croydon CR0 4YY

A CIP catalogue record for this book is available from the British Library.

ISBN 978 1 80081 073 0
eISBN 978 1 80081 075 4

CONTENTS

MAPS

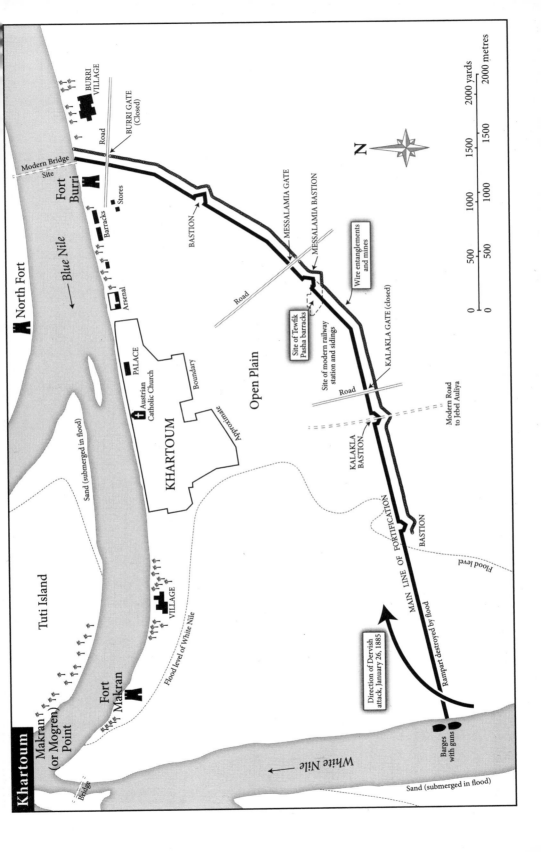

Khartoum

BURRI VILLAGE

BURRI GATE (Closed)

Road

Modern Bridge Site

Fort Burri

Stores

Barracks

BASTION

Arsenal

PALACE

Austrian Catholic Church

KHARTOUM

Boundary

Approximate

MESSALAMIA GATE

MESSALAMIA BASTION

Road

Wire entanglements and mines

Site of Tewfik Pasha barracks

Site of modern railway station and sidings

KALAKLA GATE (closed)

Road

Modern Road to Jebel Auliya

KALAKLA BASTION

Open Plain

BASTION

MAIN LINE OF FORTIFICATION

Direction of Dervish attack, January 26, 1885

Rampart destroyed by flood

Flood level

Barges with guns

White Nile

Sand (submerged in flood)

Bridge

Fort Makran

VILLAGE

Flood level of White Nile

Tuti Island

Sand (submerged in flood)

Blue Nile

North Fort

Makran (or Mogren) Point

N

0   500   1000   1500   2000 yards
0   500   1000   1500   2000 metres

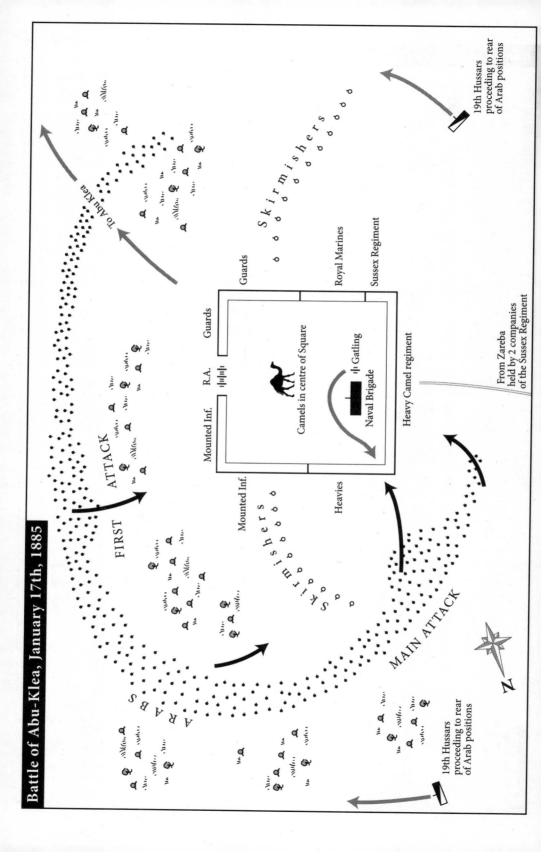

Battle of Abu-Klea, January 17th, 1885

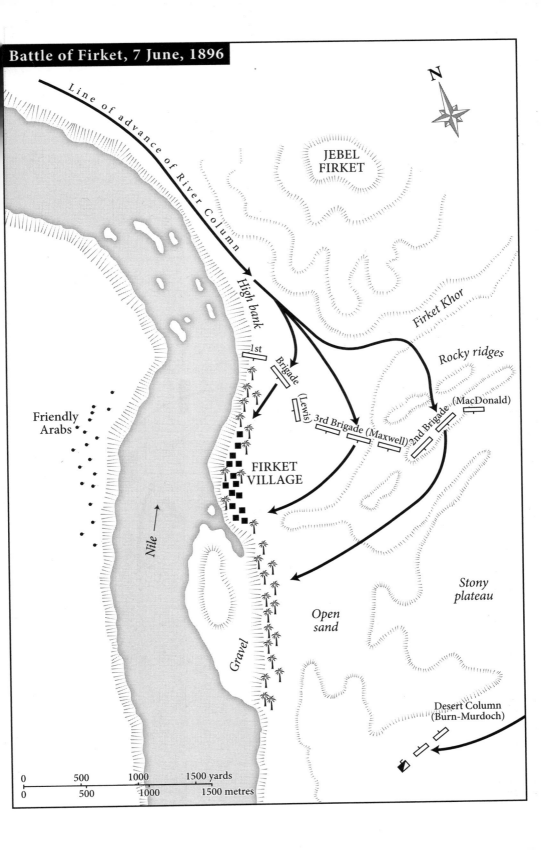

Battle of Firket, 7 June, 1896

N

Line of advance of River Column

JEBEL FIRKET

Firket Khor

High bank

Rocky ridges

1st

Brigade

(Lewis)

(MacDonald)

3rd Brigade (Maxwell)

2nd Brigade

Friendly Arabs

FIRKET VILLAGE

Nile

Stony plateau

Open sand

Gravel

Desert Column (Burn-Murdoch)

0	500	1000	1500 yards
0	500	1000	1500 metres

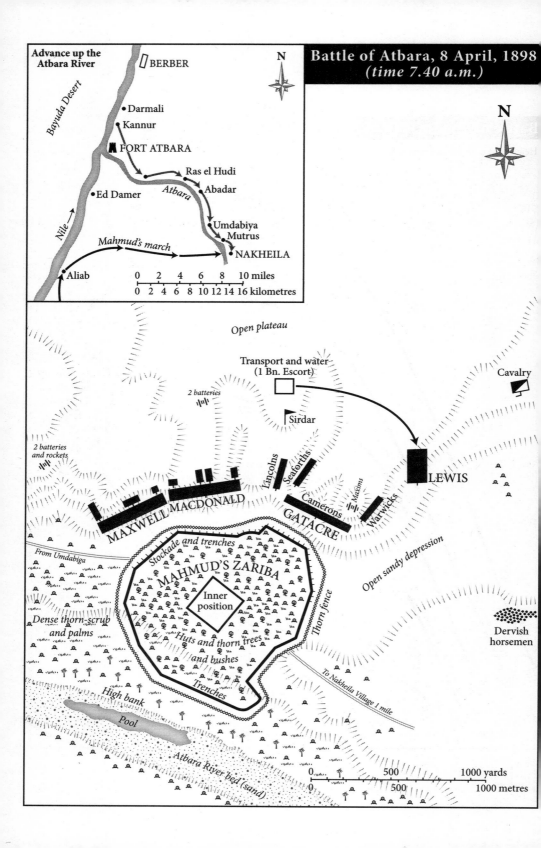

Battle of Atbara, 8 April, 1898
(time 7.40 a.m.)

Advance up the Atbara River

N

BERBER

Bayuda Desert

Darmali
Kannur
FORT ATBARA
Ras el Hudi
Abadar
Ed Damer
Atbara
Nile
Umdabiya
Mutrus
NAKHEILA
Mahmud's march
Aliab

| 0 | 2 | 4 | 6 | 8 | 10 miles |
| 0 | 2 4 6 8 10 12 14 16 kilometres |

N

Open plateau

Transport and water
(1 Bn. Escort)

Cavalry

2 batteries

Sirdar

2 batteries
and rockets

Lincolns
Seaforths
LEWIS
MAXWELL MACDONALD
Camerons
Maxims
Warwicks
GATACRE

From Umdabiga

Stockade and trenches

MAHMUD'S ZARIBA

Inner position

Open sandy depression

Thorn fence

Dense thorn-scrub
and palms

Huts and thorn trees
and bushes

Dervish horsemen

Trenches

To Nakheila Village 1 mile

High bank

Pool

Atbara River bed (sand)

| 0 | 500 | 1000 yards |
| 0 | 500 | 1000 metres |

Battle of Omdurman, 2 September, 1898, first phase

Heights are in feet above river level on 2 September, 1898

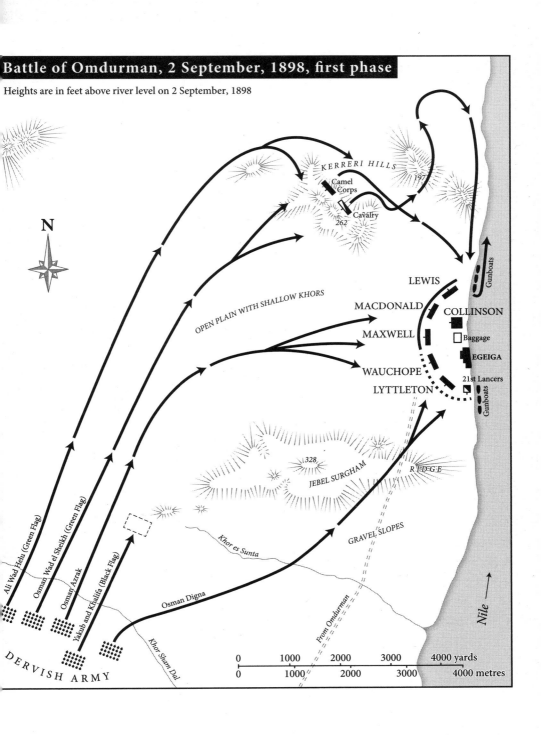

N

KERRERI HILLS

197

Camel Corps

Cavalry

262

Gunboats

LEWIS

OPEN PLAIN WITH SHALLOW KHORS

MACDONALD

COLLINSON

MAXWELL

Baggage

EGEIGA

WAUCHOPE

21st Lancers

LYTTLETON

Gunboats

328

JEBEL SURGHAM

RIDGE

Khor es Sunta

GRAVEL SLOPES

Ali Wad Helu (Green Flag)

Osman Wad el Sheikh (Green Flag)

Osman Azrak

Yakub and Khalifa (Black Flag)

Osman Digna

From Omdurman

Nile

Khor Shau Dal

DERVISH ARMY

| 0 | 1000 | 2000 | 3000 | 4000 yards |
| 0 | 1000 | 2000 | 3000 | 4000 metres |

Battle of Omdurman, 2 September, 1898, second phase

Heights are in feet above river level on 2 September, 1898

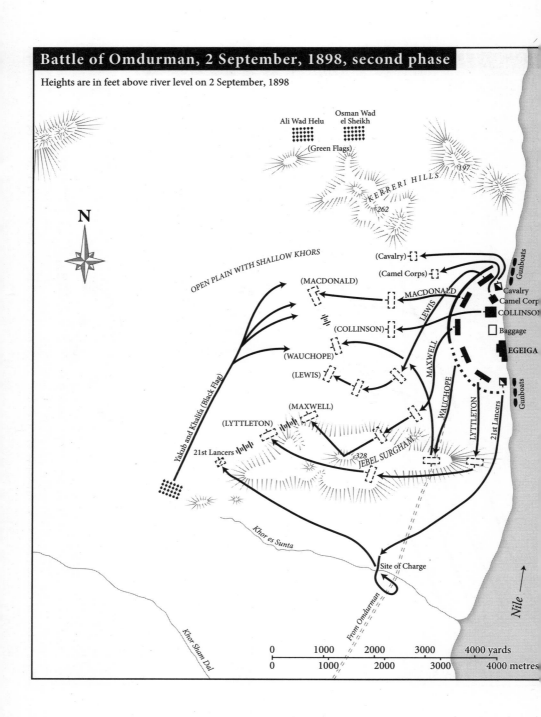

Battle of Omdurman, 2 September, 1898, third phase

Heights are in feet above river level on 2 September, 1898

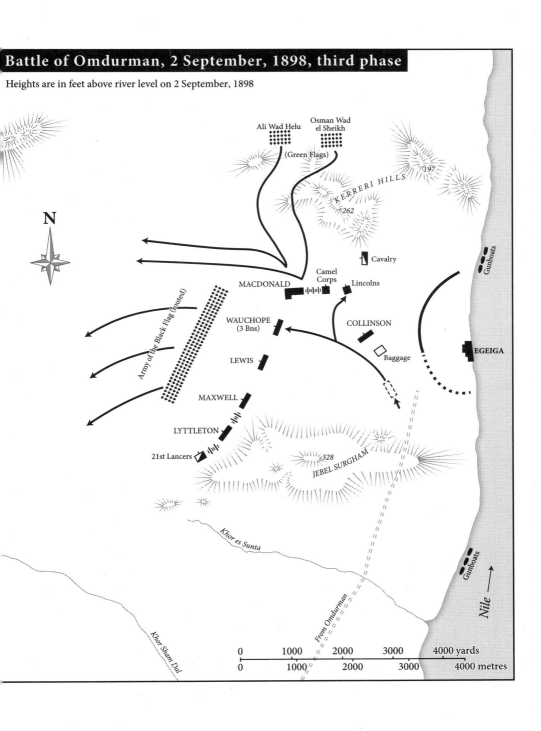

PREFACE

My fascination is with the thoughts and words of the men who face the trials of armed conflict at its worst. The Egyptian and Sudan campaigns of 1882–98 feature some of the most gripping accounts I have ever encountered. The terrain is spectacular, with its backdrop of wild deserts and the Nile River winding in and out of our story. I have made a particular effort to use the voices of officers who attained high rank in the Great War just sixteen years later – some of whom are obvious, like Winston Churchill and Herbert Kitchener, but also those such as David Beatty, Douglas Haig, Ian Hamilton, Henry Rawlinson, Horace Smith-Dorrien and Charles Townshend. These senior officers were not born old in 1914; they too had been young men, strong and virile, but often showing the military qualities that marked them out for future greatness. We now know who won each nerve-jangling battle. At the time the participants of course did not, and they often feared for their lives.

I think it unlikely that certain incidents, not fully understood or contentious at the time, can ever now be understood. All we can do is to suggest what probably happened. Men were lost in the chaos of battle, with smoke all around, their view blocked by comrades, camels and assailants, the last of which, not unnaturally, demanded most of their attention. It is not surprising that their stories sometimes differ in detail. In the years covered here there were too many battles, so I have tried to bring out different perspectives and to concentrate on those that drive forward our narrative. The political background – a complex subject that has filled hundreds of pages in too many books – is only sketched in.

I have throughout used the most common of the – many – British versions of Egyptian and Sudanese placenames. I have also, after a period of inner wrangling, decided for the most part to use the term 'Dervishes' for the brave men of the Mahdist armies. I am aware that 'Ansar' would be a more appropriate collective term, and that Dervish is a misnomer. Yet this is the term almost universally used in contemporaneous accounts, so I have opted for simplicity. Nor have I censored – and hence softened – some of the terrible racist terms occasionally used within quoted accounts. We should not 'wash it away' by pretending it never happened. Finally, I have dropped British honorifics such as 'Sir', unless within quotes, as they add nothing to our understanding.

There is no doubt that combatants on both sides behaved reprehensibly on the battlefields of 1882–98. But as many readers of this book will be British, this book may well provoke the question: are we the baddies? I do not intend to throw mud at men who for the most part were acting according to the prevalent belief systems of the time, but only to point out when their attitudes and actions might be seen as unacceptable from our perspective. In a sense, this is nothing more than a sop to our feelings, as we read sometimes chastening accounts of British imperialism, arrogance, racist bigotry, brutality and downright murder. Although in a sense we must accept that such behaviour is wrong, at the same time we need to try to understand that this occurred more than a hundred years ago when the world was a very different place. Or was it? Humankind is still riven by nationalism, imperialism and religious extremism around the world – especially in the Sudan – one of the most dangerous places on the earth.

THE REASON WHY

'When Allah made the Sudan,' say the Arabs, 'he laughed!'
You can almost hear the fiendish echo of it crackling over
the fiery sand.[1]
George Steevens, *Daily Mail*

EGYPT WAS AN ANOMALY WITHIN THE BRITISH EMPIRE, a land of
desert sands, soaked with the blood of past conflicts, full of
history, but with few apparent economic resources to be har-
vested. The irony was that originally the British had no wish
to take on Egypt as a fully fledged colony, preferring to leave
it to be controlled by the local ruler – the Khedive – under the
vague suzerainty of the Turkish Sultan. Unfortunately, in his
efforts to modernise Egypt, not wishing to be left behind other
nation states, the then Khedive, Ismail Pasha, borrowed copious
amounts of money from abroad, particularly from the British
and French governments. Much of the money was spent on
infrastructure projects – such as railways, bridges, canals, har-
bours, docks, telegraph communications, the sugar refining
industry – but a fair amount was also squandered on the pur-
chase of estates and the building of extravagant palaces. Soon
the Egyptians found themselves in a spiralling circle of debt,
with minimal prospect of the modernisations paying for themselves any time soon.

By 1875, ruin beckoned, and in desperation Ismail Pasha
sold off perhaps his greatest asset, the shares held in the Suez
Canal, conceived and constructed as a joint venture between the
Egyptian Government and the French-led Suez Canal Company.

Now, for just over £4 million, the British gained nearly 50 per cent of the shares, and the preservation of the route through the canal became an absolute priority of British foreign policy. For the Khedive the money raised was but a drop in the ocean of debt. His financial troubles resulted in the establishment of the *Caisse de la Dette Publique* in 1876. This committee represented the direct intervention by creditor European nations to investigate the Egyptian economy from top to bottom, including debt consolidation or restructuring, with the overall intent of creating an achievable repayment programme for the international debts. Although other countries were involved, the committee was dominated by British and French interests, with Evelyn Baring appointed as the British controller. The Khedive soon found his every move hedged in by this system of 'Dual Control'.

Ismail chafed under the restrictions imposed on his rule, and was soon intriguing to create trouble that would 'prove' the failure of 'Dual Control'. In 1879, after a period of turmoil, Ismail was deposed and replaced as Khedive by his son, the far more pliable Mehmet Tewfik. Yet more serious problems were bubbling beneath the surface in Egypt as the masses struggled with endemic poverty, exacerbated by a punitive tax system. All this encouraged a burgeoning Egyptian nationalistic consciousness, with unrest directed at both the Khedive and the Europeans.

One of the most influential figures in this movement was Colonel Ahmed Arabi, who, although routinely denigrated in contemporary British accounts, possessed a strength of purpose that channelled the widespread popular unrest into an effective military-led revolt against Tewfik on 9 September 1881. Unable for the moment to withstand the nationalist demands, Tewfik was forced to concede the establishment of a new chamber of deputies including several of the nationalist sympathisers. Ominously, from a certain perspective, work started on strengthening the Egyptian Army and coastal defences. The portents were obvious – this could be a threat to the control of the Suez Canal. Britain would never officially condone espionage, but in January 1882, Major Alexander Tulloch decided to investigate on his own account, combining a bit of freelance spying with shooting game. The Egyptians proved to be charming hosts, tolerant to a fault of his covert activities, which, as even Tulloch admitted, were certainly close to the knuckle.

> On one occasion I thought the chief of the staff was lifting the curtain rather too high, so I said to him plainly, 'You must not tell me too much! You and I may be on opposite platforms before long!' He laughed, saying, 'When I am abroad, I keep my eyes open, and I guess you do the same!' To sum up: I was able in my report to give not only a full detailed account of everything connected with the army – its guns, arms, stores, magazines, factories, what was on order in Europe, and what their scheme of defence was: I was also able to examine and give an account of the state of the forts at Alexandria, and along the coast, with the nature and number of their guns, etc. I managed to get an excellent French map of the Delta, which was of great use to me in reporting on the military value of the railways, the Cairo, Ismailia, and Suez fresh-water canal.[2]
> Major Alexander Tulloch, Welsh Regiment

The growing threats to the authority of the Khedive became too much for the British and French, who most of all craved stability and security for their investments in Egypt. On 8 January 1882 they sent a joint diplomatic note, which not only asserted the overall power of the Khedive but pledged to support him against all his enemies. This was a slap in the face and direct warning to the new parliamentarians and certainly to Arabi, who rejected the whole idea of foreign intervention. As the warnings were not immediately backed up by force, this merely triggered a new even more nationalistically flavoured line-up of politicians, including the appointment of Arabi as minister of war in May 1882. The first Anglo-French actions were tokenistic as they sent warships, that staple of imperial diplomacy, to take up position in Alexandria harbour and to cruise off the Egyptian coast. By this time both the Khedive and Arabi were appealing for support from the nominal ruler of Egypt, Sultan Abdul Hamid II. The response could have been predicted: the Sultan rejected the idea of deploying troops against fellow Muslims who, after all, were merely opposing the sanctions of foreign – and nominally Christian – governments; but he also hesitated to depose the Khedive who was so clearly supported by the British and French. Here was a man with little to gain and a lot to lose, whichever side he took.

That summer, the streets of Alexandria were filled with rumours of a 'reckoning' and threats of slaughter in the streets for the European population. On the afternoon of 11 June 1882 the situation exploded into a vicious riot. Soon there were massed crowds numbered in thousands rampaging through the streets. All the smouldering grievances burst to the surface in an orgy of violence and destruction. Maltese- and Greek-owned businesses were targeted, with crowds reported to be chanting, 'Death to the Christians!' European consulates were attacked and the British consul was badly wounded, only just escaping with his life. The Egyptian police and soldiers did little or nothing to intervene, some even joining in, and overall it was evident where their sympathies lay. An estimated fifty Europeans were killed, with great damage to property and businesses across the city.

Admiral Beauchamp Seymour, the commander in chief of the Mediterranean Fleet, did not land his men to intervene directly ashore, doubtless aware of the underlying hesitations of the Prime Minister William Gladstone's Liberal government, which wanted to avoid a war with Egypt. Although the riots died down by nightfall, after the belated intervention of a regiment of Arabi's soldiers, they had caused panic among the surviving Europeans who feared a resumption at any moment.

As a matter of urgency, Tulloch had been attached as a military liaison officer to Seymour's staff aboard the temporary flagship *Invincible*; indeed, after the riots his earlier reports were printed as a War Office memorandum. Tulloch had a first-hand view of the prevarications of the Gladstone government and a low-key first encounter with Herbert Kitchener, a man who will be central to our story. Although definitely not considering himself to be Irish, Kitchener, the son of army officer, was born in County Kerry on 24 June 1850. He volunteered to serve with a French field ambulance unit during the Franco-Prussian War, before being commissioned into the Royal Engineers in 1871. He had carried out notable surveying and mapping work with the Palestine Exploration Fund, during which period he had become fluent in Arabic. More mapping and survey work followed in Cyprus before he saw the opportunity for action.

> All this time our politicals and the admiral were in constant telegraphic communication with the government at home, whose motto seemed to be, 'Peace at any price!' We saw clearly enough what it would all end in, but the government were apparently of the same mind as the proverbial ostrich. One morning when I was engaged writing on board the *Invincible*, a tall thin subaltern of engineers named Kitchener came to see me: he had got a few days' leave from his general at Cyprus, and as he could speak Arabic, had come to see if he could be of any use to me. 'Certainly!' I replied.[3]
> Major Alexander Tulloch, HMS *Invincible*

From the ships they could see the Egyptians making further preparations – or from their point of view, precautions – in case of war. It was soon evident that the now *de facto* head of government, Arabi, was well aware of Tulloch's previous activities as an amateur spy.

> Arabi's preparations in mounting more guns and adding to the parapets of his batteries could not be allowed to go on, so he got a letter from the admiral that the preparations against us must cease. To this he replied he was really not aware more guns were being mounted, &c., and would

stop it at once; that he was not well acquainted with the
armaments of the forts, but if the admiral wished for information about them, he should ask Major Tulloch, because
Major Tulloch really knew far more about the forts than
he, Arabi, did.[4]

Major Alexander Tulloch, HMS *Invincible*

Tulloch was evidently pleased at such a professional compliment from his adversary.

Back in England, there was an outcry at the attacks on
British civilians under the very guns of the fleet. Gladstone's
government had decided to postpone demands for reparations
until the bulk of the vulnerable European civilians had been
evacuated. The politicians in London were still pondering their
exact course of action, but the threat to the Suez Canal proved
impossible for them to ignore. There was also the question of
the safety of British commercial investments in the region. It
was almost impossible to secure the safety of the canal without
taking Cairo, as the Egyptians could not be left in control of
the Ismailia canal or railways. Furthermore, if the nationalists
were not toppled in one swift, crunching blow, then the British
government would have to finance a permanent Suez defence
force at doubtless vast expense. From a military point of view,
it was necessary to prepare for a military expedition to 'restore
order'. Hence the recently appointed adjutant general, Lieutenant General Garnet Wolseley, as the designated commander
in chief of any future expedition, was busy undertaking the
practical preparations for the despatch of an army corps of two
divisions to Egypt, totalling some 24,000 men with the associ-
ated transport.

Wolseley was acclaimed as the greatest soldier of the age; he
was born in Dublin on 4 June 1833 to a military family and was
commissioned into the 12th Foot in 1852. He transferred to the
80th Foot and had early service in the Second Anglo-Burmese
War where he was wounded in 1853. He was again wounded
– twice – in the Crimean War in 1855, including losing an eye,

before serving during the Indian Mutiny of 1857. A series of important postings followed and as he was promoted to major general in 1877, he had become to the British public 'the very model of a modern major general' as immortalised in song by Gilbert and Sullivan's 1879 comic opera *The Pirates of Penzance*. There was even a popular expression 'Everything's all Sir Garnet!' meaning, 'All is in order!'

Now Wolseley was pondering the various tactical options open to him in the event of war. One approach was to land near Alexandria and advance from there via the Nile to Cairo and he therefore signalled to Tulloch asking him to investigate the feasibility of this route. As a result of his prior investigations, Tulloch himself favoured a landing at Ismailia near the mouth of the Suez Canal for the advance to Cairo, but he felt honour bound to check out the Alexandria route as requested, using the railway which was still open. It would prove a dangerous mission, as Tulloch was a marked man.

I decided to go up the line in disguise. The admiral did not at all like the risk of my doing so, but I said I considered it a matter of duty, so arranged to slip into the Suez train with the mail passengers next afternoon, got up as a Levantine official. I did not like cutting off my naval beard, and rather amused Kitchener by saying, as I brushed it out before clipping it for shaving, 'Well, "K", I wonder if this also' – pointing to my throat – 'will be cut today!' When a reconnaissance has to be made, there should always be at least two, to give a chance of one getting back with the required information; so 'K' went with me in the same train. He, like the rest of the passengers, was safe enough, but I knew that if recognised I should not get far. Arrived at Kaffir Zyat, I made out that I was suddenly so overcome with a painful complaint I must return for special medical advice to Alexandria; but when 'K', who remained to help the invalid, inquired about the exact time our train would leave, it was decidedly unpleasant to find that our expected return train had been taken off, and that there was but one more train to come that evening. It was the last run by the European administration and brought the few remaining English from Cairo. I thought it advisable to keep out of sight as much as possible until the train arrived and got a couch in a room in the station-master's house. Having plenty of cigarettes, I was comfortable enough. When the train came in, I saw one of the Europeans recognised me, but a quick sign was sufficient. The invalid and his companion had a carriage to themselves. Arabi's people soon heard about my little trip. Seven days afterwards a fair-complexioned Syrian was noticed in the train at Kaffir Zyat: he was taken out of the train under the impression that he was a European doing my work, and his throat cut on the platform. I doubt if Sir Garnet ever knew the risk I ran to get and wire him the information he required.[5]

Major Alexander Tulloch, HMS *Invincible*

Wolseley came up with a far-seeing plan for the campaign even before the formal outbreak of hostilities. He resolved to advance from Ismailia, using the railway lines to ease his transport requirements.

Meanwhile the Egyptians covertly intensified their attempts to strengthen the defences of Alexandria against the threat posed by the Anglo-French squadrons. They brought in more guns, built up the battery parapets and earthworks, and prepared measures to block the entrance of the harbour. In negotiations with Admiral Seymour, they promised to comply with his demands to desist, but every night, under cover of darkness, they resumed the works. Finally, Seymour had had enough of being ignored and on 10 July he issued a 24-hour ultimatum.

As hostile preparations, evidently directed against the squadron under my command, were in progress during yesterday at Forts Isali, Pharos, and Silsileh, I shall carry out the intention expressed to you in my letter of the

6th instant, at sunrise to-morrow, the 11th instant, unless previous to that hour you shall have temporarily surrendered to me, for the purpose of disarming, the batteries on the isthmus of Ras el Tin and the southern shore of the harbour of Alexandria. [6]

Admiral Beauchamp Seymour, Mediterranean Fleet

In the topsy-turvy world of nineteenth-century imperialism, preparing to defend one's port from a possible foreign invasion was clearly an aggressive act. The reply Seymour received offered to suspend the mounting of any further guns, but this was rejected out of hand. The forts *must* be disarmed. Now it came to the crunch, the Anglo-French accord fractured, as the French government ordered Admiral Conrad, commanding the French squadron, not to cooperate with the British fleet in the event of force being used to prevent the work on the batteries. The French squadron withdrew to take up station off Port Said. It would be war, but the Royal Navy would fight alone.

2

THE BOMBARDMENT OF ALEXANDRIA

It is not often one gets a chance of such a perfect view of an engagement without any risk. I thought the Egyptians showed a great deal of pluck. Until their heavy guns were actually capsized or disabled, they made a very good fight of it. They had, in reality, no chance of success from the very commencement, as only a few of their guns could penetrate the armour-plates of the ironclads, even under the most favourable circumstances, and all of these were very soon disabled.[1]

Captain Arthur Wilson, HMS *Hecla*

THIS WAS NOT A FAIR FIGHT. The Egyptian defences, so condemned by Admiral Beauchamp Seymour in his reports to the Admiralty, were no real threat to the massed guns of the Royal Navy. Alexandria was on a strip of land between the Mediterranean and Lake Mariût, with its old eastern port divided into an inner and outer harbour, and a new western port. Defending it were a string of forts, based on French fortifications, which were by this time somewhat dilapidated and, being constructed of soft limestone, could not withstand modern artillery fire. The parapets were often just sand covered with a veneer of cement, while the gun emplacements had no overhead cover, leaving the gun detachments vulnerable to shellfire. The guns were a mixture of a few relatively modern muzzle-loaded rifled Armstrong guns varying from 7- to 10-inch, less effective old smoothbore guns from 6.5- to 15-inch and a number of heavy mortars.

The British squadron that would assail them on 11 July 1882 was composed of the battleships *Alexandra, Superb, Sultan, Téméraire, Inflexible, Monarch, Invincible* and *Penelope*. They were accompanied by a torpedo boat, the *Hecla*, a despatch boat, the *Helicon*, the gun vessels *Condor* and *Bittern* and the gunboats *Beacon, Cygnet* and *Decoy*. To an eye more accustomed to Nelson's 'wooden walls', typified by the *Victory*, or the dreadnoughts of the Great War, the ironclads looked somewhat eccentric, with their mixture of central batteries and large turrets, reflecting the turmoil in warship design at that period. But they were armed with batteries of powerful modern guns and defended by thick armour, which was all but impervious to the Egyptian shells. Ships can sink, whereas forts cannot, but the Egyptians would be reliant on lucky shots to cause any real damage. The Royal Navy had the capacity to hit hard with relative impunity, barring misfortune. But then, nothing in war is ever certain.

For the attack, Seymour divided his forces into two: at 09.40, the *Sultan, Superb, Téméraire* and *Inflexible* would take up station outside the breakwater, taking on the defences of the Ras el Tin peninsula, especially the Lighthouse Fort which covered the entrance to the inner harbour. Once this had been achieved, *Sultan, Superb* and *Alexandra* were to assail Forts Pharos and Silsileh covering the new eastern harbour, while the *Téméraire* engaged Fort Marabout. Meanwhile the *Invincible, Monarch* and *Penelope* would move inside the outer harbour to batter Fort Mex.

That night, as soon as it was dark, we put out all lights, and we – that is, the *Invincible*, the *Monarch*, and *Penelope* – steamed quietly down past the shore batteries and took up our prearranged positions opposite Fort Mex. This was the enemy's strongest fort: the thick sand parapet well covered the heavy armament, consisting of, to the best of my recollection, two Armstrong 18-ton guns, three 12-ton Armstrongs, six heavy 9-inch (100 lb.) smooth-bores, and several smooth-bore 36-pounders; there were also three heavy mortars. The magazine of the fort was well covered,

and in rear, on a slight rise, was a massive masonry citadel, with smaller (40-pounder) Armstrong and smooth-bores (36-pounders). Along the front of the fort was a rocky fore-shore, and behind one flank a small-boat harbour.[2]
Major Alexander Tulloch, HMS *Invincible*

During the battle Tulloch took station in the maintop alongside a 1-inch Nordenfelt, where he had an outstanding view of the action as it unfolded. He was impressed by the way the Egyptian garrison stuck to their guns despite the torrent of fire pouring into their positions.

The enemy's gunners, considering the tremendous fire we poured into the Mex Fort, made uncommonly good shoot-ing, our waterline being apparently their special target. Placed as I was, I could see their projectiles strike the water some yards off, and then shoot along under the surface; but by the time they touched the ship their force was gone. Having abnormally good sight, I often noticed the enemy's shot coming towards us, just like cricket-balls. My compan-ion in the top, Hardy, not having been under fire before, bobbed occasionally when the shot came close. I began chaffing him – when a thing like a railway train rushed past! He had then the laugh on his side. I could not help stagger-ing back: it must have been a shell from one of the 18-ton guns, and very close to us, as it cut the signal-halliards.[3]
Major Alexander Tulloch, HMS *Invincible*

Although the thick armour plate protected the ships' vitals, the unarmoured sections suffered damage. Yet the Egyptian forts were being pounded. A couple of fort magazines were deto-nated, some of the heavy rifled guns were dismounted and rendered useless. But still the Egyptians fought on.

Charles Beresford had been promoted to captain a few days earlier. Here his role commanding the *Condor*, a gun vessel armed with just one 7-inch gun and two 40-pounder guns, was to act as a 'repeating ship' to pass on signals between the ships during the action. However, he was soon called into action to assist the *Téméraire*, which had run aground. As he did so, he became very concerned at the flanking fire at the inshore squadron emanating from the two 10-inch rifled guns based at Fort Marabout.

I ran down to her and towed her off and while doing so, saw Fort Marabout giving pepper to *Monarch, Invincible* and *Penelope*. Not one of these ships could be spared, as they were getting it hot and could not spare a gun for Marabout from the forts they were engaging. Seeing the difficulty, directly I had got the *Téméraire* afloat I steamed down at full speed and engaged Fort Marabout, on the principle that according to orders 'an opportunity' had occurred. I thought we should have a real rough time of it, as I knew of the heavy guns, and I knew that one shot fairly placed must sink us. But I hoped to be able to dodge the shoals, of which there were many, and get close in, when I was quite sure they would fire over us. That is exactly what occurred. I got in close and manoeuvred the ship on the angle of the fort, so that the heavy guns could hardly bear on me, if I was very careful. The smooth bores rained on us, but only two shots hit, the rest went short or over. One heavy shot struck the water about 6 feet from the ship, wetting everyone on the upper deck with spray, and bounded over us in a ricochet. I did not fire on the smoothbores at all until I had silenced the heavy guns which were annoying *Invincible, Monarch*, and *Penelope*. The men fired splendidly. I put all down to the lectures I have given them at target practice, telling them never to throw a shot away, but always to wait until they got the sights on. The admiral, instead of making, 'Recall *Condor!*' made, 'Well done, *Condor!*' at the suggestion of Hedworth Lambton, the flag-lieutenant. We then remained there 2½ hours, and had silenced the fort all except one gun, when the signal was made to all

the other small craft to assist *Condor*, and down they came
and pegged away. I was not sorry, as the men were getting
a bit beat.[4]
Captain Charles Beresford, HMS *Condor*

At about 14.00 the Egyptians were forced to abandon the lower
western battery of Fort Mex to shelter in the nearby citadel.
However, the guns themselves seemed intact and there were
fears that the garrison could return and reopen fire. Seymour
decided to send a volunteer shore party from the *Invincible* under
the command of Lieutenant Barton Bradford and Lieutenant
Hedworth Lambton to spike the guns. Accompanying the party
was the ubiquitous Tulloch. As they approached the shore, they
were covered by Nordenfelt fire from the gunboats.

When we got to some of the outlying rocks we stopped
steaming, and then, as the day was very hot and the water
looked inviting, I thought a swim would be very pleasant,
so, sword in hand, slung myself overboard. I was rather
out of breath on getting ashore, but managed to scuttle up
a small breach made by our fire. When half-way up I put
my foot in a shell-hole and came on my nose: the squadron, looking on, thought I was shot. I got to the crest of
the parapet, when, instead of black fellows, whom I hoped
to frighten into fits by a ferocious display of the regulation sword exercise, I found the fort was empty. If there
were any men in the citadel, they thought that with the
gunboats so close in they had better lie low. A guncotton
charge was put into the muzzle of one of the 18-ton guns,
a wire attached, and we all scrambled over the parapet,
lying down outside. The guncotton did not injure the gun,
so another method was tried. A charge was put between
the cheeks of the carriage; then we took shelter as before.
The carriage was found to be destroyed, and the gun dismounted. The commander of one of the gunboats told me
afterwards that bits of the gun carriage had gone out over

our heads to sea and cut his rigging. Whilst Bradford was attending to the other big gun, Lambton, the gunner, and I raced off with the hammer and bag of nails to spike the great smoothbores, which we did. I found one man had taken shelter under the first great gun I went for, but as he did not show signs of fight, we left him alone where he was. All this work was rapidly done, and then we decided that the sooner we were on board our cutter again the better![5]

Major Alexander Tulloch, HMS *Invincible*

Together they had destroyed two 10-inch rifled guns and six smoothbore guns.

One by one the forts fell silent, and at 17.15 Seymour ordered his ships to 'cease firing'. Although the fleet was running short of ammunition, the shells had done their work. The British casualties were negligible, estimated at five killed and twenty-eight wounded. Egyptian losses were doubtless severe – and several of the British shells had crashed into the city, causing serious damage and numerous civilian casualties. It was not quite the end. Next day, some of the batteries were seen to be still active and a partial bombardment was ordered before a truce was eventually established. By this time the European quarter of the city was ablaze, from either the shelling or arson, with widespread looting and rioting. It was unclear at first whether Arabi's forces had evacuated the city or had just fallen back to the outskirts.

The problem for Seymour was that he lacked the personnel to form an effective landing force, capable of restoring order and withstanding hostile forces, without crippling the fighting power of his ships. Still, he had to do what he could. At 10.30 on 13 July he despatched ashore an initial force of some 400 men under the overall command of Commander Tynte Hammill of the *Monarch*, who managed to rescue the Khedive from Ras el Tin palace. Following this, Captain John Fisher of the *Inflexible* took ashore a landing party to secure the outer defences of the city as a security against an attack from Arabi's forces, who had retreated several miles but who could return at any moment.

As Fisher occupied the lines around the city, he discovered the disadvantage of having a zone of total anarchy behind him. He requested assistance to calm the situation and Captain Charles Beresford landed on 14 July, accompanied by a motley party of bluejackets, some marines and a few Egyptian cavalry, collectively charged with the onerous responsibility of restoring law and order as soon as possible.

> I never saw anything so awful as the town on that Friday; streets, square, and blocks of buildings all on fire, roaring and crackling and tumbling about like a hell, let loose. Arabs murdering each other for loot under my nose, wretches running about with fire-balls and torches to light up new places, all the main thoroughfares impassable from burning fallen houses, streets with many corpses in them, mostly murdered by the Arab soldiers for loot – these corpses were Arabs murdered by each other – in fact, a pandemonium of hell and its devils. I took a chart with me and arranged the different parts of the town where I should make depots and police stations. I had only 140 men to patrol the town, to stop the looting, to stop the 'fresh burning' of houses, to bury the corpses, and to protect the lives of those who had come on shore. By quickly sending the men about in parties in different parts of the town, and by employing Arabs to inform me when and where certain houses might be burnt, I often managed to get a patrol there just in time to stop it, and the people thought there were 600 police in the town instead of 140. Neither myself nor my men slept one wink, as at 12 o'clock on two occasions an alarm was sounded that Arabi was attacking the lines, and all of us had to peg away to the front, where we had to remain until daylight, expecting attack every moment. These alarms lost many houses, as the mob set them alight while we were at the front; however, it was unavoidable.[6]
>
> Captain Charles Beresford, HMS *Condor*

He introduced a draconian system of military law, which to his own mind worked well.

> On Saturday night, I had the whole town proclaimed in Arabic, stating that persons caught firing houses would be shot, persons caught looting twice would be shot; all persons to return to their homes, etc., with confidence, and anyone wanting to get information or to lodge complaints to repair instantly to the chief of police.[7]
>
> Captain Charles Beresford, HMS *Condor*

Lieutenant Percival Marling landed and was billeted at the railway station on 18 July. Of course, military law didn't apply to a British officer.

> The heat and flies and dirt were awful. Looted all sorts of things for my room. My servant has made me a first-class tub out of a baking trough. There was an alarm in the middle of the night, and we all had to turn out and stand to our arms for half an hour. The whole city is in ruins, and lots of the houses still burning. Furniture, pianos, mattresses, chairs, and tables, and every imaginable thing are lying about the streets. Charlie Beresford, Provost Marshal, has shot and flogged about fifty or sixty Arab looters. We took seventeen watches, twenty-one rings, and twelve bracelets off one fellow, and eleven brooches and nine rings off another, and fourteen rings off a woman, who squealed like blazes![8]
>
> Lieutenant Percival Marling, 3rd King's Royal Rifle Corps

By 19 July a semblance of order had been achieved, with the fires dowsed and the corpses buried. Meanwhile several officers went ashore to investigate the gun batteries.

> I went round the batteries near Ras el Tin. Some of the sights were decidedly gruesome. I heard afterwards on

perfectly reliable authority that the casualties amongst the blacks, garrison gunners, and infantry reserves in rear, had been over 800. Cartloads of dead were taken out of the battery during the action, but there were at last, so many that a huge pit at Ras el Tin was dug, and they were thrown into it and earth over them; the top layer of bodies was visible in several places. The parapet had fallen over some, which could not in consequence be moved from where they had been killed. Under one gun, which had been cap-sized by a shell, lay the bodies of the Egyptian officer and five or six of his gallant crew. Few men could have tried to do their duty better than those who actually manned the batteries.[9]

Major Alexander Tulloch, HMS *Invincible*

One of the officers sent ashore was Captain Arthur Wilson, whose task was to make sure that the forts no longer posed any kind of a military threat. Many questioned the destruction of perfectly good guns, but orders were orders.

We have had a period of almost incessant hard work since the bombardment, but no fighting. My work has been, first, spiking or disabling all the guns in the outlying forts, which cover an extent of 8 or 9 miles, and afterwards searching for magazines and destroying ammunition. I suppose the admiral thinks I have a good nose for explosives. There is an enormous store of ammunition in the principal maga-zine that I have been working a whole week to get rid of, but I am not allowed to blow it up, and have to carry it half a mile to throw it into the sea. Before order was re-estab-lished in Alexandria, I managed to get a large quantity of it carried down by the Arabs simply by sitting down in the middle of the high road with three or four bags of biscuits and a few bluejackets to show what I wanted and bribing the passersby with biscuit to carry it down for me.[10]

Captain Arthur Wilson, HMS *Hecla*

Once the town was quiescent, Beresford was made responsible for the defence of the Mex lines and citadel, which defended the south-western boundary of Alexandria, blocking as it did the strip of land between the sea and Lake Mareotis. Meanwhile, there had also been a move to secure the village of Ramleh, about 5 miles towards Aboukir Bay, which harboured an important pumping station. With the destruction of the forts, the pacification of Alexandria and the establishment of basic defensive positions to hold back Arabi's regiments, all the sailors had to do now was wait for the arrival of the army. It would not be that long, but some observers pondered the wisdom of launching the naval attack before the army had arrived, allowing the almost complete destruction of Alexandria, and giving Arabi the chance to organise his forces.

***

ON 17 JULY, GENERAL ARCHIBALD ALISON arrived to take command of the first British battalions bolstering the Alexandria garrison – which brought the total troops available to around 5,000 including marines and naval shore parties. For the moment, Colonel Ahmed Arabi had withdrawn the bulk of his forces some 16 miles along the railway leading to Cairo to establish strong earthwork defensive positions at Kafr Dowar. Here his army was growing as more and more nationalists flocked to his banner. Some of the newly arrived British infantry found themselves assigned to picket duty outside Ramleh. Soldiers never complain but they do 'observe' a lot.

> Now we had to undertake that dreariest of all duties connected with war, viz., outpost duty, and that too in the very teeth of the enemy. This night I was placed, with six men under my charge, on the side of a belt of trees in front of the line of sentries. Between this wood and the main body of the picket was a sandy plain about 400 yards wide, while in front of it extended a tract of level green fields, which,

from our position – by the aid of an occasional flash of the electric light from our naval sentry in the bay – could be seen for a long way. Our duty was to watch, and if we saw any sign of living men in front, retire back on the main body with the intelligence. Two men were continually on the lookout, while the remainder of us reclined amongst the trees.[11]

Corporal John Philip, 2nd Duke of Cornwall's Light Infantry

All was quiet until about midnight, when suddenly the silence was broken.

Without the least warning, a sharp volley of musketry rang from the picket behind us, and the bullets crashed against the tree-tops over our head. The readers must keep in mind that this was our first angry shot, and they must bear with us patiently if we showed a little trepidation. Another and another volley followed, and now the yells of the Arabs were heard between us and the pickets. Crossing to the edge of the trees, we saw a large body of horsemen galloping madly hither and thither, within 100 yards of us. They were evidently as much surprised and frightened as we were, for they were calling loudly, 'Allah! Allah!' We crawled close to the fence skirting the wood, and, with beating hearts, waited for the crisis. Again, the rifles of the picket spoke, but the trees above got most of the bullets. We had our rifles loaded, and ammunition ready for action, but I gave instructions not to fire as we did not want those wild Bedouins to know our whereabouts and very soon, they galloped away to the left, firing a retaliating shot occasionally before they swept out of sight.[12]

Corporal John Philip, 2nd Duke of Cornwall's Light Infantry

Meanwhile, a great deal of ingenuity was demonstrated by two naval officers, Captains John Fisher of the *Inflexible* and Arthur Wilson of the *Hecla* in constructing an armoured train.

Fisher and I had put our heads together and supplied the general with an ironclad truck armed with Gatlings, which he was much taken with, and this led up to the idea of mounting a heavy gun in the same way. I had some trouble in persuading the admiral to let me try, as of course, as in duty bound, he foresaw all sorts of dangers and difficulties. I first arranged it so that I could hoist the gun out and fire it on the ground alongside the railway, but that took more than half an hour, and in case of a reverse there was every chance of being cut off. So I determined to try mounting it on the truck, so that it could be fired there. When I had got it ready yesterday afternoon, the general came out with me to see it fired, and as soon as he saw it he said, 'Oh, it is sure to smash the truck all to pieces!' We fired two rounds, and nothing happened, so he quite altered his opinion and went away delighted.[13]

Captain Arthur Wilson, HMS *Hecla*

The armoured train was protected by sandbags reinforced by iron rails. As a wise precaution it was equipped with a full set of tools and materials in case they had to repair the track. It was used to some good effect in a first reconnaissance in strength launched by Alison on 5 August 1882. Wilson was pleased with the results obtained by his brainchild that day.

Today my gun was put in front of the train which took him out to fight, and I think on the whole did good service; at all events, nothing went wrong with the gun. As Arabi had pulled the rails up, and we had not time to lay them down again, I could not get nearer than 2,300 yards, and the enemy kept so well under cover that it was very difficult to tell what effect the shot had. I was firing nearly the whole time over the heads of our own men, so it was rather nervous work. My heart was in my mouth once when one of the shots stripped and I heard it turning head over heels in [the] air as it went along. Fortunately, it fell just beyond

our men and hurt no one. I don't know in the least what
the result of our afternoon's work has been. It has certainly
shown that Arabi has a very strong position and means to
hold it – I don't think we can drive him out of it with our
present force. I thought the marines who were in front of
me behaved exceedingly well; nothing could have been
steadier than they were. The artillery fire opposed to us
was very weak, only one shell pitched close to us, and then
just as we thought they had found our range they left off
firing, and I don't know what became of them.[14]
Captain Arthur Wilson, HMS *Hecla*

It was an inconclusive engagement, but after all it was only a
reconnaissance. It had cost some three dead and twenty-three
wounded, as against the optimistic estimates of Egyptian losses
that ranged up to 300. From the interrogation of prisoners, it
was thought that Arabi's strength at Kafr Dowar consisted of
some four regiments of infantry, one regiment of cavalry, one
regiment of artillery, and around 5,000 Bedouins – in total about
16,000 men.

***

THE MIGHT OF THE BRITISH EMPIRE was gathering at Alexandria, all
awaiting the arrival of Lieutenant General Garnet Wolseley, who
had been slightly delayed by illness. Lieutenant General Edward
Hamley had arrived to command the 2nd Division of Wolseley's
army corps. As we have seen, Wolseley had already decided to
attack Cairo from the direction of Ismailia on the Suez Canal,
eschewing any approach from Alexandria. He would take with
him the 1st Division of some 6,000 men commanded by Lieutenant General George Willis. But all this remained a closely
guarded secret – although Wolseley reveals all in a letter to his
wife on 18 August.

We start from here to-morrow at noon for Aboukir Bay,

where the fleet and all the transports carrying the first Division will anchor at 4 p.m. tomorrow to pretend landing there during the night to attack Arabi's position in front of this place on Tuesday morning. Everyone here believes we intend doing so: only about three people amongst the soldiers are in the secret, and I have completely befoozled the 'press gang', who have, I know, telegraphed home that we mean to land at Aboukir. I suppose they will be furious when they find how they have been taken in, but if I can take them in, I may take in Arabi also. On Sunday evening I hope to be at Ismailia.[15]

Lieutenant General Garnet Wolseley, Headquarters

Wolseley had no love of journalists, and fooling the press was fair game, but one distinguished military personage also deceived was the unforgiving figure of Hamley whose division was to be left behind to hold Alexandria. Hamley had not the slightest idea of Wolseley's real intentions.

He led me to believe that I was to cooperate from Ramleh in a combined attack on the Egyptian position, Sir G. Wolseley with the rest of the troops advancing from Aboukir Bay on the strip of land between the Lakes Aboukir and Edkee. I observed, alluding to our conversation on the 15th, that I expected he might choose this point to advance from, and mentioned the order in which in that case I should advance, so as to give him a hand, which he approved. He then instructed me to make demonstrations this evening and Sunday, to induce the enemy to expect I should attack him. I was warned not to be surprised if I should hear firing at Aboukir on Saturday evening.[16]

Lieutenant General Edward Hamley, Headquarters, 2nd Division

On the afternoon of 18 August, eight warships and the transports carrying the 1st Division left Alexandria. Alfred Male, brought out as a military chaplain to the forces and attached to Wolseley's headquarters staff, was one of those bemused by events.

> The general impression among the staff men was that we were to bombard the strong forts in Aboukir Bay next day, land under fire, and storm the entrenchments. And, as if to carry out this idea, we steamed away from Alexandria, some eighteen transports in all, convoyed by ironclads and accompanied by the *Salamis*, with Wolseley himself aboard. When Aboukir Bay was reached we lay off, and line of battle was at once assumed. We could see plainly the batteries ashore crowded with men; and as our war-ships struck their topmasts, as if in preparation for a fight, the Egyptian gunners could be seen standing to their guns, evidently determined, if possible, to repel the anticipated attack. Thus, we lay from three o'clock in the afternoon till evening. No lights were to be shown by our ships, so that when the evening shadows fell, we were completely hidden from the sight of the men ashore. Then, just as the crescent moon was beginning to peep out from a bank of clouds, suddenly signals flashed in quick succession from the *Salamis* and in obedience to the signals we silently moved away, stealing off under cover of the darkness in single line, led by the 'old fighting *Temeraire*' or rather by her descendant and namesake. In the morning when the dawn broke the amazement of the vigilant Egyptians could be imagined as they swept the sea and found no hostile warship in sight. This was Wolseley's ruse – a feint on the batteries in Aboukir Bay – a real and rapid advance northward to seize the Suez Canal.[17]
>
> Reverend Alfred Male

Now it was game on – at a new 'playing field'. The question was: would Wolseley's masterplan work?

3

THE ADVANCE TO QASSASIN

Get lazily out of bed and hear we are to start at once. The old story of an attack at the front, hear that the enemy is within 2 miles, hope so, don't believe it. Advance a mile and a half and halt, no signs of the enemy. I thought not! On again, sand feels like London pavement in the hottest part of the season only soft, reflects the glare of the sun, like the heat of an oven, feel as if I was being fried when I lie down to rest at the halts.[1]

Lieutenant Charles Balfour, 1st Scots Guards, 1st Brigade

WOLSELEY'S DIMINUTIVE ARMADA swept through the night and appeared at dawn off Port Said to totally surprise the Egyptians. There was merit in maintaining surprise, for Colonel Ahmed Arabi could have ordered the blocking of the Suez Canal, or the defence of Port Said. But the canal was open, and Port Said lay naked before them. Wolseley had achieved his initial objective and his ships sailed up the canal, taking El Kantara and making their base at the town of Ismailia, halfway down the canal. This was the focal point of the railways to Cairo and Port Suez, but also of the Sweetwater canal which supplied drinking water taken from the Nile at Cairo. Wolseley realised that it was essential that he advance as quickly as possible to avoid Arabi's forces draining the canal and destroying the railway. As a first step, Major General Gerald Graham's 2nd Brigade advance guard moved the couple of miles to the west to seize the key rail junction at Nifisha without opposition. Behind them the main force began to disembark in force on 21 August. Ismailia was soon crowded with troops, among them Lieutenant James Grierson: a promising officer who had been posted in from India to act as an intelligence officer on Wolseley's staff.

> Ismailia is very crowded. Troops are bivouacking in every street and square, horses are picketed all along the canal banks and the place presents an animated appearance. Personally, I am as fit as possible, except my skin which is rapidly peeling off my face and hands. I have mounted a pair of goggles. You never saw anything so curious as the sight of an army wearing blue goggles, and all with blue veils over their faces. I don't like the latter and shan't wear one. It is fearfully hot simply grilling by day, but the nights are most deliciously cool and very pleasant.[2]
>
> Lieutenant James Grierson, Headquarters

Speed was of the essence, so on 24 August Wolseley moved off on a reconnaissance to the west, to determine where the Egyptian forces were. With him were three squadrons of Household Cavalry and Mounted Infantry, the York and Lancaster Regiment, the Royal Marine Light Infantry, and a couple of Royal Horse Artillery guns. Lieutenant Colonel William Butler, another intelligence officer, was entranced by the desert conditions as he explored out to the flank.

> There is nothing like it in all the world – only sand, the sand of the hourglass, but made infinite by space, just as a tumbler of sea water becomes infinite in the ocean. Sand, drifted into motionless waves, heaped in ridges, scooped into valleys, flattened, blown up into curious cones and long yellow banks, the tops of which the winds have cut into fretted patterns as it blew over them. And all so silent, so withered, and yet so fresh; so soft, so beautiful, and yet so terrible.[3]
>
> Lieutenant Colonel William Butler, Headquarters

They had only got forward a couple of miles when they found the canal dammed near El Magfar and not far beyond they could see the Egyptians were present in strength at El Mahuta.

> From where we stood, the desert for 3,000 yards rose gradually to El Mahuta, where some lofty mounds of sand and broken pottery still marked what is supposed to have been the spot at which Pharaoh decreed that the Israelites should make bricks without straw. These mounds ended the forward view; they were now black with figures, while to the right and left of them a long, open line of Arab camelmen and horsemen stretched along the skyline far into the desert on either flank. It was a very striking scene: the morning sun shone full in their faces; musket barrel and spear head flashed and glittered along the desert ridge, while behind it the heads of many more men and camels showed above the ridge; and beyond them again straight columns of black railway smoke were rising into the still, clear air of the desert, showing that the resources of civilisation had also been called into request by the Egyptian enemy, and that his infantry were being hurried up from the direction where lay Tel el Kebir to make head against our further advance.[4]
>
> Lieutenant Colonel William Butler, Headquarters

Although Wolseley estimated the Egyptians numbered some 10,000 men and ten guns, he decided it would be invidious to retreat, and decided to fight a holding action having first seized control of the El Magfar dam in front of the Egyptian positions.

> Although I had but three squadrons of cavalry, two guns and about 1,000 infantry, I felt it would not be in consonance with the traditions of Her Majesty's Army that we should retire, even temporarily, before Egyptian troops, no matter what their numbers might be. I decided, therefore, upon holding my ground until evening, by which time I

knew that the reinforcements I had sent for to Nifisha and Ismailia would reach me. I consequently took up a position, suited to the numbers at my disposal, with my left resting on the captured dam over the Canal, and the cavalry and mounted infantry covering the right. It was now 9 o'clock.[5]
Lieutenant General Garnet Wolseley, Headquarters

A rider was sent back calling for the Guards Brigade, the Duke of Cornwall's Regiment and the 3rd King's Royal Rifle Corps to march to the sound of the guns. And slowly the reinforcements began to trickle in.

From 10 to 11 o'clock the enemy continued to develop his attack upon my centre and right. His guns were served with considerable skill, the shells bursting well amongst us. Fortunately, they were common shells with percussion fuses, which sank so deep in the very soft sand before bursting, that few splinters flew upwards; when he did use shrapnel the time-fuses were badly cut. Feeling complete confidence in my ability to drive back any close attack the enemy might make, I did not allow our guns to open fire for some time after they were placed in position, hoping he might thereby be the more readily induced to advance to close quarters, under the notion that we had no artillery with us. When, however, he brought twelve guns into action, to relieve the Household Cavalry, into whose ranks and those of the Mounted Infantry he was throwing his shell with great accuracy, our two guns opened upon his twelve guns with marked effect, our practice being very good. The Household Cavalry and Mounted Infantry were skilfully manoeuvred by Major-General Drury-Lowe on the extreme right, to check the enemy's advance on that side; but the horses, just landed from a long sea-voyage and fatigued by their march across a desert deep in sand, were in no condition to charge. About noon, two Gatlings, with a party of sailors, under command of Lieutenant

King-Harman, and belonging to HMS *Orion*, arrived and took up a position for action.[6]

Lieutenant General Garnet Wolseley, Headquarters

The Duke of Cornwell's Light Infantry were back at Nifisha when the call to arms burst upon them.

Most of us were in our shirt sleeves squatting on the sand, and devouring hard regulation biscuits, waiting for the coffee to cool, when the bugles rang out the 'Assembly!' That call is answered by a sharp turnout, even in barracks; but, with the enemy in the near vicinity, it means simply a maddening charge. Coats, arms, accoutrements, etc., were thrown on in wild confusion, canteens of coffee upset in the melee for first on parade. In a space of time almost incredible to a non-military man, we were dashing from the tents and forming in the ranks, eagerly scanning the country around for a sight of the foe; but no: we had to go to them. 'Fours-right! Quick march!' came the sharply uttered command, and away we tramped through the soft sand, sinking several inches at every step. We knew from the stern looks of our respected commander, and his hurried whispering to the other officers, that some new development of the enemy had taken place which required our immediate attention.[7]

Corporal John Philip, 2nd Duke of Cornwall's Light Infantry

It was a forced march in the broiling heat, with the unblinking glare of the sun driving them to distraction. The toiling men began to suffer the agonies of thirst, which some ameliorated – at least for a while – by sucking pebbles. At last, at about 13.00, they arrived at the scene of the battle.

We made our way across an open plain in rear of our own batteries, and there the sight was sufficient to send the blood leaping through the veins with excitement and admiration.

Those brave fellows were stripped to their shirts and trousers, sleeves rolled up, the perspiration streaming from their faces as they loaded and fired like 'devils let loose'. Before a gun had ceased to rebound from the concussion of firing, half-a-dozen hands were on the wheel putting it in position again. They were fighting against fearful odds; it was a case of forty cannon to ten, but there was no flinching. The shells crashed around that little band, but they heeded them not. As my company was passing one of the batteries, I observed a tall artilleryman directing his eye along his gun, apparently taking careful aim. While so doing, his head was literally blown to pieces; but, 'ere his lifeless body had reached the ground, another was in his place, and in a twinkling an angry report rang from the muzzle as if bidding defiance to the numerous foe.[8]

Corporal John Philip, 2nd Duke of Cornwall's Light Infantry

They took up defensive positions along a line of sandbanks. Here Corporal John Philip cursed the insouciant approach of one of the attached war correspondents who, by making himself a target, attracted shells which threatened to plunge among the infantry nearby.

An occasional shell came tearing amongst us but did no damage till one of those daring fellows, war correspondents, came galloping up on horseback and dismounted on the higher ground in front. Throwing the reins over his arm, he sat down on a campstool, produced his notebook, and set to work. The enemy, no doubt eyeing him through their field glasses, and probably thinking he was devising a plan for their annihilation, poured a perfect torrent of shot and shell about his 'devoted head'. But he was made of the real stuff; for he wrote on! Sometimes he was hid from our view in a cloud of sand, raised by a shell falling within a few yards of him. As it cleared away, he was seen to shake the remnants of it from his notebook and continue his task. It eventually got too hot for his charger, for it plunged and reared to such an extent that the brave writer had to remount and seek a more safe retreat. Glad were we when he left, for the shells meant for him came dancing amongst us in a rather unpleasant manner.[9]

Corporal John Philip, 2nd Duke of Cornwall's Light Infantry

Wolseley's makeshift line held, thanks mainly to the rapid and accurate fire of his artillery. One by one the reinforcing battalions arrived at the scene. Next morning at first light the British infantry advanced on the Egyptian positions.

A front line of skirmishers moving steadily forward towards a long ridge of gradually sloping sandhills, on the summit of which could be seen the earthworks from where the guns of the enemy had poured such a deadly shower on the preceding day. Every moment we expected them to blaze out again in all their fury, accompanied, as they would be, by the still more deadly rattle of musketry, for by this time we were within range of that weapon. I can assure you that hearts beat fast with suppressed excitement. When within about 300 yards the remark passed freely along the ranks, 'Won't we catch it when they do wake up!' but no, all was silent, and a halt was ordered. An officer was seen to gallop to the brow of the hill without molestation, and then we knew the foe had fled. Instantly there was a commotion among the staff surrounding Lord Wolseley: mounted officers galloped hither and thither with new instructions to the various corps. Up dashed two batteries of Royal Horse Artillery, the 19th Hussars, and about fifty mounted infantry. They swept majestically past us in all the pride of military glory, bent on the tracks of the flying enemy.[10]

Corporal John Philip, 2nd Duke of Cornwall's Light Infantry

The Egyptians had fallen back to a camp established at Tel el Kebir about 20 miles further to the west along the railway and canal. A vigorous pursuit followed, with the cavalry sweeping aside token opposition at El Mahsama station. They certainly caught the Egyptians on the hop, for they captured seven Krupp guns, a stores depot and several loaded railway wagons. The cavalry also discovered an Egyptian dressed in civilian clothes wandering about on the station platform – no less a figure than Arabi's chief of staff and chief engineer, Mahmud Fahmi Pasha.

They then pressed on to capture the village of El Qassasin, where they found the canal lock intact. This meant the British could control the water along the stretch of the Sweetwater canal back to Ismailia. At least they could, once they had removed the dam at El Magfar. This proved easier said than done, as considerable ingenuity had been employed in its construction, with alternative layers of sand and bundles of reeds lashed together with telegraph wire. A mixed working party of sailors, sappers and soldiers struggled to pull the dam apart using picks and shovels, but even explosives had minimal effect. It took a couple of days hard graft before the canal was open for navigation up to the Qassasin lock. It also secured the water supply, although first they would have to remove the bodies the Egyptians had thrown in to pollute it.

By this time, logistical problems were becoming apparent, as Wolseley had outrun his supply chain and as a result, a temporary halt was called at El Qassasin. The recently recaptured railway line had been severed in places and would take time to repair. There was also a big problem in finding mule or camel transport. The result was that the troops had to exist on a meagre diet of biscuits, with only a dribble of polluted water to drink with it. Foraging broadened the diet with watermelons, while local farms were officially recompensed for sequestered cattle and sheep. As the canal was unblocked the navy managed to get some supplies forward with a chain of boats operating up and down the waterway. Nevertheless, it was a tough time for the men, who, lacking shelter, were also suffering from heat exhaustion and sunstroke. The conditions had certainly impacted on the Guards Brigade who were still at El Magfar.

The typical guardsman would look curious in Pall Mall. Bristly beards (some have grown very well) hair cropped as if he had been undergoing fourteen days, as brown as a Spaniard, stained serge frock of an uncertain colour, trousers and boots somewhere underneath a thick coating of dust. The men get very hard work again digging out the block on the canal and railway: while at it they work tremendously hard, as the Royal Engineers all say no ordinary infantry of the line could do the work they do.[11]
Lieutenant Charles Balfour, 1st Scots Guards, 1st Brigade

Gradually the essentials began to arrive.

Tents at last! Brought up by boat on the canal and now not only tents but kit bags and beds turn up. Here's luxury! Instantaneous rush on baths, general cleaning of teeth and brushing of hair. The tents look like a ship fully dressed – all the clothes we have worn for the last week hung out to air and a change of clothes adopted, quite a curious sensation to feel thoroughly clean.[12]
Lieutenant Charles Balfour, 1st Scots Guards, 1st Brigade

The pause also allowed the British to complete their concentration, based at Ismailia rather than Alexandria. More cavalry arrived, plus an Indian contingent. On 26 August 1882, the frustrated – and annoyed – Lieutenant General Hamley sent a pleading communication to Wolseley's chief of staff, John Adye.

Can you not tell me what you wish me to do? This place will be in good state of defence this evening. I could leave three and a half battalions and bring you four – or if sailors take the police duties, could bring you five. Shall I take any steps for embarkation?[13]
Lieutenant General Edward Hamley, Headquarters, 2nd Division

The mood of the fuming subordinate was not ameliorated by a

further two days wait before he was ordered to bring the Highland Brigade round to join Wolseley's main force.

On 28 August, while the British reorganised and prepared
for the next stage of the advance, the Egyptians launched a
couple of spoiling attacks on El Qassasin, which was being held
by Graham with 1,728 infantry, 57 cavalry, 70 mounted infantry
and two 13-pounder guns. First, a large force of Egyptian cavalry
appeared to the north of Qassasin. Graham immediately sent a
heliograph message to Major General Drury-Lowe in command
of the cavalry brigade back at Mahsama. The cavalry moved
forward, ready to intervene if called upon, but the attack failed
to develop and they returned to Mahsuma. The real thrust came
later at about 16.30, when a considerable body of Egyptian
infantry advanced behind a mile-wide line of skirmishers and
supported by heavy artillery fire. Graham realised this renewed
threat was serious, and again sent a message back to Drury-Lowe
ordering him to move forward. Meanwhile, the Cornwalls were
heavily engaged at the left of Graham's thin red line.

> The railway was on our right, made up for a distance of half-
> a-mile, forming an embankment from 20 to 30 feet high. It
> ran parallel to, and some 200 yards from the canal on our
> left. The intervening ground was rough and uneven. We
> formed deliberately up for the fray having plenty of time,
> for the enemy, though in sight, were a good way off. As they
> came nearer and within rifle range, the smoke curled above
> their lines, followed by the 'whish' of the bullets and the
> heavy roar of shells, announcing their challenge. Coolly we
> took up our position, under a galling fire, one half lining
> the railway embankment, while the other half extended
> to a thin line, each file two paces apart, at right angles and
> in the open plain, directly in front of the advancing host.[14]
> Corporal John Philip, 2nd Duke of Cornwall's Light Infantry

They soon came under heavy fire.

Bullets whistled close to our ears, their sharp 'Ping!' only to be heard when they came within a few feet, as the continuous crash of exploding shells filled the air. We waited till the front line of the opposing infantry was within 900 yards, and then opened fire with a vengeance. But the thinning process was going on; man after man, struck by the leaden hail, rolled down the embankment, clutching vainly at the sand in their descent.[15]

Corporal John Philip, 2nd Duke of Cornwall's Light Infantry

Then Philip himself had a fortuitous escape.

I received a stunning blow on the right side of the head, which sent the brain reeling, and the man rolling down the embankment. I lay for a few minutes in a semi-unconscious state, and then sat up and looked around on the ghastly sight at the bottom of the ravine which ran along below the railway side. My helmet lay beside me, the chain, which had been hooked up, cut in two, the thick puggaree round it to protect the head from the hot sun torn on one side to tatters, and part of the helmet itself away I knew not where. It was a near shave, and to the chain I believe I owed my life. It had turned the missile, and the thick folds of the puggaree had deadened the blow. I put my hand gradually up, and it was with a feeling of indescribable relief that my fingers, instead of going into the hole I imagined, passed over a ponderous lump. I breathed more freely, and, sticking on my battered helmet, scrambled up to renew the fight, feeling little or none the worse of my expected transference to another world.[16]

Corporal John Philip, 2nd Duke of Cornwall's Light Infantry

The Cornwalls held their line, but to their right the Egyptians were threatening to fall on Graham's exposed right flank. At 17.20, Graham had sent his ADC, Lieutenant Duncan Pirie, to tell Drury-Lowe to take his cavalry in wide sweep round to allow them to strike at the exposed left flank of the Egyptians. Pirie was at first unable to find Drury-Lowe in the gathering gloom. Not unnaturally, Pirie grew more and more anxious, while to make matters worse his horse was soon exhausted, and he was fortunate to be able to borrow a replacement from an artillery battery. At last, he encountered Drury-Lowe some 4 miles to the north-west of Qassasin. What happened next triggered an interesting spat between generals, as he blurted out not only that the cavalry must attack the Egyptian left as soon as possible, but also added the disturbing comment that Graham was only just able to hold his own. When this appeared in Drury-Lowe's report it triggered outrage from Graham, who in fairness had said no such thing, and from Wolseley, who felt this subaltern was criticising the security of his deployments. It became quite a *cause célèbre* in the British newspapers in the subsequent months, with various press journalists who had been present and anonymous officers chiming in to back up Pirie's interpretation of the situation. Be that as it may, on the night of 28 August, one can be pretty certain that Philip would have sided with Pirie.

It was fairly dark now, and nothing of the enemy could be seen but the flashes of their rifles and cannons, and we fired in reply at random. Our ammunition being almost done, the firing waxed feeble, and unless we got relief our stubborn stand would be of no avail. As soon as our fire died away it would only be a matter of a few minutes for the superior numbers of the Egyptians to advance and crush us, for we were only a handful of worn-out men.[17]
Corporal John Philip, 2nd Duke of Cornwall's Light Infantry

Then, not a moment too soon, the cavalry arrived. Among them was Major Reginald Talbot, who recalled the excitement of what followed.

We marched along the line of sand ridges, an occasional order to trot along breaking the silence. We must have

marched 5 or 6 miles, when it was broken by the boom
of a gun, followed by the hissing of a shell. General Lowe
shortly ordered our guns to unlimber and reply, and the 7th
Dragoon Guards to clear the front of our guns, which they
did by retiring, making us the front line. The Household
Cavalry continued to advance at a walk, when, in a moment
became visible a white line of infantry in our immediate
front, which opened a tremendous fire upon us. Not a
moment was to be lost! 'Form front in two lines! Draw
swords! Charge!' And we were upon them. Until we got
within 100 yards they continued to fire; but in one moment
the brilliant light from the firing line, the rattle of the fire,
and whirring of the bullets ceased – the white line had faced
about and was in flight. We rode them down in solid rank,
but, as they dispersed, we opened out and pursued. They
fell like ninepins, many of them unwounded, who fired and
stabbed our horses as we galloped past them. We charged
for 300 yards; then Ewart[18] called out, 'Rally!' and we set
to work to collect our men. I can imagine no more splendid sight than this moonlight charge of our fine fellows on
their dark horses, against the guns supported by the whole
line of infantry, whose fire was so brilliant in the night that
it looked just like the lightning of some grand pyrotechnic
display. Then the cheer we gave, then the few seconds of
silence and then the havoc and slaughter.[19]
Major Reginald Talbot, Household Cavalry

Even so, there was the tragic aftermath of any battle for the
exhausted survivors as they returned to their camp at Qassasin.

The companies' rolls were called, and it was with solemn
looks we heard many a well-known name shouted by the
orderly sergeants without the answering, 'Here!' There
would have been a larger dead and wounded roll had we
been a stronger party; the thinness of our lines and the
cover of the railway saved a good deal of life. As it was,

the killed and wounded amounted to about 100. I and some more went down to the side of the bridge where lay the wounded. The doctors were busy amongst them, and groans and cries of pain resounded on all sides. Some were in the throes of death; others bright and cheery, with legs or arms disabled. We did not stay long, simply bidding our best-known comrades good-bye, and then retraced our way to the camp.[20]

Corporal John Philip, 2nd Duke of Cornwall's Light Infantry

There was considerable suffering to be undergone by some of the wounded cavalrymen as well. On the night of 30 August, Major Alexander Tulloch, now back on land and attached to Wolseley as an intelligence officer, was carrying out the first of several reconnaissances of the ground between Qassasin and Tel el Kebir when he passed over the scene of the charge.

There were many dead, and, to my horror, I found several wounded men, some in a state of delirium, others very weak but still sensible. I never shall forget the eager, almost wolf-like, clutch at my [orderly's] waterbag as soon as the unfortunate man he was assisting knew what it was. I sent in at once for dhoolies from the Indian cavalry; and one poor fellow I helped to carry had his abdomen sliced open by a sword-cut. Fortunately, the bowels had not been touched; but I had to put them back in their place before I moved the man. Another was a wounded officer – a huge fellow. As I lifted him, his head, badly cut and festering, fell on my shoulder; the broken bone of his left arm was protruding through the cloth of his coat; this I did not notice until placing him flat in his dhooly. All this time the enemy's cavalry pickets were watching me at some few hundred yards' distance, but seeing what I was doing they did not advance. Four or five of the wounded I brought in recovered, amongst them the tall officer.[21]

Major Alexander Tulloch, Headquarters

The recces showed that the Egyptian Tel el Kebir defences were gaining in numbers and that some units had been transferred in from Kafr Dowar. But the British, too, were gaining in strength.

★★★

WOLSELEY'S WHOLE ARMY WAS MOVING UP IN STAGES with the aim of concentrating at Qassasin by 12 September. The Indian Brigade and the Highland Brigade were among those arriving and soon the whole corps would be ready to make the final drive on Tel el Kebir. The railway was at last back in working order, which alleviated the supply problems. On 9 September, Arabi made another attempt to disrupt the British build-up when he launched another attack on Qassasin. He had been informed by Bedouin irregular forces that they had severed communication links between Ismailia and Qassasin which they claimed was weakly held. This time it was a two-pronged assault, with one force marching east from Tel el Kebir and the other marching south from Es Salihyeh. But the British were ready for them, having amassed a force of nearly 8,000 at Qassasin, commanded by Lieutenant General George Willis, who also had plentiful reserves close at hand.

The Second Battle of Qassasin began when outpost pickets of the 13th Bengal Lancers detected their approach. Graham certainly relished the challenge as, when the alarm was raised back at Qassasin at 06.45, he swung his brigade into action.

> The Philistines are on us! Are they mad? In 5 minutes, my dispositions are made, and in 20 minutes the troops are out in line of battle. Heavy artillery fire from enemy as before, but our guns advance with the infantry, and before 9 a.m. the enemy are in full retreat.[22]
>
> Major General Gerald Graham, Headquarters, 2nd Brigade

The battle was a damp squib, for the Egyptians, disheartened by the strength and vigour of the British response, showed little inclination to attack. As the British advanced the Egyptians began to fall back, and the pursuit was continued until Wolseley brought it to a halt. Afterwards the intelligence officers interrogated the Egyptian wounded and prisoners and received confirmation of the friable state of morale in Arabi's camp.

> We received from them confirmation of the accounts of the discontent existing in the camp at Tel el Kebir, and of the desire of many to give up fighting and return to their ordinary occupations. One man told me that his officer had recommended him to lie down and pretend that he was killed, and, 'Then the English soldiers will take you prisoner and will not hurt you!' Surely a very pleasant testimony to the native confidence in the humanity of our troops! I asked him whether he was more afraid of the bullets or the shells, and he replied that he was in such a fright that he could not tell the one from the other. 'God only knows, what a fright I was in!'[23]
> Captain Charles Watson, Headquarters

However, they also learned something that would prove of value in the aftermath of the battle.

> We also learned that there was a considerable probability that unless the British advanced rapidly, the city of Cairo would be burned, not by Arabi and his soldiers, but by what were called the 'bad people', persons of similar character to those who had destroyed Alexandria after the British bombardment. It was the recollection of this danger to the city that determined the rapid ride to Cairo of our cavalry after Tel el Kebir.[24]
> Captain Charles Watson, Headquarters

Wolseley was well aware of the threat to Cairo and determined to smash the power of Ahmed Arabi and his nationalist force once and for all.

Wolseley tells me that he doesn't mean to let Arabi escape him next time, that he means to smash him altogether, and relies on me to do it. He doesn't mean him to escape into the Delta, where he can't get at him.[25]

Major General Gerald Graham, Headquarters, 2nd Brigade

And that next time would be soon.

4

THE BATTLE OF TEL EL KEBIR

Before this reaches you the news of our fight will have reached you with its disquieting butcher's bill, over which Mr. John Bull rather gloats, and thinks, when the list is a long one, that he has had something for his money. And yet how much pleasanter is death from clean bullet wounds than from loathsome diseases. To be killed in the open air with the conviction you are dying for your country, how different from rotting to death in a hospital, or dying like a consumptive girl in an artificially heated room.[1]
Lieutenant General Garnet Wolseley, Headquarters

WOLSELEY WAS READY FOR BATTLE. He had predicted it would occur at Tel el Kebir, but that did not make the task ahead of his men any easier. The Egyptians had constructed a series of extensive earthworks, stretching out some 4 miles in total, along a natural mound which dominated the desert for miles around to the north of the canal and just east of Tel el Kebir station. A ditch some 8 to 12 feet wide and 5 to 9 feet deep lay in front of a formidable breastwork up to 6 feet high. Additionally, there were intermittent formidable redoubts containing their artillery, while a further series of entrenchments was under construction from roughly the middle of the line, stretching back diagonally to the canal. There was also one strong advanced redoubt near the canal – a redoubt, furthermore, that had not been detected in prior reconnaissances. Colonel Ahmed Arabi had amassed a total force of some 22,000 troops and 75 guns. Wolseley believed he was faced by 30,000, and he had only 13,000 and 60 guns, but his force was far better trained.

His biggest problem was the flat desert approach from Qassasin, which had no cover of any kind. This would leave the advancing British exposed to heavy Egyptian artillery fire for some 5 miles – resulting in murderous casualties. Wolseley pondered his options and came up with a solution. But this too was risky.

> My desire was to fight him decisively where he was, in the open desert, before he could take up fresh positions more difficult of access in the cultivated country in his rear. That cultivated country is practically impassable to a regular army, being irrigated and cut up in every direction by deep canals. I had ascertained by frequent reconnaissance that the enemy did not push his outposts far beyond his works at night, and I had good reasons for believing that he then kept a very bad look-out. These circumstances, and the very great reliance I had in the steadiness of our splendid infantry, determined me to resort to the extremely difficult operation of a night march, to be followed by an attack before daybreak on the enemy's position.[2]
> Lieutenant General Garnet Wolseley, Headquarters

This was not Wolseley's only problem as he had to deal with his recalcitrant subordinate – Lieutenant General Edward Hamley – who was still brooding over Wolseley's earlier deception and was now unhappy with his status within the expeditionary force.

> I represented that I was being deprived of everything except a single brigade – to which he replied again that the exigencies of the service required it – and went into his tent. I returned to my camp, and, after thinking over what I had heard with the greatest surprise and concern, crossed the small bridge, and went to the chief of the staff's tent. I represented to him how deep an injury would be done both to me and to the brigadier by leaving me with only a single brigade.[3]
> Lieutenant General Edward Hamley, Headquarters, 2nd Division

Staff officer Neville Lyttleton was an amused observer at a distance as the great and the good wrangled over the question of Hamley's injured pride.

> Hamley gave a lot of trouble. One of his two brigades, under Evelyn Wood, had been left behind at Alexandria, which he regarded as a slight on him, and he made bitter complaints about this to my chief.[4]
>
> Major Neville Lyttelton, Headquarters

As a result, a makeshift 4th Brigade was created, made up of the Duke of Cornwall's Light Infantry and 3rd King's Royal Rifle Corps. That resolved, a formal briefing was carried out on the morning of 12 September as Wolseley and his generals rode out between the lines.

> Sir G. Wolseley then called us round him, and said he intended to leave the camp that night and march so as to reach the enemy's works before daybreak. He added to me, 'It will be a race between the Highland Brigade and [General Gerald] Graham!' Then, addressing all generally, he said, 'Go straight in on them, and then,' he added, stamping his foot on the ground, 'Kill them all!'[5]
>
> Lieutenant General Edward Hamley, Headquarters, 2nd Division

Wolseley planned to advance across a plateau about a mile north of the canal that offered better 'going' than the loose sand in the vicinity of the canal. Hamley's 2nd Division would be on the left, with the four battalions of Major General Archibald Alison's Highland Brigade leading the way and Colonel Cromer Ashburnham's 4th Brigade acting as a reserve. To its right was Willis's 1st Division, led by Major General Gerald Graham's 2nd Brigade, followed up by the 1st Brigade commanded by Major General The Duke of Connaught. Most of the artillery was banded together to provide concentrated support in a central position between the two divisions. To the south of the canal, marching along a narrow cultivated strip of land, was Major General Herbert Macpherson's Indian Contingent, with his Infantry Brigade commanded by Brigadier General Oriel Tanner. The camp was struck in the early evening, and the troops were briefed for their night march.

> The men of each company formed round their captain in order to catch his every word. Instructions to 'D' Company by Captain G. M. Fox were, in substance: 'Now, men, we are to march all night and at daybreak storm the trenches and take the enemy's position at the point of the bayonet. We are not to fire a shot till we have captured their position. Be as quiet as possible. Don't speak above a whisper. Remember striking of matches to light pipes is absolutely forbidden; it would endanger the whole army!' Then followed some general advice. Among other things, he told us that the closer we could keep to the ground the less would be the chance of getting hit![6]
>
> Private John Gordon, 1st Black Watch, Highland Brigade

Corporal John Philip recalled the mood as they set off at 01.30 on 13 September.

> Instead of the usual sharply uttered command, 'Quick march!' by which we were wont to start, came the low and subdued tones of the various officers directing their companies to move forward. Crossing the railway, we commenced our march over the soft and powdery sand, which, fanned by a light breeze and scattered by many feet of horses and men, rose about us in heavy clouds. Between it and the darkness of the night we could scarcely see more than 4 yards around: it was a case of feeling our way. Ere a mile had been traversed we emerged on to harder ground, and the choking dust was left behind. Above was the clear blue sky, studded with innumerable stars, by some of whose twinkling light we were guided on our way. The columns

had now separated and none of the other portions of the moving array are in sight.[7]

Corporal John Philip, 2nd Duke of Cornwall's Light Infantry, 4th Brigade

Although the route was relatively straightforward, it was crucial that the units did not collide in the dark and that they all appeared at the right positions, ready to launch a simultaneous attack. Army officers are reputed to be bad at reading maps, and it is certainly the case that on this night the navigation was entrusted to an officer from the Senior Service.

> For some distance onward the engineers had erected a line of telegraph-poles to guide us, but after they ceased the desert was absolutely trackless. Our guides were the stars – had the night been overcast the enterprise would have been impossible – and we were steered by a naval officer, Lieutenant Rawson, who had doubtless studied on previous nights the relation of these celestial beacons to the course of our march. The centre of the line was the point of direction; therefore, he rode between the centre battalions of the Highland Brigade. Frequently, in the course of the night, after duly ascertaining what dark figure I was addressing, I represented to him that his particular star was clouded over; but he always replied that he had another in view, a second string to his bow, which he showed me, and that he was convinced he had not deviated in the least from the proper direction.[8]

Lieutenant General Edward Hamley, Headquarters, 2nd Division

Like the dark shadows cast by moving clouds, the long columns of men moved across the desert.

> The formation adopted for the movement of the Army Corps across the 6 miles of open desert extending from Ninth Hill to the lines of Tel el Kebir was at once simple and yet closely calculated – simple, in order to meet the

conditions imposed by a moonless night; thoroughly thought out, because the formation in which the Army Corps started must be that in which it would engage the enemy when he was found, as it was hoped. There could be no manoeuvring, no afterthought, no rectification after these 17,500 officers and men with their sixty or seventy guns had been launched out into the night from the plateau of Ninth Hill, a gigantic bolt of flesh, steel, and iron shot westward into the darkness.[9]

Lieutenant Colonel William Butler, Headquarters

They marched with unloaded rifles to avoid accidental discharges, keeping as quiet as they could, but there were occasional breaches of the silence, of which one was quite striking. It was attributed in most accounts to a drunken Scotsman.

Suddenly to our right front a peal of wild and hilarious laughter rang out in this deep stillness. It ceased almost as abruptly as it had arisen. One expected that some alarm might have followed this weird, unwonted outburst, but the void was all still again. It afterwards transpired that a man in one of the Highland regiments of the leading brigade of the 2nd Division had carried a bottle of very strong rum with him, and his repeated application to this source for sustainment during the march had ended in a hysterical paroxysm.[10]

Lieutenant Colonel William Butler, Headquarters

Yet this brief kerfuffle apparently went unheard as the Egyptian lines remained silent. By this time the Highland Brigade, with, from the left, the 2nd Highland Light Infantry, the 1st Cameron Highlanders, the 1st Gordon Highlanders and the 1st Black Watch, were only some 150 yards from the Egyptian lines. They were fortunate indeed that their line of advance had taken them just north of the advanced redoubt, which would have raised the alarm much earlier. As it was, the first

shots from an Egyptian picket did not ring out until about
04.55.

> Just as the paling of the stars showed dawn to be near,
> but while it was still as dark as ever, a few scattered shots
> were fired in our front, probably from some sentries, or
> small pickets, outside the enemy's lines. No notice was
> taken of this, though one of the shots killed a Highland-
> er;[11] the movement was unchanged – and then a single
> bugle sounded within the enemy's lines. These were most
> welcome sounds, assuring us that we should close with
> the foe before daylight, which just before had seemed
> very doubtful. Yet a minute or two of dead silence elapsed
> after the bugle was blown, and then the whole extent of
> entrenchment in our front, hitherto unseen and unknown
> of, poured forth a stream of rifle fire. Then for the first time
> that night, I could really be said to see my men, lighted
> by the flashes – the dim phantom lines which I had been
> looking on all night suddenly woke to life, as our bugles
> sounded the charge; and responding with lusty continued
> cheers, and without a moment's pause or hesitation, the
> ranks sprang forward in steady array.[12]
>
> Lieutenant General Edward Hamley, Headquarters, 2nd Division

But 150 yards is a long way under heavy artillery and rifle fire
and men began to fall. Among them was Lieutenant Wyatt
Rawson, the naval officer who had guided them with such
accuracy – to be mortally wounded was a miserable reward
for such skill and devotion to duty. Luckily much of the fire
was aimed high, as the men coming up behind the Highland
Brigade could testify.

> With the rapidity of a thunderbolt, the whole place for
> miles in front was lighted up by one blaze of fire, while the
> roar of cannon and the din of musketry was terrific. Over
> our heads flew the bullets in a steady stream, with a sound

as if sheets of iron were hurling through the air.[13]
Corporal John Philip, 2nd Duke of Cornwall's Light Infantry, 4th Brigade

If there was a race between Alison's Highland Brigade and Graham's 2nd Brigade, then the Highlanders had 'won' as they were some 800 yards ahead of the 2nd Brigade echeloned to their right. At 05.20, the Scots fixed bayonets and charged home.

It seemed as if all the events of my then short life, taking on special significance, paraded in rapid succession before me. 'Oh my God, it's hot!' said Lieutenant John Maxwell unconsciously, as he stood near me, his sword drawn, ready to lead the charge. On the order to charge we rushed forward to the sound of bagpipes, cheering as loud as our lungs would allow, the most weird, unearthly noise imaginable; but what wonder, rising from thousands of men in a fighting line dashing at a living chain of fire.[14]
Private John Gordon, 1st Black Watch, Highland Brigade

The Egyptian infantry soon corrected their range and men began to fall. Pressing on, they jumped down into the ditch and attempted to climb the ramparts to close with their opponents. It was touch and go for a while, as one of the battalions for a moment gave way.

Just as I was moving on, there came a refluent tide of men which carried me back over the rampart and down into the ditch. It was a very critical moment. I sprang on my horse and did all I could to rally – and get the men on again. Hamley came up with his staff at the moment and exerted himself nobly. I never saw a man expose his life more recklessly. We got the men halted in the ditch – it was only the left of one regiment which had fallen back – the rest of the centre met with no check, and soon got them on again.[15]
Major General Archibald Alison, Headquarters, Highland Brigade

Hamley's personal leadership from the front had proved decisive – he may have been petulant, but he was a good fighting soldier. By this time some of the following 4th Brigade had caught up.

> When we got to the trench it was full of Highlanders. I jumped down into the ditch and a man in my company, Hall by name, gave me a leg up the parapet and pushed me up. I drew my sword as the men were hanging a little behind the parapet, and hallo'd to them to come on, and jumped or rather fell down the other side with an officer in one of the Highland regiments, it was too dark to see which, on to a dead [Egyptian]. The black Sudanese fought like blazes and our men like Trojans, and the [Egyptians] ran like hares. There was very little quarter given, it was most of it bayonet work when we once got inside.[16]
> Lieutenant Percival Marling, 3rd King's Royal Rifle Corps

Further to the north, at 05.30, the 1st Division struck home and overwhelmed the ramparts, while the Indian Contingent had also dashed home south of the canal. The consensus was that the Egyptian infantry had fought well.

> Complete surprise though it was to the Egyptian soldiers behind their entrenchments, they nevertheless fought with the greatest determination against overwhelming odds. Not a moment was given them to awake, form up, prepare, or move into position. The assault fell upon them as a thunderbolt might fall upon a man asleep. The leaders in whom they could trust were, like themselves, fellaheen; few among them knew anything of war, its arts, manoeuvres, or necessities; they were betrayed on every side, yet they fought stoutly wherever ten or twenty or fifty of them could get together. The heaps of dead lying with and across their rifles facing the up-coming sun bore eloquent testimony to that final resolve of these poor fellows.[17]
> Lieutenant Colonel William Butler, Headquarters

Hamley's men pushed on, overwhelming the secondary line that covered the Egyptian camp. Meanwhile the Cavalry Brigade had been circling round the left flank of the Egyptian line, ready to charge home.

> The enemy had previously heard the neighing of some of our horses and sent a shell as a 'feeler'. There was no need to give the order 'Mount!' each man and horse was wide awake and ready for Baker-Russell's cheery, 'Trot!' and away we went. The firing now became general, and we heard the sound, rising and falling, of British cheering on our left, from which we knew that the infantry was already fighting for possession of the trenches. Our squadron had to open out in order to pass a dismounted Krupp which had been upset by the bursting of one of their shells and underneath and about it lay five or six Egyptian artillery-men – shattered and horribly mutilated. The poor fellows were spread out all over the plain and running.[18]
> Sergeant Thomas Littlejohn, 4th Dragoon Guards

It was becoming a rout. Hamley's troops charged into the Egyptian camp to be met by a horrible sight.

> It was now broad daylight, and the havoc we had wrought lay spread out before us. The dead and wounded lay in hundreds – some with frightful bayonet wounds; others, having been shot at point-blank range, were rolling in agony, the clothes slowly burning on their bodies, and out of compassion these were immediately despatched. A number of tents were nearby, and they were cleared of the lurking and treacherous enemy, who though beaten and half-dead, in several instances were seen to raise themselves on their elbows and take aim at the passing soldiers. Those who attempted this, sounded their own death-knell, for a sharp stab with the bayonet was their reward, and their lifeblood ebbed quickly out on the sand.[19]
> Corporal John Philip, 2nd Duke of Cornwall's Light Infantry, 4th Brigade

Once the wounded had been cared for, Alfred Male turned his attention to the British dead.

> The poor bodies must be laid away to rest with Christian prayer as far as possible. At the corner of the big redoubt, where the fighting had been fiercest, we gathered some of them together, Highlanders all, and in the trench itself their comrades laid them reverently, covering them with an Egyptian cloth, while I stood on the earthwork above, and repeated the words of our beautiful burial service over them.[20]
> Reverend Alfred Male

The British casualties numbered some fifty-seven killed and 380 wounded with a further twenty-two men reported missing. Of these some 243 were from the embattled Highland Brigade. The Egyptian casualties were severe, estimated at around 2,000 dead and an unknown number of wounded. Whatever the human cost, Wolseley had the victory he craved. He had broken the power of Arabi and the nationalist movement. But could he get to Cairo before the city burned?

★★★

EARLIER INTERVIEWS WITH EGYPTIAN PRISONERS had revealed that if the British did not secure the town swiftly, Cairo was in danger of being burnt to the ground, either by defiant nationalists or accidentally on purpose by looting rioters. Arabi had escaped and was reported to be heading to Cairo intent on destruction. The lessons of the delay between the naval bombardment of Alexandria and getting troops ashore had been learnt. Captain Charles Watson had been ordered to accompany the cavalry under Major General Drury-Lowe in making a dash for Cairo on 14 September.

> There is an old Egyptian saying, 'He who holds Cairo holds Egypt; he who holds the Citadel holds Cairo!' and it was

almost certain that once the population knew that the Citadel was in the possession of the British, all resistance would collapse.[21]

Captain Charles Watson, Headquarters

The early signs were good as the Abbassia barracks, located in the desert just outside Cairo, surrendered without a shot being fired after Drury-Lowe's squadrons advanced threateningly in the late afternoon of 14 September.

> It was quite a dramatic scene; in the centre was the little group of British and Egyptian officers discussing the terms of surrender, while on the one side were the British and Indian troopers, and on the other the squadron of Egyptian cavalry; behind, the white mass of Abbassia Barracks, about which we could see a great number of Egyptian soldiers, some drawn up in a column, and some wandering here and there, like sheep without a shepherd. Then, as a background, Cairo in the distance, and beyond all the eastern sky, bright with the red gleam of the setting sun.[22]
>
> Captain Charles Watson, Headquarters

After dark, a small force of cavalry under Watson's command was despatched to capture the Citadel before the Egyptians had a chance to realise just how few troops had reached Cairo. He had eighty-nine of the 4th Dragoon Guards and a further fifty-eight mounted infantry under a Captain Richard Lawrence. By the time they reached Cairo it was pitch dark. Though unmet by resistance thus far, the situation was still tense as Watson and some Egyptian officers went forward to see what was happening. The Citadel commandant was dug out of bed and Watson acted with the kind of utter confidence that was designed to intimidate.

> I said that he must parade the whole garrison without any delay and send them down to the Kasir el Nil Barracks in the

lower part of Cairo. I said that I had brought a British force to garrison the Citadel, and that the keys of all the gates were to be handed over to me at once. He seemed a little doubtful at first, but not having any idea how many men we had, he decided to comply, and sent for the keeper of the keys, who brought a number of very large keys in a beautiful bag and handed them over. I had ordered them to go to Kasir el Nil Barracks; but a considerable number never arrived there, as they took the opportunity, while marching through the streets of Cairo in the dark, of slipping away and going to their homes; this, however, was a good thing, as they were useful messengers to spread the news of how they had been turned out of the Citadel by the 'English Army'.[23]
Captain Charles Watson, Headquarters

Watson estimated there had been about 6,000 troops at the Citadel. They were not, however, the only inhabitants, as Lawrence discovered.

Hearing a loud murmur of voices and clanking sounds, I came round a corner unseen before to find some hundreds of men and women sitting round a fire that was burning on the ground, busy knocking iron shackles off their legs! It appeared that there were two prisons in the Citadel, and the departing troops had played us a nasty trick by letting the prisoners loose before they marched out themselves! These people had then broken open an armourer's shop and obtained tools to suit their needs. I ordered up at once two guards from the Dragoons, and we rushed all the poor wretches back into their prisons, and slammed the doors on those dark, evil-smelling holes! Leaving the guards on these two doors, I found some cells with European prisoners, or men of a better class, and seeing them safely shut in, passed along on my rounds.[24]
Captain Richard Lawrence, Mounted Infantry, Cavalry Division

The key to Cairo was in British hands.

On 15 September, Wolseley arrived in Cairo, accompanied by the Guards. Among them was Lieutenant Charles Balfour.

> Suddenly the bugles sounded, the train has arrived, and we start at once. We get our things on and fall in, and march down to the station. Very tired; train pretty crammed; sleep out of the question; jolting is a mild expression to apply to this train. It resembles the transit of the modest kind of country cart over gigantic boulders of rock. At intervals stop and chat with regiments bivouacked on the line: at length we reach Zagazig where we have to wait an hour or two. The Pyramids in sight and at last Cairo about 11.30 a.m. (15 September). All the available male population swarm out to see us. Quite an unexpected surprise to wait only half an hour or so before starting. The pipes struck up 'Hieland Laddie' and we marched into the streets. The women make a most extraordinary shrill screaming noise from the top storied windows of the houses to express joy, and certainly they treated us to a full dose of it.[25]
> Lieutenant Charles Balfour, 1st Scots Guards, 1st Brigade

At 15.30 on 25 September a grand parade of Wolseley's force marked the arrival of Egypt's nominal ruler, who was driven in an open-topped carriage from the train station.

> As the procession came along the bands played the *Khedive's March* and the troops presented arms, but not a sound not even a salaam from the crowd. The Khedive looked a pale, sallow creature. Alongside him sat the Duke of Connaught, and opposite Sir Garnet and Sir Beauchamp Seymour. Behind followed all the staff. In the evening there were illuminations.[26]
> Lieutenant James Grierson, Headquarters

The Khedive was most grateful to the British forces that had 'saved' him from the nationalists. Many of the nationalist leaders and key supporters were arrested and would stand trial for their 'treason'. The trial of Arabi would be symbolic, for the British insisted he should have a fair trial. But the trial also showed some unpleasant truths about the British involvement.

> Whether the trial was a bona-fide one or a farce was never sufficiently clear. Certain it is that Arabi for treason was condemned to death. Equally certain that this judgment was at once cancelled and that of exile substituted. I sat quite close to him at the time of his sentence and had opportunity of studying the face and the man. A broad, and, for an oriental, an honest face, there was something which appealed to your sympathy a good deal. He looked crushed by his misfortunes, yet there was still a dignity of bearing, which compared favourably with his judges. Certainly, the facts which were opened up at the trial dispelled many delusions. We had gone to war, not with the Egyptian nation, but to crush a rebel movement which had thrown the country into a state of anarchy, and which threatened the safety of our highway to India. The facts which transpired at that trial showed this rebel movement to have been really a national protest against the tyranny of a government, with a weak viceroy at its head, and men alien to the country as its ministers. Arabi showed singleness of purpose in his aims. He truly had the nation at his back. No participation in, or approval of, the Alexandrian massacres could be brought home to him. He was a poor man when he began his movement; he was no richer when he ended – a strange fact, indeed, had he been nothing but an adventurer. Had he succeeded he would have been an Oliver Cromwell.[27]
>
> Reverend Alfred Male

He was not alone in his suspicions over British actions. There was a considerable minority in Britain who opposed imperialism as being not only harmful to the British reputation for espousing liberalism and the eradication of slavery, but also damaging to the home country. However, such doubting voices were all but drowned out in a country in thrall to jingoism.

With the fighting over, Evelyn Baring was appointed to act as Consul General to Egypt and for more than two decades would be the real power at the heart of the Egyptian government. Although a parliament was established, authority was only granted to Egyptian politicians willing to follow the British line, while control was channelled through British officials in what became known as the 'Veiled Protectorate'.

Wolseley had triumphed at the Battle of Tel el Kebir, but there was a considerable amount of controversy as to the detail within his despatches reporting the battle. He was accused of giving far too much credit to the men of Graham's 1st Division, of ignoring the key contributions of Hamley's 2nd Division and in particular of the gallant Highland Brigade. The various generals and their supporters would spend a great deal of time writing to the press, making claims and counterclaims designed to show themselves in a good light. Lieutenant Colonel William Butler had an inkling of the truth of it in that too many cooks can spoil the broth!

On taking the three arms – infantry, cavalry, and artillery – together, there was a general to every 900 men. At first sight this plethora of the highest rank might seem of small account, but in reality, in war, it was certain to prove a serious injury. Even in a campaign of exceptional activity, the days of actual fighting must bear small relation to the days when there is no external fighting. When there is no external fighting going on, internal squabbles are apt to show themselves in camp or on the march. Staffs are also belligerently disposed on these occasions. The feathers of the domestic cock have for many years been used to distinguish general and staff officers in the British Army. 'Fine feathers make fine birds' is an old saying; and why should not the plumage of the rooster, fluttering gaily in the cocked hat of generals and staff officers, have some effect upon the heads of the men who are called 'the brains of the army'?[28]

Lieutenant Colonel William Butler, Headquarters

Still, they had triumphed and brought a victory that seemed to cement Wolseley's reputation as a great general. Yet even as the British celebrated their victory there were stirrings in the Sudan provinces that would change everything.

5

THE RISE OF THE MAHDI

Hicks did his best and was a gallant officer, but he was from
the first a doomed man, as Gordon after him was doomed.
The fact of their Christianity, and of their holding Tewfik's commission, made it impossible for either of them to
succeed in stemming the rebellion.[1]
Wilfred Blunt

THE SUDAN WAS A HELL ON EARTH that seemed to attract religious
fundamentalists. If it is true that extreme religious or political
beliefs are inculcated by extreme oppression, corruption and
mass human misery, then the Sudan was the ideal breeding
ground. The Sudan's history was one of Arab conquest, with
successive incursions preying on the indigenous African population. Some Arabs bred camels or kept cattle, but there was also
a thriving slave trade. The result was a patchwork of feuding
Arab tribes, a subservient underclass and no cohesive system
of government – it was a wild country. Surrounded by hostile
deserts and dense equatorial forests it was difficult to conquer
until Mohammed Ali, the Pasha of Egypt, made a determined
effort to overcome the obstacles and sent strong expeditionary
forces to fight their way up the Nile. A new administrative and
government centre was founded in Khartoum, at the junction
of the Blue and White Niles, but this was only the start. Over
the years the invaders pushed ever further to the south, taking
control of the huge Kordofan, Darfur and Equatorial provinces.
Although Egypt paid lip-service to abolishing the slave trade,
her officials did little or nothing to stop the main culprits, who

not only thrived but also set up their own suzerainties within the Sudanese borders. Awareness of the militant disapproval of the British government to any vestiges of the slave trade led the Khedive to appoint a British governor of the Equatorial province as a fig leaf, to avoid retribution. The first, Samuel Baker, was in 1874 succeeded in the post by Colonel Charles Gordon, a distinguished officer of the Royal Engineers. Perceiving the experiment to have been relatively successful, Gordon was appointed as the governor of the whole of the Sudan in 1877.

Gordon was born to a military family on 28 January 1833. He joined the Royal Engineers in 1852, served with distinction in the Crimean War in 1855 and took part at the close of the Second Anglo-Chinese War in 1860. In 1863, he was appointed to command Chinese forces and performed brilliantly in saving the emperor from the Taiping rebels, rising to the local rank of general. By the time of his return to Britain in 1865, he became known to the popular press as 'Chinese Gordon'. After a period of more humdrum duties, he had been plucked back from obscurity by the Khedive's call to the Sudan. He proved a dynamic governor, lambasting the corrupt Egyptian officials and attempting to stamp out the slave trade. He had some impact in restricting the activities of slave traders, but the lack of any real authoritative direction or control from either the Khedive in Egypt or the Turkish Sultan left a power vacuum in the Sudan, which Gordon could not fill on his own. In 1879, he was further irritated when the Khedive Ismail Pasha was removed in favour of his son, Tewfik. Although, as we have seen, this was done at the instigation of the British and French governments, Gordon felt he should have been consulted before such a drastic action was taken. His response to a combination of these pressures and ill health was to resign as the Sudan governor in 1879. The Sudan soon reverted to its old ways under the far more laissez-faire suzerainty of his Egyptian replacement, Raouf Pasha. The slave traders resumed their evil business without any real hindrance, and the poor and needy of Sudan once again suffered unbearable cruelty and oppression.

In the light of this terrible predicament, the whirlwind rise of Mohammed Ahmed was something to behold. Born in Dongola around 1844, he was devoutly religious, studying the Islamic texts under the foremost Sudanese scholars. He travelled widely, spreading the word, gaining a reputation as a powerful preacher, combining passion with an incendiary message from his trance-like visions that he was the chosen one, the prophesised 'Mahdi', who would be guided by God to secure the universal acceptance and dominance of the Islamic faith, bringing an era of justice and prosperity for all, before going on to preside over the Day of Judgement. This offered a golden future and a place in heaven for those who fell in with striving to achieve the Mahdi's vision. What did they have to lose?

Mohammed Ahmed announced his status as the Mahdi publicly in May 1881. On 11 August, the first clash occurred when a company of Egyptian troops armed with Remington rifles descended on the 300 barely armed supporters that the Mahdi had gathered on Aba Island on the White Nile. The result was a shock as the sheer elan of the Mahdists overwhelmed the Egyptian troops. The Mahdi then avoided immediate retribution by retiring into the Nuba mountains of South Kordofan, from there spreading his messianic message and gaining recruits wherever he went. His strength grew rapidly. When two more Egyptian companies pursued him, they too were ambushed and destroyed at the Battle of Jabel Quadir on 9 December 1881. Word of these victories spread and many of the local tribes joined the Mahdist forces, known as the Ansar, which soon were numbered in thousands.

Meanwhile, the Egyptian government was being distracted first by the nationalist revolt by Colonel Ahmed Arabi, and then by the British retaliation with the Egyptian War of 1882. The resulting power lacuna was the ideal opportunity – it was not missed.

The Mahdi moved on to El Obeid, where he suffered a painful rebuff in an initial attack made on 8 September 1882. He attributed this to the crude frontal assault tactics employed, and resolved in future to simply surround such well-defended localities, relying on starvation to deliver his enemies to him without heavy losses. This would set the pattern for future operations, including the siege of Khartoum. As for the Egyptian forces, they were still in disarray. A relief expedition for El Obeid ended up being besieged itself at the town of Bara. In January 1883, both Bara and El Obeid were finally starved out, with the surviving soldiers assimilated into the Ansar hosts and the leaders executed. With El Obeid now serving as the Mahdist capital, the huge provinces of Kordofan and most of Darfur had fallen to the rebellion. The word was spreading fast.

★★★

IN EGYPT THE WAR WAS OVER and, thanks to the intervention of the British, Tewfik Pasha had regained his status as the Khedive. Arabi's army had disintegrated since the Battle of Tel el Kebir, but a start was made under British guidance in setting up a new army – initially to be some 6,000 strong. This was in accordance with the long-standing policy of empires throughout history to maintain domination of a country by building up a local army under the control of the invaders. This had been the tried and trusted technique in India, and it would be applied wholesale in Egypt, even though this was not formally part of the British Empire. On 21 December 1882, Major General Evelyn Wood was appointed as 'Sirdar' or commander in chief of this reformatted army, which would be rebuilt from the bottom upwards. To assist him, several British officers were despatched to take control of the regiments – given Egyptian ranks a grade or two higher than their British Army status. Captain Charles Watson was one of the Royal Engineer officers called back to Egypt. He would become Wood's righthand man and even stood in as Sirdar on occasion.

> My principal work is to look after the way in which the War Minister spends the money, and keep a 'general eye'

over all matters of artillery stores, etc. I have had plenty to
do already – and find that I must speak Arabic. Just fancy: I
was inspecting the clothing establishment today and had to
discuss the new patterns of cloth with the director of it, a
nice old gentleman who knew not a word of any European
language. However, I managed to get along![2]

Major Charles Watson, Egyptian Army

Another Royal Engineer recruited to the Egyptian Army was
Herbert Kitchener, who in 1883 had finally escaped his service
in Cyprus and had been posted as a captain to be second in
command of the sole Egyptian cavalry regiment. He soon
earned a reputation as a hardworking officer, determined to
train his men to a high standard. Andrew Haggard was also
appointed as a second in command, this time of the newly
reformed 4th Egyptian Battalion, where he identified a number
of problems that had to be resolved before they could become
effective officers.

Our chief difficulty was of course at first the language,
or rather the languages, in which we had to carry on our
work. Our second difficulty was the drill – that is, to find
out the best kind of drill to suit the Egyptians. As regards
the former, we had to talk French to such of the officers as
understood it, and to conduct all our correspondence in
French and Arabic. Secondly, we had to deal with all the
non-commissioned officers and soldiers in Arabic alone;
and thirdly, the actual words of command, which we had
to pick up ourselves before we could roll them off the chest
in fine sonorous tones to the soldiers, had to be in Turkish,
of which the soldiers themselves understood just about as
much as we did. To tell the truth, it was a very bastard
Turkish that we used in those words of command, many
of which we manufactured for ourselves as time went on;
but still the old non-commissioned officers and the officers
from whom we learnt it, many of whom were half-Turks

and Circassians, understood what it was meant for, which was all that was wanted. As we all worked very hard from morning till night, and as the Egyptian has naturally a wonderful aptitude, or to be more accurate, a wonderful affection, for drill, we very soon found things going along splendidly. Of course, we made some frightful mistakes to begin with, but that did not matter – all pioneers make mistakes.[3]

Major Andrew Haggard, 4th Egyptian Battalion

Few could have imagined that in less than twenty years these Egyptian army battalions would be front and centre in the victories achieved.

★★★

TO THE BRITISH GOVERNMENT THE SUDAN was an unwelcome sideshow, an Egyptian problem that was the responsibility of the hapless Khedive Tewfik to resolve. The 'new' Egyptian Army was too small and too 'new' (and at this point intended for service in Egypt only), to be of any use in suppressing the huge Mahdist revolt. But something had to be done. In desperation, Tewfik, recalled some 10,000 of Arabi's former army to the colours for service in the Sudan. To secure a reassuring professional leadership, a number of British officers were recruited. Foremost among these was Colonel William Hicks, who had retired from service in the Indian Army in 1880, after a long career including service in the Indian Mutiny and on the staff of the Abyssinian expedition of 1867–8. He was now raised to the rank of major general and appointed as chief of staff to the nominal Commander in Chief Sudan: Suliman Niazi Pasha. On his arrival in Khartoum, Hicks consulted with Lieutenant Colonel John Hamill Stewart, a British intelligence officer who had been sent out to assess the situation. The outlook was certainly grim, isolated as they were, with unreliable troops, whose pay was often months adrift, faced by superior numbers of well-motivated opponents and with a logistical incoherence plaguing anything they might try to do.

At first it seemed that, against the odds, Hicks might be successful. In April 1883, he led some 5,000 men to try and clear the territory between the Blue and White Niles. He vengefully destroyed all evidence of the Mahdi's time on Aba Island, before fighting a battle with around 5,000 Dervishes at the Battle of Marabieh on 29 April. Adopting a square formation which exposed no flanks, and blessed by the presence of two machine guns, Hicks's force managed to keep their nerve, and their firepower flayed the Dervishes who were armed for the most part only with spears and swords. Following this success, Hicks fell back to Khartoum to reorganise. Unhappy with what he perceived as interference from Suliman Niazi Pasha, Hicks threatened to resign, but any impasse was prevented when his superior was made governor of East Sudan, while Hicks was promoted to overall command with the rank of lieutenant general.

Also present in Khartoum was a twenty-five-year-old journalist and artist, Frank Power, who had only arrived that August, but was appalled by the sheer brutality and venality of the Egyptian regime that Hicks had to cope with.

> I pity Hicks, he is an able, good and energetic man, but he has to do with wretched Egyptians, who take a pleasure in being incompetent, thwarting one, delaying and lying.[4]
> Frank Power, *The Times*

On 9 September 1883, having gained command and emboldened by his success at Marabieh, Hicks launched an ambitious expedition to reconquer El Obeid and the Kordofan province. This time he advanced with the Sudan Field Force consisting of some 8,100 infantry, 900 cavalry and 300 gunners deploying four field guns, ten mountain guns and six machine guns. All this accompanied by some 2,000 camp followers, 5,500 camels and 500 horses. This was a major expedition in numbers, but the overall quality of the personnel was dire. Power accompanied

Hicks, but a dreadful bout of dysentery that reduced him from over 14 stone to only just 9 stone caused him to be sent back from Deum to Khartoum. His bowels would save his life.

Hicks and his army began the long march to El Obeid from Deum. One of the journalists accompanying him seems to have been aware of their predicament.

> You know I am by this time, after an experience of many years, pretty well accustomed to dangers of most kinds, even some extra. Yet I assure you I feel it terrible to face deadly peril far away from civilized ideas, and where no mercy is to be met with, in company with cravens that you expect to see run at every moment, and who will leave you behind to face the worst.[5]
> Edmund O'Donovan, *Daily News*

Hick's command was plagued by disputes between feuding British and Egyptian officers. The men were still not capable of anything but marching in a clumsy square formation, as they could not be guaranteed to quickly form square if attacked. They had to carry everything they needed, which meant a shortage of water soon became a desperate problem. Morale was poor, something which the Mahdi's agents played upon, infiltrating into the camp and spreading the word of his divine mission. Desertions were frequent. Gradually the Mahdi amassed his forces and, as they grew in strength, began to leech away the strength of the Sudan Field Force. Stragglers were picked off by Dervish horsemen, while the overnight zeribas were harassed by rifle fire.

At 10.30 on 5 November 1883, the Mahdi and his generals struck, having amassed a force of approximately 40,000 men. The terrain dotted with trees had forced Hicks to divide his force into three squares, one leading the way, with the other two following on some 300 yards apart. Under attack by hordes of determined warriors, the already demoralised Egyptian infantry were helpless, and one by one the squares collapsed as the killing began. One anonymous Arab boy left an account in a later set of detailed interviews.

> It was near noon – a rush, terrible and sudden, sweeping down like the torrent from the mountain, was made. The Arabs burst upon our front face in overwhelming numbers. It was swept away like chaff before the wind. Seeing this, the other sides of the square turned inwards, and commenced a death dealing fusillade both on the Arabs pressing into the square and on each other crossways. A terrible slaughter commenced. Hicks Pasha and the very few English officers left with him, seeing all hope of restoring order gone, spurred their horses, and sprang out of the confused mass of wounded, dead, and dying. These officers fired away their revolvers, clearing a space for themselves, till all their ammunition was expended. They killed many. They had got clear outside. They then took to their swords and fought till they fell. Hicks Pasha now alone remained. He kept them all at bay, but he was struck on the wrist with a sword, and he dropped his own. He then fell. I was covered with blood, and I got under a dead body and pretended to be dead while the struggling and yelling, uproar, fighting, and slaughtering was going on, as it did for 3 hours. They felt me and found I was alive; they pricked me with a spear. I was made prisoner.[6]
> Anon.

Although there may be an element of 'telling people what they want to hear', with Hicks identified as the last to fall, the intelligence officers gave credence to this account. It was estimated some 11,000 men were killed in half an hour of havoc, including Edmond O'Donovan. Only around 300 were taken prisoner.

Back in Khartoum, the Europeans were aware that they were living in a tinderbox, with little real support for their cause in the city. The news of the massacre had reached them soon enough, but if that was not bad enough, it was followed by reports of a new seat of rebellion.

In August 1883, a former slave trader, Osman Digna, had taken advantage of the chaos to ferment revolt in the Suakin area, a key port on the Red Sea coast. Whether he was inspired by religious fervour or a desire to return to his former profession is not entirely clear, but the revolt gained a ready traction among the martial east coast tribes, particularly among the Hadendawa tribesmen. Local successes enabled him to dominate much of the Red Sea coastal area outside of the towns of Suakin and Sinkat. A column of some 550 men was sent out to suppress the revolt, accompanied by the local British consul Lynedoch Moncrieff, a veteran of the Zulu Wars, who had decided to go along for the experience. On 4 November 1883, the column was ambushed at the hamlet of El Teb by a party of Hadendawa. They tried to form square, but it collapsed under the onslaught, and although many escaped, Moncrieff was not one of them. This triumph meant a large number of Remingtons and copious ammunition fell into Osman Digna's hands. As the flames of this secondary revolt began to spread, the seat of government in Khartoum was threatened on two fronts.

Hicks had left the defence of Khartoum in the hands of one of his British officers, Colonel Henry de Coetlogan, a recently retired officer who had served in the Indian Army. On news of the disaster, he had recalled garrisons from vulnerable outposts, concentrating what forces were left at Khartoum. With him he had reporter Frank Power, who was asked to act as the British consul in the absence of any other candidates. They set to work to greatly strengthen the defences by ordering the construction of a formidable ditch and ramparts between the White Nile and Fort Burri next to the Blue Nile. They used considerable imagination to deny an easy approach to the rebels.

> We have paved the bottom of the ditch and side of the fortification with spear-heads, and have for 100 yards the ground in front strewn with iron crows' feet, things that have three short spikes up however they are thrown,, and then beyond, for 500 yards, broken bottles – you know the

Mahdi's men are all in their bare feet; at intervals we have put tin biscuit-boxes full of powder, nails, and bullets, at 2 feet underground, with electric wires to them, so Messieurs the rebels will have a *mauvais quart d'heure* before they get to the ditch.[7]
Frank Power, *The Times*

De Coetlogan managed to amass a garrison of around 8,000 men, although many lacked military virtues. He appealed to the Khedive for more troops to bolster the defences but was denied in a peremptory fashion that enraged Power.

This morning Colonel de Coetlogan gets a telegram from the Khedive to say that, 'He believes he cannot get together a column to relieve us, so we must depend on the neighbouring sheiks for assistance.' This is really rich, as the Khedive knows very well that there is not a sheik in the Sudan who would, or dare, help us; and the fact of our sending to a tribe for help would confess our weakness and bring it down on us like a hundred of bricks.[8]
Frank Power, *The Times*

The Mahdi was gaining power and influence at an exponential rate and even Gladstone and his Liberal Government could not ignore the burgeoning threat to Egypt – and hence to the Suez Canal. But what were they to do?

★★★

WHILE GLADSTONE AND HIS MINISTERS PONDERED, the British press – as so often – knew exactly what should be done! It was started innocently enough when the explorer Samuel Baker wrote a letter suggesting that the former governor general Charles Gordon should be sent back to sort things out. This was picked up by William Stead, the pugnacious editor of the *Pall Mall Gazette*. He had developed a reputation for controversial press campaigns; indeed, he has been cited as the precursor of modern tabloid journalism. He was intrigued by Baker's proposal and arranged for Gordon to be interviewed. Some of the interview reflected the time-honoured concerns of British imperialists at the prospect of a victory by Muslim forces acting as a contagion across the world. The rest was a clear exposition of what Gordon thought, which was *not* what government policy was edging towards – the evacuation of the Sudan.

> You have 6,000 men in Khartoum. What are you going to do with them? You have garrisons in Darfur, in Bahr Gazelle, and Gondokoro. Are they to be sacrificed? Their only offence is their loyalty to their Sovereign. For their fidelity you are going to abandon them to their fate. How will you move your 6,000 men from Khartoum and all the Europeans in that city, through the desert to Wadi Haifa? Where are you going to get the camels to take them away? Will the Mahdi supply them? If they are to escape with their lives, the garrison will not be allowed to leave with a coat on their backs. They will be plundered to the skin, and even then, their lives may not be spared. Whatever you may decide about evacuation, you cannot evacuate, because your army cannot be moved. You must either surrender absolutely to the Mahdi or defend Khartoum at all hazards. The latter is the only course which ought to be entertained. There is no serious difficulty about it. The Mahdi's forces will fall to pieces of themselves.[9]
> Major General Charles Gordon

This last typifies the confidence borne of a somewhat naïve ignorance of the scale of the danger posed by the Mahdi and his forces.

Nevertheless, the press became enthused with the idea that Gordon was the only candidate capable of taking over the reins of power in the Sudan. Gordon was a self-confident loose cannon, of eccentric religious views, unwilling to fall in with the views of others, convinced that his way was the right way in all matters. He would follow his instincts, push his ethical opinions to the end, and seemed to have no fear of death – if the Mahdi was a zealot, then so too was Gordon. But Gordon was right about the fundamental unsoundness of the adopted strategy of evacuating Khartoum. How exactly was it to be done? Yet still he was to be sent out assisted only by Lieutenant Colonel John Hamill Stewart. This was a disaster waiting to happen.

Voices from Egypt had an idea of the dangers run in considering Gordon. The Consul Evelyn Baring had refused to consider Gordon earlier, feeling that to send such a demonstrative Christian to Khartoum to face a religious movement led by the Mahdi would be counterproductive. He also feared Gordon's erratic changes of mind on any given subject.

> Gordon would be the best man if he will pledge himself
> to carry out the policy of withdrawing from the Sudan as
> quickly as is possible consistently with saving life. He must
> also fully understand that he must take his instructions from
> the British representative in Egypt and report to him.[10]
> Evelyn Baring

Gladstone seems to have shared these fears that Gordon would need controlling.

Yet Gladstone left the briefing of Gordon to a committee led by Secretary of State for War, Lord Hartington. In retrospect this may have been a mistake. For after the briefings there somehow remained a fatal ambiguity as to whether Gordon was simply to report on the situation in the Sudan, arrange to evacuate European civilians and the Egyptian troops garrisoning the Sudan, to negotiate a lasting settlement with the Mahdi, or, by some unspecified means, secure a military victory over the Mahdi and his ever-increasing armies. All but the first of these options were impossible from the start.

Gordon left London on 18 January 1884. In an early sign of what was to come, he tried to bypass Port Said and sail through the Suez Canal direct to the Red Sea port of Suakin, to avoid having to discuss the situation with either Evelyn Baring or the Khedive Tewfik Pasha. His stratagem was detected, and he was ordered to report to Cairo first. Gordon's reception committee included Colonel Francis Grenfell, who recorded his impressions.

> He was a strange and interesting man, who, once seen, could not be forgotten – short and spare, his hair tinged with grey, with a curious detached look in his blue eyes. His appearance was 'not of the earth earthy' but that of a communer with the unseen, as indeed he was. He lived in a world of his own, and practical business with him was almost impossible. The only orders he implicitly obeyed were those evolved by himself after consultation with his Bible.[11]
> Colonel Francis Grenfell, Headquarters, Egyptian Army

An old friend of Gordon's, Gerald Graham, left us his memories of Gordon's meeting with the Khedive, which makes for somewhat uncomfortable reading – for there was more than a touch of arrogance on display.

> After breakfast Gordon sent for the Sultan [Khedive] and his brothers, treating them with civility, but as inferiors and with no ceremony, telling them to sit down, and dismissing them when done with. He talked Arabic utterly regardless of grammar, as he does French, but he rarely seems at a loss for a word – when he is he refers to his interpreter – and he always seems to make himself understood. Gordon's telegram to Khartoum yesterday was, 'Don't be panic-stricken; you are men, not women; I am coming!'[12]
> Major General Gerald Graham

In a sign of the growing uncertainty, despite the oft-expressed reservations of Baring, Tewfik appointed Gordon as his governor general of the Sudan; clearly, Gordon was no longer just reporting back to the British government. Confusion in aims and objectives was proliferating between Gordon and the powers that be in London and Cairo – a recipe for disaster against such a focused and formidable opponent as the Mahdi.

While in Cairo, Gordon met Zubeir Pasha, one of his old slave trader adversaries, who had been a powerful figure in the Sudan in addition to his many nefarious activities. Although at times useful to the Khedive, Zubeir had grown too powerful, and he had been placed under detention in Cairo for the last six years. Gordon concluded that in the existing circumstances the best that could be hoped for was to hand over power in Sudan to Zubeir. Although still an unreconstructed advocate of slavery, Zubeir had a strong existing powerbase in the Sudan, which Gordon hoped might counter the advance of the Mahdi. Despite their former enmity, Gordon considered that Zubeir was 'a man they could do business with'. Baring reluctantly fell in with Gordon's arguments, but he had a far more difficult task in convincing the politicians back in London. Far from the intractable problem of the Sudan, but all too close to the outrage that would be expressed by the Liberal politicians and newspapers, the powerful anti-slavery lobby and the British voters, the British government wavered for several months, before eventually telling Baring in March 1884 that Zubeir was simply not acceptable. Better a Sudan in flames than a return to the slavers.

With the Sudan policy still undecided, Gordon and Stewart set off for Khartoum on 26 January 1884. Their mission was hopeless from the start. They were just two men, without the backing of the kind of strong British expeditionary force that might have given them a chance of successfully evacuating Khartoum. With the existing relatively small garrison of poorly trained Egyptian troops they would be lucky to survive. Gerald Graham never forgot his last parting with Gordon at Korosko on the Nile on 2 February.

The place where I last saw Gordon is wild and desolate. The desert there is covered with a series of volcanic hills, nothing between the hills but black basins, or ravines, dry, dark, and destitute of all vegetation, looking like separate entrances to the pit where those who entered might leave hope behind. I climbed up the highest of these hills and through a glass watched Gordon and the small caravan as his camels threaded their way along a sandy valley, hoping that he would turn round that I might give him one more sign; but he rode on until he turned the dark side of one of the hills, and I saw him no more. Sadly, we returned to our steamer, and I felt a gloomy foreboding that I should never see Gordon again.[13]

Major General Gerald Graham

He never did.

6

BATTLES OF SUAKIN, 1884

They were certainly the most fearless creatures I have seen. One felt quite sorry such brave men should be killed, but there was no help for it. If they only learnt to use their rifles in the same fearless way they use their spears I don't think our men would have had much chance with them.[1]

Captain Arthur Wilson, HMS *Hecla*

OSMAN DIGNA WAS A THORN IN THE SIDE of the Egyptian authorities. His rebellion in the Suakin area had moved from an irritation to a serious threat. The death of the British consul, Colonel Lynedoch Moncrieff, was a signpost to the future and a decision had to be made whether to continue to garrison Suakin or surrender it to the rebels. The answer was to send a former British officer, Valentine Baker, to take command.

Baker had a promising future as an innovative cavalry officer, rising to command the 10th Hussars, before an incident in 1875 led to him being cashiered and imprisoned after what was either a misunderstanding or an attempted assault on a young woman in a railway carriage. It was a true *cause célèbre* that appeared to end his career prospects, reviled as he was by almost everyone from top to bottom in society. On his release, he took service under the Sultan in the Turkish Army during the Russo-Turkish War of 1877–8. His combination of military skills, reckless courage and aggressive tactics led to rapid promotion to lieutenant general, and great success on the battlefield. He also re-encountered another classic Victorian adventurer, Colonel Fred Burnaby, with whom he had already shared several adventures. Burnaby was still serving with the Household Cavalry, but as was his wont, had taken a long leave to visit the latest war zone. Baker was then employed in an administrative capacity in Armenia from 1878–82, but had travelled to Cairo, hoping to be appointed as Sirdar, by Khedive Tefil Pasha. This was too much for Queen Victoria, still outraged by Baker's alleged conduct, who blocked the appointment in favour of Evelyn Wood. As a sop to Baker, he was given command of the semi-military Egyptian gendarmerie. With the crisis in Suakin demanding military resources, Baker was the man selected, like Gordon, as a sacrificial lamb, to bring order to the Red Sea Littoral. Baker's gendarmerie was hastily reconstituted as two infantry battalions and a cavalry regiment, and he would be further reinforced by three battalions of Sudanese infantry, one raised with the help of Zubeir Pasha, and the others from garrison towns. Finally, a Turko-Egyptian battalion was raised. Many of these men had not really signed up for service outside Egypt and were thus both mutinous and deserting in droves. Baker reached Suakin in December 1883, and began the work of trying to convert his unwilling men into soldiers. One welcome addition to Baker's ranks was Burnaby, who sensed another wild adventure was in the offing and once again took leave from his regiment to join the fray. Burnaby was a consummate soldier, even though he did not look the part.

His complexion was a sickly fish belly white, which was made even more conspicuous by the tiny dead black moustache he wore. I never saw him in the magnificent panoply of the 'Blues' full dress, but in 'civies' he was slovenly to grotesqueness. On that eventful day he went forth to battle clothed in an old blue yachting suit, with two soiled dress ties knotted below his knees – navy fashion – and with his neck wrapped in a black silk muffler. A broad-brimmed pith-hat, green-lined, with the chin strap worn as gunners do, and a straight double-edged, dervish sword in a red leather sheath completed the picture.[2]

Frank Scudamore, *The Times*

Somehow Baker persuaded himself that his force was strong enough to relieve the besieged garrison at Tokar. On 28 January 1884 they sailed down to land at the port of Trinkitat. Here they established Fort Baker to act as a firm base, before moving inland. Next day, they began to advance inland behind a cavalry screen, initially in two columns, followed by four Krupp guns, two Gatling guns, a small escort and some 300 baggage camels.

> A screen of cavalry surrounded our front and flanks at a distance of about a mile. Our infantry was drawn up in double echelon of squares. The guns were in the centre of the large square, the camels and baggage were between the two smaller squares and about 200 cavalry were in two squadrons. Small scouting parties were sent out considerably in advance and beyond the cavalry screen. The ground was sandy – very flat; a few tufts of grass here and there broke the monotony of the scene. Small parties of the enemy occasionally showed themselves on our left front and skirmishers on camels on our front and right front.[3]
>
> Colonel Fred Burnaby

They had not gone far that day when the First Battle of El Teb burst upon them. British journalist John Macdonald, who was accompanying the force, saw the beginning of the action.

> About nine o'clock shots were heard from the vedettes on our left front, where a number of the enemy were soon visible. The enemy were dispersed by three rounds of Krupps. Bands of rebels then appeared on the ridges in front and towards the right. In the latter direction a small body of the rebel cavalry suddenly came in sight. Clearly the enemy's intention was to rush upon us on all sides. Major Giles, commanding the Turkish cavalry, received orders to charge the Arab horse.[4]
>
> John Macdonald, *London Daily News*

The ill-disciplined cavalry set off and were soon in disarray, despite the best efforts of Baker and Burnaby.

> Baker advanced a troop of cavalry to drive them off. Our cavalrymen got out of hand; three troops advanced instead of one and pursued in straggling order for a distance of about 1½ miles. The general seeing this, ordered Major Harvey to recall them. I rode on with this object and by cutting a corner I eventually came up with some of the men, Major Harvey endeavouring to get them into line. At this moment a very heavy fire could be heard on my left rear, and half a dozen Arabs on horses appeared from a piece of rapidly sloping ground in our front. Harvey endeavoured to make the cavalry move forward. It was hopeless; they swung round at a rapid trot. The six enemy horses approaching at a gallop, some of our men fired at them on the move; it is needless to say, with no result. One of the enemy Arabs became emboldened; he galloped straight into our squadron and began to cut down men right and left. His companions had given up the chase, but not this man, who, alone, was putting to flight the whole squadron who made no attempt to defend themselves but begged for mercy and were killed like sheep. General Baker was endeavouring to rally his men, but it was an impossible task. I shot down some, but this would not stop the rest, and whilst Baker was endeavouring to make the cowards stop, I could see that they were only pursued by a handful of men with spears. A good squadron of cavalry could have driven all the Arabs back, but our cavalry were as timid as our infantry. It was a *sauve qui peut*.[5]
> Colonel Fred Burnaby

Meanwhile the infantry had been engaged in forming one large brigade strength square. It had not gone well: training on a barrack square was different from the reality in the face of a determined enemy.

The infantry had been gradually reforming for the purpose of getting into a single large square in front and on the left flank, and also on part of the right; but in the remaining part and along the whole of what was intended to be the rear side of the square the companies were a noisy confused rabble. The sight filled one with dismay. This was the state of things when the enemy, numbers of whom, in spite of the vigilance of the cavalry vedettes and scouts, had concealed themselves in the brushwood, rushed down with loud yells, delivering their chief attack upon the left side of the square and the left portion of the front line. The frantic efforts of the Egyptians to get into proper formation, the confused din of orders, and the chaos in the rear, where 300 camels, with the whole of the transport and commissariat, were struggling to force their way inside the square, defies description.[6]

John Macdonald, *London Daily News*

The square was never properly constituted. Worst of all was the rear face, which degenerated into a seething mass of horses, camels and men all tightly wedged together, and incapable of defending themselves.

The Egyptian cavalry, with many riderless horses, rushed past in a stream. They were wild with terror. In their panic the infantry in their so-called square fired anywhere and anyhow. Baker Pasha, outside the square, narrowly escaped being shot by his own men. An Egyptian soldier within 3 yards of me fell by a shot from his own comrades. Captain Cavalieri was killed in the same way. Finally, the scene became one of pure savage massacre. The Egyptian infantry, throwing away their weapons, knelt down, raised their clasped hands, and prayed for mercy. The Arabs seized them by the neck, speared them through the back, and then cut their throats. The yells of the Arabs and the cries of their Egyptian victims were appalling.[7]

John Macdonald, *London Daily News*

The possession of a horse proved a vital attribute in the race back to Fort Baker and a small number including Baker, Macdonald and Burnaby were able to escape. The scale of the defeat was shocking as the Dervish opponents were outnumbered by around three to one. But their military skills, determination and excellent morale made these odds irrelevant. Of the estimated 3,650 men who had marched out that morning, some 2,362 other ranks were killed. Amid shameful scenes of panic, the survivors were embarked at Trinkitat and returned by sea to Suakin.

What mattered now was the defence of Suakin, pending the arrival of British reinforcements, as even Gladstone could not ignore such an affront to British prestige. As Evelyn Baring ruefully recorded, everyone seemed to be all for military action.

> British public opinion was greatly excited about Sudan affairs. Party politicians were sure not to allow so good an opportunity for attacking the government to escape. Mr. Forster, who was a leading member of the Anti-Slavery Society and the chief of the party of bellicose philanthropy, attacked the government. When, eventually, it was decided to send an expedition to Suakin, Mr. Forster said (February 14), 'I rejoice that the Government have taken their present policy. By that, they are more likely to strike a blow against slavery than anything we have yet done!' There was no mistaking this language. The government were invited to undertake a military campaign against slavery.[8]
> Evelyn Baring

The port of Suakin was a strange place. Most of the important buildings were on a small island, linked by a causeway to the less than salubrious mainland suburbs. With the garrison all but useless, it was just as well that two Royal Navy ships, HMS *Ranger* and HMS *Coquette*, were able to form a more resolute basis for the defence of the town. Naval parties manned the ditch and earthen rampart defences. Once further reinforced by the arrival of Rear Admiral William Hewett and HMS *Euryalus* from the East India Squadron, the town was relatively secure. The hapless remnants of Baker's force were despatched back to Egypt as being useless.

The British Empire could at times move with relative speed, and it certainly did on this occasion. Command of a new Suakin Expedition was given to Major General Gerald Graham, who was regarded as a safe pair of hands. Two British brigades were despatched swiftly, and three battalions drawn from the army still occupying Egypt. To this were added units which happened to be on their way back from service in India and one battalion from Aden. There were also eight 7-pounder screw guns, and a naval party with six Gardner and Gatling guns. Burnaby and Baker would accompany them as extra intelligence officers. Altogether, this was a powerful force, very different from the ramshackle forces poor Baker had originally been assigned. However, although soldiers never complain, the 10th Hussars comprising the Cavalry Brigade alongside the 19th Hussars were not happy with the horses which they inherited.

> We were soon landed and moved into camp and took over the horses of the Egyptian cavalry, Arab horses they called them the one I got hold of was the most miserable looking pony I ever saw – it would not have been hired out on Hampstead Heath and the saddlery was like brown paper! I did not feel eager for the fray when I saw this state of things![9]
> Private J. A. Starr, 10th Hussars

The forces allotted may have changed, but the plan of action remained much the same. Once again they sailed down the coast to land at Trinkitat and concentrated at Fort Baker. They would then advance to recapture the town of Tokar which had recently fallen to the Mahdist forces. At 08.00 on 29 February they set off heading for the village of El Teb. Ahead of them was a screen of cavalry, who saw a depressing reminder of human mortality as they passed the scene of the First Battle of El Teb on their left.

We soon came to the dead bodies of Baker's army rotting in the sun a fearful sight although one soon gets accustomed to it, but not the stench! We were kindly permitted to smoke whenever we chose but I fell back on the old Indian remedy – a small bag of camphor around my neck![10]
Private J. A. Starr, 10th Hussars

Behind them the infantry and artillery were advancing in columns, but ready to form a single strong square if attacked. The Dervishes had fortified a low ridge that lay about 10 feet above the desert, building two strong earthwork redoubts, reinforced by sandbags, and each containing two captured Krupp guns, as well as numerous rifle pits, creating a strong defensive position. Graham had hoped the Dervishes would launch a death or glory attack, but they remained ensconced in their redoubts. He would have to storm home. With the column as a spectator was the captain of HMS *Hecla*. He did not want to miss the battle.

We could see the enemy in the hills in the distance before we had left Fort Baker more than about a mile, but as we approached, they all disappeared, and we saw nobody – nothing but two Krupp guns, which they had captured from Baker the other day, looking over a sort of parapet at us. We marched steadily past them, as if we were going to leave them on the left, and still we saw no sign of the Arabs until we were nearly abreast of the battery and 900 or 1,000 yards from it, when they opened fire with their Krupp guns and with rifles. We marched steadily on without replying until we were right behind them and had them between us and where we landed. Then we halted, and for some little time a sort of duel was kept up between the Royal Artillery with their 7-pounders and the Krupp guns in the fort, the naval machine guns occasionally joining also, but with no result of any importance on either side except occasionally a man or a horse being struck in the square; but most of the shots were kind enough to pass through without hurting anybody.[11]

Captain Arthur Wilson, HMS *Hecla*

The British square had edged past the ridge with the intention of assaulting the left rear of the position, while the cavalry swirled on past to be in place to cut off any easy avenue of retreat. As they closed, a vicious melee began.

One fellow got in close to me and made a dig with his spear at the soldier on my left. He failed to reach him, and left his whole side exposed, so that I had a cool prod at him. He seemed to be beastly hard, and my sword broke against his ribs. The man on my right was a plucky fellow and collared him round the neck and tried to throw him. The Arab still held on to his spear, so I hacked at him in a futile kind of way with the stump of my sword, and while I was doing so a second Arab came up and hit me over the head with a sword. My pith helmet took the greater part of the blow, so it only just cut the scalp, and I hardly felt it. Both Arabs were shot and bayoneted on the ground almost instantly. If I could only have got a basin of water and washed my face, I should have escaped notoriety, but I only had a little cold tea in my water bottle, and until we got to the wells there was no water to be got, so the blood ran all over my face, and the correspondents spotted me. General Buller, who was close behind, congratulated me in his cheery way, and he has since recommended me for the VC. It has been a wonderful piece of luck, as I only walked out in the morning as a loafer just to see the fight. Nothing was further from my thoughts than going in for distinction of any kind, but as I happened to stumble into a hot corner, I could not possibly have done anything but what I did, unless I took to my heels![12]

Captain Arthur Wilson, HMS *Hecla*

Wilson was indeed awarded a Victoria Cross. Near him in the fighting was the journalist Bennett Burleigh who saw a terrible incident.

> An Arab running out, spear in hand, rushed for one of the soldiers. The man fired, and at 8 yards' distance missed the savage; then the soldier appeared to be swayed by two instantaneous impulses – one to charge and give his foe the bayonet, the other to fall back to the line out of which he and other equally rash comrades had run to engage the Arabs. It ended by his furtively looking over his shoulder, swaying to the rear for a step or two, and the Arab, who had not halted, bounded upon him, burying his lance deep in the wretched man's throat. Before the soldier had time to fall, he was lanced again and again; but the savage was [at] the same moment himself shot and bayoneted by two of the 65th – too late to rescue, but in time to avenge.[13]
> Bennett Burleigh, *Daily Telegraph*

At the forefront of the fighting was the force of nature that was Burnaby, armed with a borrowed sword and a double-barrelled shotgun borrowed from a naval officer. He had already received a flesh wound in the left arm and been unhorsed as his horse dropped dead. This did not daunt the 6 foot 4 inch colossus.

> He had topped the parapet and certainly seemed to be doing some remarkable execution among the Arabs with his shotgun. Three natives protecting the Krupp gun rushed at him, but he calmly plugged into them with his left and right. The first charge of buckshot at close quarters knocked the one clean off his feet; the other two, staggering with the sting of the pellets, were subsequently bayoneted by some of the Highlanders following closely on Burnaby's heels.[14]
> Frederick Villiers, War Artist

When Burnaby's use of a shotgun was later used against him by his political opponents safe back in England, who accused him of wanton murder of Arabs as a non-combatant, his robust reply can well be imagined.

The cavalry under the command of Brigadier General Herbert Stewart thought that the parties of Dervishes sighted in the scrublands behind the ridge were fleeing, and in accordance with his orders launched a charge to cut them down. They were too early. The warriors they had sighted were by no means retreating and more than ready for a fight.

> The Arabs did not seem the least afraid of us and faced us with uplifted spears and giving forth the most fiendish yells. Their favourite mode of attack was to throw a curved stick, a sort of 'Boomerang' and cause the horse to fall and then spear the rider, or to drop round the rear and hamstring the horses. I saw the horse of Lieutenant Probyn – who fell just in rear of me – had been served in this manner. I watched it trying to rise to its hind quarters for some time. The officer commanding my troop very wisely dismounted the best shots and we soon cleared the front and continued the firing until they got out of range. A chum and I had a couple of shots at a fellow on a camel 800 yards distant and had the pleasure of seeing him drop. Poor Major Slade had been killed. I saw one of our men with a horrible gash in the face – it seemed as though half his face was hanging down. Most miraculous – this man recovered – although minus the sight of one eye, the loss of his nerve, and one ear and part of his skull. We lost seven men in the action.[15]
> Private J. A. Starr, 10th Hussars

Among those in grave danger was the colonel of the 19th Hussars.

> Having been wounded through my left arm and side, and my horse having been killed, I found myself on the ground

surrounded by the enemy and by my own men, who were
charging, and passed quickly over me. I held out my right
hand, which was seized by Quartermaster Sergeant Mar-
shall, who stayed behind with me, and dragged me through
the enemy, and took me back to the regiment. Had I been
left behind I must have been killed.[16]

Lieutenant Colonel Percy Barrow, 19th Hussars

When the last vestiges of resistance had been stamped out, after
3 hours of bitter fighting it was all over. The British lost some
30 killed and 162 wounded at the Second Battle of El Teb, while
the Mahdist losses were estimated at over 1,500, although only
825 bodies were there to be counted. Next day Tokar was recaptured unopposed. One benefit of the speed of the advance was
that most of the weapons and munitions captured from Baker's
ill-fated expedition were recovered.

Meanwhile, Private Starr's troop of the 10th Hussars was
assigned to accompany the wounded back to the ships at
Trinkitat.

I had a good look at Baker Pasha he had been struck by a
piece of shell in the face and his gay uniform was smothered
in [blood]. Also, Colonel Burnaby who had been wounded
in the arm, but seemed quite cheerful about it, for when
we left them at Fort Baker he bade us good night and said,
'We'll have another go at them tomorrow!' I believe he had
already made himself felt among the enemy![17]

Private J. A. Starr, 10th Hussars

On their return to El Teb there was an incident which draws
attention to a besetting problem throughout the Mahdist wars
– the unwillingness of the Dervish wounded to surrender – and
the consequent merciless retribution in the slightest case of
doubt.

As I was scouting across the country, I found a wounded

man. The Arab motioned and begged for water. I made signals to the officer, who then rode up and ordered him to be shot. Unmerciful perhaps you may say, but they were not to be trusted, for cases occurred where they counterfeited death and when anyone passed, they sprang up and disembowelled them![18]

Private J. A. Starr, 10th Hussars

★★★

MAJOR GENERAL GERALD GRAHAM was not disposed to rest on his laurels. Having returned to Suakin, he resolved to strike hard and fast at Digna's camps at Tamai and Tamanieb near the Khor Ghob Wells. On 13 March 1884, Graham's forces were approaching Tamai in two echeloned squares: the 1st Brigade square commanded by Major General John Davis, with the 2nd Brigade square commanded by Brigadier General Redvers Buller some 800 yards staggered back to the right rear. They were rather further apart than had been intended, but Graham, who was in the first square, pressed on regardless. In front of them were a screen of mounted infantry. As they approached the *khor* (gully) the Mounted Infantry screen had an unwelcome surprise.

I sent back word to Brigadier General Stewart to say the ravine was full of fuzzy-wuzzies. The ravine was about 200 to 500 yards wide in places, 20 to 50 feet deep, and full of bushes. I thought there were some 6,000 fuzzie-wuzzies, but the bush was so thick one could only guess. I went again to look over the edge of the ravine with Freddy Thornton and some twenty men dismounted. An Arab about 20 feet below us shoved up his long gun and shot Private Morley, who was about 8 feet from me, in the stomach, and about 2,000 [Dervishes] scrambled up the side of the ravine. I emptied my revolver into the brown of them.[19]

Lieutenant Percival Marling, Mounted Infantry

With the square rumbling forward, the mounted infantry had to remount in haste to clear the field of fire. The Dervishes were getting closer, and bullets were spattering all around them. But they were determined not to leave Private Morley behind.

> My orderly brought up my horse and put Morley up in front of me, but after going with him a short way he fell off, I couldn't hold him on. I then got off and put him across my saddle, and held him on with another fellow, Hunter, a Rifleman and a right gallant fellow. Private Cliff, led the horse. We got him back about 200 yards to a place not quite so dangerous, and I went into the square to get a stretcher to put Morley on.[20]
> Lieutenant Percival Marling, Mounted Infantry

It would all be in vain as Morley would die. But Lieutenant Percival Marling was awarded the VC for his courage.

Meanwhile the 1st Brigade square was grievously mishandled as it approached the lip of the khor. Graham ordered the Black Watch to charge forward, an order that does not appear to have initially reached the other half of the front rank, the York and Lancasters, although they belatedly sought to conform. The 'charge' did not last for long, as the front of the square became disrupted, just as a mass of Dervishes erupted from the nullah to strike at the right front corner of the square, over-running the naval machine guns.

> To my horror on looking round behind, I saw crowds of Arabs at the Gatlings, one was on the top of the gun and threw himself on me with a spear, but it passed over my left shoulder and I hit him in the jaw with hand and sent him flying, another came at me from under the gun and I had just time to kick him in the mouth. We fell back crushed as it were by a weight and then my trusty claymore found its way to the hilt into several black devils. I clove a piece out of one of their heads just as one does an egg for breakfast

and saw his white brain exposed. I was mad with rage and fury and had I not been a strong man I must have been thrown down and killed. I think God must have put a coat of armour on me that day. They are most awfully plucky; I saw one man just dead, and he was crawling towards us to kill a white man before he died. I took a splendid spear and killed a great many wounded men with it, it went into their hearts like lightning and their blood flowed out on the sand.[21]

Captain Andrew Scott-Stevenson, 1st Black Watch

The square fell back some 600 yards, just about holding together, greatly assisted by the crossfire support from Buller's 2nd Brigade square as it came up alongside on their right. Another mass of warriors charged from the khor, but the attacks were shot to pieces by the disciplined volleys of the Royal Irish Fusiliers and Gordon Highlanders. After a reorganisation the two brigades resumed their advance in tandem on the khor, recapturing the lost machine guns as they went. The relatively unscathed 1st Brigade then advanced to complete the capture of the village and wells. It had been a close-run thing, but the Battle of Tamai had been won. The British suffered 110 fatalities and a further 110 wounded; Dervish casualties were estimated at between 1,500 to 2,000. Few of the Dervish wounded survived. One of those ordered to massacre any that resisted was Private Starr. From their perspective it was like walking among vipers, but it was a merciless business.

My troop had a most unpleasant duty to perform – that of dispatching the wounded who would not accept quarter but threw their spears at us when we approached them in their dying moments. I saw a hand-to-hand encounter between a wounded Arab and a Highlander who bayoneted the Arab – and then the Arab managed to stab him – what became of the Highlander I never knew. The groans and shrieks of the dying was awful. It was an awful scene such as I can never forget and hope I may never see again![22]

Private J. A. Starr, 10th Hussars

Of course, such ruthless treatment of the wounded made them even less likely to 'go quietly into the night' and so begat further violence.

Graham looked to maximise the advantage of his victory by moving swiftly forward to capture the nearby wells at Tamanieb. There was no doubt that he had inflicted severe damage on Osman Digna's forces. The question was what to do now? Graham had no doubts: the best way he could assist Gordon in the evacuation – or defence – of Khartoum was by maximising the advantage gained at El Teb and Tamai. Military success should be followed by a political offensive to neutralise the impact of Osman Digna and the Mahdi among the Red Sea Littoral tribes; this could only work if the British continued to maintain a strong military presence at Suakin. But Graham looked to do even more.

> Present position of affairs is that two heavy blows have been dealt at rebels and followers of the Mahdi, who are profoundly discouraged. They say, however, that the English troops can do no more, must re-embark, and leave the country to them. To follow up these victories, and bring waverers to our side, we should not proclaim our intention of leaving, but rather make a demonstration of an advance towards Berber and induce a belief that we can march anywhere we please. I propose, therefore, making as great a show as possible without harassing troops. A strong battalion, with regiment of cavalry, advances tomorrow to Handoub, and thence a reconnaissance will be made along the Berber road.[23]
>
> Major General Gerald Graham, Headquarters, Suakin Force

Graham would always regret not having taken the initiative and launched a serious advance on Berber, rather than merely asking for permission. What followed was a disgrace: his immediate superior in Cairo, Lieutenant General Frederick Stephenson (commanding British forces in Egypt) was sceptical, due to his fears of an adequate water supply on the route to Berber. In late March 1884 Gladstone ordered a complete withdrawal, leaving only a tiny garrison at Suakin, thereby at a stroke negating everything Graham had achieved and rendering his battles pointless. It was also one more nail in Gordon's coffin.

7

THE SIEGE OF KHARTOUM

> No one could be astonished at my reluctance to make a bolt of it without the garrisons, for it virtually makes out all our toils, for the last seven months, as utterly useless; we had, to all intents and purposes, better have surrendered months ago. One feels such a mean brute to go egging on men to fight, and then to let it end with a skedaddle.[1]
>
> Major General Charles Gordon, Khartoum Garrison

GORDON WAS NO KNIGHT in shining armour, just as Khartoum was no fabled city of the East. It was a dishevelled-looking collection of unremarkable buildings that lay on the left bank of the Blue Nile just a mile above the confluence with the White Nile. En route, at Berber, Gordon had proclaimed his intention to hand over the country to the descendants of the original rulers, an unwise demonstration of weakness that would further undermine the confidence of local leaders who were already sceptical as to British or Egyptian willingness to support them against the Mahdi. If they were to be abandoned, then why on earth would they fight on alone? If they were not to fight, then best to throw in their lot with the Mahdi as early as possible.

Meanwhile, in Khartoum the journalist-turned-interim British consul, Frank Power, had decided to remain in post – and he welcomed the arrival of Gordon.

> Gordon is a most lovable character – quiet, mild, gentle, and strong; he is so humble too. The way he pats you on the shoulder when he says, 'Look here, dear fellow, now

what do you advise?' would make you love him. When he goes out of doors there are always crowds of Arab men and women at the gate to kiss his feet, and twice today the furious women, wishing to lift his feet to kiss them, threw him over. He is Dictator here; the Mahdi has gone down before him, and today sent him a 'salaam', or message of welcome. It is wonderful that one man could have such an influence on 200,000 people. Numbers of women flock here every day to ask him to touch their children to cure them; they call him the 'Father and the Saviour of the Soudan'. He is, indeed, I believe, the greatest and best man of this century. I stay on here to the end. I'll stop while he stays.[2]

Frank Power, *The Times*

This saintlike depiction should be tempered by some reference to other views which point to his reliance on instinct rather than reason, his stubbornness, irascibility, and occasional petulance. Nonetheless he was an extraordinary administrator with the charisma to make most people overlook his faults.

Gordon began attempting to restore confidence in the Egyptian rule pending withdrawal. Various popular measures were enacted including the novel idea of ensuring that the Egyptian soldiers – upon whom the survival of the population depended – were actually paid! Public debts were cancelled, prisoners released,and food supplies disseminated to the deserving poor. Gordon also attempted to open negotiations with the Mahdi to permit the peaceful withdrawal of the Egyptian soldiers, officials, women and children; this was something in which he had placed considerable faith in his earlier assessment of the Sudan imbroglio. Yet the Mahdi was a very different proposition to the Sudanese leaders Gordon had previously encountered. This was a man just as committed, just as driven to his cause. Gordon's request met with short shrift. The Mahdi called on him to adopt the Muslim faith and to surrender. He also despatched forces to begin the investment of Khartoum. On 12 March, some 4,000

Mahdists advanced up the east bank of the Blue Nile, pushing on to besiege the town of Halfaya. Next day, one of Gordon's steamers was fired on as it reconnoitred the situation. The siege of Khartoum had begun.

The arrival of Gordon had marked the departure of Colonel Henry de Coetlogon who had played such a key part in constructing the early defence works. Gordon sent him back to Cairo with an open letter saying that 'Khartoum was as safe as Cairo or Kensington Park'.[3]

In view of subsequent events, this was unfortunate. For a while, the situation remained calm enough in Khartoum itself, but elsewhere the Mahdi's forces were fast gaining ground, and not just in the immediate vicinity. By April 1884, it was apparent that many of the tribes between Berber and Khartoum had turned over to the Mahdi. When Gordon heard from Baring that there were no plans to despatch Major General Gerald Graham's force from Suakin to take and hold Berber – and hence secure the only feasible evacuation route – he vented his considerable spleen.

> As far as I can understand, the situation is this: you state your intention of not sending any relief force up here or to Berber, and you refuse me Zubeir. I consider myself free to act according to circumstances. I shall hold on here as long as I can, and, if I can suppress the rebellion, I shall do so. If I cannot, I shall retire to the Equator and leave you the indelible disgrace of abandoning the garrisons of Sennar, Kassala, Berber and Dongola, with the certainty that you will eventually be forced to smash up the Mahdi under great difficulties if you would retain peace in Egypt.[4]
> Major General Charles Gordon, Khartoum Garrison

If he was to fight, then he wanted more reliable troops than the Egyptian garrison he had inherited. To this end he made a special effort to recruit Sudanese troops which he placed under the command of one of their own, Faragh Pasha. They would prove his most reliable 'fighting' soldiers. In all he had some 2,400 regular Egyptian and Sudanese troops and 5,000 irregulars. Most were armed with Remington rifles, but he also had twenty-nine artillery pieces of various shapes and sizes.

Gordon had also taken several measures to further improve the city defences. The main defensive embankment was raised to some 7 feet high and 14 feet thick, topped in places by a loopholed wall some 5 foot high, while the ditch was both widened and deepened until it was a significant obstacle some 6–8 feet deep and 10 feet wide. The improvised obstructions of broken bottles and caltrops were also extended to stretch for some 600 yards in front of the ramparts. Using the arms, ammunition and materials of war laid down in the armoury during his previous period as governor general, he augmented the ditch and approaches to the ramparts with barbed wire and a layer of percussion mines improvised from 20-pound shells which could be detonated by fuses to create huge explosions. These would prove very effective. A number of forts were established, based usually on strongly built brick buildings, loopholed and protected by ramparts and ditch defences: they consisted of Fort Burri, at the north end of the ramparts by the Blue Nile; North Fort, on the opposite bank of the Blue Nile; Makran Fort, at the junction of the two rivers; and the stronger, purpose-built Fort Omdurman which lay some 1,200 yards back from the riverbank on the other side of the White Nile. Another four smaller bastions were built into main ramparts, each holding two or three small artillery pieces.

We have been almost daily engaged with the rebels, who now thoroughly surround Khartoum. General Gordon is busily engaged laying out mines in front of the works in all directions. Yesterday and today the rebels came down to a village opposite and fired heavily on the palace. We returned the fire with artillery and musketry, and on both occasions the Arabs soon retreated. There was no loss on our side. The town is quiet. Over half the population before the siege began went over to the rebels, thus weeding out all bad characters. General Gordon is issuing rations to the poor. Food is very dear. We have corn and biscuits for about four months. General Gordon has issued paper money, as our treasure is still at Berber. The merchants accept it as money, and all the arrears to the soldiers can be thus paid off. General Gordon has sent emissaries to offer to all the slaves of the rebels their freedom if they abandon their masters and come in. If they do this, it will be a fearful blow to the rebels. The general has hired the large mission premises on the river and has moved all the ammunition there; in case of attack with artillery on the fortifications, it will be perfectly safe.[5]

Frank Power, *The Times*

With the capture of Berber on 26 May, any hopes of a line of retreat that way was finally severed, as was the telegraph line. Henceforth communications between Cairo and Khartoum would have to rely on a mixture of spies and messengers.

Throughout, Gordon was the heart and soul of the garrison. He was all things to all men – civilian administrator, commander in chief and engineer – visiting the outlying defence works, personally supervising the laying of the mines and monitoring the repairs to any damage suffered in the ramparts. Even when he was back in his palace next to the Blue Nile, the all-seeing eye of his telescope was ranging round the forts to watch out for any signs of men falling asleep or otherwise neglecting their duties. Anyone caught transgressing was flogged; his liberalism only went so far, and this was life or death.

Gordon had used his training as a Royal Engineer officer to good effect, but he was assisted by the annual flooding of the Nile rivers which lasted from April to September. This flooded the ground to the south of Khartoum and impeded the Mahdi's forces in moving up from the Kordofan province to mass around Khartoum. As the river levels rose this also allowed a new string to Gordon's bow. He had used his arsenal to fit bullet-proof armour plating to the steamers and created six armoured barges mounting guns, with which he was able to launch raids up and down the rivers to forage for supplies, while also taking every opportunity to harass and disrupt the Dervishes. Frank Power describes one such raid, launched on 29 July, under the command of Mohammed Ali Bey.

> A flotilla of five armoured steamers and four armoured barges with castles on them went up to Gareff, on the Blue Nile. I went with them. On the way up we cleared thirteen small forts, but at Gareff found two large strong forts – earthworks rivetted with trunks of palm-trees. There were two cannons in one. For 8 hours we engaged these forts, and with the Krupp 20-pounder disabled their two cannons. The Arab fire was terrific, but, owing to the bullet-proof armour on all the vessels, our loss was only three killed and twelve or thirteen wounded. Towards the evening we drove the rebels, who were in great numbers, out of the forts.[6]
>
> Frank Power, *The Times*

More successful raids followed, boosting morale, capturing munitions and considerably augmenting food stocks, which boosted the garrison's ability to resist.

Then came disaster. After raiding the village of El Eilafun, Mohammed Ali Bey set off inland on the trail of Sheikh El Obeid, this despite warnings from Gordon not to leave the river. Advancing through wooded terrain, guided by local tribesmen, they were ambushed by vastly superior numbers and Ali and up to 1,000 of his men were slaughtered. This was a terrible blow to any offensive capacity Gordon had retained. Forced to adopt a more passive approach, the Mahdi's forces grew bolder and ever closer. Gradually, the food supplies began to run out. The Mahdist forces made no real attempts to frontally storm Khartoum, probably as a result of the Mahdi's painful experience a couple of years before in his first assault on El Obeid.

They were prepared to wait until the garrison were starved out, or too weak to defend themselves. The Nile waters were also beginning their seasonal fall, exposing an undefended section of shelving ground adjacent to the White Nile, and also facilitating the arrival of fresh Mahdist forces from the Kordofan. It was evident that something had to be done.

On 7 September, Gordon permitted the steamer *Abbas* to make an attempt to break the blockade, carrying Lieutenant Colonel John Hamill Stewart, the British consul, Frank Power, the French consul, Francois Herbin and an escort of some nineteen Greeks. They were to carry a letter to Baring which was intended to hammer home the message that Khartoum was in mortal danger.

> How many times have we written asking for reinforcements, calling your serious attention to the Sudan! No answer at all has come to us as to what has been decided in the matter, and the hearts of men have become weary at this delay. While you are eating and drinking and resting on good beds, we and those with us, both soldiers and servants, are watching by night and day, endeavouring to quell the movement of this false Mahdi. The reason why I have now sent Colonel Stewart is because you have been silent all this while and neglected us, and lost time without doing any good. If troops were sent, as soon as they reach Berber, this rebellion will cease, and the inhabitants will return to their former occupations. It is therefore hoped that you will listen to all that is told you by Stewart and the consuls and look at it seriously, and send troops as we have asked without any delay.[7]
> Major General Charles Gordon, Khartoum Garrison

Gordon subsequently explained his decision to let his closest aides depart on the *Abbas*, a small paddlewheel steamer.

> Why did you let them go? The matter was thus. I determined

to send the *Abbas* down with an Arab captain. Herbin asked
to be allowed to go. I jumped at his offer. Then Stewart
said he would go if I would exonerate him from deserting
me. I said you do not desert me. I cannot go; but if you
go, you do great service. I then wrote him an official – he
wanted me to write him an order. I said 'No, for though
I fear not responsibility, I will not put you in any danger
in which I am not myself.' I wrote them a letter, couched
thus: '*Abbas* is going down; you say you are willing to go
in her, if I think you can do so in honour – you can go in
honour, for you can do nothing here, and if you go you do
me service in telegraphing my views.' You will notice the
number of Greeks. They were a bodyguard I ordered and
paid highly, to prevent any treachery on the part of the
crew. Thus, the question of treachery was duly weighed
by me and guarded against, as far as I could – both on the
part of the crew and on the part of the inhabitants – and
I told them to anchor mid-stream, and not to take wood
except in isolated spots. I escorted them by two steamers
past every place where danger could be apprehended, viz.,
Berber and Shendy.[8]

Major General Charles Gordon, Khartoum Garrison

Gordon arranged for two steamers, the *Safieh* and the *Mansura*
to escort the *Abbas* to just beyond Berber, while four nuggars
(small Arab sailing boats) would provide an alternative means of
transport should the *Abbas* fail to get through the cataracts. Unfortunately, Stewart then blundered in releasing the two nuggars,
and proceeded alone. Still, all was well, until they came to a place
where the river split into two channels and the skipper made a
calamitous mistake and chose the wrong one, impaling the *Abbas*
on a rock. There was no shifting her and they had no nuggars
to take them further down the river, so they were forced to go
ashore and seek help from friendly villagers. What happened next
was remembered in later years by an anonymous stoker.

On September 18, the steamer struck on a rock near a small island in the Wad Gamr country. We had previously seen many of the people running away to the hills on both banks of the river. Everything was landed on the island by means of a small boat. Colonel Stewart drove a nail into the steamer's gun, filed off the projecting end, and then threw the gun and its ammunition overboard. Meanwhile, several people came down to the bank shouting, 'Give us peace and grain!' We told them we had brought peace. Suleiman Wad Gamr, living in a house on the bank of the river, being asked for camels to take the party to Merawi, said that he would provide them, and invited Colonel Stewart and the two consuls to the house of a blind man, named Fakrietman, telling them to come unarmed, lest the people should be frightened. The camels were not given us. We all went unarmed, except Colonel Stewart, who had a small revolver in his belt. Presently I saw Suleiman come out and make a sign to the people standing about the village, armed with swords and spears. These immediately divided into two parties, one running to the house of the blind man, the other to where the rest of Colonel Stewart's party were assembled. I was with the latter. When the natives charged, we threw ourselves into the river. The natives fired and killed many of us, and others were drowned. I landed on a small island, and remained there until it was dark, when I swam over to the left bank.[9]

Anon. Stoker, *Abass*

The other party of assailants murdered Stewart, Power and Herbin and threw their bodies in the river. Now Gordon was truly alone.

The falling Nile waters, coupled with the arrival of more powerful Dervish artillery made Gordon decide to send most of his remaining steamers under the command of Nushi Pasha to go down the Nile to meet the hoped for relieving forces at Shendi. This left only the *Ismailia* and *Husseinyeh* at Khartoum.

***

On 23 October, the Mahdi reached Khartoum with his whole vast army of tens of thousands. Again, the Mahdi offered his surrender terms, this time via letters written at his behest by Rudolf Slatin, one of the Mahdi's hostages. Slatin might be considered a bit of a wild card – an Austrian adventurer who found his way to the Sudan and rose to be governor of Darfur. Here he was engaged in a series of battles with the Mahdi's forces and had in desperation renounced his somewhat tenuous Catholicism to become a Muslim in the hope it would encourage his men. All to no avail, as he was ultimately forced to surrender. His conversion saved his life, but condemned him to an uncertain life as a prisoner/interpreter to the Mahdi. As an apostate to Christianity, he was of course anathema to Gordon, who rejected the idea of conversion out of hand; he could never abandon or betray his religion. However, as was not unnatural, Gordon began to fixate on when exactly any relief expedition would arrive – if ever. He began writing a remarkable daily journal, most of which survived, and it reflects his increasing bitterness at the failure of others. Thus, on 26 September, he wrote:

> It is a curious fact that any effort to relieve the garrisons made from the outside is contemporaneous with the expiration of the period stated in March of the time they could hold out, viz., six months. There are some ugly suspicious circumstances all the way through! The consequence will be a far greater expense. Had efforts been made quietly between March and August to span with proper transport between Wadi Halfa and Hannek, much of the present difficulties to an advance would have been got over, and security would have been felt everywhere that efforts were really being made.[10]
> Major General Charles Gordon, Khartoum Garrison

By 13 October there was no doubt that he despaired of the Gladstone administration and a dark and prophetic pessimism began to appear in his journal writings.

We are a wonderful people; it was never our government
which made us a great nation; our government has been
ever the drag on our wheels. It is, of course, on the cards
that Khartoum is taken under the nose of the expeditionary force, which will be *just too late*. The expeditionary force
will perhaps think it necessary to retake it; but that will
be of no use, and will cause loss of life uselessly on both
sides. It had far better quietly return, with its tail between
its legs; for once Khartoum is taken, it matters little if the
opposition say. 'You gave up Khartoum!' If Khartoum falls,
then go quietly back to Cairo, for you will only lose men
and spend money uselessly in carrying on the campaign.[11]
Major General Charles Gordon, Khartoum Garrison

On 9 November he restated his basic position – he would not
desert his garrison or his people at any cost, even though it
might cost him his life.

I declare *positively* and *once for all that I will not leave the
Sudan until everyone who wants to go down is given the chance
to do so* unless a government in established which relieves
me of the charge: therefore if any emissary or letter comes
up here ordering me to come down, *I will not obey it but will
stay here and fall with the town and run all risks.*[12]
Major General Charles Gordon, Khartoum Garrison

It is clear Gordon was 'not for turning' even at this late stage of
the siege.

The situation was by now desperate. Food supplies were
reduced to almost nothing and the Mahdist forces were gradually
chipping away at the defences. Commencing on 12 November,
sustained attempts had been launched to capture the Omdurman Fort, and despite a desperate resistance aided and abetted
by the fire of the last two steamers sailing up and down the
White Nile, the fort was completely cut off. But even *in extremis*
Gordon displayed occasional flashes of humour, as for instance

in his journal entry for 26 November, when he fondly imagined the dotage of the main protagonists in the drama they were sharing, despite a somewhat bleak punchline.

> We seldom realise our position. In 10 or 12 years' time Baring, Lord Wolseley, myself, Evelyn Wood, and etc., will have no teeth, and will be deaf; some of us will be quite passé; no one will come and court us; new Barings, new Lord Wolseleys, will have arisen, who will call us 'twaddlers'. 'Is that dreadful bore coming? If once he gets alongside you, you are in for half an hour!' will be the remark of some young captain on seeing you enter the club! This is very humiliating, for we, each one, think we are immortal. That poor old general who for years vegetated! Who ever visited him? Better a ball in the brain than to flicker out unheeded, like he did.[13]
>
> Major General Charles Gordon, Khartoum Garrison

By December, the Dervishes had set up a battery of guns on the opposite bank of the Blue Nile, from where they could batter Gordon's palace from a range of just 2,000 yards. Worse still, as the Nile waters fell, the defences had to be extended to cover the gaps between the receding waters of the White Nile and the ramparts.

On 14 December, Gordon sets another deadline, writing in his journal.

> Now *mark this*, if the Expeditionary Force, and I ask for no more than 200 men, does not come in ten days, *the town may fall:* I have done my best for the honour of our country. Goodbye.[14]
>
> Major General Charles Gordon, Khartoum Garrison

But even at this late date the relief forces he yearned for were nowhere near reaching Khartoum. There was no possible rescue for the heroic garrison within the timetable he laid out. Could they hold on? Or were they really doomed?

8

THE STARTING GATE

I enjoy the Nile scenery very much. In some places we
steam along the foot of precipitous sandstone cliffs, and
then along alluvial valley lands. Saw several temples in the
faces of cliffs. Ran on a mud bank this afternoon but got off
directly. We find it most cool, in fact too cool. The sunsets
are grand.[1]

Lieutenant Charles Townshend, Royal Marine Light Infantry

GLADSTONE DITHERED, WAITED, PREVARICATED some more and then
finally in late September reluctantly despatched an expedition
under Wolseley, the current adjutant general. The hero of the
Ashanti War and the Egyptian Campaign of 1882 would now be
charged with rescuing Gordon. The British Army at the time was
riven with rivalry, divided into schools of patronage following
the leading lights, of which there is no doubt that the 'Wolseley
Ring' had gained predominance. When Wolseley was appointed
to command the Gordon Relief Expedition he had an important
choice to make in the route to be adopted to Khartoum. There
were two possible routes: one, the time-honoured caravan route
of some 280 miles from Suakin to Berber, which left then only a
relatively easy journey of 200 miles along the Nile to Khartoum;
the other option was to use the Nile to travel most of the 1,650
miles from Cairo to Khartoum. As *de facto* chief of staff of the
British Army, Wolseley had been considering the question as
early as April 1884 and he had already made his selection, from
which he never wavered. Inspired by his own experiences as the
commander of the successful Red River Expedition to stamp

out a rebellion in Canada back in 1870, he resolved to follow the Nile route.

This was the 'past' Wolseley chose to follow, rather than the accumulated wisdom of the centuries. In his own mind he equated the problems he had faced and overcome in his journey across rivers and lakes in Canada with the problems posed by the Nile. _

I would propose to send all the dismounted portion of the force up the Nile to Khartoum in boats, as we sent the little expeditionary force from Lake Superior to Fort Garry on the Red River in 1870. That force had to traverse a desert region, destitute of supplies, for a distance of 600 miles, taking provisions with it for three months in boats. It had to pass over a range of hills (800 feet where we crossed them). I find the difference in level between Wadi Halfa and Berber is about 720 feet, but there is no descent, whereas in the Red River Expedition we had to mount up 800 feet, and go down the other side of the hills (about 600 feet) to Fort Garry. Of the total distance by river from Wadi Halfa to Berber (666 miles) 224 miles of that distance is navigable by steamers at one stretch, and a railway is finished for 33 miles, and only requires the rails to finish 22 miles further. There are also two stretches of about 70 miles each, easily navigable by light draft steamers at high Nile, and by ordinary sailing boats. In fact, there would only be about 200 miles of difficult navigation between Wadi Halfa and Berber. Remembering the great superiority of river over land transport, the ease with which stores of all sorts are carried in boats, the great distance, comparatively speaking, that can be traversed daily in boats, and the vast saving that there would be in expense, I have no hesitation whatever in saying that the river route from Wadi Halfa to Khartoum is infinitely preferable to any other.[2]

Lieutenant General Garnet Wolseley

But the Nile proved a far more difficult obstacle due to its series of six great cataracts that would have to be overcome. These were lengths of mostly uncharted whitewater rapids, with the surface of the water broken by numerous rocks and small islets. The General Officer Commanding in Egypt, Lieutenant General Frederick Stephenson, estimated it would take at least four months to reach Khartoum by this route. In contrast, even if the relief force could only advance 10 miles a day, they would be at Berber within a month following the Suakin–Berber route. But there were still plentiful local Dervishes to provide opposition, while the blazing desert and scarcity of practical wells meant that most of the water they needed would have to be carried with them, with all the additional transport problems that entailed. Furthermore, as Berber had fallen to the Mahdi's forces back in May 1884, they would have to arrive there in a fit state to fight what might prove a tough battle. It is fair to say that there was no easy option.

But Wolseley's star was in the ascendent at the War Office; he defended his scheme robustly and managed to overwhelm the doubts of the Admiralty as to the feasibility of the plans. Throughout, Wolseley was obdurate, in essence refusing to consider any alternative to his own scheme, and regarding any difference of opinion as a personal affront. Stephenson began all the preparations required for the Nile operations, but he also continued to express his doubts in telegrams back to London. The result was inevitable and on 26 August the War Office acted to appoint Wolseley in command of the expedition.

> After anxious consideration, Her Majesty's Government have come to the conclusion that it is unjust to you to ask you to be responsible for directing an operation which, after full knowledge of plan, you consider to be impracticable. They have therefore decided to send Lord Wolseley to take temporarily the chief command in Egypt. Government highly appreciate the manner in which you have carried out the important and difficult duties of your

command, and earnestly hope that you may feel yourself able to remain in Egypt whilst Lord Wolseley is there, and assist him with your advice. Lord Wolseley goes out with Lord Northbrook.[3]

War Office

Stephenson would show exemplary loyalty to the cause by continuing to stay in his position based in Cairo and would give his usurper every support.

Wolseley planned the construction of a fleet of some 400 rowing boats similar to those he had used in Canada. But where to find them? When the government finally made its mind up to proceed with the expedition, he knew just the man. And this was not a naval officer, but one of his own favourites who had served with him on the Red River Expedition and on his staff at Tel el Kebir – Lieutenant Colonel William Butler.

On the 4 August, I received a telegram from Lord Wolseley, who was then the adjutant-general of the War Office. It merely said, 'I want to see you here to-morrow!' Of course, I guessed what it meant. The Nile route had been selected for the attempt to reach Khartoum. Next morning, I was in Pall Mall, but only to find that the final word had not been spoken by the Government. Even at this eleventh hour all that could be said was, 'We have it in contemplation to despatch a strong brigade of British troops to or towards Dongola by the Nile route. Proceed at once to find 400 boats similar to those used in the Red River Expedition. If you cannot find such boats, you will have to build them.' By the evening of the 6 August two things were clear: not in England could be found 400 new, sound boats fit for the work they would have to do – build them we must.'[4]

Lieutenant Colonel William Butler

If they were to build them then they had to have a clear template delineating the ideal shape, size and weight of the boat. As early as 7 August he had organised a meeting at Portsmouth.

> We got together in the dockyard the load the boat would have to carry – biscuit, preserved meat, groceries, tent, arms, ammunition sufficient for twelve men during one hundred days. We put the load with twelve men into a man-of-war gig in the basin, found that load was too heavy for the boat, and the boat too heavy for the work we wanted; and then and there we laid the lines of our new, ideal 'Nile whaler.' She was to be 30 feet in length, 6 feet 6 inches in beam, 2 feet 3 inches in depth; to weigh, with fittings complete, about 1,000 pounds. Before any official sanction could be given to spend a five-pound note on this work, we had designs, specifications, dimensions, all finished; a trial boat actually being built at Portsmouth in one week.[5]
> Lieutenant Colonel William Butler

This would be the crunch – how to get the money required upfront from a notoriously parsimonious government. Then on 12 August, Butler was called to a meeting of several heads of contracts and finance departments.

> The parliamentary official began by observing that he understood I had been charged with inquiries and arrangements as to boatbuilding on an extensive scale. I answered that that was so; that our work of design, preparation, and inquiries had for some days been finished; and that we only awaited the word 'go' to proceed to immediate action. Then there came a slight pause, broken by the high official asking in a doubtful tone if I really thought those 400 boats could be built and shipped from England in the time he had seen stated in a paper of mine – one month? I answered that I had not much doubt of the general correctness of that estimate. Then came another little pause, followed by the official's writing a few words upon a

half-sheet of notepaper, which he handed to me. I read, 'Colonel Butler, you may proceed with the construction of 400 boats!' That was good, but his next spoken words were better: 'Gentlemen,' he said, turning to the representatives of the departments of finance, contracts, and control, 'I have assembled you here to tell you that Colonel Butler has a blank cheque for the building and equipment of these boats, and his decisions as to expenditure are not to be questioned!' I bowed and retired. That evening forty-seven telegrams to forty-seven boatbuilders went out. The Nile Expedition had begun. But what a cloud hung over it! Turn it in one's mind in any way, the problem came back to the same point – the 12th of August! How easy it would all have been had this decision been given two months earlier![6]
Lieutenant Colonel William Butler

Nevertheless, this was still a great victory over the forces of bureaucracy. A lesser man would surely have been swamped by officialdom and the delays multiplied in consequence. An additional order for another 400 was later put in. As built, they were rather like the normal naval whaler but fuller in the body, which allowed them to carry more weight, which of course was vital due to the huge quantities of stores and provisions that would have to be carried. They were fitted for twelve oarsmen and in addition had two masts for sails. In all they could carry ten soldiers, two boatmen and some 1,000 rations as well as ammunition.

One officer had been rather quicker off the mark. In July 1884, Captain Herbert Kitchener had begun the hazardous solo journey, disguised as an Arab and with only a small escort, making his way as far forward as Dongola. Here he attempted to divine the mood of the local governor towards the Mahdi before moving further on to Ed Debba, where he engaged in a series of recces to determine the best route to Khartoum, while continuing to spy on the local Mahdists. This was a risky business, and he took to carrying poison to allow for a rapid suicide rather than any prolonged torture. He also managed to establish some communications via various intermediaries with Gordon, who seemed to be impressed – even suggesting at times that Kitchener might be a future governor.

Wolseley arrived at Cairo on 9 September, but on the way he had developed a second strand to his plan. He had clearly become concerned at the delays that would be caused by the great bend in the Nile after Korti, where it bent back some 150 miles to the north-east to Abu Hamed, before turning back another 150 miles to Berber to the south-east, and only then turning back to the south-west towards Khartoum. In following the Nile, they would be travelling round three sides of an oblong which could take weeks. Wolseley wanted a contingency plan in case of excessive delays, and he decided to create an extra force able to cut directly across the desert that formed the fourth side of the oblong – and he knew just who he wanted for that force. He intended to create an elite Camel Corps, of four 'regiments' roughly the size of a brigade, composed of volunteer-only detachments from the Guards regiments, the Rifle Brigade, and the various light cavalry regiments and infantry regiments already serving in Egypt. Other units and elements would be added at a later stage, but this ludicrous idea was accepted, despite it going against almost every accepted military principle of the virtues of long-term training and working under known NCOs and officers. But Wolseley had his way. This campaign would be his vision – and his alone.

★★★

LOGISTICS IS AT THE HEART OF ANY CAMPAIGN, but never more so than the Nile expedition to relieve Khartoum. The man in charge of the lines of communication was the Sirdar, Major General Evelyn Wood, still commander in chief of the Egyptian Army, but like Stephenson, the former GOC Egypt, he had been side-lined for the campaign. Nonetheless, Wood still had a key role in organising all the depots and staging posts along the route to the intended base at Korti. This was a stupendous undertaking, but given the distances and difficulties involved it was entirely understandable that things went wrong. The shortage of camels was not something that could be easily rectified, and this would be a problem for the whole campaign. The whalers were being built and would soon arrive, but in the interim, there were several venerable Nile steamers that were pressed into service. Captain Charles Beresford was sent to oversee the arrangements for water transport as far as Wadi Halfa, which was an obvious base camp, lying as it did just below the Second Cataract. This was a fearsome prospect, but there was a need for at least some of the steamers to get through the maelstrom to operate further to the south towards Korti.

Here the Nile divides into two, flowing on either side of a group of rocks and islands for about 20 miles, and at the other (or upper) end of the group of rocks and islands, on the east (or left) bank, is the sickle-shaped gorge of Bab el Kebir. At this time, although the river was falling, the roar of the torrent pouring through the Bab was so tremendous, that no voice could be heard, and we communicated with one another by semaphore. Lord Wolseley told me that he was informed that it was impossible to haul the steamers up the Second Cataract and asked me if I could do it. I replied that nothing was impossible until it was proved to be impossible; and that, in the case under consideration, I would admit the impossibility when I had smashed two steamers in trying to get them through; while if I smashed only one, I might thereby get experience which would enable me to succeed with the other. The steamers were hauled through successfully while the Bab el Kebir was still full and roaring, the current being so powerful that the steamers forging against it trembled like a whip. Some 4,000 natives were put on the hawser of the first steamer; and as they hauled her up, she had but a foot's clearance between her sides and the rocks. The torrent flung her against them, and if she

had not been defended by timber and mats, she would have been smashed to pieces. About the middle of the gorge the natives could move her no farther. Whereupon they cried to Allah to strengthen them, and to order the rope to pull harder and to slacken the water. But as their prayers availed not, I eased the steamer back again, and put about 1,500 British soldiers on the hawser. They did not pray; indeed, their language was as it were the reverse of prayer; but they dragged the steamer right through. Theologically speaking, the victory should have gone to the natives. I put the problem to a bishop, but he was unable to solve it![7]
Captain Charles Beresford, Naval Brigade

By such means he managed to get six steamers safely through.

The whalers had begun to arrive at the Second Cataract in mid October. They had already undergone a long journey from their British boatbuilders. But then a delay occurred as Wood tried to maximise the work he could get out of the local steamers and nuggars, the flat-bottomed, shallow drafts sail boats used to carry cargo on the Nile. He therefore prioritised getting them through the Second Cataract before falling seasonal water levels would make it impractical for such craft. This delay infuriated Butler, who had far more faith in his whalers.

Here, again, the plan was marred by that worst of all combinations – the men who won't see and the men who don't see. They were in [a] high place, and I was powerless against their ruling. At this point that ruling was destined eventually to kill the expedition. The order was given that the English boats, now numbering 130, were to remain idly at anchor at the foot of the Second Cataract, while some sixty or seventy heavy native craft were to have the right-of-way through the Bab el Kebir (the Big Gate of the Cataract). This decision cost us a loss of ten days. We had, in fact, been doing too well up to this point. It was but seven weeks since these boats had their keels laid in England, and here we had over 100 of them 1,000 miles up the Nile, and the remainder were coming on in quick succession. The Second Cataract of the Nile has lived in my memory since October 1884 as a spot in the world where I suffered mental torture of the acutest kind – that which results from seeing terrible disaster ahead and being powerless to prevent it![8]

Lieutenant Colonel William Butler

As the Nile waters began to fall, it left the rocks infesting the Bab el Kebir gorge that much closer to the surface, leaving minimal clearance for the boats. Beresford was then given the task of getting the whalers amassed at Wadi Halfa to the next staging post the other side of the Second Cataract at Gemai – a distance of some 17 miles.

My plan was to haul the boats up to the entrance of the Bab and then to carry them across the neck of land formed by the curve of the Bab, a distance of 2,488 yards, which required 400 men, who should be divided into sections of forty to each boat. The boat was hauled on shore, her masts, oars, and poles laid on the ground to serve as bearers; the boat was laid on these keel uppermost, and was then lifted and carried, the masts, oars, and poles resting on the men's shoulders, and other men supporting the boat by resting thwarts and gunwale on their shoulders. My scheme was at first received with incredulity by all except Lord Wolseley. But I made a trial trip with thirty men, and had the boat across the portage, including six stoppages for rest, and in the water with all her gear without a scratch, in an hour and twenty minutes. The passage of Bab el Kebir, low as the water had become, would have taken at least 6 hours, with great risk of disaster.[9]

Captain Charles Beresford, Naval Brigade

By 27 November, 687 boats had been passed through or round the Second Cataract, only four had been lost and twenty-seven men drowned, which given the foaming torrents and jagged rocks was a great achievement. The process was eased after the arrival of the Canadian and Mohawk voyageurs in late October 1884. These had been recruited in response to Wolseley's admiration for their achievements in the Red River Expedition. Time and time again they were tested to the very limits of their skills – as in this typical incident.

> As the boat rebounded off the rock, the rope was slacked for a moment, only 2 or 3 seconds, just long enough to permit one of the crew to take a hitch round a rowlock, thus swinging us round straight into the stream, saving us from drifting into sure destruction, and enabling all onboard to take a firm hold on the rope, you may bet your life it was a firm grip this time, and we try the upward movement again and with greater success. Heavens, but the strain was a terror, inch by inch we crept up to the top, hung there for a moment, touch and go, then slowly forge ahead and out of danger, for a moment and but a moment only, out fly the oars, and pull, my hearties, for your lives! 'Pull! Pull!' is the word. Four oars scraping the bank, and four moving the boat around a sharp turn just about 30 feet from the head of the heavy pitch, where if we failed to connect it was all over with us. Boat and men would have run their last trip.[10]
> John Sherlock

John Sherlock would earn a reputation as one of the most skilful boatmen. It is sad to note that after surviving the worst the Nile could throw at him, Sherlock died of smallpox on 26 March 1885.

After completing his task at the Second Cataract, Beresford then began the boat journey up the next section of the Nile to Dal.

> Our daily routine along the river began at 4.30: all hands turn out, make up tent – if there were one – breakfast, and start, sailing or tracking or rowing according to the state

of the river. But whether you sailed or tracked or rowed, before long the river changed, and you must row instead of track or sail instead of row. Then you would come to a difficult place, and you would heave the cargo on shore, and get the empty boat up a fall or a heavy rush of water and portage the cargo on to the boat. So on to midday, when an hour was allowed for dinner; then at it again, sailing, tracking, rowing, in and out cargo, till sundown. Then haul into the bank and eat bully beef without vegetables. After supper, roll in a blanket and sleep on the soft sand the profound and delicious slumber of weary men. Occasionally a boat would strike a rock; or at rare intervals an accident would happen, and part of a crew would be lost, and the boat's gear swept away; or a hole would be knocked in the boat, when she would be emptied of gear and cargo, hauled up, and patched. Under these circumstances, the boats often made no more than 3 or 4 miles advance in a day. Overloaded as were many of the boats, they served their purpose admirably well. At the big cataracts were stationed working parties, which emptied the boats of gear and cargo, portaged them overland, and hauled the boats through the rapids. So we struggled up the broad and rushing river from Gemai to Dal, sailing and towing and rowing, capsized and righting again. And one night a sandstorm waltzed out of the desert and blew away our tent and with it knives, forks, slippers, lamp, candles, matches and everything. And the next morning Peel dropped his knife, and in trying to save it he upset our whole breakfast of sardines and coffee into Colbourne's boots. Half my kit was stolen, and I was reduced to one broken pair of boots, and the natives stole my tooth powder and baked bread with it. We had boils all over us like the man in the Bible, because every little scratch was poisoned by the innumerable flies of Egypt. But we were so busy that nothing mattered.[11]

Captain Charles Beresford, Royal Navy

In such desert conditions it would not be appropriate to say that it never rained but it poured.

★★★

IT WAS AN INCREDIBLE JOURNEY for the British troops moving up the Nile. It has to be remembered that their journey did not start at Wadi Halfa – just getting there was an odyssey of some 800 miles. Great temples, symbols of long dead ancient civilisations, the sights that unfolded before them as they sailed up the great river were staggering. At Wadi Halfa, the men of the composite Guards Camel Regiment were introduced to their camels. It was not love at first sight.

> Mounting a frisky camel is exciting work for the beginner, and nearly always results in a cropper. The mode of procedure should be thus: having made your camel to kneel by clearing your throat loudly at him and tugging at his rope, shorten your rein till you bring his head round to his shoulder, put your foot in the stirrup, and throw your leg over. With his head jammed like that, he cannot rise, and must wait till you give him his head. Unless you do as directed, he will get up before your leg is over; if this happens, stand in the stirrup till he is up, and then throw your leg over, otherwise you will infallibly meet with a hideous catastrophe.[12]
> Lieutenant Lord Gleichen, Guards Camel Regiment

The Guards Camel Regiment made their own way riding along the banks of the Nile. It was still a long long way via Dongola to the final base depot at Korti.

> Our road lay more or less along the Nile the whole way, the detachment encamping on the river at night, at settled stations, and making an average of 20 miles during the day. As one day was very much like another, I will only

describe the usual mode of procedure. Starting at five or
six in the morning, according to the distance to be done,
we walked, dragging our camels after us, for 4 or 5 miles
in the cool of the morning. When the sun got hot, which
it did unpleasantly soon, we mounted and rode, with only
half-an-hour's interval at noon, straight on end for 8 or 9
hours. Walking like this is most fearfully monotonous, and
it's no use hurrying the camel up; he simply won't hurry.
On he goes at his 2¾ miles an hour pace, with sickening
regularity; and beyond keeping the men in their proper
places there is absolutely nothing whatever to do. I tried
reading, I tried writing – no good! The only thing in which
I met with any success was going to sleep! After a time, we
all trained ourselves to sleep in the saddle for short periods
– generally very short, as we fell off at the slightest irreg-
ularity of pace. However, any excitement was better than
nodding in the hot sun for hours, only rousing yourself to
abuse your camel for not going faster, and your men for
not keeping together. We adopted all sorts of formation on
the march, according to the ground we came to: column of
companies, fours, two deep, or even single file over some
of the rocky passes.[13]

Lieutenant Lord Gleichen, Guards Camel Regiment

Gleichen even came to a sort of rapprochement with his camel.

I cherished a great affection for my own camel, I named
Potiphar, a great upstanding white beast of some twenty-two hands, who reciprocated it by bellowing every time
I came near and making playful rushes at me. I really think
I succeeded in making him know and care for me after a
time, for he ceased his attacks, and reduced his bellow to
a grumble; but he got no further in his love than that. His
pace was usually very slow, and required continual whack-
ing, but when excited he walked away from the others; his
trot was not one of his good points – in fact, his chief talent

lay in doing more work and breaking down less than any
of the others.[14]
Lieutenant Lord Gleichen, Guards Camel Regiment

The camels may have seemed indestructible to the casual eye,
but they were prone to many maladies, made worse by the inner
contrariness that marked them out from other beasts.

> Great care had to be taken with the camels, as they are
> really delicate animals, and had all sorts of unknown ail-
> ments if carelessly looked after. When taken down to the
> river, some camels would look aimlessly about, exhausting
> the patience of the man by not drinking for 10 minutes
> or more, and sometimes not drinking at all if the least
> jostled. They used to get colds in their noses, too, at night,
> especially the flank ones; sometimes they caught cold if
> the saddles were removed too soon; sometimes, also, they
> fought in the lines, and got their ropes into fearful con-
> fusion. They used to break away at times, and wander all
> over the lines, causing great sorrow to their riders, who
> came to seek them. Besides this, on the march a camel
> would occasionally go slower and slower, and at last kneel
> down without warning, refusing to get up; no examination
> would discover the seat of the sickness or injury (if any),
> so he was whacked till he did go on. Altogether they were
> a sad trouble.[15]
> Lieutenant Lord Gleichen, Guards Camel Regiment

Meanwhile, the infantry went by boat. For every battalion it
was an amazing rite of passage, but one of the more amusing
accounts of a journey by whaler from Sarras to Korti in mid
December was left by an anonymous officer of the 1st Royal
Irish Regiment. Our protagonist was an inexperienced subaltern
who found himself faced with a series of unanticipated challenges to his authority.

Greatcoats and nothing else was the favourite kit with the men of my boat, who prided themselves on their dress and were anxious to save one good suit of khaki in which, they said, they would march into Khartoum. It was a handy costume when you [are] stuck on a sandbank or struck upon a rock, as you could be overboard in a second to shove the boat off. Very often my men used to row in their birthday suits! Just before we started up the Nile I had been transferred to a new company, and my skipper left the detailing of the crews of the boats to the colour-sergeant, who took advantage of my youth and innocence (?) to put into my boat ten of the biggest blackguards in the company, and a really good corporal of the old stamp – Corporal George McKee. Though I was new to the company, my future boat's crew were well known to me by name and sight as being constant attenders at the orderly room, so I thought a 'few kind words' would do them no harm, and consequently informed them that I knew them well, but that we were going to have no damned nonsense in my boat, or out of it they would go to sink or swim! A grin of amusement was all the answer I got to my short speech.[16]
Anon. Officer, 1st Royal Irish Regiment

Anyone familiar with the ways of the Regular Army would smile at this. The British Army is not renowned for its rowing skills – and somehow our anonymous hero had to get his gang of ruffians rowing like Boat Race oarsmen. At first it did not go well.

When we started off the corporal and I were the only two men who had ever handled an oar in their lives. Luckily the corporal was a good tough nut, and had been stroke in the regimental boat some years previously when we were in Malta. That first day's row is still a nightmare to me. We left Sarras at 12 noon, the corporal and I doing the rowing, while the remainder did their best to imitate us, but only

succeeded for the most part in 'catching crabs'. The current for the Nile was slight – but except quite close inshore it ran at about 3 miles an hour. Unfortunately, our cox, never having handled a tiller before, kept alternately running us out into the stream or into the banks. The distance from Sarras to Gemai was only 12 or 14 miles, but we did not get there till 8 p.m., and I thought we should never get there. I was more dead-beat than I have ever been before or since.[17]
Anon. Officer, 1st Royal Irish Regiment

At Gemai, he was relieved when one of the Canadian voyageurs was attached to his boat. The cataracts were tidal races that it seemed impossible to navigate skilfully and where, without the voyageurs, they would no doubt have come to grief.

The ordinary monotony of the journey was broken at places like Dal, where one had to pull for 4 solid hours up a gigantic millstream, sometimes only gaining a few feet after half an hour's pull, when one's muscles felt as if they would crack. It was most exciting work, and at first the task looked an impossible one, but the skill with which the voyageurs took advantage of every back water and shot past the most dangerous-looking places was perfectly marvellous.[18]
Anon. Officer, 1st Royal Irish Regiment

His men also mastered the skills required by boatmen on the Nile.

It was marvellous how quickly the men took to rowing. In a few days they were pulling powerful if not stylish oars, and they certainly put their hearts and their backs into it. My crew of blackguards were simply splendid, and we never had any difference of opinion. On one occasion we came to a very stiff bit of water, and I turned round and said, 'Now, boys, we'll have to pull here!' And the man behind – one of the biggest and sturdiest scamps in the battalion, said,

'Begorrah, Sir, we'll pull to hell with you!' And a voice from the bows added, 'And out the other side, Sir!'[19]
Anon. Officer, 1st Royal Irish Regiment

The days began to blend into each other as they toiled against the current.

The day's work did not vary much: we awoke at the first streak of dawn – had some tea or coffee and biscuit – bully beef if you cared for it, and then used to sail if the wind was really strong – which to us seemed very seldom – to sail and row, if the wind was only moderate. If there was no wind, or an adverse one, it was a case of rowing, or towing if the bank was favourable, the latter being a quicker mode of progression than rowing against the strong current. If we had a really good sailing breeze, we didn't like to waste it, and had cold bully beef and biscuit at about midday as we sailed along, but if we had had a tough morning's row or two, we used to halt for about an hour to have a hot meal. At about sunset the leading boat of the company would halt for the night at some suitable spot, and the others if possible closed up. This often was not possible, owing to the numerous mishaps that were always taking place from bumps on rocks and sandbanks. The boats, when the Royal Irish took them over, had done several trips already, and were for the most part in a pretty rotten condition, and the materials for repairing them had run out, so that we had to use any expedients such as biscuit tins, etc., to patch them up. I thought myself lucky if on arrival at the night halting-place there was no damaged boat to mend, and that in consequence I could get a full night's sleep – such a splendid sleep it was, too, under the clear sky of the Sudan winter.[20]
Anon. Officer, 1st Royal Irish Regiment

His growing friendship and overall faith in the voyageur attached to his boat did not prevent his Canadian chum from taking advantage of the innocence of the young officer.

> Each boat had a box labelled 'medical comforts' which was on no account to be opened. Very foolishly the authorities had a printed label on the box showing its contents, which in addition to beef-tea, arrowroot, etc., also consisted of two bottles of brandy and two of port wine. It had been reported that no box of medical comforts had reached its destination intact. I determined that my boat should be the exception, so the box was put in the stern of the boat, so that I could keep my eye on it during the day while I pulled stroke, and at night I slept on it in the boat. Never did it go out of my sight except at the portages, when my friend George, the Canadian, volunteered to carry it for safety's (?) sake. I drew the line at carrying boxes at portages, and trusted George. When, however, my box was examined on arrival at Korti, though it appeared quite untouched, the liquor was all gone, the arrowroot, etc., were, however, quite complete; George had no use for them![21]
>
> Anon. Officer, 1st Royal Irish Regiment

It was not until late January that the Royal Irish Regiment boats reached Korti. Here they could rest at last but were further cheered by the collective award of a £100 cheque awarded by Lord Wolseley to the quickest battalion to make the Nile passage. And so, the British forces gathered at Korti. The quickest they may have been, but were they quick enough to rescue Gordon?

9

THE DESERT COLUMN

Next moment they charged like a whirlwind. We opened
fire and they fell in scores and in hundreds, but through
the dense smoke which soon gathered around us we could
see their wild forms ever springing forward over the heap
of dead and dying and in less than it takes to tell they were
on us![1]
Captain Willoughby Verner, Headquarters, Desert Column

DELAYS BREED MORE DELAYS and there was soon no doubt that
despite Lieutenant General Garnet Wolseley's efforts to chivvy
things along, it was evident that his secondary plan of an overland Desert Column in addition to the river route would indeed
be necessary. He had to get a force to Khartoum by the quickest possible method, but time was fast running out. Gordon's
messages were more infrequent and by December 1884 it was
evident that he could not last out much longer. The river route
would still be central to Wolseley's plans, but a corner had to be
cut – literally and figuratively.

His new plan was for a River Column based on four infantry
battalions to push up the Nile with their whalers by the circu-
itous route via Abu Hamed and Berber as originally planned
under the command of a gruff experienced old campaigner,
Major General William Earle. Meanwhile, a smaller, but sup-
posedly fast-moving Desert Column, under the command of
Brigadier General Herbert Stewart, would march the roughly
175 miles across the open Bayuda Desert to the vicinity of the
Dervish-held town of Metemmeh which they were to capture.

Here they would rendezvous with Gordon's surviving river steamers, who would carry the chief intelligence officer, Colonel Charles Wilson, to meet Gordon at Khartoum, so that he could report back first-hand on the real state of the siege. Meanwhile, Stewart would organise supply columns and stores depots back along his route across the desert, while awaiting the arrival of the River Column. In hindsight, there was a great deal wrong with this plan, but at the time there was a mood of optimism in the Korti camp as Wolseley arrived and the Desert Column readied itself for its departure.

> Lord Wolseley arrived here just at dusk I was on the bank in a crowd of soldiers and officers – almost the first thing I heard was Lord 'W' saying, 'Is Major Kitchener there?' Then someone said, 'Yes!' and he then said, 'Let him come on board at once I wish to see him!' I had to go down a broad flight of steps and on board he shook hands and asked the news which I told him. Next day I met him walking about and he called me and said some very nice things about my services – I dined with him the same evening. However, the greatest honour was done to me last night, Xmas, the men had a bonfire and sang songs – Lord 'W' and everyone was there. After the songs cheers were given for Lord 'W', General Stewart, and then someone shouted out, 'Major "K"!' so 2,000 throats were distended in my honour. I am very proud of that moment and shall not forget it in a hurry – after that General Buller was cheered – I expect we shall be at Khartoum before you get this letter.[2]
>
> Major Herbert Kitchener, Headquarters

It was not to be.

At 15.00 on Tuesday 30 December the Desert Column set off from Korti after a march past Wolseley to bid them on their way. By this time, it consisted of the Heavy Camel Corps (Guards and heavy cavalry detachments), the Light Camel Regiment (detachments mainly from hussar regiments), the Guards Camel

Regiment (detachments from the Guards infantry regiments), and the Mounted Infantry Camel Regiment (detachments from the Egypt infantry troops). In addition, it would ultimately have the 1st Royal Sussex Regiment, a small Naval Brigade, three 7-pounder guns and the usual ancillary services. It was a tough march, sure enough, but Lieutenant Charles Townshend took some pleasure in the New Year celebrations.

> At midnight – the last moment of the old year, 'Auld Lang Syne' was sung from front to rear whilst on the march, the effect being very fine. The air was quite still, and the long column presented a weird appearance in the moonlight. At 1 a.m., we reached the wells of El Howeyiat. Here we halted and slept on the ground in our accoutrements. There was very little water in these wells, and that was muddy. Sentries had to be placed over the water skins. We halted at midday for the men's dinners. A ration of one pint of water to each man was served out, and there was a good deal of grumbling among the men. This was most irritating as the best means possible were taken by the officers, and the men seemed to have no idea as to the necessity of economising the water. That pint of water had to serve for everything until the next day, when we hoped to reach the Gakdul Wells. None of us had washed since leaving Korti, and one felt very dirty. I always managed to save a little tea in my pannikin for shaving purposes.[3]
> Lieutenant Charles Townshend, Royal Marine Light Infantry

They reached Gakdul Wells, where there was a good and plentiful source of water, on 5 January. Here they were about half way to Metemmeh, but logistical confusion disabled any attempt to 'hurry' onwards in their journey. Haste would surely have been advisable if they were to have any hope of coming down 'like a wolf on the fold' on a surprised Dervish garrison. But this could never be a 'dash' across the desert because the endemic shortage of camels meant that they would have to travel in awkward

stages, tracing and retracing their steps in a crab-like motion.
The plan was to leave the Guards Camel Regiment to set up
a base at Gakdul, while Stewart and the main force took the
camels and returned all the way back to Korti to pick up more
stores and allow the 1st Royal Sussex to ride the camels on the
return of the column to Gakdul. Until the column returned,
the Guards Camel Regiment was somewhat vulnerable if the
Dervishes noticed they were there.

> Outpost duty was rather severe, especially at night. Since
> we were by no means sure that the enemy might not be
> meditating a night attack on our cul-de-sac, we had to keep
> many sentries going. Two officers and some sixty-five men
> were on outpost duty every 24 hours. Since several high hills
> commanded all the tracks, ravines, and gullies by which we
> might be attacked, it was easy enough to post sentries during
> the day to see for many miles round. At night, however, it
> was different; a chain of sentries had to be established round
> the whole place, and with so many glens and gullies it was
> impossible to command the whole satisfactorily with a
> few men on a pitch-dark night. Oh, the agony of going the
> rounds four or five times a night! The whole distance on a
> map would not exceed three-quarters of a mile, if as much,
> but the fastest time on record was 48 minutes for the whole
> round. Uphill and downhill, over those sharp rocks, no path
> visible, as your lantern would be sure to go out at the first
> cropper, skinning your shins over every big stone, climb-
> ing down precipices you would never attempt by daylight,
> losing your way, your hat, your bearings.[4]
> Lieutenant Lord Gleichen, Guards Camel Regiment

They knew the main column would not return for around ten
days, but the Guards Camel Regiment made good use of the
time, organising separate pools and troughs for men and camels,
clearing a road and camp sites and building two redoubts on the
heights above the gorge.

Stewart did not even set off from Korti until 8 January. With the second tranche was a small Naval Brigade of five officers and fifty-three men, which had been placed under the command of Captain Charles Beresford. It would be their role to assist in taking Gordon's steamers to Khartoum. Beresford had made sensible preparations that he struggled to explain to landlubbers.

The intervening days being occupied in preparations. An essential part of my own arrangements consisted in obtaining spare boilerplates, rivets, oakum, lubricating oil, and engineers' stores generally, as I foresaw that these would be needed for the steamers, which had already been knocking about the Nile in a hostile country for some three months. At first, Sir Redvers Buller refused to let me have either the stores or the camels upon which to carry them. He was most good-natured and sympathetic, but he did not immediately perceive the necessity. 'What do you want boilerplates for?' he said. 'Are you going to mend the camels with them?' But he let me have what I wanted. With other stores, I took eight boilerplates, and a quantity of rivets. One of those plates, and a couple of dozen of those rivets, saved the column. The Gardner gun of the Naval Brigade was carried in pieces on four camels. Number One carried the barrels, Number Two training and elevating gear and wheels, Number Three the trail, Number Four, four boxes of hoppers. The limber was abolished for the sake of handiness. The gun was unloaded, mounted, feed-plate full, and ready to march in under 4 minutes. When marching with the gun, the men hauled it with dragropes, muzzle first, the trail being lifted and carried upon a light pole. Upon going into action, the trail was dropped and the gun was ready, all the confusion and delay caused by unlimbering in a crowded space being thus avoided.[5]
Captain Charles Beresford, Naval Brigade

The journeys to and from Korti were as rushed as possible, as

Stewart was desperate to save time, but in doing so he further undermined the already inadequate camel resources of the Desert Column. The camels were not only often overloaded, but they also lacked rest, foraging opportunities, fodder and water. The consequences of this may not have been immediately obvious, but as they prepared for the next leg of their journey to Metemmeh, many of the camels were already suffering from exhaustion. Beresford did his best to reduce the damage suffered.

> The whole progress of the expedition depended upon camels as the sole means of transport. When a camel falls from exhaustion, it rolls over upon its side, and is unable to rise. But it is not going to die unless it stretches its head back; and it has still a store of latent energy; for a beast will seldom of its own accord go on to the last. It may sound cruel; but in that expedition it was a case of a man's life or a camel's suffering. When I came across a fallen camel, I had it hove upright with a gun-pole, loaded men upon it, and so got them over another 30 or 40 miles. I superintended the feeding of the camels myself. If a camel was exhausted, I treated it as I would treat a tired hunter, which, after a long day, refuses its food. I gave the exhausted camels food by handfuls, putting them upon a piece of cloth or canvas, instead of throwing the whole ration upon the ground at once.[6]
>
> Captain Charles Beresford, Naval Brigade

On 12 December, Stewart and the main column arrived back at Gakdul. One of the officers attached to the column was an intelligence officer, Captain Willoughby Verner, who set to work with Wilson to interview the prisoners that had been taken in the immediate vicinity of Gakdul. They were trying to ascertain the strength of the Dervish forces that might lie ahead of them.

Occupied all day in examining the prisoners taken at Gakdul. They of course lied like true 'Believers', but one of the seven, a lad, split on them and by a little *judicial* pressure, his brother also came to a more sensible frame of mind. Metemmeh they describe as being some distance from the river, with some wells, and a strongly built town of considerable size. All the men there wear the Mahdi's uniform, and they make all people do so who wish to trade there. Hence our poor innocents appearing in the garb. When taken prisoner they made a great show of tearing off the badges and swore they had been forced to wear them. The people at Metemmeh have got two or three mountain guns and there are some 2,000 men who will fight. One account says 1,200.[7]

Captain Willoughby Verner, Headquarters, Desert Column

Another arrival at Gakdul was Lieutenant Colonel Fred Burnaby, as ever in search of adventure, and designated to be the garrison commander of Metemmeh once it was captured.

At 14.00 on 14 January the Desert Column at long last set off for Metemmeh. The first stage was over an open expanse of flat gravelly plain, and it was not long before they noticed that their water containers, which, to say the least, were important in the desert, were totally inadequate.

As much water as possible was taken in iron camel-tanks, two to a camel, but the condition of our private water-skins and leather bottles was pitiable. Every man had been served out afresh with both skin and bottle on starting from Korti, and yet barely 20 per cent of the skins held their full complement of water. Even after every visible hole had been carefully sewn up, and the whole skin thoroughly greased, at the end of the first day's march you would find more than half your water evaporated; next day the skin would be a damp, flabby bag, and the day after, a dried, shrivelled-up article without an atom of water in it. How

a committee of intelligent officers can ever have selected such an article beats my comprehension.[8]
Lieutenant Lord Gleichen, Guards Camel Regiment

They stopped for the night at about 18.00 and began the tedious, time-consuming business of unloading and feeding the camels. Then they had to feed themselves, set the sentries and get what sleep they could.

Reveille woke us next morning at 3 a.m., and by 4.30 we had had our breakfasts and were on the move. It is very cold in the early morning in the desert, especially during January, and the comfort of a steaming cup of cocoa or tea, with biscuit and cold 'bully' beef, must be felt to be appreciated. Although I own 'bully' is not inviting at midday, when floating about the tin in red, warm, stringy masses, yet it has its period of beauty, in the early mornings, when the cold night has solidified it into respectable-looking cold beef; at that time a quarter of a pound of it inside you, washed down with hot drink, makes a deal of difference in the way you are disposed to look at things on a dark and cold morning.[9]
Lieutenant Lord Gleichen, Guards Camel Regiment

As they progressed across the desert, they were preceded by patrols by the attached squadron of 19th Hussars, commanded by Lieutenant Colonel Percy Barrow, but also including Major John French. This was essential, for any chance of a surprise attack had been lost with the protracted gathering at Gakdul. The Dervishes must know they were coming, the question was what would they do? Or even more pertinently, when would they strike?

It was no real surprise when a patrol led by French encountered a strong party of Dervishes on the morning of 16 January. As the Hussars fell back, they managed to secure the rocky defile that led through a range of hills, through which the main body was able to pass into the wide valley that led to the Abu Klea Wells. By the time they were all through, there was only 3 hours of daylight left and they bivouacked for the night. Charles Beresford describes the construction of their overnight defensive positions.

Through glasses we could clearly distinguish innumerable white-robed figures of Arabs, relieved upon the black cliffs dominating the pass, leaping and gesticulating. Here and there were puffs of smoke, followed after an interval by a faint report; but the range was too far and no bullet arrived. The Naval Brigade with the Mounted Infantry, which were on the left of the column, were ordered to ascend the hill on the left of the line of advance, to guard the flank of the column. We dragged up the Gardner gun, placed it in position, and built a breastwork of loose stones. By the time we had finished, it was about 4 o'clock. Beyond and beneath us, a line of green and white flags was strung across the valley, fluttering above the scrub, and these, with a large tent, denoted the headquarters of the enemy. The rest of the column were hurriedly building a zeriba in the valley. As the twilight fell, a party of the enemy crept to the summit of the hill on the right flank, opposite to our fort, and dropped bullets at long range into the column below, which replied with a couple of screw guns. As the darkness thickened, there arose that maddening noise of tom-toms, whose hollow and menacing beat, endlessly and pitilessly repeated, haunts those who have heard it to the last day of their lives. Swelling and falling, it sounds now hard at hand, and again far away. That night, we lay behind the breastwork, sleepless and very cold; and the deadly throbbing of the drums filled the air, mingled with the murmur of many voices and the rustle as of many feet, and punctuated with the sullen crack of rifles, now firing singly, now in a volley, and the whine of bullets.[10]

Captain Charles Beresford, Naval Brigade

It was a long night. It was difficult to sleep under intermittent fire, with the relentless beating of the drums rising and falling with gusts of breeze. And the men had other needs that gnawed away at them – water and tobacco.

> We were very hard up for water and the men were suffering agonies of thirst. Some of the reserve supply was issued to the men. But we were all impatient to occupy the wells and satisfy our thirst. As soon as it became dark orders were given that no light should be shown. Notwithstanding this a man would light his pipe now and then – shouts of, 'Put that pipe out!' then brought a volley from the enemy.[11]
> Lieutenant Charles Townshend, Royal Marine Light Infantry

The night was punctuated by occasional alarms caused by over-strained nerves that an attack was underway.

> On more than one occasion the whole force, right down the line, stood simultaneously to their posts, with bayonets fixed and eyes peering into the darkness. It was during one of those alarms that from the direction of the enemy we heard the tramp of a horse's feet on the gravel advancing towards us, and, curiously enough, straight to our detachment. The end of a cigar glowed in the darkness and with an instinctive knowledge of his man, one of my troopers exclaimed. 'It must be the colonel!' He was right, it was Burnaby returning from a solitary visit of observation to the enemy's lines. I got over the wall and went up to him, and explained the state of affairs, and how annoying it was that my men could not go to sleep. He laughed his cheery laugh. 'Ah! Never mind', he said, 'boys will be boys!' Somewhat shamefacedly the word was passed down the line and there were no more alarms that night.[12]
> Lieutenant Colonel Lord Binning, Heavy Camel Regiment

Dawn on 17 January brought an increased volume of fire, which seemed to presage an attack, so the British strengthened the zeriba made of cut mimosa bushes, and used biscuit boxes and camel saddles to create a gun position from which the 7-pounders could return fire. As Stewart rode out to try and see what was happening he came under heavy fire.

> Sir Herbert Stewart and Colonel Burnaby were riding about on high ground, a mark for the enemy. I saw the general's bugler drop close beside him, and running up, implored both him and Burnaby to dismount, but they would not. I had hardly returned to my place when I heard another bullet strike, and saw Burnaby's horse fall, throwing its rider. I went to help Burnaby to his feet, and as I picked him up, he said a curious thing. He said, 'I'm not in luck today, Charlie!'[13]
>
> Captain Charles Beresford, Naval Brigade

A large mass of Dervishes was seen manoeuvring across the valley and for a while Stewart must have hoped that they would attack, which would have maximised the advantage of his superior firepower from a strong defensive position. It was not to be.

> The enemy's main body showed itself, advancing up the wadi in two lines, the second very strong and reckoned at about 5,000 men. They halted on a ridge about 1,000 yards from us and appeared to be dressing their ranks. Numerous bright banners floated out in the breeze, chiefly red and white, and the early sun shone on the spearheads of the dense crowd of savages. I don't know what Sir Herbert thought of this business, but I at once made up my mind that we had a big job on hand and that the force opposed to us must be some of the Mahdi's regulars. The enemy's tactics were evidently to make us leave our zeriba and fight in the open, whereas we had hoped they would come on and attack us. This, it soon became very certain they would not do.[14]
>
> Captain Willoughby Verner, Headquarters, Desert Column

Short of water as he was, Stewart had little choice but to resume the advance on the Abu Klea Wells. He would leave two and a half companies of the 1st Royal Sussex in the zeriba with the Royal Engineers, a proportion of the baggage camels and the makeshift hospital that had been established to look after the wounded.

At 09.00 on 17 January the 19th Hussars were sent out to guard the flanks of the line of advance. By 10.00, the cumbersome square formation began its advance.

> Directly we left the zareba, the enemy got our range, keeping up a ceaseless fire with deadly effect. A private in my company was the first of the Marines to be hit. He was shot through the chest, rolled over, tearing the ground with his hands, and died almost immediately. The cries for 'Stretcher!' rapidly increased. 'Tommy Atkins' does not like to be inactive under a heavy fire: nothing is so trying both to the patience and nerves of the men, and we all became very impatient to have the fight settled. But a movement in square is necessarily a slow one in order to preserve formation. We scarcely went a snail's pace and were further impeded by the wounded and the camels in the centre of the square. Every now and then the square would halt, lie down and fire volleys.[15]
>
> Lieutenant Charles Townshend, Royal Marine Light Infantry

The terrain was not helpful; this was no flat desert. Everything seemed to be against them.

> The route, studded with rocky knolls, furrowed with watercourses, and sharply rising and falling, was almost impassable for the camels. They lagged behind, slipping and falling, and we of the rear face were all tangled up with a grunting, squealing, reeking mass of struggling animals. Their drivers, terrified by the murderous fire coming from the right, were pressing back towards the left rear angle.

By dint of the most splendid exertions, the sailors kept up, dragging the Gardner gun. Men were dropping, and halts must be made while they were hoisted into the cacolets and their camels forced into the square.[16]
Captain Charles Beresford, Naval Brigade

They had a line of skirmishers out on both flanks, trying to force back the Dervish snipers. The 19th Hussars had already been dragged into a vigorous skirmish with a mass of Dervishes on the far left of the line of advance and were hence unable to scout ahead. Stewart ordered the square to incline to the right to avoid a very rough area of rising ground.

The trouble was that the rear of the square, defended by the Heavy Camel Regiment, was no longer attached to the rest of the formation. The camels meant to be in the centre of the square were unhappy with the ground underfoot and in lagging behind, had wrecked the left rear face which was in considerable disarray.

Swiftly and with almost appalling silence, they came on, and then suddenly espying the weak spot in our defence, they wheeled like a flock of pigeons and made for the gap in our left rear. At the same moment the two bodies we had already seen wheeled about and joined in the charge. Our men, though completely taken by surprise, fell steadily back in an endeavour to close the rear face. I could see Burnaby on his pony riding to and fro, and urging our men on to fall back quickly, but our riflemen, who were out skirmishing, masked our fire, and it was not until the last of them had managed to crawl in on hands and knees to avoid the bullets of our own men, that an effective fire could be brought to bear.[17]
Lieutenant Colonel Lord Binning, Heavy Camel Regiment

The Dervishes came on in a three-pointed phalanx led on horseback by their Emirs, with their banners and the footmen racing up behind. The skirmishers on the left face and rear of the square side were hopelessly isolated.

> Our skirmishers were racing in for their lives. The last man
> was overtaken and speared. At this moment the left rear
> angle of the square was still unformed. The camels were
> still struggling into it. Several camels, laden with wounded,
> had lain down at the foot of the slope and their drivers had
> fled into the square; and these animals were being dragged
> in by soldiers. The appalling danger of this open corner
> was instantly evident.[18]

Captain Charles Beresford, Naval Brigade

Beresford and Burnaby saw the danger of the left rear face, and both took precipitate action: Beresford by deploying his Gardner to augment the firepower at the danger point; and Burnaby by opening out his rear two companies to extend the left face of the square – and as he thought to directly face the threat. The problem was that both actions left them, and their men, exposed 'outside' the square – such as it was – and further weakened its overall integrity by leaving a flank for the Dervishes to exploit by simply going round the extended line.

> Then I ordered the crew of the Gardner gun to run it
> outside the square to the left flank. At the same time,
> Colonel Burnaby wheeled Number 3 Company (4th and
> 5th Dragoon Guards) from the rear face to the left flank.
> Number 4 Company (Scots Greys and Royals) had already
> wheeled from the rear to the left flank, so that they were just
> behind me. Five or six paces outside the square we dropped
> the trail of the gun. So swiftly did these things happen that
> the leading ranks of the enemy were still 400 yards away.
> They were tearing down upon us with a roar like the roar
> of the sea, an immense surging wave of white-slashed black
> forms brandishing bright spears and long flashing swords;
> and all were chanting, as they leaped and ran, the war-song

of their faith, 'La ilaha ill! Allah Mohammedu rasul Allah'; and the terrible rain of bullets poured into them by the Mounted Infantry and the Guards stayed them not. They wore the loose white robe of the Mahdi's uniform, looped over the left shoulder, and the straw skullcap. These things we heard and saw in a flash, as the formidable wave swept steadily nearer.[19]

Captain Charles Beresford, Naval Brigade

Verner was one of those who helped Beresford deploy his Gardner.

I was helping to close-up the Heavies and was somewhere in the rear of the 5th Lancers, when Beresford came bursting through the mob with a Gardner, to bring it into action on that face. As he ran it out, I pulled back two Lancers who were then on the knee and whose heads were in the way of the gun. As the enemy came on, they were met with a tremendous fire from Captain Pigott's company of the Mounted Infantry and the Rifle Company, and they fell by scores. The mass then swung off to their right and made for the Lancers and Dragoons. These men did not deliver an effective fire and fell back on their camels. A great body of the enemy continued this outflanking rush and swept round the rear face of the square. Several horsemen and men on foot with banners preceded them. These were all shot down in the advance, but the crowd of spearmen surged over everything and in less than a minute from their first appearance were right into us, hurling spears and stabbing and slashing.[20]

Captain Willoughby Verner, Headquarters, Desert Column

Beresford was now outside the square and desperate to get his Gardner into action.

I laid the Gardner gun myself to make sure. As I fired, I

saw the enemy mown down in rows, dropping like ninepins; but as the men killed were in rear of the front rank,
after firing about forty rounds (eight turns of the lever), I
lowered the elevation. I was putting in most effective work
on the leading ranks and had fired about thirty rounds
when the gun jammed. The extraction had pulled the head
from a discharged cartridge, leaving the empty cylinder
in the barrel. William Rhodes, chief boatswain's mate,
and myself immediately set to work to unscrew the feed-
plate in order to clear the barrel or to take out its lock.
The next moment the enemy were on top of us. The feed-
plate dropped on my head, knocking me under the gun
and across its trail. Simultaneously a spear was thrust right
through poor Rhodes, who was instantly killed at my side.
Walter Miller the armourer was speared beside the gun at
the same time. I was knocked off the trail of the gun by a
blow with the handle of an axe, the blade of which missed
me. An Arab thrust at me with his spear, and I caught the
blade, cutting my hand, and before he could recover his
weapon a bullet dropped him.[21]

Captain Charles Beresford, Naval Brigade

Beresford was caught in a mass of Dervishes, only the press of
bodies saved him in those frenzied moments – a life lived or
ended in seconds.

Struggling to my feet, I was carried bodily backwards by
the tremendous impact of the rush, right back upon the
front rank of the men of Number 4 Company, who stood
like rocks. I can compare the press to nothing but the crush
of a theatre crowd alarmed by a cry of fire. Immediately
facing me was an Arab holding a spear over his head, the
staff of the weapon being jammed against his back by
the pressure behind him. I could draw neither sword nor
pistol. The front ranks of our men could not use rifle or
bayonet for a few moments. But the pressure, forcing our

men backwards up the hill, presently enabled the rear rank, now occupying a position of a few inches higher than the enemy, to fire over the heads of the front rank right into the mass of the Arabs. The bullets whizzed close by my head; and one passed through my helmet.[22]

Captain Charles Beresford, Naval Brigade

Another man caught outside the square was Burnaby. It all happened in a matter of moments, but he seems to have realised his error and tried to recall the Heavy Camel Regiment companies to bring them back into line and close the rear face of the square. Then, seeing that some of his skirmishers were still struggling to get back, he drew his sword and rode out to meet his enemies face-to-face. He may have made a mistake, but he put his body on the line to try and put things right. It was too late.

For a moment through the smoke, I caught a glimpse of Burnaby, his arm outstretched, his four barrelled Lancaster pistol in his hand. It was only a momentary glimpse, and I did not see him again until all was over. I made my way as best I could to the spot where I had seen the colonel, foreboding in my heart. But I was not the first to find him. A young private, in the Blues, a mere lad, was already beside him, endeavouring to support his head on his knee. The lad's genuine grief, with tears running down his cheeks, was as touching as were his simple words, 'Oh! Sir, here is the bravest man in England dying, and no one to help him!' It was too true, a glance showed him to be beyond help. A spear had inflicted a terrible wound on the right side of his neck and throat, and his skull had been cleft from a blow from a double-edged sword – probably as he fell forward on his pony's neck. Either wound would have proved fatal for the marvel was that he was still alive. As I took his hand, a feeble pressure, and a faint look of recognition in his eyes, told me he still breathed, but life was ebbing fast, and it was only a matter of a few moments before he was gone. He

was killed some 30 yards from the square, and no friendly form lay near him, save one, for under a pile of dead fanatics, we found the body, scarcely recognisable, of Corporal Mackintosh, of my detachment, who had perished in a gallant attempt to save his colonel.[23]
Lieutenant Colonel Lord Binning, Heavy Camel Regiment

Burnaby had been riding Lieutenant Percival Marling's pony Moses, which was also stabbed and cut to pieces. Although many consider that Beresford and Burnaby had erred in their deployments, perhaps not too much criticism should be made. Neither were infantry officers, who might have better understood what was required, and they were reacting in haste to a desperate situation.

The whole rear of the square was now in total chaos. It had not been 'broken' as such, because it had never actually been formed. But the Dervishes were inside, and it was truly mayhem. It was then that the accursed camels became a blessing in disguise, forming a barrier in the centre of the square.

The square became a mob, huddled back-to-back retreating from the Arabs, who were now among us, cutting and slashing with their long straight swords and stabbing the men with their long spears like so many sheep. The crush was so great that at one time I could not get my arms down to my sides and remained with sword and pistol up in the air, doing my utmost to keep my feet. Although it was afterwards said that no camel ought to have been in the square, that they impeded us, etc., I personally believe that they were our salvation on that hard-fought day for, being in the centre, they held the square, as it were, together. The Arabs were stabbing even our wounded who lay helpless in the cacolets fastened to the sides of the camels.[24]
Lieutenant Charles Townshend, Royal Marine Light Infantry

Wilson and Stewart were caught up in the bitter fighting inside the square. Wilson drew his revolver, always a sign of a desperate situation with a British officer, but here it was difficult to miss the Dervishes – they were so close.

> The Arabs began running in under the camels to the front part of the square. Some of the rear rank now faced about and began firing. By this fire Herbert Stewart's horse was shot, and as he fell three Arabs ran at him. I was close to his horse's tail, and disposed of the one nearest to me, about three paces off; and the others were, I think, killed by the Mounted Infantry officers close by.[25]
>
> Colonel Charles Wilson, Headquarters, Desert Column

Lieutenant Lord Gleichen was on the right-hand face of the square. As the rear folded up, his men came under a tremendous pressure from the sheer weight of bodies surging against them. What the hell was happening? Remember it was impossible to see more than a few yards in the crush.

> Telling the men to stand fast, I forced my way through the jam to see what had happened. Heavies, Sussex, and camels of all sorts were pressing with terrific force on our thin double rank, and it seemed every moment as if it must give; but it didn't. On getting through to the other side of the press, a gruesome sight was seen. I shouted myself hoarse trying to get the men to aim carefully, but my voice was lost in the din. A rain of bullets whizzed dangerously close past my head from the rifles behind into the fighting mass in front. Numbers of the Arabs went down in that hail, and I fear several Englishmen too. Everything depended on the front and right faces standing fast. And well did they stick to it. With the rear rank faced about, the men stubbornly withstood the pressure, and, do what they would, the Arabs could not break in the solid mass of men and camels.[26]
>
> Lieutenant Lord Gleichen, Guards Camel Regiment

Slowly the Dervishes that had got into the square were hunted down and slaughtered. Wilson never forgot the phlegmatic courage of one of the Emirs.

> I saw a fine old sheikh on horseback plant his banner in the centre of the square, behind the camels. He was at once shot down, falling on his banner. He turned out to be Musa, Emir of the Duguaim Arabs, from Kordofan. I had noticed him in the advance, with his banner in one hand and a book of prayers in the other, and never saw anything finer. The old man never swerved to the right or left, and never ceased chanting his prayers until he had planted his banner in our square. If any man deserved a place in the Moslem Paradise, he did.[27]
> Colonel Charles Wilson, Headquarters, Desert Column

But there were many such examples of incredible courage witnessed in the fighting.

> Their desperate courage was marvellous. I saw a boy of some twelve years of age, who had been shot through the stomach, walk slowly up through a storm of bullets and thrust his spear at one of our men. I saw several Arabs writhe from out [of] a pile of dead and wounded, and charge some 80 yards under fire towards us, and one of them ran right up to the bayonets and flung himself upon them and was killed. I saw an Arab, who was wounded in the legs, sit up, and hurl his spear at a passing soldier. As the soldier stopped to load his rifle, the Arab tried to reach another spear, and failing, caught up stones and cast them at his foe; and then, when the soldier presented his rifle and took a deliberate aim, the Arab sat perfectly still looking down the barrel, till the bullet killed him.[28]
> Captain Charles Beresford, Naval Brigade

It had been too 'hot' to last that long. Firepower told and at last the Dervishes began to waver, then retreated over the ridge line and out of sight.

As the shooting died down the square was reformed and moved a short distance away from the mass of dead bodies – a terrible scene of butchery.

> Our square was reformed 200 yards clear of the place where it had fought, and we proceeded to gather the wounded and reckon our losses. I was ordered to count the enemy's killed. Close up to where the left face had stood lay over 400 in heaps, in some places two or three deep, whilst there were 500 more between us and the valley they had emerged from. The wadi itself was full of dead and wounded. The scene where we had stood and fought was simply indescribable. Within a space of about 50 yards square were heaped up some 130 British soldiers with fifty or sixty camels and horses and scores of Dervishes who had broken into the square and been slain. Perhaps the saddest sight was our wounded men who had been hit early in the fight and who had been speared as they lay. Our losses were very heavy, considering our small number, over 150 killed and wounded – about one in twelve. Amongst the killed was the celebrated Colonel Burnaby, a man who literally knew not fear. A few minutes before he was speared, he passed me, and giving me a hearty slap on the back, ejaculated, 'Isn't this fine sport, my boy!'[29]
> Captain Willoughby Verner, Headquarters, Desert Column

One of the more disturbing aspects of the battle was the treatment of the Dervish wounded. This would prove to be the great moral conundrum of fighting an opponent who will not surrender – something which the British find admirable in their own soldiers, but which they were not willing to condone or tolerate in others.

I got a party of Life Guards and went out to collect

ammunition and arms. We got altogether seventeen boxes
of small arms ammunition off the dead and wounded
camels and destroyed over thirty Martini rifles and hundreds of spears and swords. We threw all into a fire. Whilst
thus occupied, there was a cry of, 'Look out!' and I saw
about six men charging furiously towards the square. Of
course, everybody fired and they all fell, the last actually
reached the bayonets and delivered a sword cut in amongst
the men. These men had been lying amongst the dead
feigning. In general, their wounded were very troublesome. One fired at me with a Remington at 5 yards distance
and I had to 'aid' him. In consequence of similar cases, all
the wounded had to be despatched. Most of them were
horribly injured and would have died, for the Sudanese is
like a cat and only 'comes down' when he gets a genuine
smash.[30]

Captain Willoughby Verner, Headquarters, Desert Column

One can see the difficulty, for to assist the Dervish wounded
was to risk death. But it is not pleasant to read such accounts
– and to note the different layers of special pleading involved.
The Dervish losses were estimated to have been around 1,100
dead, which is in chastening contrast to the 74 dead and some 94
wounded suffered by the British.

The reaction to the news of the Battle of Abu Klea by the
poet and literary critic Wilfred Blunt shows the level of frustration coursing through the pens of the anti-imperialists as they
raged from the sidelines.

These English soldiers are mere murderers, and I confess
I would rather see them all at perdition than that a single
Arab more should die. What are they? A mongrel scum of
thieves from Whitechapel and Seven Dials, commanded by
young fellows whose ideal is the green room of the *Gaiety*,
without beliefs, without traditions, without other principle
of action than just to get their promotion and have a little

fun. On the other side men with the memory of a thousand years of freedom, with chivalry inherited from the Saracens, the noblest of ancestors, with a creed the purest the world ever knew, worshipping God and serving him in arms like the heroes of the ancient world they are. It is over the death of these that we rejoice. No, I desire in my heart to see their blood avenged, and every man of Stewart's butchering host butchered in their turn and sent to hell. Gladstone! Great God, is there no vengeance for this pitiful man of blood, who has not even the courage to be at the same time a man of iron? What is he that he should have cost the world a single life? A pedant, a babbler, an impotent old fool.[31]
Wilfred Blunt

Harsh words indeed.

It was late afternoon on 17 January, before the Desert Column was ready and able to move on the remaining few miles to the Abu Klea Wells. The men were tired and parched, but many were called upon to assist with transporting the wounded, as there were now too few camels left to carry them all.

By the time the wounded were picked up, the dead counted, and their weapons destroyed, and the square was ready to start, it was half-past three in the afternoon. There was no food, and hardly any water. The soldiers suffered dreadfully from thirst; their tongues were so swollen as to cause intense pain, their lips black, their mouths covered with white mucus. Several men fainted. Luckily, I had put a skin of water upon a camel just before the action, so that the men of the Naval Brigade all had a drink, and there was a little water over for the wounded. The sailors persisted in smoking; they said it did them good; so, I let them![32]
Captain Charles Beresford, Naval Brigade

It seemed an age before they reached the wells. Even then there seemed to be no end to the work that had to carried out.

A large square was formed for the night on some rising ground close to the wells, for the chances of another attack were not yet by any means over. Three hundred volunteers were then called to march back to the zeriba and bring up all the baggage before daylight. They were soon started off, and then began for us quite the coldest night we ever experienced; the wounded must have suffered fearfully. Of course, we had no extra clothing or covering of any sort, nothing between us and the freezing night air but a shirt and a very thin serge jacket. I tried to get shelter between two camels, but directly I began to get warm the brutes would feel me and lurch over on top of me, till I was driven into the open again. Hardly a wink of sleep did one of us get that night, and fearfully hungry we were too. Half a dozen of us huddled together, giving up sleep as a bad job, and made the time pass, by sucking in turns at a solitary pipe – a great preventive of pangs of emptiness in the stomach region. At last, the cold grey dawn began to break, and, glad of any movement, we stood to our arms.[33]
Lieutenant Lord Gleichen, Guards Camel Regiment

After such a battle many must have thought over what had happened and there is no doubt that some harsh judgements were made.

It was a mistake to turn cavalry into infantry and make them fight in square with an arm they were not accustomed to. Add to this, the cavalry were detachments from different regiments, only brought together a few days before we left Korti. A cavalry man is taught never to be still, and that a square can be broken. How can you expect him in a moment to forget all his training, stand like a rock, and believe no one can get inside a square? Then a cavalry man has a short handy carbine; he is given a long rifle and bayonet and uses them for the first time in his life when a determined enemy is charging him. The Heavy Camel Corps had little drill as infantry. Those who were near the Heavies told me that as the men fired, they moved back involuntarily – not being taught, as infantry men are, to stand in a rigid line; they thus got clubbed together. The sailors were pressed back with the cavalry and lost heavily: they get very excited and would storm a work or do anything of that kind well; but they are trained to fight in ships, and you cannot expect them to stand shoulder to shoulder in a square like grenadiers.[34]

Colonel Charles Wilson, Headquarters, Desert Column

This is not a matter of lack of courage, but of different skill sets. There was also widespread criticism of the weapons they had to fight with. When men are engaged in life-or-death combat, they want – and deserve – weapons that can be relied on.

Nearly half the British rifles jammed, owing to the use of leaf cartridges. The Remington rifles used by the Mahdi's soldiers had solid drawn cartridges which did not jam. During the action of Abu Klea, the officers were almost entirely employed in clearing jammed rifles passed back to them by the men. The British bayonets and cutlasses bent and twisted, the result of a combination of knavery and laziness on the part of those who were trusted to supply the soldier with weapons upon which his life depends. The bayonets were blunt, because no one had thought of sharpening them.[35]

Captain Charles Beresford, Naval Brigade

These were common complaints. It is also true that prior experience in desert conditions was invaluable in keeping rifles in a condition where jamming was reduced to a minimum.

I am certain many rifles jammed through dust having got into the breech blocks. In our company we always kept pieces of linen, leather, etc., bound round the breech-blocks as guards when the rifle was not required for use in action: but we marines were the only ones who used this precaution. Even inside a holster, a revolver would become useless through the fine sand, unless protected by something. I always kept a silk handkerchief bound round the hammer of my own.[36]
Lieutenant Charles Townshend, Royal Marine Light Infantry

***

THEY AWOKE THE FOLLOWING DAY to ponder their next move. There were still over 20 miles to go before they reached Metemmeh and the Nile. The question uppermost in many minds was could their dwindling force get to their destination without fighting another battle? Their ranks were being fast eroded. The intelligence officers were soon in action.

Sir Charles Wilson and I were busily engaged in examining prisoners who had come in after the fight. We learnt from them that Omdurman (Gordon's north fort) had surrendered to the Mahdi a few days previously and the force we had defeated was 12,000 strong and included some 8,000 Baggara Arabs despatched by the Mahdi to oppose us. Another piece of news of serious import to us was that the Mahdi had sent a second contingent to bar our road to the river which still lay 24 miles ahead of us. Sir Herbert at once decided to push on at all risks and thus gain the river before this new force could oppose us.[37]
Captain Willoughby Verner, Headquarters, Desert Column

At 16.00 on 18 January, they set off again, leaving two companies of the Royal Sussex to build a makeshift redoubt to guard the vital water supply and protect the wounded. This would be an all-night march in an attempt to reach the Nile by dawn on 19 January. As with so much about this expedition it was a forlorn hope with only approximately 1,500 men left of the Desert Column. Verner was given the task of leading the way. This was to some extent a case of the blind leading the blind as he had no personal experience of the route.

> We marched for 2 hours across an open and undulating country, and at 6 o'clock darkness set in, our course being about south by east. Soon after 10 o'clock we reached the belt of scrub and the camels, which had been moving as usual on a broad front, got into great confusion. At 1 a.m., after 3 hours of incessant halts and delays owing to camels falling etc., we emerged from the scrub, and I reckoned we had covered 15 to 18 miles. Sir Herbert now directed me to try and hit off the river opposite the west corner of the Island of Gubat – and we thereupon left the camel track and struck off through the scrub, our course being south by west. The great column of camels had now got into inextricable confusion and my task of leading was at times rendered almost impossible by the numerous parties of men and stray camels which kept on surging forward past me on either flank and wheeling across my front. By dint, however, of incessant halts and constant closing up, we managed to advance about 4 miles in the 5 hours preceding dawn.[38]
> Captain Willoughby Verner, Headquarters, Desert Column

With the break of dawn, there was a feeling that it couldn't be much further, but the Nile was still not in sight. They did not want to run straight into Metemmeh, which was the presumed concentration point for the Dervish forces sent by the Mahdi.

> A halt was called, and the general decided to take what the natives assured him was the shortest line to the river. So convinced was I that this would take him to exactly the point

he most wished to avoid, namely Metemmeh, that I asked
for and obtained a small escort of Hussars on their small
Syrian ponies and rode off alone on a reconnaissance in the
direction I felt the Nile must lie. Nor was I disappointed,
for, on going a couple of miles ahead, I reached some rising
ground whence the Nile valley was clearly visible only 4
miles distant. But I also saw to my left front, a portion of
the town of Metemmeh and troops in formation marching
out apparently to occupy a ridge just north of it.[39]
Captain Willoughby Verner, Headquarters, Desert Column

He galloped back to report to Stewart, who decided to advance
to occupy the ridge from which Verner had seen the Nile. But
they were thwarted by the approach of a threatening mass of
Dervish rifleman who forced them to fight where they were –
about half a mile short of the gravel ridge just above the Nile
– which was then occupied by a large force drawn up as if ready
for battle. So began the Battle of Abu Kru on 19 January.

We collected all our transport into the centre and made
a rough line of defence around it with camel saddles and
boxes containing biscuit and bully beef. Meanwhile the
Dervishes moved rapidly round so as to bar our route to
the river, and soon brought a concentric fire to bear on us
from the scrub on three sides. Our situation was somewhat
trying, the men had been marching all night and were worn
out and hungry, for remember it was the third consecutive
night during which they had had no sleep.[40]
Captain Willoughby Verner, Headquarters, Desert Column

The packed zeriba was an easy target for the surrounding
Dervish riflemen and soon the casualties began to mount. Then
a serious blow as Stewart was badly hit in the groin.

About 10.15am, Stewart was wounded and carried to the
hospital. The command then devolved upon me as senior

officer. After a short talk with Boscawen, who was next senior officer, we went together to Stewart, and found him very cool and collected, and apparently not in great pain; but on my saying I hoped he would soon be well, he at once replied that he was certain the wound was fatal, and that his soldiering days were over. I said what I could to cheer him.[41]

Colonel Charles Wilson, Headquarters, Desert Column

Wilson had no command experience and was forced to rely heavily on Lieutenant Colonel Evelyn Boscawen (commanding the Guards Camel Regiment), who would act as his chief of staff. At that point their only hope was that the Dervishes would throw caution to the winds and charge the zeriba. Sadly, they proved happy enough to stay back and fire into such a tempting target.

A breastwork of biscuit boxes and camel saddles was made, but before this was completed and our camels double knee lashed inside the square, the bullets of their riflemen began to sing about us as they crept closer and closer. There was a small rise of ground about 200 yards in front of our square, and hearing Burleigh, the correspondent, point this out and suggest that this should be occupied, I at once asked permission to go and make a breastwork. About half a dozen of us, officers, and Burleigh ran as hard as we could with camel saddles and boxes to the knoll, piling them one on the other. It was warm work, for their riflemen, only about 400 yards distant, devoted all their energies to us.[42]

Lieutenant Charles Townshend, Royal Marine Light Infantry

As they worked, the intrepid volunteers were helped by covering fire from the zeriba, including from Lord Gleichen and his men in the Guards Camel Company. This too proved a risky occupation.

Every one of my men was extended flat on his stomach as
the enemy's bullets were whistling close over our heads,
so I prudently assumed the same position at first, but
found I couldn't bring my field-glasses to bear comfortably.
Accordingly, I sat up, and was prospecting round satisfac-
torily, when suddenly I received a violent blow in the pit of
the stomach. I staggered up, and immediately fell down flat
– my wind was entirely gone, so I lay and gasped. A couple
of my men immediately rushed up, caught hold of me,
and, at a sepulchral, 'Take him away!' bore me off between
them at a fast 'double' for the hospital. My first idea was
that I was badly hit, but somehow I didn't seem to feel the
bullet inside; the further, too, I went, the better I felt, and
by the time we arrived at the zeriba I had recovered just
sufficient breath to gasp out to the men that I didn't think
I was very bad. So I clambered over the wall of saddles
and things, and sat down to get my wind and see what
damage had been done. It was chiefly to my clothes; the
brass button that had saved my life was carried away, ditto
watch and compass, and my pockets were half torn away.
Further investigation only revealed a large bruise. It must
have been a ricochet bullet, but it was as near a 'squeak' as
I ever wish to have.[43]
Lieutenant Lord Gleichen, Guards Camel Regiment

He had been fortunate indeed. As he recovered, he could see
that things were going from bad to worse in the zeriba.

A continuous rain of bullets went into and over the camel
zeriba. Every other minute a dead or wounded man was
carried past on a stretcher. Scores of camels were shot; you
would hear that sickening, 'Fft!' go into a camel close by
you, and see the poor brute patiently lying there, with a
stream of blood trickling from his shoulder or neck. After
a time, his head would drop lower and lower, till the neck
got that peculiar kink in it that betokens the approach of

the end, and over he would roll, quite silently. They never bellowed or tried to move when they were hit; nothing but an occasional shake or shiver would tell that a bullet was in them.[44]

Lieutenant Lord Gleichen, Guards Camel Regiment

The dwindling force was in an impossible position; something had to be done or they were doomed – but what?

At first, we managed to keep down their fire by steady section volleys into the scrub at 75 to 800 yards, but no sooner was the fire checked in one spot than it broke out in another. Meanwhile the bullets rained in, hitting men and camels, crashing through biscuit boxes or clanging against iron camel saddles. The hospital soon became full of wounded, and the surgeons at work, as well as the wounded, were as exposed as anybody to the fire, and many a wounded man was shot over again. It became apparent at last that the only chance of saving the force was to go out and attack the Dervishes, so arrangements were made to strengthen the defences and, leaving a strong garrison to guard the wounded, to form a small fighting square of 800 men with rifles and sally out, and fight our way down to the river.[45]

Captain Willoughby Verner, Headquarters, Desert Column

This really was a desperate undertaking as neither the defenders of the zeriba nor the advancing square looked strong enough to withstand a full-on assault. Few men thought that the two halves of the Desert Column would ever live to meet again. Yet this was their only real chance of survival.

When we got clear of the redoubt, we made for a gravel ridge on which a large force of the enemy was collected with their banners, and behind which we knew lay the Nile. We did not go straight, but zigzag, to keep as much

Chain of Fire

as possible on the bare gravel patches, over which men and camels could march more freely than through the sayas grass; and we went at a sauntering pace in consequence of the camels in the square. The enemy's sharpshooters, who were well concealed in the long grass, and behind and beneath the trees and bushes, kept up a continuous fire on the square during its march. We could not send out skirmishers to reply to them, for fear of a sudden rush of spearmen as at Abu Klea; and the ground was much more dangerous, and likely to conceal large bodies of men, than that of the Abu Klea valley. All we could do was, when we got into a warm spot, to lie down and fire volleys at the puffs of smoke in the long grass.[46]

Colonel Charles Wilson, Headquarters, Desert Column

At every halt of the square, the bush in front was blasted by volleys to clear a way, before the slow advance continued, pushing onward into a horseshoe-shaped valley in the gravelly ridge in front of the Nile. But the Dervish return fire was fast thinning their ranks.

The sun was getting low when we got within about 600 yards of the ridge. Here we got into a very hot place: seven men were shot dead, and men fell so quickly that the cacolets and stretchers were filled. Things began to look ugly, and some of the officers told me afterwards that they thought we should have been obliged to turn back without reaching the Nile. That, however, we should never have done, as failure meant annihilation. I was walking just behind the Marines, and one poor fellow fell dead almost into my arms. The men were quite steady, with a set, determined look about their faces, and I knew they could be trusted.[47]

Colonel Charles Wilson, Headquarters, Desert Column

Then, without rhyme or reason, the Dervishes launched an

all-out assault. Presumably their leaders thought the square was
faltering and falling apart. Perversely this was a blessed relief; it
was exactly what the British might have prayed for as it gave the
British the chance to deploy their firepower to maximum effect,
to shatter the strength of the Mahdi's forces, instead of being
slowly eroded to nothing by the relentless sniping.

> All at once, the firing ceased, and the enemy's spearmen
> came running down the hill at a great pace, with several
> horsemen in front. It was a relief to know the crisis had
> come. The square was at once halted to receive the charge,
> and the men gave vent to their feelings in a wild sponta-
> neous cheer. Then they set to work, firing as they would
> have done at an Aldershot field-day. At first the fire had little
> effect, and the bugle sounded 'cease firing' the men, much
> to my surprise, answering to the call. The momentary rest
> steadied them, and when the enemy got within about 300
> yards, they responded to the call 'commence firing' with
> deadly effect. All the leaders with their fluttering banners
> went down, and no one got within 50 yards of the square.
> It only lasted a few minutes: the whole of the front ranks
> were swept away; and then we saw a backward movement,
> followed by the rapid disappearance of the Arabs in front
> of and all round us. We had won – and gave three ringing
> cheers – but we had still to reach the Nile with our heavy
> train of wounded, and men weary with constant excite-
> ment and want of sleep.[48]
> Colonel Charles Wilson, Headquarters, Desert Column

The relief was incredible as the Dervishes fell back in disarray.
The Battle of Abu Kru had been won, but again the aftermath
was dreadful.

> The cheering was tremendous as the enemy, including the
> spectators from the villages, began to fly in all directions.
> The wounded Arabs lying about were all bayoneted, for

it was found that they would slash at our men as they lay wounded on the ground, and one of our marines had his brains blown out by a wounded Arab who was apparently dead.[49]

Lieutenant Charles Townshend, Royal Marine Light Infantry

In the extended action the British suffered 26 killed and 100 wounded, while the Dervishes suffered an unknown number of casualties with estimates ranging from 300 to 1,000. It is significant that the great charge which caused so much damage to the Dervish forces had not caused any casualties to the square. After gathering up the wounded, Wilson pushed on towards the Nile, with Verner resuming his post as the guide.

I led in a southerly direction. Some of the enemy's cavalry now threatened our rear and the square halted and fired at them and they made off. I struck a wadi just at dusk and followed it down and shortly saw a white bank in front of me which seemed to be mist. Soon I saw it was water and then, as I topped a sandy ridge, I saw to my front a silver band of the Nile trending off to Khartoum. The last rays of the setting sun were just visible as the square came down to the water. I got a drink before anybody, and then got back up the bank. I then lay down, thoroughly beat.[50]

Captain Willoughby Verner, Headquarters, Desert Column

It was an incredible relief, one that had seemed impossible before the misguided Dervish charge. The men were utterly drained and who could blame them. Perhaps even worse was the condition of their camels.

Our camels are getting fearful sores on their humps. I could put my fist into some of the holes, and they get full of the most loathsome maggots. We rode in big wooden saddles covered with red leather and had stirrups. The saddles weighed 80 lb. As the camels lost condition from hard

work, insufficient food, and very little water, their humps got smaller and smaller, and the saddles didn't fit. From 7.45 a.m. January 14th to 4 p.m. January 20th our camels never got a drop of water, and only 9 lb of dhurra. No wonder they got thin, poor devils.[51]
Lieutenant Percival Marling, Mounted Infantry, Camel Regiment

The lack of sleep, the shortage of water, the stress and strain of constant danger culminating in their miraculous escape from the likelihood that they would all die: they slept where they dropped by the banks of the Nile.

★★★

THEY HAD BEEN THROUGH SO MUCH, but they had only just begun. To recap their orders from Wolseley: the Desert Column was now to establish a base, capture Metemmeh, secure a rendez-vous with Gordon's river steamers, despatch Charles Beresford and Charles Wilson upriver to check the situation at Khartoum, before returning to Metemmeh, to send messages back to Wolseley and await the arrival of the River Column before moving forward together to relieve Khartoum. On 28 January, when news of the serious wounds suffered by Stewart reached Wolseley, he appointed Major General Redvers Buller to take over the command, with Major General Evelyn Wood to act as chief of staff. Buller and the 1st Royal Irish Regiment were to be despatched as soon as possible to make the journey via Gakdul Wells to Gubat.

Meanwhile, the original Desert Column made a start by occupying the nearby few baked-mud buildings that made up the village of Gubat, which were soon put into a state of defence and used as a store depot and makeshift hospital. They also cele-brated the safe arrival of the 'other half' of the force left behind before the Battle of Abu Kru. On 21 January Wilson ordered an attempt to be made to capture the town of Metemmeh in accordance with Wolseley's original orders. It proved a damp squib despite the cooperation of some 250 men who had come ashore from four of Gordon's steamers – the *Bordein, Safieh, Tel-ahawiyeh* and *Tawfikieh* – which had arrived off Gubat at about 11.00. The town was strongly held, and it was soon evident that the British 7-pounder guns were incapable of bringing down the defending mud walls. Wilson's forces were far too weak to carry on with what seemed like a hopeless endeavour, and he abandoned the attempt, ordering a return to the fortified camp at Gubat.

The commander of the Khartoum steamers was Muhammed Nushi Pasha, and the news he brought was grim indeed. Khartoum was only just holding out – and that news was already a month old. From this time on there is a fatal confusion in the storyline of the Desert Column. What had been intended as a reconnaissance to Khartoum by the intelligence officers aboard the river steamers suddenly became characterised as an attempt to 'save' Gordon. Yet this was manifestly impossible with the forces Wilson had at his disposal. He had the Dervish fortress of Metemmeh immediately behind him, and he had intelligence reports of two more strong Dervish forces making their way towards his base at Gubat – one from the direction of Berber downstream and one from Omdurman. His own forces had been sorely depleted while his camels were evidently in desperate need of a good long rest before they would be capable of serious operations. Wilson summed it up succinctly.

> The original programme had failed. It was that Stewart was to occupy Metemmeh; then that Beresford was to man the steamers with his Naval Brigade, and take me to Khartoum, and that I was to leave Burnaby in command. Burnaby was dead, Stewart dangerously wounded.[52]
> Colonel Charles Wilson, Headquarters, Desert Column

Barrow's 19th Hussars were sent upstream to check whether the Omdurman forces were near. Nothing was sighted, so on 22 January Wilson carried out a reconnaissance in three of

Gordon's steamers, looking for any approach of Dervish forces from Berber. Only when he felt Gubat was secure did he begin to turn his mind to the journey up the Nile to Khartoum. Then there were more delays – the steamers were not really fit for purpose.

> These vessels, about the size and build of the old penny steamboats on the Thames, had been ingeniously protected and armed. In the bows was a small turret constructed of baulks of timber and containing a 9-pounder brass howitzer to fire ahead; amidships, between the paddle-boxes, was the central turret, also built of timber, and mounting a gun to fire over the paddle-boxes. Astern, on the roof of the deckhouse, was an enclosure of boilerplate, protecting the wheel and giving shelter to riflemen. The sides and bulwarks were covered with boilerplate, above which was fixed a rail of thick timber, leaving a space through which to fire. The boiler, which projected above the deck, was jacketed with logs of wood. The improvised armour of wood and iron would stop a bullet but was pervious by shell. The ships' companies were an interesting example of river piracy. The steamers had been cruising up and down the Nile since October, a period of four months, during which the crews lived on the country, raiding and fighting. Everything was filthy and neglected except the engines.[53]
> Captain Charles Beresford, Naval Brigade

Beresford's naval party got the steamers ready for their fantastic voyage.

> An engine-room artificer from the Naval Brigade was sent on board each steamer, in which they went to work to repair defects. Wood for the steamers was obtained by cutting up the waterwheels, up and down the river, a slow process as performed by natives receiving orders through interpreters. The *Talahawiyeh* towed a nuggar carrying

about fifty Sudanese soldiers and a cargo of grain for Khartoum. According to Gordon's express desire, the British troops were clad in red tunics, which, being borrowed from the Guards and the Heavy Camel Regiment, were far from being a regimental fit. By the time the preparations were complete, it was too late to start that night, and the Royal Sussex, folded in their red tunics, bivouacked on the bank.[54]
Captain Charles Beresford, Naval Brigade

Meanwhile Beresford himself had fallen ill, afflicted by a monstrous carbuncle, so Wilson decided to leave him behind, even though he was by this time the only naval officer left standing.

At 08.00 on 24 January, Wilson set off aboard the *Bordein* accompanied by Captain Frederick Gascoigne and his ten chosen men from the Royal Sussex Regiment, with another 110 of Gordon's Sudanese soldiers. Alongside them was the *Talahawiyeh* and a towed nuggar, holding Captain Lionel Trafford, Lieutenant Edward Stuart-Wortley, ten more of the Royal Sussex and in total another 120 Sudanese soldiers. There is no doubt that Wilson had a realistic grasp of their chances of success.

Now what was it we were going to do? We were going to fight our way up the river and into Khartoum in two steamers of the size of 'penny' steamers on the Thames, which a single well-directed shell would send to the bottom.[55]
Colonel Charles Wilson, *Bordein*

Wilson was a worried man – and with good reason. With the forces at his disposal there was little he could hope to achieve against the thousands under the command of the Mahdi.

The outlook was not bright; my only hope was that, with the steamers and the few Englishmen, we might make a sortie before I left which would shake the enemy and bring in provisions. I try not to show anxiety. I do not know whether I succeed. Everyone else is in high spirits; they think

all is finished or nearly so, and that the safety of Gordon and Khartoum is assured. I wish I could feel the same, but I do not see how he is to hold on till the middle of March. When I did get to sleep it was only for a short time, for the rats held high carnival races round the cabin, and my slightly thatched skull was evidently the landing-place after a jump. In self-defence I had to muffle myself up, leaving only a small blowhole to escape suffocation.[56]
Colonel Charles Wilson, *Bordein*

That was if they ever got to Khartoum. They first had to overcome the problems posed by the dangerous rapids of the Sixth Cataract, and the narrow Shabluka gorge where the Nile passed through towering granite hills. The *Bordein* ran aground twice, but after more interminable delays managed to get free. Time was passing and however much they cursed the Nile, nothing seemed to go right. On the 27 January, they at last escaped the clutches of the cataract. Then came the first inkling of disaster.

During the afternoon a man on the left bank shouted out to us that a camel-man had just passed down with the news that Khartoum was taken – and Gordon killed. We did not believe it, nor did Khashm el Mus, who said that such reports had been flying about for the last two months. We dined together in high spirits at the prospects of running the blockade next day, and at last meeting General Gordon after his famous siege.[57]
Colonel Charles Wilson, *Bordein*

At 06.00 on 28 January, Wilson began his final approach to Khartoum, with the *Bordein* leading. The river having been – for the moment – conquered, they now had to get past the Dervish batteries covering the approach to the city.

After they had passed Halfiyeh, and grew closer to Khartoum, the firing became ever more intensive. Wilson took up station in the makeshift forward gun turret as they ran the gauntlet.

A heavy fire was opened upon us from four guns and many rifles at from 600 to 700 yards. The guns were well placed, one in a sakieh pit, two in a little battery above, and one in the village. The bullets began to fly pretty thickly, tapping like hail against the ship's sides, whilst the shells went screeching overhead or threw up jets of water in the stream round us. Our men replied cheerily, and the gun in the turret was capitally served by the black gunners under their captain Abdullah Effendi, who laid the gun each time and fired it himself. The gunners, who had nothing on but a cloth round their waists, looked more like demons than men in the thick smoke; and one huge giant was the very incarnation of savagery drunk with war.[58]
Colonel Charles Wilson, *Bordein*

Both ships managed to get through without damage and then – at last – they could see the promised land of Khartoum.

We could see the large government house at Khartoum plainly above the trees. Khashm was very anxious to know whether we could see the Egyptian flag, which he said Gordon always kept flying; but neither Gascoigne nor I could see a trace of one anywhere. Khashm now began to get anxious, and said he felt certain something must have happened at Khartoum, and that the place must be in the Mahdi's hands, otherwise there would have been no boats at Halfiyeh, and the flag would be flying. I could not believe this; at any rate, we could not stop now until we were certain all was over.[59]
Colonel Charles Wilson, *Bordein*

As the pressed on, they once again came under heavy fire.

We got into such a fire as I hope never to pass through again in a 'penny steamer'. Two or more guns opened upon us from Omdurman fort, and three or four from Khartoum or the upper end of Tuti; the roll of musketry from each side was continuous; and high above that could be heard the grunting of a Nordenfeldt or a mitrailleuse, and the loud rushing noise of the Krupp shells, fired either from Khartoum itself or from the upper end of Tuti Island. We kept on to the junction of the two Niles, when it became plain to everyone that Khartoum had fallen into the Mahdi's hands; for not only were there hundreds of Dervishes ranged under their banners, standing on the sandspit close to the town ready to resist our landing, but no flag was flying in Khartoum and not a shot was fired in our assistance; here, too, if not before, we should have met the two steamers I knew Gordon still had at Khartoum. I at once gave the order to turn and run full speed down the river. It was hopeless to attempt a landing or to communicate with the shore under such a fire.[60]

Colonel Charles Wilson, *Bordein*

What had happened?

★★★

KHARTOUM WAS IN DIRE STRAITS by January 1885. Deadlines had come and gone, but still the garrison held out. But the end was nigh. They were desperately short of food. As the grain and food supplies were exhausted, people were reduced to eating camels and donkeys, hunting down cats and dogs – even rats – so desperate were they for food. Ironically, the rats may have had plenty to eat as corpses littered the streets with people too tired and too weak to bury them. The garrison soldiers were protected for as long as possible, but they too began to suffer the effects of malnutrition. As their bodies weakened, other illnesses took their chance with outbreaks of virulent dysentery and enteritis. Men became too weak to stand their guard or attend to the endless task of maintaining the defences – and worse still, the backbreaking work of extending them over the dry land revealed by the receding waters of the Nile. On 5 January, Fort Omdurman, cut off and battered by the Mahdi's guns for the best part of a month, had finally fallen. It meant that the guns could be sited along the opposing bank of the White Nile, able to fire into the rear of the main line of fortifications. The falling water levels of the White Nile had already further exposed that flank. Gordon announced that those civilians who wished to leave and go over to the Mahdi were welcome to do so. Many took advantage of this offer, but some 14,000 remained, unwilling to risk the Mahdi's reaction – and thus they still had to be fed. But on what? It would not be long.

Then on 20 January, news of the Dervish defeat at the Battle of Abu Klea reached the Mahdi. For just a moment, he seems to have considered raising the siege, but after some debate he instead resolved to finish the job once and for all. Gordon must have hoped, against the odds, for a last-minute rescue – perhaps gazing from the roof of the palace with his trusty telescope for some sign of deliverance. Resolute to the last, he refused to consider surrender, rebuffing all attempts to persuade him.

The denouement came on the night of 25/26 January 1885. Gordon had detected signs of an imminent assault and tried to get everything ready, but his men were physically beyond serious military resistance. The main attack was launched using a sandbank uncovered by the retreating waters of the White Nile. The Dervishes turned the right flank of Gordon's main defensive line, after which one party charged along the ramparts killing all that were capable of resisting – and many that were not. Another party crossed the open ground and attacked the town, slaughtering some 4,000 people. Gordon is reported to have fought to the end using first a rooftop gun from the palace, before going down to meet a heroic death; a death which has become the stuff of legend despite contradictory versions from somewhat unreliable witnesses. His body was despoiled, and his head cut off. One prisoner of the Mahdi, Rudolf Slatin, who was erroneously believed by some of the Dervishes to be related to Gordon, watched on in horror.

I crawled out of my tent and scanned the camp; a great crowd had collected before the quarters of the Mahdi and the Khalifa, which were not far distant. Then there was a movement in the direction of my tent, and I could see plainly that they were coming towards me. Three black soldiers marched in front. One, named Shatta carried in his hands a blood-stained cloth in which something was wrapped. Behind him followed a crowd of weeping people. The slaves had now reached my tent and stood before me with insulting gestures. Shatta unwound the cloth and showed me the head of General Gordon! The blood rushed to my temples and my heart seemed to stop beating; but, with a tremendous effort of self-control, I managed to gaze in silence at this ghastly spectacle. His blue eyes were half-opened; the mouth was perfectly natural; his short whiskers were almost completely white. 'Is this not the head of your uncle the unbeliever?' said Shatta, holding the head up in front of me. 'What of it?' I replied quietly. 'A brave soldier who fell at his post. Happy is he to have fallen; his sufferings are over.' The procession moved on with its grisly trophy.[61]
Rudolf Slatin

When Gordon's head was subsequently presented with a flourish to the Mahdi, his reaction was one of fury – no doubt he saw the value of such a high prestige prisoner.

★★★

THE EVIDENCE OF HIS OWN EYES left Wilson reeling. He had after all been a personal friend of Gordon. Although he had had his doubts, increasing with each hour that passed, he had still hoped against hope that this was an adventure which would all end happily ever after – but apparently not. He was devastated as his dreams were smashed.

To me the blow was crushing – Khartoum fallen and Gordon dead – for I never for a moment believed he would allow himself to fall into the Mahdi's hands alive – such was the ending of all our labours and of his perilous enterprise. I could not realise it, and yet there was a heavy feeling at the heart telling of some awful disaster. For months I had been looking forward to the time when I should meet Gordon again and tell him what everyone thought of his splendid defence of Khartoum – and now all was over; it seemed too cruel to be true.[62]

Colonel Charles Wilson, *Bordein*

They had all suffered so much, all risked so much, all for nothing. As the *Bordein* and *Talahawiyeh* reversed direction the only remaining question was: could Wilson and his men escape? They were surrounded by bursting shells and the pitter-patter of countless bullets all around them. It seemed unlikely they would get away. Perhaps they wouldn't have made it, but for a nameless Sudanese soldier.

A fragment of a shell went through the funnel, cutting the stay and letting a rush of flame out, which soon set fire to the large wooden block left swinging in the air. I was rather anxious, as the sparks began to fly about, and the deck was littered with open ammunition-boxes; but on calling for help, a plucky Sudan soldier jumped up, and after a few minutes managed to get down the flaming bit of wood and throw it overboard. If an Englishman, he would have had the Victoria Cross. He was afterwards shot, just as we were getting out of danger.[63]

Colonel Charles Wilson, *Bordein*

For the next couple of days, the journey downstream was a miserable affair. Sandbanks held them up, the steamers' sides had been peppered with bullets and shell fragments, with many leaks needing to be plugged. And still the Sixth Cataract lay ahead of them. With the seasonal drop in water levels beginning to bite, the rapids would be ever more fearsome. This time they took a toll as the *Talahawiyeh* struck a sunken rock, the waters rushed in, and she began to sink. Luckily everybody aboard managed to transfer to the large nuggar they were towing and got through the rest of the rapids unscathed. Now they had to escape past the fort of Wad Habeshi, which had appeared unmanned on the journey upriver, but which they realised might well now be manned and pose a real threat with all guns blazing. Then came a sudden terrible shock.

> We were congratulating ourselves on having got down the cataract safely and speculating on our chances of running past the battery without serious injury, when the *Bordein* ran on a sunken rock with a crash that shook us all; but she came off at once, and we hoped that no great harm had been done. I rushed out of the cabin to the fore part of the ship, and on looking down into the fore-hold, saw that the water had already covered the bottom, and was coming in with great force. I shouted to Ibrahim to tell the captain to lay her alongside a sandspit close at hand, and then went back to the cabin, where the others had remained, thinking we were all right. They would hardly believe me when I said, 'It is all up; we are wrecked, and the ship is sinking fast!'[64]
>
> Colonel Charles Wilson, *Bordein*

She was run aground on the sandspit at the end of a nearby small island. Turning to with a will they managed to get all the men, guns and ammunition off the *Bordein* and get them to the nearby island of Mernat. Wilson then despatched Wortley in a small felucca with just four British soldiers and eight Sudanese to sail back to Gubat, to pass on the news of the accumulated mishaps, and to request that a steamer come to collect them as soon as possible. With such small numbers Wilson was intensely vulnerable to being attacked and overwhelmed by vastly superior forces. The question was would the relief boat come in time? Would Wilson be luckier than Gordon?

Back at Gubat, Beresford had recovered his health, and furthermore the second tranche of his Naval Brigade arrived on 31 January, with a strong column of much-needed reinforcements led by Buller. Beresford was an energetic officer and he had busied himself in putting the *Safieh* into a shipshape condition ready for any eventuality that might arise. This was just as well.

> Very early in the morning of the 1st February, I was awakened by a voice hailing the *Safieh*. I ran to the rail, and there, in the first light of the dawn, was a boat, and Stuart-Wortley's face was lifted to mine. He climbed aboard. 'Gordon is killed and Khartoum has fallen!' he said. Then Stuart-Wortley told me how Sir Charles Wilson's two steamers were wrecked, how his force was isolated up the river, and how the Mahdi might be marching down with his whole triumphant horde armed with all the guns and rifles of the fallen city.[65]
>
> Captain Charles Beresford, *Safieh*

At 14.00 the same day, Beresford set off, accompanied by Lieutenants Colin Keppel and Edmund Van Koughnet, with forty-five of the newly arrived naval party acting as his crew. They were armed with two small 4-pounder guns and two Gardner guns. He also had an extra twenty men of the King's Royal Rifle Corps aboard ship. They had some 36 miles to steam upstream from Gubat to the Mermat Island where Stuart-Wortley had reported Wilson and his men were trapped. The problem was that they would have to pass the fort of Wad Habeshi first. On 2 February they anchored up some 3 or 4 miles from the fort.

> By 7.30 a.m. we were within 1,200 yards of the fort, and I opened fire with the bow gun. Wad Habeshi was a strong earthwork, with four embrasures, mounting four guns,

and manned, according to Stuart-Wortley's report, by 5,000 riflemen. The only practicable channel ran within 80 yards of the fort. We could only crawl past the battery, and as we were defenceless against gunfire, our only chance was to maintain so overwhelming a fire upon the embrasures as to demoralise the guns' crews. It was an extreme instance of the principle that the best defence resides in gunfire rather than in armour; for we had no effective armour. But so deadly was the fire we poured into the embrasures of the fort, that the enemy could not fire the two guns bearing upon the *Safieh* while she was bore abeam of them. We passed the fort, and by the time we had left it about 200 yards astern, our fire necessarily slackened, as our guns no longer bore upon the battery.[66]

Captain Charles Beresford, *Safieh*

Unfortunately, this gave the fort gunners their chance to get correct their aim.

Suddenly a great cloud of steam or smoke rose from the after hatchway. Instantly the fire of the enemy increased. Chief Engineer Benbow, who was standing with me on the quarter-deck, ran to the engine room. A Maltese carpenter rushed up to me crying, 'All is lost, Sir, myself and my brother, Sir! The ship he sink, Sir!' and was promptly kicked out of the way. I saw the black stokers rushing up from the stokehold hatchway. At the moment, it was uncertain whether the ship was on fire, or the boiler injured; but as she still had way upon her, I ordered her to be headed towards the bank, away from the fort, and so gained another few yards. The carpenter's mate reported that there were 3 feet of water in the well, and that the vessel was sinking. Then she stopped. In the meantime, our fire upon the side embrasure of the fort was continued by the riflemen; and it went on without pause, lest the enemy should get another shot in. I dropped anchor and addressed the men. I told

them that the vessel was all right, as she had only a foot
of water under her bottom; that the stores and ammunition must be got up on deck in case she settled down; that
no relief was possible; but that not a single Dervish would
come on board while one of us was alive. The men were
quite cool and jovial. 'It's all right, Sir,' said one cheerfully.
'We'll make it 'ot for the beggars!'[67]
Captain Charles Beresford, *Safieh*

Investigations revealed that the *Safieh* boiler had been pierced
by a Dervish shell and the reported water below decks was
pouring out from the pierced boiler. It was a critical situation, not only for themselves but for Wilson's marooned party
further upstream. Their survival was dependent on the ability
of Chief Engineer Henry Benbow to repair the boiler. Luckily,
they had aboard some of the metal plate and other essentials
– essentials that it may be recalled Buller had tried to remove
from Beresford's camels before the Desert Column set off back
in early January.

Mr Benbow, with no other assistance than that of the leading
stoker, had to cut a plate, 16 inches by 14, drill the holes in
it to receive the bolts, drill holes in the injured boiler plate
corresponding to the first to a fraction, and cut the threads
of the screws upon bolts and nuts. The new plate being too
thin to take the pressure, he also had to bolt an iron bar
across it, drilling the holes through the bar, through the
new plate, and through the injured boiler plate. During the
whole time he was below in the stifling hot engine-room at
work upon a task demanding at once great exertion and the
utmost nicety, the fire from the fort never ceased. Bullets
pattered continually upon the hull, some of them piercing
it, and striking the wounded men who lay below. At any
moment another shell might burst into the engine-room.
But Mr Benbow went on with his work. On deck, we continued to maintain a steady fire, hour after hour, upon the

fort. It was our only chance. The slightest cessation, and they would bring their gun to bear on us.[68]

Captain Charles Beresford, *Safieh*

Meanwhile, on Mermat Island, Wilson was aware of the approach of the relieving force.

We suddenly heard the report of a gun downstream, and the effect was electrical. There was a general shout of 'Ingliz! Ingliz!' and every one's spirits rose 100 per cent. I sent a man up a high tree close to the place where we slept, who reported that he could see the steamer – he was not sure whether there was one or two – keeping up a fire on the fort. I was listening to the cannonade, rather surprised at its long continuance, when Gascoigne came running back to report, and crossed over to the small island to hoist the flags on the *Bordein* so as to show our exact position; and I had the gun pointing towards the river loaded to fire the three shots agreed upon with Wortley to show we were all right. As it turned out, the relieving party were so busily engaged themselves they never saw the flags or heard our guns. As soon as the enemy on the left bank saw the flags run up, they opened fire upon us; and we replied with our Remingtons, and shell from the gun.[69]

Colonel Charles Wilson, *Bordein*

Wilson realised that the steamer must be in trouble and that immediate action was needed. He used another felucca to ferry back and forth to get his whole force from the island to the right bank of the Nile. He then marched downstream to the sound of the guns, until he was opposite the Wad Habeshi earthworks. Thus, he was able to augment the fire from the *Safieh*.

Captain Frederick Gascoigne, accompanied by a couple of engine room artificers, volunteered to row out to the beleaguered *Safieh*. It was a risky business.

Gascoigne's boat was received with a hot but badly directed fire, and he managed to go and return without having a man hit. He told us they were all well and cheery on board, and had lost one officer wounded, a seaman killed, and several men badly scalded by the rush of steam out of the boiler. The boiler would be mended by sunset, and Beresford wished us to keep up our fire till dark, so as to take off the enemy's attention from his steamer. Unfortunately, we had only saved enough ammunition for one gun, and even some of that was damp, so that the shells did not burst as well as they ought to have done. Abdullah Effendi made, however, on the whole very fair practice; and two or three of our shells burst in the battery. The enemy replied to us with solid shot, but not with much spirit, and their shot went screaming over our heads. Their rifle fire was also somewhat wild, and the bullets fell 50 or 60 yards behind us.[70]

Colonel Charles Wilson, *Bordein*

The two engine-room artificers stayed aboard the *Safieh* and proved invaluable in assisting the redoubtable Benbow's repairs to the stricken boiler.

It was about two o'clock when the artificers joined him, so that he had already been toiling single-handed, except for the leading stoker, for 3 hours. After another 3 hours, at 5 o'clock, the plate and bar were made, the holes drilled in them and in the boiler, and the threads cut upon the bolts and nuts. But the boiler was still so hot, that it was impossible for a man to be in it, and the plate could not be fixed, because it was necessary to pass the bolts through the plates from inside the boiler. Mr Benbow pumped cold water into the boiler and out again once or twice; but by 6 o'clock the heat was still too great for a white man to endure. We smeared a [Sudanese] boy with tallow, and I promised him a reward if he would go into the boiler. He was delighted. He was lowered down, to climb out again faster than he went in. After a short pause, he had another try. This time, in a frying heat that only a black skin could bear, he stayed inside, passing the bolts through, while Mr. Benbow caulked plates and bolts and screwed them home. The boy was none the worse in body and richer in possessions than ever in his life! [71]

Captain Charles Beresford, *Safieh*

At last, the repairs were completed by nightfall on 3 February. Meanwhile, Beresford had come up with a cunning plan to not only escape his current predicament but also rescue Wilson's party.

It was my object to delude the enemy into the belief that we had abandoned the steamer; for, if they thought she was empty, they would not fire upon her, lest they should damage an invaluable prize. Therefore, in the hope of deceiving the enemy, as the darkness gathered, the four boats brought down to embark Wilson's party were ostentatiously hauled alongside, as if to take off the ship's company. Then all firing stopped; and after that 13 hours' furious fusillade, the immense and crystal silence of the desert submerged us like the sea. Talking above a whisper was forbidden; every aperture was closed below, where the lamps were burning to light Mr Benbow at his work, and no spark of light was allowed on deck. The men lit their pipes at a slow match burning in a bucket and smoked under cover. [72]

Captain Charles Beresford, *Safieh*

Amazingly the simple ruse seemed to work.

They had run the guns outside the fort in the interval, and fired a few rounds at us, accompanied by a heavy rifle fire. But the *Safieh* remained dumb and motionless. The firing ceased, the enemy evidently believing that we had abandoned the vessel. I slept in snatches on deck, waking every now and then to look round. At five o'clock the next morning Mr Benbow lit the fires, using the utmost caution, keeping the ash-pit draught plates almost shut, in order to prevent sparks, which would instantly betray us, from flying up the funnel. On deck, we were in suspense, all staring at the shot-riddled funnel. It kept its secret for 50 minutes; then suddenly it belched a fountain of hot ashes. It was then within 10 minutes of daylight. Almost at the same moment a great shouting broke out in the fort, and a convulsive beating of tom-toms. Then the guns and rifles began to speak again. Instantly we weighed anchor. The moment the steamer began to move, such a yell of rage went up from the Dervishes in the fort, as I never heard before or since. Leaping and screaming on the bank, they took up handfuls of sand and flung them towards us. They had thought us fled, and the steamer theirs. And there we were, and there was the steamer moving away up-river towards Khartoum; and the men of Wad Habeshi were naturally disappointed.[73]

Captain Charles Beresford, *Safieh*

Beresford took the *Safieh* a little way further up the Nile, so that he could turn round in safety. Then he made the run back past the fort's guns. Beresford had arranged to meet Wilson's party a little further downstream, while Gascoigne would brave the gauntlet of running past the fort in the nuggar. A new problem arose when Gascoigne ran aground on a sandbank just a few hundred yards from the fort. Now he would have to be rescued!

As we came abreast of Wad Habeshi, we turned both Gardners and both howitzers upon the embrasures, in one of which we burst a shell; while the twenty soldiers and the fourteen bluejackets maintained their steady rifle fire. We were running now with the stream instead of against it, and our speed was the greater, and we stormed past the fort without a single casualty; and then, just as we thought we were clear, lo! there was Gascoigne's hapless nuggar, stuck and helpless some 400 yards below Wad Habeshi, and in full bearing of its side embrasure. As all depended upon the safe passage of the *Safieh*, I ran on until we were a mile from the fort and out of its range, and then dropped anchor.[74]

Captain Charles Beresford, *Safieh*

He then sent Keppel and a few sailors in a rowing boat to assist in freeing the grounded nuggar. When this was accomplished, Beresford sailed a further mile downstream where he was able to embark the main body of Wilson's men. It had been a smart piece of work – apparently not all high-risk rescue missions were failures. Wilson was still distraught, but he consoled himself by reflecting that his part in the last dash to Khartoum was doomed to failure.

I thought at the time that, if we had reached Khartoum before it fell, the presence of two armed steamers with a small detachment of British soldiers (twenty) might have turned the scale in General Gordon's favour. The fuller knowledge which I now possess of the condition of the garrison, and of the determination of the Mahdi to attack Khartoum before the English arrived, leads me to believe that if the steamers had left Gubat a week earlier, the result would have been the same; and that even if it had been possible for them to have reached Khartoum on the 25th January, their presence would not have averted the fall of the city.[75]

Colonel Charles Wilson, *Bordein*

He was right, but Wilson has since been made a scapegoat, with every day's delay analysed and condemned as if his meagre force could have rescued Gordon 'if only' he had proceeded with more haste and determination. It was nonsense. Gordon could have left on the steamers at any time; he wouldn't for reasons which may be admirable but show a distinct lack of common sense. The garrison and the civilian population of Khartoum were not 'saved' by his presence, every additional day of the siege only added to their suffering and did nothing to change the underlying situation. Those who would be slaughtered were still destined to be slaughtered; those who could 'turn their coats' and join the Mahdist forces duly did so. Gordon's stance lacked logic – he was doomed by a combination of his own contrary nature, Gladstone's woeful prevarications and Wolseley's planning. But what a story it was.

10

ALL HOPES FADE AWAY

Twenty millions, a vast sum for those days, was spent in emulating the Duke of York who marched up a hill and then marched down, except that in the more modern version we rowed up the river and then ran down it.

Captain Ian Hamilton, 1st Gordon Highlanders

WHERE WAS THE RIVER COLUMN? How were they faring on the murky waters of the Nile while Brigadier General Herbert Stewart's dusty warriors plodded across the desert? The short answer was badly. The River Column was commanded by a gruff martinet, Major General William Earle, who was generally considered a good soldier of the 'old school', but not over-blessed with organisational skills. To counterbalance this, Wolseley had assigned Colonel Henry Brackenbury to act as chief of the staff and second in command. The River Column, which set off from near Korti on 24 January 1885, consisted of four strong British battalions: the 2nd Duke of Cornwall's Light Infantry, the 1st South Staffordshire Regiment, the 1st Black Watch and the 1st Gordon Highlanders. This was a cohesive force in contrast to the 'pick-and-mix' composition of the Desert Column. With them was the perennial 'know it all' Captain Ian Hamilton.

My company took their seats in eleven small rowboats to struggle hundreds of miles up the Nile in order to save Gordon: a vague and typically British adventure – just like a fairy tale. It was incessant toil, much of it waist-deep in water; bad food, broken nights, the lack of any drink but

sand and water; the resultant scurvy; all these wore health
and nerves to fiddle-strings. Never in their whole lives had
the men worked so hard. The mere thought of such a job
would make a modern labour union call a strike! Yet, there
was no crime, no stinting of effort, no grumbling.

Captain Ian Hamilton, 1st Gordon Highlanders

It was indeed a period of hard graft. Ahead of them riding
along the banks of the Nile were the attached squadrons of
the 19th Hussars and the Egyptian Camel Corps, which were
commanded by Colonel William Butler. They were acting as an
advance guard, checking out what lay ahead of the whalers and
working out the best spot for the next overnight bivouac.

One had to keep an eye all round the compass: in front and
on the right flank for the enemy, on the river to the left, and
to the rear upon our own people. By this time, I had come
to know the various values of the Nile waters pretty accurately, what our boats could do against the Nile, and what
the Nile could do at its worst against our boats. Thus, I was
able by noon each day to form an estimate of the spot on
the river shore which a force of four companies of infantry
would be able to reach by evening. I then looked about for
the best camping place on the shore, waited until the first
boat had arrived there, gave orders for the thorn bushes
to be cut, laid out the ground for the zeriba, and then
went forward again with the forty hussars and the score
of camel men to explore the rocks in front for 6 or 8 miles,
getting back at nightfall to find the advanced guard of four
or six companies assembled there, and all made ready for
the night. The main body of the River Column would be
camped from 2 to 6 miles behind, according to the difficulties their boats had met in the day's ascent through the
cataracts. These latter were even more formidable than any
we had encountered below Dongola, but our men were
now thoroughly seasoned; they had become exceedingly

expert in all kinds of bad water, and, but for the necessities imposed by the presence of an active enemy always only a few miles in our front, it would have been possible for the column to make an average distance of perhaps 8 or 10 miles daily. With an enemy, however, in proximity, it became necessary to keep the battalions concentrated at night, excepting the advanced guard under my command, which had its separate camp some miles in front of the main body.

Lieutenant Colonel William Butler, 19th Hussars

There were reports from spies of gatherings of up to 3,000 Dervishes lying ahead, but they fell back before the advance of the British. Brackenbury began to get the measure of the various spies and informants that came into their camp at night.

I had learnt by experience that native reports might generally be classed under two heads: those of spies, who said what they thought we should like to hear; and those of professed deserters, which were intended to frighten us. We had constantly heard from our spies that the tribes were frightened; that the Mahdi's troops were deserting him; that this tribe and that had refused to join him; that the enemy would not fight but join us when we advanced. We as constantly heard from men who came to us, professing to be deserters, greatly exaggerated accounts of the enemy's numbers and determination to fight.

Colonel Henry Brackenbury, Headquarters, River Column

They were making progress, but it was slow. As a relief force for Khartoum, it was doomed to failure, given the fact Khartoum had fallen just two days after they commenced their dangerous voyage. Then on 5 February – right out of the blue – came an order to stop all further movement forward. What had happened?

***

NEWS OF THE FALL OF KHARTOUM had reached Wolseley's headquarters at Korti on the evening of 4 February. All lingering
hopes were dashed, and they were left to reflect on a dismal
situation: Gordon was probably dead, Khartoum had fallen, the
Mahdist forces were gathering.

> At 7 p.m., just as I was going to dinner, I received letters
> from Gubat and from Buller at Gakdul. I was certainly
> knocked out of tune by the dreadful intelligence that Khar-
> toum was taken by Mahdi's troops on 26th January and
> that Gordon's fate was uncertain, but he was said to have
> been killed. I earnestly pray he may have been killed, for to
> him death was always looked forward to as the beginning
> of a glorious and new life, whereas if he be alive, he may
> be kept for years in prison by this cruel monster Mahomed
> Ahmed.
>
> Lieutenant General Garnet Wolseley, Headquarters

Wolseley was already setting up in his own mind a 'narrative'
that success had been snatched away at the very last minute.

> If the traitors who admitted the Mahdi's troops into the
> city had but waited another few days, the arrival of Wilson
> at Khartoum would I believe have burst the whole siege
> up. The moral effect of English soldiers having reached
> the place, and brought in provisions, no matter how little,
> would have given such heart to the defenders and so
> depressed the besiegers, that the Mahdi's game would have
> been up. God has however willed it otherwise for His own
> divine reasons, and we must bow our heads accordingly,
> and say 'Thy will be done'.
>
> Lieutenant General Garnet Wolseley, Headquarters

Wolseley was in a torment of frustration, as the government
had denied him the freedom to move to the front, and he thus
could not wrest control of affairs and was left to direct from

afar. What on earth were they going to do now? The fall of Khartoum meant that the Mahdi and his generals could concentrate all their forces against Wolseley's isolated two columns, with the Desert Column marooned out at Gubat being in the most obvious danger. With his mission over, the decisions required were dependent on the Liberal Government's future policy towards the Sudan. Wolseley ordered his forces to stand fast where they were for the moment, and telegrammed home to London for instructions as a matter of urgency.

> I telegraphed all this news at length to Lord Hartington and asked for instructions. What a business there will be in England over the news! If anything can kill old Gladstone this news ought to, for he cannot, self-illusionist though he be, disguise from himself the fact that he is directly responsible for the fall of Khartoum and all the bloodshed it entails: that it was owing to his influence, active measures for the relief of Gordon were not undertaken in time. Whilst Gordon was starving, this arrogant minister who poses as a great statesman, but without any just claim to be considered one, was discussing to himself whether Gordon was 'hemmed in' or 'surrounded' and no one could persuade him that Khartoum was besieged or Gordon in any danger. Never were the destinies of any great nation committed to a more incompetent pilot. And yet a pack of fools and theoretical vestrymen contrive to worship him with an almost idolatrous reverence. What an ending to all our labour, and all our bright hopes.
>
> Lieutenant General Garnet Wolseley, Headquarters

The response from London was somewhat unexpected and loaded with the stench of party politics. Gladstone defended himself as best he could, but his position was almost impossible against a background of near hysteria from every side. The news had indeed created an outcry across Britain. Even Queen Victoria had been moved to express her dissatisfaction to her benighted prime minister. Reeling before this tidal wave of public opprobrium, Gladstone's government changed its tack. Wolseley was not impressed when he got the news.

About 9.30 p.m., I received the decision of the home government and of all the surprises I have had, it has been the greatest. They have actually picked up enough courage to tell me to protect from the Mahdi the districts 'now undisturbed'. They don't wish any retrograde movements and are prepared to support me in every possible way, by sending troops to Suakin etc., adding they did not wish to prevent me from going to Berber, if I thought such an operation desirable. I have replied that I require some more explicit declaration of their policy. Do they mean us eventually to destroy the Mahdi's power? If not, any advance upon Berber, which I think they wish me to attempt, would be merely undertaken for party purposes to keep Mr Gladstone in office. In fact, the Cabinet today have realized that nothing could save them except a spirited policy, and their telegram to me is the result. It smells far more of the caucus than patriotism. 'Let all your soldiers,' they say, 'grill for the summer in the Sudan, let many of them be killed and wounded, we care not, so long as the country will recognize that we have at last roused ourselves and adopted a spirited policy.' This seems to be their reasoning. They do not seem to realize how the fall of Khartoum has completely changed the military position. The Mahdi has now a large army at his disposal, and the reports I have had from Gabat say that with the capture of Khartoum 15,000 rifles and 15 camel guns with plenty of ammunition fell into the Mahdi's hands. He is quickly becoming a great military power. When surrounding Khartoum he suffered from sickness amongst his troops, wanted money and had very little food. Now the prestige of his success will cause the tribes to join him. He will be regarded as irresistible. The government intends us to remain in the Sudan all the

summer – I fear our mortality will be great as British soldiers do not stand tropical heat well, and the dullness of
their lives, reacting upon the want of any military enterprise or object to work for, will break them down in spirit.
Lieutenant General Garnet Wolseley, Headquarters

For the moment, though, the die was cast. The campaign would
go on.

★★★

AFTER WOLSELEY TELEGRAMMED THE NEWS to his subordinates,
the River Column resumed its advance on 8 February, but it
soon became apparent that it was about to face its first serious
opposition from the Mahdi's forces who had taken up a strong
defensive position based on the 300-feet-tall heights of the Kirbekan ridge which blocked the further progress of the British.
What followed was the Battle of Kirbekan on 10 February 1885.
The Dervishes were in stone sangars stretching along the top
of the Kirbekan ridge and on four small hillocks which covered
the ground from the main ridge to the Nile. It was a somewhat
fearsome prospect.

That old martinet General Earle had to make up his
mind. Half his life had been spent trying to inculcate and
enforce incredible standards of military punctilio, dress,
deportment, drill. Now he was up against a live thing, the
Mohammedan faith, and he rose to his chance; he was
inspired to act like Frederick the Great. None of your Abu
Klea or Metemmeh squares. We would have been shot to
bits by their riflemen had we tried sheep tactics against
shock tactics.[1]
Captain Ian Hamilton, 1st Gordon Highlanders

Perhaps it is fortunate that Earle had at his side Butler, who not
days before had explored the vicinity on one of his reconnaissance

rides ahead of the column. Butler suggested that while the attention of the Dervishes was drawn to a frontal demonstration, a strong column of the South Staffordshires should follow a rocky valley that Butler asserted – and had checked – ran all the way around the flank of the Dervish position, cutting them off and allowing a combined assault to be made on the smaller hillocks from both front and rear. It was a bold plan and it worked perfectly.

> The moment the head of our column appeared round the enemy's left flank, a precipitate retreat of the main body began from behind the position to their camp, at the entrance of the Shukook Pass. Our little body of hussars pounded along as best their tired horses could go. Of the Dervishes, some jumped into the river on their left; others hid in the clumps of boulders and had a shot at us as we appeared. A few were killed, but by far the larger number reached the Shukook and got away into its labyrinths. Meanwhile the vanguard on the ridge and in the kopjes, about 300 in number, abandoned to their fate, met their death bravely, and only succumbed to volleys of the infantry.[2]
>
> Lieutenant Colonel William Butler, 19th Hussars

There was one unfortunate incident which rather removed the gloss from the victory.

> Between the crests of the two main kopjes there was a depression forming a small flat plateau, on which was built a stone hut some 10 feet square, with a thatched roof. General Earle was engaged in forming up the men in the ranks on this plateau, not more than 10 yards from the hut, when a sergeant of the Black Watch said, 'There are a lot of men in that hut, and they have just shot one of our men!' General Earle ordered the roof to be set on fire; but on its being said that there was a quantity of ammunition

in the hut, he ordered the roof to be pulled down, and himself approached the hut. I was close to him, and said, 'Take care, Sir, the hut is full of men!' Our men had set the roof on fire, and my attention was attracted for a moment by seeing a native who rushed out from the side door of the hut bayoneted by one of our men. As I turned my head back towards the general, I saw him fall, shot through the head from a small square window in the hut, close to which he had approached. He lived only a few minutes, tended to the last by his aide-de-camp Lieutenant St Aubyn, and by the senior medical officer, Surgeon-Major Harvey.[3]

Colonel Henry Brackenbury, Headquarters, River Column

This left Brackenbury in command of the River Column. Ian Hamilton was typically scathing in his assessment of their new commander.

Earle was a bold man who had kept himself in touch with the rank and file and was out for fighting. He was succeeded automatically by the next senior, Henry Brackenbury, the purest example then going of a type since become more common; the bureaucratic, scholastic soldier. Without any exception Brackenbury was the most competent administrator in our Army. As an organizer also he was far ahead of his time for he was an ardent advocate of the General Staff at a date when no one else at the War Office knew exactly what a general staff was: he had been an instructor at the Royal Military Academy. In sheer brain power he was chronologically 1,000 years in advance of his predecessor, Earle. He knew millions of things Earle did not know as well as the relations of the things to one another; and he realized their relation to other things. On the other hand, he hated cataracts, night alarms and live soldiers. On paper he appreciated them well; that is to say he wrote what military instructors barbarously call 'appreciations' about them, but Brackenbury, the real Brackenbury, hated them in practice. He had never worked with soldiers; never kept in touch with them; always tried to keep out of can-non-shot range of them.[4]

Captain Ian Hamilton, 1st Gordon Highlanders

This is unfair, but it did represent one point of view amongst the regimental officers. There had always been an animosity with 'staff officers' who were often caricatured in this sneering fashion as all brains and lacking the 'guts' for the real soldiering.

The River Column resumed its slow advance up the river. On the next day, a piece of intelligence fell into their hands which confirmed the death of Gordon in the fall of Khartoum.

By merest chance, as the crew of one of the boats were at their old work of towing along the shore, a soldier of the Cornwalls noticed a small native saddle lying amongst the tumbled rocks, evidently dropped there by a fugitive from the fight of the day before. A black goatskin bag was fastened to the saddle, and in the bag the man found a scrap of soiled paper. He might well have thrown the crumpled scrap away, but his intelligence prompted him to bring it to his captain. From the captain it passed to the colonel of the battalion (Richardson). On my return to camp before sunset, I learnt that the Arabic writing on the bit of paper had been deciphered sufficiently to let us know it contained bad news. Later on, the whole was made clear. This is what it said, 'On the night of the 26th January the army of the Mahdi entered Khartoum and took the forts, city, and vessels in the river: the traitor Gordon was killed. Inform your troops of this signal triumph which God has given to the arms of the Prophet of His Prophet.' This was a copy of an original letter sent from Berber by Mohammed el Khier, the Emir of the Mahdi, to Abdul Wad el Kailik, the head Emir opposed to us here. I took the letter to the lower camp. It was the first news we had had of the fate of

Gordon. We knew, six days previously, that Khartoum had fallen; now we knew Gordon was dead.[5]
Lieutenant Colonel William Butler, 19th Hussars

On 12 February, there came another telegram from Korti, updating them as to the current situation.

It informed me that the Government had decided that we were to stay in the Sudan till the Mahdi's power at Khartoum was destroyed. If we could not do this before the hot weather, we must wait until autumn. Buller had left Gakdul on the 8th for Gubat and would take Metemmeh as soon as the Royal Irish reached Gubat. It was assumed that I could reach Berber on the 28th February, or have reported my proximity to it. Buller would be in the neighbourhood, with four or six guns and about 1,500 men, on the left bank. If I did not think I could reach Berber by that date, I was to name a date, in order that Buller might meet me and cooperate in the attack on Berber. The desert road to Gubat would be held, and a garrison left there, with a view to subsequent operations of the united columns against Khartoum. I was therefore to push forward with all possible speed compatible with safety. I was to leave a garrison of 200 men at Abu Hamed, instead of 300 as previously ordered, with 250 rounds of ammunition per man, and sixty days' provisions. To this telegram I replied that I did not think it possible to reach Berber by the 28th February, and that any date given must be pure conjecture, the time being dependent upon condition of unknown rapids and unknown movements of the enemy. I said it was impossible to pass more than one battalion-a-day through the rapids here; and if the enemy were holding the Shukook, I must again concentrate the whole or part of my force. When we reached Salamat, I should be able to give an approximate date for reaching Abu Hamed, and at that place an approximate date for reaching Berber. Now I could only say I did not think we could reach the latter place under one month from this date. [6]

Colonel Henry Brackenbury, Headquarters, River Column

This meant he did not anticipate reaching Berber before 12 March. Progress continued to be slow, despite Brackenbury's best organisational efforts. On 15 February, the advance parties of the River Column occupied Salamat and then the village of Hebbeh, where they took their revenge on the locals deemed responsible for the ambush and massacre of Colonel John Hamill Stewart and Frank Power when their steamboat ran aground on Sherri Island.

By 23 February, they had reached the village of Huella, where Brackenbury was able to concentrate all his force of some 3,000 men in the one camp site for the first time. They still had some 30 miles to go to reach Abu Hamed while it was still some 150 miles to Berber. Yet the tempestuous cataracts of the Nile were mostly behind them, and the calmer waters of the river offered hope of an accelerated progress. Brackenbury was in an optimistic frame of mind.

This day's work had been the best ever performed by the troops. Two hundred and fifteen boats had been rowed by their strong arms through 10 or 11 miles of the swiftest water possible to contend with. The men were in high spirits; and there were two battalions, neither of which had yet been in action, longing for the chance of emulating those who had fought so gallantly at Kirbekan. It was the first time I had seen the whole force in one bivouac; and I lay down with a feeling of perfect confidence in their power to conquer any host of Arabs that the Mahdi could bring against them from the farthest corners of the Soudan. In four days, I said to myself, we shall be at Abu Hamed. We shall open up the Korosko desert-route, and our doing so will ring through the Sudan, and weaken the knees of the followers of Mahomet Achmet. [7]

Colonel Henry Brackenbury, Headquarters, River Column

Even Ian Hamilton was in a good mood as his whaler pulled into the campsite.

> For weeks we had only seen broken water and now at last the river came gliding to us smoothly from the west. In two or three days' time we looked to have Abu Hamed in our hands and to get filled up with fresh supplies the Joalin Arabs were bringing us across the caravan route from Wadi Haifa. I don't think that ever in my life I had felt so uplifted, so confident, as I did when the sunlight turned the drops of water on our uplifted oar blades into diamonds.[8]
>
> Captain Ian Hamilton, 1st Gordon Highlanders

It seemed that nothing could go wrong now. But it already had.

★★★

MAJOR GENERAL REDVERS BULLER was following in the path of the original Desert Column towards Gubat with the reinforcements that he hoped would revitalise the forces there and allow them to take Metemmeh and secure their position. On 8 February, Buller had set off from Gakdul. He took with him the 1st Royal Irish Regiment and the irrepressible figure of Major Herbert Kitchener. The infantry marched at night, accompanied by enough baggage camels to carry the water they would need. Progress was fast and it was evident that there had been no need for the original Desert Column to be mounted on camels. They would arrive at Gubat on 11 February.

Meanwhile Colonel Charles Wilson was travelling in the opposite direction to report his grim tidings personally to Lieutenant General Garnet Wolseley. He left behind him a demoralised force.

> The awful news that Gordon was dead, and that Khartoum had fallen was whispered around. We endeavoured to keep it a secret from the men, but they soon heard of it. It was

most dispiriting, and we now thought that overwhelming forces of the Mahdi might be expected every day as we were, at the most, only three marches from Khartoum. The longer we stayed at Gubat, the more critical became our position: it seemed as if a second Hicks Pasha's expedition was to be enacted.[9]

Lieutenant Charles Townshend, Royal Marine Light Infantry

Although the arrival of Buller at Gubat cheered them up a smidgeon, the underlying situation had not really changed. One battalion did not counterbalance the massed Dervish armies that would be freed by the fall of Khartoum.

Sir Redvers Buller arrived with the Royal Irish who had marched on foot across the desert. With him came Major Kitchener, [who] took command of the Intelligence Department which I had been running since Sir Charles Wilson's departure for Khartoum on 24th January. Some spies I had sent to Khartoum returned on this day with information that the Mahdi was sending down a strong force with guns to attack us. The following day another spy returned with further information of the imminent approach of the Dervishes on both banks of the river.[10]

Captain Willoughby Verner, Headquarters, Desert Column

At first Buller was full of optimism and sceptical as to the failure of Wilson to capture Metemmeh. This soon dissipated after briefings from his officers on the spot. Beresford was particularly influential.

At his request, I stated to him my view of the situation, which was, briefly, that unless we departed swiftly, we should be eaten up by the enemy, who were known to be advancing in immense force. I also reported officially that until the Nile rose, the two steamers remaining to us were practically useless: a consideration which proved conclusive. Sir Redvers Buller's dispatch, dated at Gubat 12th February, and addressed to the chief of staff, describes the conclusions to which he came after having carefully reviewed the situation. The camels were greatly reduced in number and were nearly worn out; but if the Column were to attempt any further enterprise, the camels must be sent to Jakdul and back to bring supplies, a journey which would take at least ten days. This circumstance was virtually conclusive.[11]

Captain Charles Beresford, Naval Brigade

The combination of a threatening enemy and logistical incoherence was damning – and to his credit Buller soon made up his mind to withdraw back to Abu Klea pending developments – although in his heart he must have realised that a retreat all the way back to Korti was inevitable. He sent a series of messages back to Wolseley briefing him as to the reasons behind his actions.

On 13 February, Buller sent back a preliminary convoy made up of various elements of the original Camel Regiments, totalling some 300 men, under the command of Lieutenant Colonel Reginald Talbot. With them went the seventy-five wounded men mostly carried in the camel cacolets, but the most serious, including Stewart, who was just about clinging to life, were carried on stretchers by Egyptian bearers. It was symptomatic of the danger they were in that a nasty clash with a force of Dervishes for a while threatened another disaster before they eventually managed to drive them off and fight their way through to Abu Klea.

Next day, the main column left Gubat after attempting to destroy everything that would have been of value to the Mahdi's forces.

I disposed of the poor old *Safieh* and the *Tawfikieh*, lest upon our departure they should be taken by the enemy. The six brass guns were spiked and thrown overboard,

the ammunition was destroyed, the eccentric straps were removed from the machinery, and finally the valves were opened, and the vessels sunk. Then came the sad destruc-tion of the stores for which we had no transport. The number of camels would only suffice to carry rations for three days, by the end of which the Column would have arrived at Abu Klea, where there were more stores.[12]
Captain Charles Beresford, Naval Brigade

The frustration of the soldiers who had been existing on meagre rations who were ordered to throw good food into the river can well be imagined.

At 06.30 on 14 February, the main body of the Desert Column, about 1,700 men, set off back across the desert. Every step a tacit admission of utter failure. First, they passed the battlefield of Abu Kru, marked by an unburied masse of malodorous human and camel corpses. They arrived at Abu Klea the next day where they set up camp, while Talbot's column pushed on for Gakdul. Sadly, a couple of days later Herbert Stewart died, having lived just long enough to hear of his promotion to major general for his services. The water supply provided from the wells was inadequate for the needs of Buller's force, moreover there was nothing to feed the camels. There was no choice but to split his forces again and send on a substantial force to bridge the gap to Gakdul while they still could. On 16 February, another column was despatched under the command of Lieutenant Colonel Percy Barrow, this time consisting of the remnants of his 19th Hussars and another tranche of the Camel Regiments.

These departures left Buller's command reduced to just the 1st Royal Irish Fusiliers, the 1st Royal Sussex Regiment, the artil-lery, Beresford's Naval Brigade and the final remnants of the Camel Regiments. If they were to stay, they needed to establish some kind of defence, so the men were set to work to build three forts from biscuit boxes and arranged to be able to support each other in the event of an attack. Gradually the Mahdist forces con-gregating in the area began to spatter their camp with bullets.

A party of Dervishes had followed us from the river and seized the hills where I had been sketching in the morning, whence they were sending in Remington bullets pretty sharply. As it was impossible to tell what force they were in, we had simply to grin and bear it. They fired into our bivouacs all night and next morning brought up a gun and opened up on us with common shell. Our 7-pounders soon stopped this game and the Gardners, getting the range of the stone breastworks, which they had constructed during the night, cleared them out soon after midday. Our casualties were four officers and about thirty men killed and wounded, but it was a very unpleasant sort of fighting, and we were glad when they desisted from their attentions.[13]
Captain Willoughby Verner, Headquarters, Desert Column

They remained at the wells for about ten days. Captain Willoughby Verner was sharing an improvised shelter with Kitchener.

Kitchener would take a nap lying on an Arab prayer carpet while I was taking my turn of duty. We were the happiest of comrades and the only subject we ever differed on was about our afternoon tea. He insisted on having it well-boiled, so as to get what he called 'A good grip on it!'[14]
Captain Willoughby Verner, Headquarters, Desert Column

Wolseley remained unaware of the true parlous state of the Desert Column and had been busy concocting plans for them to cut across the desert to Merowe, some 30 miles further up the Nile from where they could support the River Column. These hopes were stillborn when Evelyn Wood pointed out the true situation facing the Desert Column, and this was coupled with the arrival of Brackenbury's depressingly realistic assessment that he could not reach Berber before 12 March. It was only when Wolseley digested these reports that he issued orders for both the Desert Columns and the River Column to withdraw entirely – all the way back to Korti. But how? Time was running out for the remnants of the Desert Column at Abu Klea.

> Our camels are dying in numbers every day. My own was so weak it could not get up with me on it. Buller ordered a church parade at 4 p.m. Two or three bullets from a long range nearly hit our padre. I think most of us prayed we might get back all right. I know I did. As my camel was dying, we shot him and ate part of his hump, and gave the rest to my men. It was horribly tough and full of maggots, but a change from the everlasting bully beef.[15]
> Lieutenant Percival Marling, Mounted Infantry, Camel Regiment

To make matters worse, reports came in that the Dervishes were approaching on 23 February.

> A large force of Dervishes about 8,000 strong, of which two-thirds had rifles, arrived on the scene and halted at some wells about 2 miles from our little post, whither the force who had attacked us had withdrawn. Sir Redvers Buller was at first inclined to remain and fight them, but the impossibility of carrying away our wounded after even the most successful action, induced him to order a retreat across the 52 miles of waterless desert which lay between us and Gakdul.[16]
> Captain Willoughby Verner, Headquarters, Desert Column

The question was clear: how were they to break contact and get away across the broken ground – where they had been ambushed at the Battle of Abu Klea? It fell to a naval officer to suggest a solution.

> Perhaps the column had never been in more imminent danger than it was at that moment. Sir Redvers Buller discussed the situation with me. I expressed the opinion that the large force of the enemy would cut off our advance,

rush us, and then move upon Gakdul and so on to Korti itself; and remarked that the column was short of transport and of provisions, and would be short of water. 'What would you do if you were in command?' said Buller. I told him that in the evening I would light a larger number of campfires than usual, and, leaving them burning in order to deceive the enemy, I would then depart in silence and with speed. 'For a sailor ashore,' said Buller, 'you've a good head! I'll do it!' And he did. At two o'clock the same afternoon, Sir Redvers Buller sent on his sick and wounded – thirty-two of all ranks – with a convoy of 300 men commanded by Colonel Stanley Clarke; and that night, at 7.30, the rest of the column stole forth into the desert, leaving a ring of campfires flaming in the dark behind us.[17]
Captain Charles Beresford, Naval Brigade

Before they departed, they had filled in the wells, blocking them with dumped camel saddles and sand, to further impede the Mahdist forces.

We only moved out just in time. I don't suppose they found out we had gone until next morning, and then pretty late, as they would not have approached the place except very cautiously. It was a very nasty place to get out of, as for about 6 miles the road or track runs in a valley with commanding hills on both sides, and had the enemy made any attempt to hold the ground at the head, where it emerges into the desert, very few of us would have got out without scratches. Once in the desert we did not mind how many came on us.[18]
Lieutenant Beauchamp Doran, 1st Royal Irish Regiment

Once again, the Desert Column, what remained of it, had teetered close to disaster. But they had got away. After a four-hour march they bivouacked still undisturbed. Next day, although there was the occasional shot from isolated Dervish scouts, they could march across the desert plain on the long road to Gakdul. It was hard marching, with minimal food rations and still short of water. There was one amusing incident to raise their depressed spirits.

> I was riding as usual ahead of the column, the Naval Brigade with their guns on camels being close behind. Presently a camel fell, and a halt was made. Sounds of struggling were to be heard followed by a hollow sound, as the blue-jacket in charge kicked the poor brute in the ribs in the vain hope of making it get up. Next moment a clear, hard voice resounded afar through the still desert air, 'It ain't no use, the beggar wants new boilers!' In an instant the silence was broken, and roars of laughter were heard far and wide.[19]
> Captain Willoughby Verner, Headquarters, Desert Column

And Lieutenant Lord Gleichen reported at least one terrifying encounter during the retreat.

> That evening, as we lay comfortably in the sand after dinner, smoking our pipes before we turned in, two gigantic spiders made their appearance in our midst. Up we all jumped, over went lanterns and plates, and it was not till 'C' had valiantly slain the beasts with a slipper that we ventured to return to our places. It's all very well to laugh and to treat spiders with contempt, but a bite from one of these brutes is no joke. Imagine a yellow brute with two pairs of beaks, a body rather longer than your thumb, and eight long legs, covered with stiff and spiky red hairs, the whole beast barely to be contained in a soup-plate, and you have an idea of the apparitions which made for us that night They devour little birds, their bite is by way of being poisonous, and they are horrible to look at. No wonder we bolted.[20]
> Lieutenant Lord Gleichen, Guards Camel Regiment

The Desert Column got safely back to Gakdul, but it too was soon abandoned, and they marched all the way back to Korti, which they reached on 16 March. The great adventure was over.

***

BAD NEWS DOES NOT ALWAYS TRAVEL FAST, but for Brackenbury and the River Column it arrived on 24 February, just as the whalers were about to leave the consolidated camp. Brackenbury opened the despatch from Wolseley. It was a confusing mishmash of bad news, directions for the column's future conduct, but still leaving a considerable degree of discretion to Brackenbury.

Korti, 20th February. Buller evacuated Gubat. His main body went to Gakdul with all sick and wounded. He remains with about 1,500 men at Abu Klea. The enemy have now begun to fire into his camp there and have killed and wounded some of his men. He awaits camels to fall back on Gakdul, which I hope he will begin to do tomorrow, the 21st instant; but owing to the weak state of his camels, all his men must go on foot. I have abandoned all hope of going to Berber before the autumn campaign begins. You will therefore not go to Abu Hamed, but having burned and destroyed everything in the neighbourhood where Stewart was murdered, you will withdraw all your force to Abu Dom, near Merawi, bringing all the Mudir's troops with you. Please express to the troops Lord Wolseley's high appreciation of their gallant conduct in action, and of the military spirit they have displayed in overcoming the great difficulties presented by the river. Having punished the Monassir people for Stewart's murder, it is not intended to undertake any further military operations until after the approaching hot season. Further orders will be sent to you upon your reaching Abu Dom. Until you have occupied the Shukook pass, and made sure of everyone through it, you had better keep this telegram entirely to yourself and

Butler. Of course, if you are in the presence of the enemy
when you receive this, you must defeat him before turning
back. If you do not receive this before you have reached
Abu Hamed or are so near to it that it is merely a question
of occupying it without opposition, you must halt there,
and send back information at once to me, when I will start
the convoy from Korosko, which I do not otherwise mean
to despatch. Of course, it is impossible at this distance to
give you positive orders, but Lord Wolseley has every confidence in your military discretion.[21]
Lieutenant General Garnet Wolseley, Headquarters

Brackenbury was a competent staff officer who could read
between the lines.

Little time was needed for decision. The cup was snatched
from our lips, but we must bear the disappointment bravely.
The conditions in which I found myself gave no reasonable
excuse for pressing on. And lightly as the message touched
upon General Buller's difficulties, there was sufficient in it
to give cause for anxiety as to the result of his retreat. That
he had not retired one hour before it was necessary to do
so was a certainty. If his troops should be surrounded by
vast numbers of the late besiegers of Khartoum, who had
already had three weeks within which to collect to oppose
him, his situation might be full of peril. I knew Lord Wolseley could have but a handful of men at Korti, and the
flower of his force was here in the River Column. I had but
one course open to me – to make my way to Abu Dom
with all possible speed. I showed the telegram to Colonel
Butler. He entirely agreed with me.[22]
Colonel Henry Brackenbury, Headquarters, River Column

However, the orders to retreat dismayed many of his officers,
especially those constitutionally unable to understand military
realities.

In half an hour we got our new orders. We were to go about turn and hook it; putting the desert as fast as we could between ourselves and the warriors we had come so far to fight. A letter had come in by runner from Wolseley telling Brackenbury that Stewart was dead, and Buller was retiring with the Desert Column from before Metemmeh. Wolseley advised us to come back but left an option. There was no more hesitation or consultation than there was under similar conditions at the Dardanelles. Brackenbury took his seat in my boat; I took the helm; the bugle rang out with the, 'Retire!' We turned on our tracks and flew back on the plume-less, foam-flecked wings of the cataract which had so furiously fought against our advance. Not a shot was fired at us on the way down.[23]

Captain Ian Hamilton, 1st Gordon Highlanders

It was indeed an easier return 'going with the flow' as it were sailing down the Nile, rather than struggling up it. The River Column pulled into Korti on 7 March, some nine days before the long-suffering Desert Column. The expedition was over. The troops would go into summer camps along the Nile.

***

BITTERNESS SPEWED LIKE BILE from many of the participants in the blasted campaign for the 'Relief of Khartoum' and Charles Gordon. Gladstone was – quietly – unrepentant.

Gordon was a hero, and a hero of heroes; but we ought to have known that a hero of heroes is not the proper person to give effect at a distant point, and in most diffi-cult circumstances, to the views of ordinary men. It was unfortunate that he should claim the hero's privilege by turning upside down and inside out every idea and inten-tion with which he had left England, and for which he had obtained our approval. My own opinion is that it is harder to justify our doing so much to rescue him, than our not doing more.[24]

William Gladstone

Lord Salisbury, the Leader of the Opposition, caught the popular mood when he moved a vote to censure Gladstone's government for both the failure of the relief expedition, but also for the abandonment of the Sudan as being against the interests of the Empire.

> The conduct of Her Majesty's Government has been an alternation of periods of slumber and periods of rush; and the rush, however vehement, has always been too unprepared and too unintelligent to repair the damage which the period of slumber has effected.[25]
>
> Lord Salisbury

Secondly, blame was attributed to the valiant Gordon, who refused to change tack and stuck to his self-appointed 'post' when he could – in truth – have left at any time right up to the end. But as we have seen his character forbade such a course of action – as Baring later conceded.

> Looking back at what occurred after a space of many years, two points are to my mind clear. The first is that no Englishman should have been sent to Khartoum. The second is that, if anyone had to be sent, General Gordon was not the right man to send.[26]
>
> Evelyn Baring

Gordon's refusal to leave did not save anyone from the Mahdi's revenge, nor did it prevent the survivors of his garrison from joining the Dervish armies. It was a futile action by a man whose life had become entwined with a cult of Christian martyrdom.

Wolseley was the next to be justifiably blamed, although many of his critics were vindictive and driven by personal spite.

The Desert Column was an act of desperation prompted by the multiplying delays caused by first Gladstone's obduracy, and then Wolseley's fixation with a River Column carried on whalers. That might have worked when he first came up with the idea in April 1884, if it had been carried out in the summer of that year and timed to relieve Gordon before winter set in and the Nile waters fell to make the river almost impassable. But Wolseley insisted on sticking to his Nile scheme, even when necessity of building and transporting the whalers, plus all the other logistical delays rendered it unfeasible. For the rest of his life, Wolseley stuck to his guns.

> I have of course been intensely disappointed and believe that my plans were well laid and for a long time everything was bright: I could almost in imagination feel the grasp of my friend Gordon's hand. It was only a question of a few days, a few hours. But I lost my best soldier when Stewart fell, and everything was indecision and nerveless afterwards. Days that were worth a nation's ransom were squandered in doing nothing. Never was a commander as near making a great coup as I was.[27]
> Lieutenant General Garnet Wolseley, Headquarters

The depths of his self-delusion are staggering.

Then there were the torrents of blame poured upon the almost blameless. First, Colonel Charles Wilson who was trashed for his so-called delays in launching the last desperate dash on the steamers. Yet that was never part of his mission orders – he was to reconnoitre and report back. Wilson was an inexperienced commander, true, but he conducted himself in a sensible manner, consulting with his more experienced subordinates and acting with exemplary military logic in checking out reported threats to his base camp at Gubat before setting off for Khartoum. His riverboat adventures showed his determination, pressing as close as he could to Khartoum under heavy fire to be absolutely certain that the city had fallen, and that

Gordon could be presumed dead or a prisoner. He did not fail to rescue Gordon by a mere two days – his force was trivial in the extreme. The real relief force was the River Column, which was meant to combine with the Desert Column at Metemmeh before launching a combined effort. That was literally two to three months away. The River Column had only started off two days before Khartoum fell. They were an irrelevance at best. Yet some blamed Brackenbury for deciding to abandon his mission when invited to do so by Wolseley.

> The River Column though weak was homogeneous. There was nothing in the Sudan which could prevent them getting to Berber, thence with reinforcements to fight an earlier Omdurman; to save millions of lives; to save Gladstone's soul; to save Wolseley's prestige from the knock from which it never recovered; to save heaven knows how many millions of money. There was nothing to prevent this but the crack up of the will of one man who might have said 'Advance' and did say 'Retire'.[28]
> Captain Ian Hamilton, 1st Gordon Highlanders

Brackenbury may not have been the inspirational leader Hamilton wished for, but he was a competent officer who made a sound military judgement when placed on the spot by his superior. One might have hoped that Hamilton would learn the lesson of when it was important to retreat from a hopeless situation. Thirty years later Gallipoli would show that he did not.

11

BATTLES OF SUAKIN, 1885

> We knew that, being soldiers, we went where we were told, and did what we were told when we got there, but beyond this I do not believe there was a man in the whole of this magnificent force who could have given you any intelligible reason for which we were fighting, if indeed his ingenuity enabled him to give you any reason at all.[1]
>
> Captain Ernest Gambier-Parry, Commissariat and Transport Corps

HISTORY REPEATS ITSELF AS A FARCE. The Suakin campaign had been abandoned against all logic after Major General Gerald Graham's victories over Osman Digna at the Battles of El Teb and Tamai in March 1884. Now the campaign was to be resuscitated as a desperate effort to deflect attention from the crushing effect of the fall of Khartoum. This was about being seen to do something, anything, not a rational well-thought-out military expedition. Left alone for a year, Osman Digna had rebuilt much of his former power base, through a combination of the messianic influence of the Mahdist message for people who had nothing, a degree of intimidation of tribes unwilling to heed that call, and a growing realisation that the Red Sea littoral was open to exploitation after the departure of the British force.

A new Suakin Field Force was created and, given the circumstances, the British government was taking no chances. This would be a well-funded powerful force that could be almost guaranteed to deliver victory as a sop to the British press and voters. Once again, Graham was placed in command, now promoted to the rank of a lieutenant general. Some 13,000 troops

were allotted including the Guards Brigade commanded by
Major General Arthur Lyon Freemantle (1st Coldstream Guards,
3rd Grenadier Guards, and 2nd Scots Guards); the 2nd Brigade
commanded by Major General John McNeill (1st Bedfordshire
Regiment, 2nd East Surrey Regiment and a Battalion of the
Royal Marine Light Infantry); an Indian Brigade commanded by
Brigadier General John Hudson (15th Sikhs, 17th Bengal Native
Infantry and 28th Bombay Native Infantry); and a Cavalry
Brigade commanded by Brigadier General Henry Ewart (5th
Lancers, 20th Hussars, 9th Bengal Cavalry and a regiment of
Mounted Infantry). The empire was bestirring itself to bring
Osman Digna to heel once and for all, secure the pacification of
the whole of the Red Sea littoral, and construct a railway line
from Suakin to Berber.

As the various regiments arrived at Suakin in March 1885,
they were accommodated in a series of camps which, although
inside the outer redoubts, were outside the defensive walls
around Suakin. With no logical layout, or organised fields of
fire, these camps were vulnerable to incursions from small
bands of Dervishes.

Lying all night long, either waiting for an expected attack,
or peering into the darkness till every bush in front took the
form of a man on the move, began to tell on our nerves.
Then there was that sense of insecurity and the uncertainty
of what might happen in the night, for none of us knew
when we lay down at night whether we should be alive in
the morning. I was lying on my camp bed with my sword
on and my revolver ready to my hand. It must have been
about half-past ten o'clock, and I may have been dozing.
There had been no firing for an hour; and now that the
sentries had been stopped calling 'All's well!' the quiet of
the camp was only broken by the neighing of a horse or
the grunt or moan of a camel, when suddenly the stillness
was interrupted by the most awful scream that it has ever
been my lot to hear – a loud, long wail of agony – as of a

man mortally wounded, crying out with his last breath. It was a sound that absolutely seemed to curdle the very blood in one's veins. Then came a rush through the camp as those men who had been in their tents turned out. A few random shots were fired without effect, and the enemy, if ever seen at all, had disappeared. With the stealth of a wild beast, and with the wriggle of an eel, a party of Arabs must have entered the camp unnoticed by the sentries, and then rushing in through one door of a tent have stabbed and hacked with their long spears as they rushed through and out of the tent the other side. One poor fellow had been stuck with a spear right through the stomach, and with a last frightful and pitiful yell had expired at once. How the Arabs managed to enter the camps we never discovered; but this sort of thing was repeated by them over and over again in the face of double sentries and guards and pickets all over the place.[2]

Captain Ernest Gambier-Parry, Commissariat and Transport Corps

If anything, the situation was made worse by nervous sentries, shouting out challenges and firing shots at dim shadows in the night, in a fashion that disturbed everyone's sleep. When Graham arrived to take over his command on 12 March, he was soon aware of the problems and ordered a series of remedial actions, which should have been carried out far earlier: a more logical compact layout, the use of zeribas and a control on firing. This brought the problem under control. As a leader, Graham was not a man who sought popularity among his men.

Broad-shouldered and tall, above the average height of even tall men, with iron-grey hair and strikingly handsome features, so far as looks went he was the beau ideal of a soldier, and wore his loose cotton dress, on the breast of which was the coveted ribbon of the Victoria Cross, with an easy grace which stamped him as a man used to fashionable society, and free from the pipeclay stiffness of the camp. His voice was good, but his manner of speech slow, and he said very little at a time, while his eyes had a placid expression which reminded one somehow of the calm gaze of an ox – a placidity that never left him, I believe, even in the moment of danger; indeed, danger was nothing to him – he enjoyed the whistle of a bullet as other people like the scent of a flower. He looked you full in the face when speaking, but his features rarely lit up, and were not characterised by that bright alertness of expression, neither did he often offer a suggestion, simply saying, 'I want to do so and so, can it be done?' and apparently caring little to inquire into detail. He was so profoundly reticent, that the heads of departments were sometimes only informed of his plans at a date when it was very difficult to execute them properly; and, as orders were frequently changed at the last moment, a sort of uneasy feeling prevailed that no definite line of action had been decided on. This was certainly unjust; but reticence, though a valuable quality in a commander, may be carried to such a point that it will shake the confidence of his troops.[3]

Major Emilius De Cosson, Suakin Field Force

Although Graham had experience of desert fighting, many of his newly arrived troops had never undergone desert conditions and needed a considerable degree of acclimatisation.

Of course, we all very soon had the skin burnt off our faces, not only by the direct heat of the sun, but by the refraction from the sand, which is almost as bad. One thing which nearly all of us suffered from was sore lips. Our lower lips would swell up to an enormous size and then break and fester. It was very painful, but when once cured we were not troubled again in this way. A good thick moustache was the best preventative, and I am sure a beard protected one's face a great deal. Another thing most of us did was to have our hair cut off quite short to the head, but I am not sure

1. Colonel Ahmed Arab

2. Tewfik Pasha

3. Admiral Beauchamp Seymour

4. Captain Charles Beresford

5. The British naval bombardment of the Alexandria forts, 11 July 1882

6. The charge of the Black Watch at the Battle of Tel el Kebir, 13 September 1882

7. The Naval Brigade at the Battle of El Teb, 29 February 1884

8. The Desert Column in their doomed attempt to relieve Khartoum, January 1885

9. Lieutenant General Garnet Wolseley

10. Major General Gerald Graham

11. General Charles Gordon

12. The Mahdi

13. General William Hicks

14. General Herbert Stewart

15. Colonel Henry Brackenbury

16. Bennett Burleigh

17. The ferocious fighting at the Battle of Abu Klea, 17 January 1885

18. The traditional heroic depiction of General Gordon's
death at Khartoum, 26 January 1885

19. Captain Charles Beresford's dash in the Safieh up the Nile to
rescue Charles Wilson after he had run aground, January 1885

20. Tribesmen of the Sudanese Beja clan in 1885. Their distinctive hair gave rise to the derogative term 'Fuzzie Wuzzy'

21. A soldier of the 8th Sudanese Battalion, Egyptian Army

22. Men of the 1st Lincolnshire Regiment resting on the long march to Atbara

23. Cameron Highlanders at the Battle of Atbara, 8 April 1898

24. Emir Mahmud in his bloodstained jibbah after his capture at the Battle of Atbara

25. Major General Herbert Kitchener meets Emir Mahmud
after the Battle of Atbara, April 1898

26. The Queen's Own Cameron Highlanders leaving Wad Hamid, August 1898

27. The 1st Lincolnshire Regiment waiting for the Dervish
assault at the Battle of Omdurman, 2 September 1898

28. The 12th Sudanese Battalion in their trenches during
the Battle of Omdurman, 2 September 1898

29. Heroic depiction of the brave but somewhat futile charge
of the 21st Lancers at Omdurman, 2 September 1898

30. Lieutenant Raymond de Montmorency VC of the 21st Lancers

31. Captain Douglas Haig attached to the Egyptian Cavalry

32. Lieutenant General Herbert Kitchener

33. Major General Archibald Hunter

34. Colonel Hector Macdonald who excelled at Omdurman

35. In the aftermath of the Battle of Omdurman many of the Dervish wounded lying on the battlefield were despatched with no mercy

36. The Mahdi's Tomb at Omdurman showing the damage done by British shells

37. The Grenadier Guards landing at Khartoum, September 1898

that this was a good thing. It was cooler and more easily kept clean, certainly; but in a hot climate a good crop of hair is a protection from the sun, hair being a non-conductor of heat.[4]

Captain Ernest Gambier-Parry, Commissariat and Transport Corps

The regular khamsin winds caused further distress, whipping up sandstorms.

The whole of this part of the plain is covered with a dense cloud of whirling sand which penetrates everything – eyes, nose, ears, clothes, watches and boots, mixing with the water one drinks, and the bread that one eats, till it grates like cinders between the teeth. When we looked out of the tent this morning, we could hardly distinguish objects 20 yards off, in fact it was as bad as a London fog, only the fog was palpable and hit you in the face; nor do I know anything more exquisitely painful than to have to ride against the wind during one of these storms. There was no use in closing the tent doors, for the sand still came in through every chink and crevice, covering everything with a thick coating of dust, no doubt plentifully laden with microbes, bacilli, etc.; the germs disseminated by the dead camels and other objectionable matter about the camp. As a protection against these sandstorms and the glare of the sun, our men were all provided with blue goggles and gauze veils, attired in which the British soldier presented a very grotesque appearance.[5]

Major Emilius De Cosson, Suakin Field Force

Many of the men discarded these as next to useless.

Graham had received intelligence that Osman Digna's forces were once more gathering his men at Tamai, some 14 miles to the south-west, with a forward base reported at the tiny village of Hashin, 7 miles west of Suakin. After considering his options, Graham decided to first move on Hashin, intending to leave the

2nd East Surreys and a couple of artillery pieces in four stone and sandbag redoubts on top of the Zeriba Hills – just short of the Hashin village – to secure his right flank and rear from any attack when he moved south to attack Tamai. A preliminary cavalry reconnaissance of the Hashin area found the village deserted.

On 20 March, Graham marched his force out heading straight for Hashin. His three infantry brigades were in a single huge formation, which would allow them to swiftly form square should they be attacked in force. Ahead they had a strong cavalry screen. At first all went according to plan and the 2nd East Surreys were soon busy building their redoubts on Zeriba Hill.

> They suddenly came full upon the square of the Guards Brigade drawn up in the plain below it, who had hitherto been standing idly listening to the bullets whistling over their heads, but seeing little of what was going on, owing to the thick nature of the bush. To do our enemies justice they never hesitated for a moment, but raising a frantic yell flung themselves straight on the square with reckless gallantry, led by a youth on a white riding camel, who had become quite a celebrity in the camp at Suakin, for at every night attack, this youth on the white camel was always to be seen flitting ghostlike round our lines under the hottest fire, and bearing apparently a charmed life. Steadily and methodically, as if on parade, the Guards levelled their rifles and poured volley after volley into the dark mass of rushing shouting Arabs, who fell before the fiery blast like corn under the sickle; the poor youth and his white camel being among the first to bite the dust, the latter riddled with bullets, though the youth himself, I believe, was taken prisoner only slightly wounded. So effective was the fire, that I was told none of the enemy succeeded in getting within 15 yards of the square.[6]
>
> Major Emilius De Cosson, Suakin Field Force

More and more Dervishes appeared out of the scrub, and at around 12.30, Graham decided to fall back, having achieved his objective in establishing a defensible position for the East Surreys on Zeriba Hill. The disengagement was carried out successfully, the brigades falling back in stages, covering each other and with their volley fire discouraging pursuit. The Battle of Hashin was not a major engagement, but it showed that Osman Digna's forces were game enough when they saw a chance to hit home hard.

Having secured his right flank at Hashin, Graham now sought to establish a forward strongpoint and supply depot some 8 miles from Osman Digna's stronghold at Tamai. He gave this task to a mixed force commanded by Major General John McNeill and consisting of his own 2nd Berkshires, the Royal Marine Light Infantry, the Indian Brigade, a strong company of Royal Engineers to help in constructing a zeriba, four Gardner machine guns, and a squadron of the 5th Lancers to act as a screen. In his calculations, Graham seems to have ignored recent intelligence reports which specifically warned that Osman Digna was aware that an attack would be made on Tamai – after all, that was the obvious move and followed the pattern of the year before. More to the point, they warned that in response, Osman Digna intended to attack the British column well before it got to Tamia, and before an overnight zeriba could be completed. It was unfortunate that this intelligence was not shared with McNeill.

They set off on 22 March, marching in two squares, with the Indian Brigade square holding the 1,500 assorted camels and mules that were needed to carry the supplies ammunition and water. Progress was slow, as Graham had assigned them a route directly across a scrub infested area of the desert. The prickly head-high scrub was a real obstacle, scratching the men, pulling the measured formations apart, and they needed frequent halts to dress their ranks. But worst of all it was almost impossible to see whether they were under threat of attack – all they could see was scrub. The delays multiplied and soon it was apparent that they had run out of time and would have to stop where they were – at roughly the 6-mile point at a place known as Tofrek – to construct the zeribas required for overnight defence. At about 10.30, a relatively clear area of ground was selected and the work began. They were building three interlinked zeribas: in the centre zeriba was the area reserved for the transport and all the supplies. In the northern corner was a zeriba that was to be manned by the Royal Marines, while diagonally opposite on the southern corner there would be a zeriba for the Berkshire Regiment, both of these units having an attached Gardner gun to augment their firepower. While the zeribas were under construction, the camels and mules were all gathered to the east of the clearing, and were slowly being unloaded, while the Marines and Berkshires had piled their arms and were relaxing.

> We laughed and jested, as men will on the eve of a cataclysm, unconscious of the impending danger. We had expected, in a general sort of way, that we should be attacked on our march out, but we had met with no opposition for over 4 hours, and had remained for as long again in peaceful possession of our clearing, without a vestige of the enemy being seen beyond small parties; it is not to be wondered at, therefore, if few of us on that hot Sunday afternoon had any thought of immediate peril. Around me was the busy hum of voices, hearty English voices, laughing and chatting confidently, as if they were at a picnic; for the English soldier is the same wherever he goes, and, though the work had been hard and the day hot, the men who had come off work were good-tempered and cheerful, as they lay beside their piled arms, smoking their pipes or drinking their coffee, for several camp-fires had already been lighted, and, exchanging rough 'chaff', which, if not particularly new or witty, seemed to have lost none of its power of amusing them by being transplanted to the Sudan. The working parties were mostly in their shirtsleeves, with

their braces hanging down behind, and 'Tommy Atkins' was busy cutting down trees.[7]

Major Emilius De Cosson, Suakin Field Force

The Indian Brigade, which was intended to march back to Suakin once the defensive post was properly established, had taken up defensive positions which formed a three-sided square around the whole position, facing out to the south, west and north – the directions from which Osman Digna's forces were most likely to attack. About 100 yards in front of them were four-man pickets to give early warning of attack. By now it was apparent that in this terrain, one squadron of cavalry was inadequate to screen such a position. All they could do was establish their own four-man posts some 1,000 yards further out, where they were hopelessly isolated, and still unable to see what was going on around them in the thick scrub; or at least not until it was too late.

By 14.00, the Royal Marine zeriba with its sandbag redoubt for the two Gardners in the north-east corner was completed and occupied. The Berkshire zeriba was also approaching completion, but time was pressing before the Indian Brigade would depart, so half the battalion was ordered to pile arms, then move in front of the Indian lines to cut more scrub, to allow the tiring engineers to finish the defences.

Major Norman Stewart was a staff officer with the Indian Brigade, and to him all seemed calm. But then a terrible surprise.

Some of the 5th Lancers came galloping in by the left flank of the 15th Sikhs and right of the 17th Native Infantry and on in the direction of Suakin. As no enemy was to be seen, and all was quiet, the last thing to enter my mind was an impending fight, more especially as only a few minutes before I had seen General Hudson at lunch and noticed Sir John McNeill chatting with a group of officers. For these reasons it is hardly surprising little, or no notice was taken of the galloping Lancers. The next

instant, however, the Arabs were rushing us from every direction.[8]
Major Norman Stewart, Headquarters, Indian Brigade

Some of the Berkshires had wandered, unarmed, over 100 yards into the scrub. In a few moments there was chaos as the assorted Indian, cavalry and Berkshires all ran for their lives back to the zeribas.

> The cavalry outposts came clattering in, dashing through the working parties, and a heavy fire was poured upon us from the enemy, who seemed all at once to have sprung out of the earth where but a second before all had seemed so quiet and so still. There was a cry all round, 'Stand to your arms, men! Stand to your arms!' but, alas! some of the men were without arms, for they had put them down on the ground while they were toiling away at their work. There was a rush to the partially formed zeribas, and, mixed up together, Englishmen and Indians stood back-to-back fighting for life against an overwhelming force.[9]
> Captain Ernest Gambier-Parry, Commissariat and Transport Corps

Panic spread and on the south face, the double lines of the 17th Bengal Native Infantry fell apart in a few terrible moments.

> All seemed to grasp the situation except the 17th Bengal Infantry, who only had to open fire as they stood, instead of which this regiment for the moment seemed paralysed, remained at the slope, and actually watched their commanding officer being killed by an Arab, who jumped up behind him on his horse's back and plunged a spear through his body! Still the men fired not, and appeared incapable of action, so great was their consternation. The next instant they began to look about, and then step back, breaking their formation, and lastly, they went. It wasn't a case of a stampede, it was more 'a bolt at a walk'. Anyhow, nothing

could be done with them, and God knows their British officers did all in their power as well as many of their native
officers and non-commissioned officers.[10]
Major Norman Stewart, Headquarters, Indian Brigade

Some of the 17th Bengal Native Infantry fell back to join the
Berkshire Regiment zeriba, but most fled into the central zeriba
and into the massed transport animals and drivers who were
also under attack. The result was total chaos.

A large body of the Arabs had at the same time attacked
the mass of camels and transport animals, who turned
round and, like a vast surging sea, came onward towards
the zeribas, crashing through the bush, swaying with their
mighty weight, and trampling down everything in their
course as they swept forward enveloped in a dense cloud
of dust, maddened and terrified. The Arabs were among
them, hacking, hewing right and left, hamstringing and
ripping up the wretched camels, and cutting down merci-
lessly the poor miserable native drivers who, unarmed and
helpless, were hemmed in and carried onward by the flood.
Many of our own men and officers, too, were in this way
driven forward, unable to extricate themselves or even to
draw their swords. Mules, horses and camels were huddled
into one hopeless mass of inextricable confusion, while the
air was filled with the screams of men and animals and the
roar of the musketry. By far the greater part were killed
and wounded at the first onslaught, but when the stampede took place they very soon scattered in all directions,
and as far as the eye could reach, all over the plain were
camels, riderless horses, mules kicking themselves free of
broken harness, drivers running for their lives, and our own
men cut off from the zeribas, sharing a common fate with
the rest, and falling either speared by the enemy or shot
down by the reckless fire of some of the Native Infantry.[11]
Captain Ernest Gambier-Parry, Commissariat and Transport Corps

Major Emilius De Cosson had also been with his transport
column, but he somehow struggled through the stampeding
mob of beasts and men and joined the marines in their zeriba.
Many others, in their desperation to escape, trampled right
through the thorn fences, but overall, the marines kept their
discipline and managed to hold the Dervishes back, before re-es-
tablishing the integrity of the zeriba.

> We had hardly been in the zeriba a moment, when they
> came jumping over the hedge at the other side and tried to
> rush across brandishing their spears, while others swept
> round outside, or fired into it from the bushes. The noise
> and smoke were tremendous, and the men fought back-
> to-back, huddled together at the two lower corners of the
> square, firing both into the enclosure and out of it. All round
> the grey-green mimosa bushes swarm with swiftly moving
> black figures, who seem to court destruction, so recklessly
> do they rush on the hail of bullets that now pours from the
> zeriba, striking desperately with their spears and swords
> even after they are mortally wounded, and hardly ever
> missing their blow. Around the zeriba a wreath of white
> smoke hangs over the heads of all, broken here and there
> by the yellow flashes of the rifles and the gleam of the bay-
> onets shining through it. The men, with hard, stern faces,
> are clustered together in knots firing desperately fast; and
> the mounted officers, revolver in hand, are trying to control
> their terrified horses and steady their men's firing. Through
> the whirling wreaths of smoke some dark figures, bran-
> dishing swords and spears, come running across the square,
> only to totter and fall before they reach the centre under the
> furious shower of bullets that are whizzing in all directions.
> At my feet a dead soldier, who has been shot beside me, pale
> and motionless, a splash of blood across his young brow,
> the intense stillness and tranquillity of his face contrasting
> strangely with the fierce action and turmoil all round.[12]
> Major Emilius De Cosson, Suakin Field Force

Meanwhile the Berkshire Regiment was caught in two halves, some out cutting fence materials for the zeriba, and the rest forming a small defensive square just east of the zeribas. Lieutenant Southey was one of those caught out in the bush; he and his men had to frantically dash back, grab their weapons and swing into action.

> I rushed off to the zeriba with the company, who were stripped and unarmed. We got in at the same moment the enemy began to penetrate the left corner of our zeriba. General Sir J. McNeill came up to me and said, 'Take your men across to the opposite side at once!' We all went over at the double to the left face of the zeriba, bayoneted and shot down men inside, who had already got over and hamstrung several mules and camels. Then we formed up along half the side and fired furiously at the enemy who were emerging from the brushwood in hundreds. They went down like ninepins, but bullets were flying about us and spears were thrown at us by the enemy who got up near enough. After we once got to the side of the zeriba no more managed to get inside again.[13]
> Lieutenant Southey, 1st Berkshire Regiment

The other half of the Berkshires managed by dint of repeated volleys to keep the Dervishes back. In the circumstances, the Berkshires performed admirably, and the regiment would subsequently be awarded the honour of becoming 'The Royal Berkshire Regiment'.

Though many British accounts focus on the collapse of the 17th Bengal Native Infantry, by contrast the 15th Sikhs and the 28th Bombay Native Infantry were as steady as a rock, lined up in their double lines facing out to the west and north.

> As soon as all the Arabs who had penetrated the ground between the two zeribas had been killed, I found my way to my general behind the right flank of the 15th Sikhs whence

one was able to watch the fight to the end. The 15th Sikhs
and 28th Bombay N.I. had no protection in front of them.
The fight was now at its height, and only a few yards separated our men from the Arabs, who were pressing the
attack home to such an extent that more than once the
Sikhs had to use their bayonets, charging out by companies
a few yards, to enable them to make their weight tell, and
back again into the line to pump in more lead on the next
rush. It was a truly marvellous sight. Our fire was simply
terrific, it was impossible for men to load faster, and yet it
didn't seem nearly fast enough, for several hand-to-hand
fights were going on all along the line of these two regiments, and at the same time every face of the two zarebas
was engaged nearly as heavily as our two regiments in the
open.[14]

Major Norman Stewart, Headquarters, Indian Brigade

If the Indian troops had given way a disaster might have resulted,
but they held firm. For about 30 minutes the battle raged, with
repeated desperate charges from the scrub. Few men had any
idea of what was happening just yards away.

The bush was so thick, in spite of the large quantity
of scrub we had cut down, that it was quite impossible
to guess how much longer the fight would continue. It
was a very anxious moment, practically the whole of
our reserve ammunition had been carried away when the
mules stampeded at the commencement of the fight, and
the men were already asking for more, in fact some had
fired every round. Another very serious matter was the
condition of the men's hands, as the rifle barrels were
now almost red hot. As regards ammunition, the Marines
and Berkshires were better off, as they had their regimental reserve to fall back on. In front of the 28th Bombay
Infantry the scrub was thicker than elsewhere, besides
being only a few yards off, giving absolute cover to the

Arabs. Any unsteadiness on the part of this regiment would have been fatal to us.[15]

Major Norman Stewart, Headquarters, Indian Brigade

Gradually the fighting died down and by 16.30 the Battle of Tofrek was all over. The aftermath was grim.

The inside of the zeriba seemed to be stained everywhere with blood, and almost everyone was spattered with it. Many men, for the first few moments after the fight was over, simply fell down from exhaustion and dropped off to sleep, so with their blood-stained jackets it was difficult to tell who was wounded and who was not. It was impossible to drag the dead bodies of the animals outside the zeribas that night, as everyone was too tired to do anything but look after the wounded. Of course, the inside of the zeriba was littered with every imaginable thing – broken rifles, spears, shields, swords, parts of kits, helmets, empty cartridge-cases in thousands, blood-stained caps and jackets, bayonets twisted in all sorts of shapes, and thrown away as useless. The darkness at length closed around the zeribas and shut out from the eye for a time the ghastly sights around. There was perfect silence inside the three squares as a quarter of the force stood lining the hedges and peering into the night. No lights were to be seen except where the doctors worked incessantly at the mass of suffering around them. The dawn was breaking long before they had completed their sickening task.[16]

Captain Ernest Gambier-Parry, Commissariat and Transport Corps

The British forces suffered around 141 killed and 155 wounded, but among the transport personnel there were another 157 killed and 19 wounded. The Dervish casualties were terrible – possibly as high as 1,500 dead. The treatment of their wounded was, as usual, complicated by the fact that they were still dangerous, even when badly injured. The result was brutal.

If our own wounded knew how to bear their fate with silent fortitude, so also did those of the enemy, and hardly a groan was to be heard from the ghastly heaps of bodies, over a thousand in number, lying round the zareba. These desert warriors die hard, and it was reported by the parties sent out to bring in the wounded, that they crept bleeding on all fours with their spears in their teeth to attack them, and even hobbled on broken legs towards them. I fear this led to some of the enemy's wounded being shot in cold blood.[17]

Major Emilius De Cosson, Suakin Field Force

For 'some' perhaps read 'most'.

The total surprise achieved by Osman Digna's men caused a substantial amount of criticism directed at both McNeill and Graham.

Of course, you know by now all about the disgraceful business of Sunday, when McNeill, simply through the most criminal carelessness, was the cause of so many poor fellows being helplessly butchered. Had it not been for those splendid fellows the Marines, we should all have shared the same fate. It was a most terrible day, and what is much worse, it might so easily have been prevented. If I had my way, I would have McNeil tried by court martial and shot. He knew 10 minutes at least before the rush was made that the enemy was in force near us, because it was heliographed from the hills at Hashin, and besides I heard an aide tell him – and yet he made no preparations what- ever. There were no scouts out, and the poor wretched soldiers were scattered all round in the bush digging and cutting – and 300 yards from their arms. The whole camp is rampant with rage and disgust, and both Graham and McNeill are vilified by both officers and men. Now we are in the pleasant position of a force engaged in a desperate war, without one grain of confidence left in their leaders.

Tomorrow, we move out to Tamai where we are to have the final battle. And heaven only knows whether wretchedly incompetent VC, KCBs[18] and all the rest of it won't go to make some fatal blunder and get us all massacred. It's as like as not![19]

Captain Henry Paget, 7th Hussars

Paget was bitter, and overstates his case, but he does make some valid points. The two gallant generals, both recipients of the Victoria Cross, had made basic military blunders. First, Graham in his force selection had not provided enough cavalry to provide a strong screen capable of giving an early warning of an attack, nor any artillery to pack a punch in defence. Second, he had failed to pass on warnings to McNeill of the intelligence reports that Osman Digna planned to attack the column. And whereas McNeill might have taken more precautions if he had been forewarned, that is no excuse for not taking adequate defensive precautions in a clearing surrounded by dense scrub and – perhaps – of ignoring early warnings of an imminent attack. And yet for all the ifs, buts and maybes, the battle was still a British victory. Unnecessarily painful perhaps, but the losses inflicted on the Dervishes reverberated right through Osman Digna's loose alliance of tribesmen. If this was the price to be paid, then perhaps it was too painful, and they lost much of their enthusiasm for the rebellion.

The preparations for the next stage of the advance on Tamai continued, with convoys trekking backwards and forwards across the desert between Suakin and McNeill's zeriba suffering only harassing attacks. Private Frank Ferguson had a narrow escape while part of the cavalry screen.

I was out as right flanker when two of the rebels ran from behind a bush and threw a spear at me, but missed me and struck the nosebag which was half full of corn hanging by the side of the horse – so I lifted my carbine, which we carry loaded always when out in small parties, and fired at

the fellow who still had a spear and hit him in the breast and he fell. The Arab without any spear drew his dagger and I did not have time to load my carbine again but brought the butt on top of his head and stunned him – drew my sword and finished the two – but I have hurt my wrist swinging the carbine. I have got the spear and dagger, which I intend to bring home with me.[20]
Private Frank Ferguson, 20th Hussars

During one of these convoys a balloon was used for the first time on active service. It was about 23 feet in diameter, covered with netting and inflated with 7,000 cubic feet of gas. It could lift a basket capable of carrying an observer to scan the country ahead for any signs of a Dervish attack.

The balloon began to rise slowly to a height of about 200 feet, being fastened to the ground by two lines attached to the car. An admiring crowd of natives witnessed the ascent in silence, and did not seem in the least surprised, much to my disappointment, as I had expected to see them struck with amazement at the sight of a man floating about in the air. When the convoy was ready to move, the balloon, still 200 feet up, was made fast to a cart in the centre of the square. It was rather difficult to avoid jerking the cords which held it, and thus running the chance of breaking them; but extreme care was taken when crossing any rough pieces of ground, as it would not have been pleasant for the occupant of the car if he had suddenly found himself floating quietly towards the mountains, miles beyond the reach of any friends. Communication was kept up with the balloon by means of written messages, and it was not long before a letter came down telling us that the enemy were still pursuing the stampeded camels down towards the sea and killing them as soon as they got up with them. The enemy could also be seen in force retiring in the Tamai direction; and later on, a large body of them were standing

gaping up at the balloon only 300 or 400 yards distant from the convoy, though quite unseen by us on the ground. The force reached the zeribas at last unmolested, when the balloon was hauled down and packed up, the gas being as far as possible saved for future use. Thus, the first ascent may be chronicled as a success.[21]
Captain Ernest Gambier-Parry, Commissariat and Transport Corps

At 04.30 on 2 April, Graham began the final advance on Tamia. They reached the Tofrek zeriba, where they breakfasted, before resuming the march. They tried to use the balloon again, having pre-inflated it at the zeriba. This time things did not go well as the day was quite unsuited for ballooning.

The wind was very strong, and the captive balloon, which accompanied the force held by two stout ropes, was blown down upon the thorny jungle through which we were passing. The consequence was that the silk of the balloon was caught and torn by the thorns, the gas escaped, and the balloon collapsed. We were deploring this misfortune when one of the parties threw us into fits of laughter by the remark that it did not matter, as there was gas enough among the headquarters staff to inflate a dozen balloons.[22]
Brigade Surgeon James Thornton, Headquarters, Indian Brigade

At 16.30, they reached Tesela Hill, where the whole force bivouacked for the night. Many of the men were exhausted.

After our hot, dusty, and very fatiguing march we were all glad to get some refreshment and rest. We had come without tents and almost without baggage. I had nothing with me but my military overcoat, a waterproof sheet, and an old tweed wrapper, all of which had been rolled up and strapped to my saddle, so I put on the overcoat, gave the wrapper to my syce (groom) who had nothing to cover him, spread the waterproof sheet on the sand, and lay down upon it as I was, using a sandy bank as a pillow. We had a pretty quiet night; a few shots, however, were fired by the enemy at long ranges, costing us one British soldier killed and two wounded. I heard several bullets pass overhead, and one struck a metal water-keg close by with great force, but fortunately no one belonging to the Indian Brigade was hit.[23]

Brigade Surgeon James Thornton, Headquarters, Indian Brigade

On 3 April, they began the final approach to Tamai. Previously, at the Battle of Tamai in 1884, Graham had been attacked by thousands concealed in a khor, but this time the valley was empty, as was the village – Osman Digna and his men had retreated further into the hills. Tamai was burnt, then the expedition retraced its steps to Suakin, getting back about noon on 4 April.

Graham decided not to pursue Osman Digna into the hills, due to the imminent onset of summer temperatures, and the increasing difficulties in securing an adequate water supply the further they got from Suakin. Instead, he opened channels of communication with the local tribes, looking for those that might have been disenchanted with Osman Digna, and offering them peace terms. This was coupled with strong mobile expeditions to stamp out signs of continuing hostility. Under this classic combination of the velvet glove and iron fist the revolt was falling apart.

★★★

GRAHAM HAD ALSO BEEN TASKED WITH the ambitious task of building a Suakin to Berber railway. which would allow British troops to penetrate to the heart of the Sudan without the constraints of marching endless miles across a desert with attendant logistical problems. Yet building the railway was itself a huge undertaking, demanding the establishment of outposts to defend the route all the way to Berber – some 270 miles in total.

The first part of the line was easy enough. The ground was firm and perfectly level, and so the work progressed with vigour; but it was a different matter when the sandy, bush-grown country beyond the camp was reached, and 'drifts' had to be cut through the thorny mimosa. All this – the severest part of the work – fell to the lot of the army. The line was ballasted by the soldiers, the sleepers were carried forward in carts by our transport animals, and the rails had to be dragged from the point up to which they were brought by the train, by teams of mules or horses. The contractor's work, and that performed by the navvies, was merely placing the sleepers at the proper intervals, and fixing the rails. For this the navvies received the princely remuneration of 12 shillings a day, and time work, a free ration, and a free kit; while our soldiers received only as many pennies extra working pay as the navvies did shillings. The additional labour thrown on the troops of guarding the head of the line, and the workmen during their labours, was also extremely heavy. Nothing could possibly have been worse for the men than this. They were exposed to the sun and had nothing to do but stand about and think. A few tent roofs were sent out to protect them from the sun, but it was not always possible to use these. I do not think more than from 1,000 to 1,200 yards were laid in a day over this, the easiest part of the country, from Suakin to Handub. The rate of progression in the hills would necessarily be reduced, and at this rate the line would probably reach Berber by the end of August next year, or in other words, the army would have been dragging its weary way along a track, exposed to a 1,000 hardships and privations, for a period of something like seventeen months.[24]

Captain Ernest Gambier-Parry, Commissariat and Transport Corps

This pessimistic viewpoint rather ignores the fact that there was *no* easy way of securing logistical coherence for a campaign in the centre of the Sudan. As they worked, the navvies themselves caused much snobbish amusement among the officers.

> Every shovelful of sand they threw up seemed to bring down two with it, causing many unique expressions of disgust; but the climax was reached when our Indian coolies were formed into gangs to work with their British comrades. The Indians could not realise the use of the wheelbarrow, which when filled they immediately hoisted on to the heads of two and carried bodily off to the bank under construction. This completely beat the British workmen, and produced remarks which I wish I could repeat.[25]
> Major Norman Stewart, Headquarters, Indian Brigade

A makeshift Camel Corps was formed to patrol the ground on either side of the railway line, while two strong defensive posts were completed at Handub and then at Otao, some 18 miles from Suakin, which the railway reached on 30 April.

Back in England, the immediate political furore over the fall of Khartoum and death of Gordon having abated, the Gladstone government was reconsidering its decision to launch a fully fledged campaign to gain revenge on the Mahdi. On 30 March 1885, a Russian force had attacked a fort on the Afghanistan border. This was seen as a threat to British interests in India and for a while it looked as if war might break out. Yet Gladstone also saw this as an opportunity to cut his losses in the Sudan. By diverting attention to this possible war with Russia, he could legitimately abandon the idea of gaining 'revenge' for Gordon. On 14 April, Wolseley received a warning telegram from Lord Hartington – which made him incandescent with rage.

> I found a telegram from Hartington, 'Secret and Confidential' informing me that Imperial interests might necessitate withdrawal of all troops from Sudan and the concentration in Egypt of all those now up the Nile. That I was to

prepare in secret for carrying out this concentration. What a blow to all my hopes, and what a policy to adopt! The old imposter Gladstone is afraid of the radicals who are dead against all forward policy in Egypt, so he is only too anxious to avail himself of the excuse of a threatened war with Russia – which he never means to embark in, if he can possibly avoid it. Gladstone has taught the uneducated classes to mock at national honour or national renown. But please God his day of punishment is at hand. May he be torn limb from limb by the people he has deceived.[26]
Lieutenant General Garnet Wolseley, Headquarters

Gladstone's government had decided that all military resources, including those at Suakin, were to be available for service wherever required. This was a deliberate form of words. Wolseley's vehement protests at abandoning the Sudan were ignored and the evacuation was ordered. While the battalions stationed along the Nile route retraced their steps to Wadi Halfa, the Suakin Field Force was also ordered to retire. Despite suffering from diarrhoea, Wolseley travelled by sea to Suakin to break the news. His imminent arrival occasioned some humour among his officers.

The news that Lord Wolseley will soon arrive is causing a general brush up all round, and it is wonderful how fast the beards have disappeared from many a hirsute chin, which erst used to grace our mess, for it is understood that Lord Wolseley is an advocate of the razor; those who have suddenly taken to shaving are called the sycophants, and an officer on being chaffed the other day replied pathetically, 'One *has* to be a sycophant nowadays, you know!'[27]
Major Emilius De Cosson, Suakin Field Force

On 2 May Wolseley arrived at Suakin. Whether it was his upset stomach, or the accumulation of stress is uncertain, but James Grierson noticed a change in the great man.

He has aged very much since 1882. His moustache has lost
the point it had then, and he has not the same jaunty air. In
fact, he looks 10 years older, and I have no doubt he feels it,
as the strain on his mind caused by the Khartoum expedition must have been a heavy one.[28]

Lieutenant James Grierson, Headquarters, Suakin Field Force

On 17 May 1885, the Suakin Field Force began its evacuation.
Wolseley returned to his role as adjutant general back in
Britain, handing back control to Lieutenant General Frederick
Stephenson.

The main protagonists in the Khartoum story had not fared
well. Gordon was dead, while his great adversary the Mahdi had
succumbed to what seems to have been typhoid on 20 June 1885.
The British retreat had left the Sudan as the theocracy he had
dreamed of, free from the cursed foreigners, but he had not lived
to enjoy it. His replacement was the Khalifa Abdullah el Taaisha,
one of his most trusted warlords. Wolseley seems to have been
broken by his failure. Though he never accepted any blame, his
subsequent career was a rapid descent to mediocrity. Although
he was only fifty-two, no age for a general, he never held a field
command again, and rapidly lost all the vigour, vitality and the
intellectual acumen that had seen him stand out from his military peer group. Although he became commander in chief of the
army in 1895, the post by then was a sinecure and his influence
was marginal. And Gladstone? Despite manoeuvring to avoid
blame, his popularity waned dramatically following the death
of Gordon. His nickname of GOM (Grand Old Man) mutated
in certain circles to MOG (Murderer of Gordon). He would be
cast out of power in the general election of 1885. As one might
expect for a wily politician, his career was not finished, but Khartoum would haunt him for the rest of his days.

The Mahdi had dreamed of an expansionist Muslim empire,
with the conquest of Egypt as the first step to global dominance. The Khalifa was willing to follow that vision and during
the summer and autumn of 1885 his forces edged north. In

response, just as Gordon had predicted, to counter the threat the British had to deploy more troops to the border area. An Anglo-Egyptian frontier force was created under a new Sirdar, Major General Francis Grenfell, with an advanced brigade stationed under the promoted Brigadier General William Butler at Wadi Halfa. Butler was a proactive figure who realised he needed to buy time to build up his forces, so he constructed a strong outpost at Kosheh which was occupied by the 1st Cameron Highlanders, with another post the other side of the river occupied by the newly raised 9th Sudanese Battalion. Once the forces were amassed, Stephenson assumed command, and on 30 December led his forces out to attack at the Battle of Ginnis, in what would be the last battle where most of British forces wore redcoats. It was a well-executed battle, with a pinning force attacking frontally to attract attention, while a flanking force under Butler circled round to win the race to seize control of the key ridge dominating the Dervish main camp at the village of Ginnis. There was some bitter fighting, but the Khalifa's forces were forced into a retreat. One key element to the battle was the excellent performance of the Egyptian units, particularly the 1st Egyptian Battalion, commanded by Major Andrew Haggard. This was a signpost to the future. It was also an end to the Khalifa's attempt to conquer Egypt. For the British, it was all over bar the shouting, and a vague sensation that they were not yet done with the Sudan. They would have their revenge, but when?

12

SOFTLY SOFTLY: THE DONGOLA CAMPAIGN OF 1896–7

I should like to govern Khartoum and to have access to the black countries of Shilluk, Dinka, and Nuba, and I could raise armies that would conquer all Africa and settle the hash of meddling French and Belgians and Germans and Portuguese and Dutch *et les autres*. And if we do right that will come to pass someday though it may not be my fate to see it or help carry it out.[1]

Lieutenant Colonel Archibald Hunter, Egyptian Army

THE BRITISH EMPIRE WAS NOT a peace-loving institution. It was home to many shades of opinion, but within it lay a core of steely determination to expand, to grow, to dominate the world. In Egypt that instrument of conquest and control was the Egyptian Army, developed to be capable of standing against the Khalifa and his Ansar. From little acorns quite big oak trees grow, and so it was with the battalions of Egyptian and Sudanese recruits. Over the years that followed, the Egyptian Army expanded to eighteen battalions of infantry, ten cavalry squadrons, five artillery batteries, a camel corps, and an officer cadet school for the training of young officers. Most of the men were Egyptian conscripts, but six of the battalions were voluntary recruits from the Sudan. Many of the officers were drawn from the British Army. This was the chance for the more adventurous and ambitious to break free from the narrow confines of British regimental service. Barrack life seemed stale, dominated by the drill book, with hidebound senior officers who had learnt everything there was to learn about soldiering decades before, and who stamped on any display of initiative. In contrast, for the young British officer given a local rank of major or 'bimbashi', the Egyptian Army offered a variety of service and a degree of responsibility that hitherto they could only dream of – as Major Ivor Maxse gleefully recalled on joining the 13th Sudanese Battalion.

> To join it after some years of garrison duty at home was like walking into fresh air after a journey on the old underground railway. Whether it be hauling steamers up cataracts, furnishing escorts to gunboat patrols, acting as a station master, postmaster, or supply officer, commanding a squadron, battery, camelry, or a fort, as brigade major or as staff officer – wherever British supervision is required there the bimbashi is to be seen, directing native officers and men, and discharging duties which in European armies are often entrusted to generals. With such varied and continuous employments during the intervals between important actions, is it surprising that, compared with his brother in England, he becomes a handyman and a distinct personage – useful in peace and invaluable in war?[2]
> Major Ivor Maxse, 13th Sudanese Battalion

Maxse was biased, but he also waxed lyrical as to the impact of officers like himself, contrasting them with the corruption, neglect and cowardice of the previous Egyptian officers.

> The young British officers who subsequently undertook to organise and command the squadrons, batteries and battalions of the new army started the machine with a totally different conception of duty and military service to any which had hitherto prevailed. Indeed, the change was so bewildering to the native officers and men that at first the task seemed hopeless. However, with stubborn insular determination they persevered on their own lines, without

compromise, and without appearing to see any difficulty. Exact pay was handed out to the men on fixed dates; good barracks, solid food and clean clothing were provided; the discipline was strict and carefully enforced; promotion went solely by merit and no intrigue could avail to alter a selection; furloughs were granted each year, and the men went home to their squalid villages smart in appearance and with plenty of money in their pockets. They were no longer ashamed of themselves or their calling. When their term of six years' service expired, they left the colours to become local policemen. The fellaheen soldier began to feel he was a man, in fact became one. He at last understood his British officers, those curious foreigners who insisted on everyone doing his duty without shrinking, and who did it themselves! In action there they were always in front, never excited; in cholera camp, still they were present, working like slaves to stamp out the pestilence: always cheerful and approachable – yet maintaining their position as officers and the respect due to their rank.[3]

Major Ivor Maxse, 13th Sudanese Battalion

There were still flare-ups and fighting around the southern border of Egypt, as for instance on 3 August 1889, when the Khalifa sent an invasion force to test the strength of resistance and met a brigade of the Egyptian Army under the command of a promising young officer, Major Archibald Hunter, at the Battle of Toski. The Egyptian Army passed the test.

The brigade I had the honour to command did all the work and most of the killing. We charged three different positions and drove them out or shot them down or killed with the bayonet. Once they charged us: the most glorious sight I ever saw. We shot about 400 in that charge alone. I managed to get a slight jab on the right forearm from a spear, which is quite right nearly now, at least they have taken out the stitches. I thought my cup of bliss was full, but it was more gratifying to know after our last charge at Toski that the Dervish army was a thing of the past and the proudest moment of my life was when the men rallied round me and cheered in their wild impetuous way. Man, it was grand and worth living for – I shall never forget it – never.[4]

Major Archibald Hunter, Egyptian Army

In retrospect, Toski can be seen as a turning point in the war against the Khalifa. Hunter was rewarded by promotion to lieutenant colonel a couple of months later. He had a simple – if extreme and genocidal – solution to the Sudanese question.

These people are not human and never will be. I have always said and firmly believe now more than ever that there is only one solution of the Sudan question and that is the extermination of the Arab and the deportation of a black population from the interior to take their place. The country can never be exploited under present conditions. The Arab won't cultivate. The climate is not suited to Europeans doing field labour; therefore, people must be brought in who *will* cultivate. The Arab who came from the east as a conqueror and fastened on here like a parasite must be effaced or absorbed or regenerated – and the last process is as doubtful as [a] leopard changing its spots.[5]

Lieutenant Colonel Archibald Hunter, Egyptian Army

It is a revealing window into the chilling perspective of a British officer. Hunter was by no means alone in such opinions.

A former bit-part player in our story, one officer in the Egyptian Army now takes centre stage in the next act of the Sudan saga: Major Herbert Kitchener. He was appointed governor of Suakin in 1886, where with a force of some 2,500 men he fought to defend the tiny garrison against the threat from the revitalised forces of Osman Digna, but also sought to win over the support of the various local tribes not yet affiliated to the revolt.

He was promoted to colonel, in which capacity he commanded a cavalry brigade at the Battle of Toski in 1889, and in April 1892, as the 'coming man', was promoted to major general and made Sirdar to replace Major General Francis Grenfell. There is no doubt that right from the start, Kitchener yearned to avenge Gordon, but he also knew he had to bide his time, especially as Gladstone had returned to power as prime minister in the General Election of that year. Evelyn Baring remained as Consul General, although since the baronetcy granted him in 1892, he was known as Lord Cromer.

That same year the Khedive Tewfik died, to be replaced by his son Abbas Hilmi. Although largely a figurehead, he was an impulsive young man who struggled to accept that status and was a constant irritant to Kitchener. This came to a head at an official inspection of the Egyptian Army, where the Khedive found fault with everything and everyone. Eventually Kitchener lost his temper and threatened to resign, which caused Hilmi to reign back his criticisms. He remained a negative influence in the background from this point onwards, but the real power still lay with the Sirdar and Lord Cromer rather than him.

Kitchener continued the work of strengthening the Egyptian Army, all the while seeking to avoid increasing the budget, which might upset his parsimonious masters back in London. One key move, which would prove of inestimable value, was the appointment of Reginald Wingate as his Director of Military Intelligence in 1889. Wingate had been an artillery officer serving in Aden and India, before he secured a posting as a brevet major to the 4th Egyptian Battalion in 1883. He was assiduous in his Arabic studies and secured the role of military secretary to first Evelyn Wood and then Grenfell, before concentrating on intelligence work. Here his linguistic skills, his grasp of Sudanese and Arabic politics, and familiarity with every aspect of the Mahdist infrastructure, enabled him to operate as a spider at the centre of a web of agents. These were either dissatisfied with their place under the Khalifa, open to bribery, or easily coerced by threats. Whatever their motivation, they supplied intelligence of inestimable value in judging the strength of Dervish forces, their future intentions and in tracking their movements. It was a risky business, with death the penalty of being caught. Some were double agents, also accepting the coin of the Khalifa, while others reported only what they thought the British would want to hear – yet somehow Wingate seemed able to divine the truth that lay behind conflicting sources. He used his agents to facilitate the escape of various religious captives of the Khalifa, whose memoirs he then used as a fertile source of propaganda to inflame the British public opinion as to the iniquities of the Khalifa's regime. In an even greater coup, he secured the escape of Rudolf Slatin after twelve long years of imprisonment. Slatin had an encyclopaedic knowledge of the Sudan and the key figures dominant within the Khalifa's entourage. He would prove an invaluable Assistant Director of Military Intelligence following his appointment to that post in 1895.

In June 1895, there was a sea change in British politics when the Conservative Lord Salisbury won the general election. The removal of Gladstone's influence was evident in the changed policy towards the whole question of the Sudan. This was the height of aggressive European colonialism, and it was evident that the 'vacuum' created by the Sudan situation was causing other greedy European eyes to fall on the Upper Nile regions. In particular there was a fear that the 'old' enemy, the French, might be intent on annexing the southernmost Equatorial Province, which was only weakly held by the Khalifa's forces. Then on 1 March 1896, an Italian calamity brough the situation to a head. An invading Italian expeditionary force from their Eritrean colony had been thrashed soundly by an Abyssinian host at the Battle of Adowa. This defeat caused the Italian ambassador to appeal to Lord Salisbury for the commencement of serious operations in the Sudan to prevent the Khalifa from taking advantage of the Italian weakness by attacking the Eritrean border. In March 1896, all these complex colonial imperatives led Salisbury to send telegrams ordering Lord Cromer and Kitchener to commence an advance to recapture the Dongola

Province of northern Sudan – yet all the while observing the strictest financial economy. It did not go without notice that this would establish a firm base within striking distance of Khartoum. The game was afoot.

***

IN JUNE 1896, KITCHENER ADVANCED from the forward base established at Akasha to strike at the Khalifa's border post at Firket. With him were ten infantry battalions, fifteen cavalry or camel corps squadrons, and three batteries of artillery. Except for four British Maxim machine gun teams manned by the men of the 1st North Staffordshire Regiment, all the units deployed were from the Egyptian Army. As Kitchener was no tactical maestro, indeed it was only Cromer's support that had prevented his supersession by a more qualified British general, he relied on the advice and expertise of Lieutenant Colonel Archibald Hunter. Thus, it was Hunter who carried out a preliminary recce of Firket on 1 June.

> I started on the reconnaissance job at 2 a.m. and saw into the enemy's camp and made up my mind where to camp the force and how to attack and was back at 11 a.m. at Akasha, wrote out the detail of times and numbers, what was to go and what was not to go etcetera and then rode to meet Kitchener who was on his way to the front then – I rode over 80 miles that day and explained the whole thing to him, which he accepted in toto.[6]
> Lieutenant Colonel Archibald Hunter, Egyptian Army

The plan was an adaptation of a tried and tested methodology: a cavalry column under the command of Major John Burn-Murdoch was to make a night march out into the desert, and then cut back in south of Firket, just in time to join in a simultaneous attack with the main force that would be making a direct assault from the north. Burn-Murdoch realised the complexity of working out timings of distance at night and he conducted his own detailed recce plotting out the exact route he needed to take to get as far as the ridge overlooking the Dervish camp. His mobile columns would consist of cavalry, the 12th Sudanese Battalion mounted on camels and horse artillery. They set off on the night of 6/7 June. Despite his recce it was a difficult business keeping the disparate elements of his column on track as they got really close to Firket – beyond the ground he had been able to recce.

> The guiding now became more difficult as none of us knew no more than the direction. A slight improvement in the light had taken place as a poor thing of a moon had risen. We worked on. I was in a state of dread lest I should be too late. At 4.30 I was within touch of the ridge and could have sent my horse artillery and cavalry in if I had heard a shot fired from the north, The light was improving every minute. At 5 a.m. we were on the ridge and could see the Dervish camp apparently without having been alarmed. A shot was now heard as I opened fire with my artillery at 5.10 a.m.[7]
>
> Major John Burn-Murdoch, Headquarters, Desert Column

The Dervish camp burst into life at this rude awakening. Lieutenant Colonel Charles Townshend was in command of the 12th Sudanese Battalion, which now dismounted from their camels.

> I could, from this ridge, see the plain below, with the village of Firket quite close, about 80 yards away. We were on a line of small hills overlooking it from the south-east. The Horse Artillery guns made good practice on Firket. I have since heard that the Dervishes were taken completely by surprise and the first shell from our gun killed eight men. The Camel Corps had dismounted and were attacking a clump of rocks held by the Dervishes south of Firket. They advanced by rushes up to a point just in front of the Dervish rocks, but did not push on any further, remaining

stationary and exchanging lively fire with the Dervishes, both sides being well under cover. The cavalry were in the plain further south; the Maxims were west, towards the river. It was about 5.30 a.m. when we heard the main body of the troops under the Sirdar attacking Firket from the north, the attack being announced by a tremendous fire, a ceaseless hailstorm of independent firing. I never heard such a tremendous fire, and the Dervishes in Firket must have found it hellish. About 7,000 men were firing into it! The Dervishes very soon began running on all sides, and we could see them being bundled over, lying like dead pigeons in their white clothes.[8]

Lieutenant Colonel Charles Townshend, 12th Sudanese Battalion

Burn-Murdoch spotted the Dervishes retiring in the face of the main attack and trying to get away down a gully – a khor – to his right rear. He took immediate action.

Burn-Murdoch sent his galloper to me to say that numbers of Dervishes were about to break out on our right, where the guns had gone, and ordered me to proceed there and head them back. I took the two companies left with me at the double. When we topped the rise I deployed on the move, moving on in line, and could then see the Dervishes in white groups coming out of a nullah in the rocks in front, but evidently wavering. I poured a hot fire into them, and they fled right and left. The show was over. It was a case of *sauve qui peut* for the Dervishes. I could see them running away into the desert. I now got a message from Burn-Murdoch to bring up my men, as he was moving south for the pursuit. We could see the Sirdar's troops swarming down the slopes in Firket.[9]

Lieutenant Colonel Charles Townshend, 12th Sudanese Battalion

As the Dervishes fled the scene they were pursued by Burn-Murdoch's cavalry, who cut them to pieces.

Although Kitchener's forces had outnumbered the Dervish forces and were armed with far more modern weapons, the Battle of Firket was still considered to have been a notable victory, and another proof of the increased reliability and overall military skills of his new Egyptian Army. Kitchener was able to push forward to Suarda, which became the new advanced base. Perhaps Hunter was slightly rueful when he realised that all the credit would go to Kitchener, but he considered himself above all a team player.

> Now of course it is called his night march, and his brilliant tactics, and quite right too. He was responsible and, if it had failed, he would have been blamed, and so I am quite satisfied he will do me justice when the proper time comes. I know he trusts me. He knows I am as keen for his success as he is himself, in fact we sink or swim, and so does everyone in the show, together, and [we] are a united and not an unhappy family.[10]
> Lieutenant Colonel Archibald Hunter, Egyptian Army

Hunter would earn the popular accolade of 'Kitchener's Sword Arm'. It would be well-earned.

Yet Kitchener was far more than a mere tactician; he was a master of logistics. Not for him Wolseley's blind trust in whalers and the vagaries of the Nile cataracts. He would augment river transport with that symbol of the modern age: the railway. This would dissolve away the desert miles and bypass the rapids. It was the obvious answer and had in part been tried before, along with the aborted attempt at Suakin. Yet Kitchener brought a focused attention and steely determination to the construction of the Sudan Military Railway. Pre-existing sections of the line were renovated, with a deliberate attempt to reuse materiel wherever possible to cut costs, while a railway battalion of some 800 Egyptian and Sudanese workers was amassed to speed up construction. The engineering was dealt with by Lieutenant Percy Girouard, who had worked on the railways in Canada, before being commissioned and taking charge of the Woolwich Arsenal Railway. His experience was invaluable, in sourcing the right materials, training the workforce and supervising every stage of the process. As the rail track edged forwards, stations and small garrisoned forts were set up to deter Dervish spoiling attacks. Throughout 1896, whenever the army advanced, so too did the railway, first to the forward base at Akasha and then on, via Firket, to Kerma. One delay was caused by a series of exceptionally severe storms which began on 25 August, washing away several sections of the line where hitherto dry wadis were suddenly filled with raging torrents. Kitchener reacted instantly and deployed a veritable army of some 5,000 soldiers, working flat out under his personal guidance to repair the damage. As a result, the line was restored by 6 September. Side by side with the railway went the establishment of a telegraph system, which was the only means of rapid communication in that vast country.

Kitchener certainly did not neglect river transport, or the offensive potential of gunboats. He made arrangements to supplement the usual Nile steamboats with three specially commissioned larger, faster armoured gunboats. These were built back in British shipyards and transported out in sections, travelling by rail until they were re-assembled ready for service on the Nile. It was sod's law that the first of these, the *Zafir*, had a broken cylinder, which blew up a boiler on her maiden voyage on 11 September with Kitchener aboard! He was distraught, but the *Zafir* would be useless until the required spare cylinder was transported forward, which would not be for several weeks. The amassing of the flotilla was also hampered by the delayed rise in the Nile, as the unseasonable low waters made the Second Cataract all but impassable until early August. Major Aylmer Hunter-Weston had been assigned as a special service Royal Engineer officer to survey the worst obstructions in the cataracts. It was dangerous work.

> I started my work alone, assisted by such of the natives as were likely to have a special knowledge of the subject. As

I was a fairly good swimmer and had had experience of using mashaks (inflated skins) in India, I was able to carry out reconnaissance to Kitchener's satisfaction. My costume was simple, artistic, and well suited to the purpose, for it consisted only of a large helmet, a sun umbrella and my birthday suit! The simplicity of this attire, however, evoked considerable merriment in the force, and in due course a picture of the cataracts appeared in the *London Illustrated News* with crocodiles in the background and me in my artistic costume in the foreground.[11]

Major Aylmer Hunter-Weston, Royal Engineers

His work was passed to the naval officers responsible for getting the steamboats through using the same kind of methods devised by Captain Charles Beresford back in 1884. With teams of up to 1,000 men straining away at blocks and tackles, they managed to pull the steamboats up the rapids. Thanks to their sterling efforts four gunboats and three steamers were got through to assist in the fighting operations, while seventy large gyassas (sailing boats) were got through to assist with the transport of men and stores.

A further cause of delays was a virulent outbreak of cholera that resulted in hundreds of fatalities. This was not something that could be ignored as it raged through the camps that summer.

The riverbank was constantly patrolled to prevent the men from bathing, washing clothes, or drinking in it. They were not even allowed to approach it save when they were sent down in parties to draw water for the camp at the appointed places, which were above all the pools that had been infected and at points where the water ran fast under the bank. A severe flogging was the punishment for any infringement of the regulations. In the camp itself everything was done to isolate the cases as they occurred. Disinfection was of course carried out in a thorough manner, and the men who were engaged on burial parties incurred no risk, as

the blankets in which the corpses were rolled were soaked
with a very powerful disinfectant.[12]
Edward Knight, *The Times*

To try and protect them from the worst of the infections, the
then only British battalion in the army, the North Staffordshires,
was moved some 6 miles away from the main camp to Gemai,
but they could not avoid the cholera.

Through practically the whole of July not a day passed
without one or more deaths. A man would report sick in
the morning, or fall out from parade, and his company officers would attend his funeral that night. The burials took
place after dark, about 10 p.m., and a little party headed by
a couple of lanterns, might be seen wending slowly up the
hill to the place of burial, to the refrain of a comic song rendered by some comedian at the smoking concert, which by
the colonel's orders was held nightly. Only the most cheerful songs were to be sung, but, judging by the rapturous
applause with which the most morbid ones were received,
they much preferred the other sort. It was amazing how
cheerful the men kept; nothing would get them down,
although our surroundings were far from inspiring, to say
the least of it; a few scattered date palms growing along
the edge of the river, and for the rest sand and rocks and
blistering heat.[13]
Lieutenant James Farley, 1st North Staffordshire Regiment

One incident caused considerable amusement, concerning the
imbecility of two of the young officers, and the splendid reactions of a grizzled veteran.

We were in lascar tents, and in the next one to mine were
two of the junior subalterns. To pass the time one afternoon they were playing with their revolvers; one asked the
other to lend him a cartridge as he wished to see if it would

fit both weapons; he found that it did – which is not surprising as they were both forty-fives. He then proceeded to take a careful aim and snap at the top button of the other's jacket, who was sitting on the opposite side of the tent. He aimed and snapped several times, and then, glancing out of the door of the tent he saw, about 50 yards away, Sergeant McNulty, the master cook, a veteran of the battle of Rorke's Drift, with a dixie in each hand, just starting to dish up the men's teas. McNulty seemed a more sporting target, so he took a careful aim at him and pressed the trigger! The crash, bang that followed turned out the whole camp. I happened to be looking at McNulty through the door of my tent and I have never seen a better demonstration of the way to take cover! Both dixies went flying and he was down behind the railway embankment in much less time than it would take to tell it. I dashed out to find the other two outside their tent, shaking as if with ague and having hysterics. The next one on the scene was Captain Marwood, the adjutant, and the way he set about those two unfortunate youngsters was a delight and a privilege to listen to – and not one word of profanity from start to finish![14]

Lieutenant James Farley, 1st North Staffordshire Regiment

His self-control in the face of such stupid behaviour is highly commendable.

★★★

AT LAST, THEY WERE READY for the advance on Dongola. The advance was triggered by intelligence reports that the Dongola governor, Muhammed Wad el Bishara, was massing a large force to resist Kitchener's advance at Kerma on the east bank of the Nile near the Third Cataract. In fact, as the Khalifa had refused Wad el Bishara's desperate requests for strong reinforcements, there were only some 5,600 Dervishes to defend Dongola. Using both the railhead and the Nile to the maximum amount possible, Kitchener had succeeded in building up a strong, well-balanced Dongola Expeditionary Force of some 15,000 men divided into four brigades of three battalions each, the North Staffordshires, a strong mobile force of cavalry and camel corps, and two Egyptian Field Batteries. All this was supported by the four Nile gunboats – the *Tamai*, *Metemmeh Abu Klea* and the *El Teb*, all formidably armed with a 12-pounder quick-firing gun, a Nordenfelt 1-inch pom-pom gun and four Maxim machine guns. The Dervishes would be outnumbered by around 3:1 and given the disparity of weapons systems, this would not be a fair fight.

Among the gunboat commanders was Lieutenant David Beatty, who had already distinguished himself when commanding the gunboat *Abu Klea* in the 1896 campaign, in particular, when he threw overboard an unexploded shell threatening the ship's magazine. Lieutenant James Farley recalled his first meeting with him as they approached Kerma.

Wilson and I entertained a large party on board the *Kalbar*, including all our officers, Beatty of the gunboats, and many others, at which fun and laughter were the order of the day. Beatty, especially, was in tremendous form; he showed us his helmet with a bullet hole through it, and said he showed it as a joke, to the newspaper correspondents without telling them the circumstances, and they got a great kick out of it, writing to their papers the story of his remarkable escape. As a matter of fact, he said his helmet was hanging on a peg in his cabin at the time and his revolver went off accidently while he was cleaning it, the bullet going through his helmet.[15]
Lieutenant James Farley, 1st North Staffordshire Regiment

Next day, 19 September, was the Battle of Hafir. Here Wad el Bishara sprang a surprise as except for a token force, he had at the very last possible moment evacuated the fort at Kerma, crossed the river which at this point was some 600 yards wide, and occupied the Hafir fort on the opposing west bank. Farley watched the action from the *Kalbar* steamboat.

They had a mud breastwork, protected by a ditch close to the river and extending for about a 1,000 yards; in it were two gun positions, with embrasures, one for six of Hicks Pasha's Krupp guns; the other at the southern end of their trench for one or two guns. At the back of this position was a thick grove of date palms, and about half a mile further south was the old steamer, *El Tahira*, moored alongside the bank and surrounded by the twenty-seven gyassas. When we and the *Kalbar* appeared on the scene the gunboats were shelling the Dervish position, under heavy fire from the enemy. The *Kalbar* could not approach too near to the position as we were unprotected with armour plating, and half company volleys at extreme range were not very satisfactory. At the beginning of the action the gunboats approached to within 500 or 600 yards of the position with their guns blazing, when suddenly the Dervishes opened up with everything they had: Krupp guns, Remington rifles and here and there an old elephant gun, and what have you! They must have had an ample supply of ammunition judging by the innumerable jets of spray kicked up by bullets of every description. The gunboats quickly put about and got out of the hailstorm, to repeat the manoeuvre and receive an equally warm reception. The Dervish fire was kept up practically the whole morning with hardly any slackening, but they must have suffered heavily from our shelling; not only were our gunboats pounding them all the time, but our guns were shelling them from across the river.[16]

Lieutenant James Farley, 1st North Staffordshire Regiment

At first it seemed that nothing would dislodge Wad el Bishara's forces, and the gunboats withdrew. Kitchener was not defeated though: he concentrated all his artillery and Maxims on an island in the Nile close to the Hafir fort and commenced an incredible barrage.

The Dervishes certainly deserved and obtained our highest admiration for the way they stuck to their position. Colonel Parsons had managed to get his brigade of field artillery and the Maxims ferried across on to an island in midstream, and from this comparatively short range they must have done greater execution than the gunboats. About 11 o'clock the gunboats suddenly headed upriver, *Tamai* leading, and the other two following in the rear at 100 yards or so distance between them. As they passed us, they shouted, 'We are off to Dongola!'[17]
Lieutenant James Farley, 1st North Staffordshire Regiment

As the gunboats headed upstream towards Dongola, they at a stroke outflanked the Dervish position and threatened their base. Wad el Bishara himself had been wounded and he had little option but to order his men to abandon Hafir and fall back on Dongola. Next morning, Kitchener was able to occupy the Hafir fort and commenced an advance on Dongola which they reached on 23 September. That morning it appeared as if there would be a battle as both sides were lined up and ready. But appearances were deceptive.

At about 7 a.m. we sighted the enemy drawn up on a hill, in their white jibbas, with their spears flashing in the sun, and we all thought to ourselves, 'This is it!' We deployed into line, and I loaded my revolver, our swords had been sharpened by the armourer sergeant in Wadi Halfa. In the meantime, the gunboats had been shelling them, and we could see shells falling in their midst. As we drew nearer, they retired to a fresh position, and soon we came on a group of dead, lying in a great pool of blood – and very horrible they looked – their gigantic black bodies sprawled across each other and all mixed up as they had fallen, legs and arms sticking out every way, jibbas all blood-stained, teeth gleaming and the expression of ferocious hate on their faces. My company passed right over them and had to open out so as to avoid stepping on them.[18]

Lieutenant James Farley, 1st North Staffordshire Regiment

What followed was also a damp squib, as the town fell with only minimal opposition.

> We were now approaching the city of Dongola, an immense collection of mud huts. The battalion on our left went through the city proper, and we through the western suburb. A lot of scattered fighting took place here; a huge Dervish darted out of a house that two of our scouts were on the point of entering, and springing on a horse that was standing at the door saddled and bridled, attempted to escape! What a hope! Several rifles cracked and he rolled backwards off the horse. The most fanatical were the Baggara, distinguished by their red patches and they died to a man, fighting to the last, calling upon Allah who was deaf to their appeals.[19]
>
> Lieutenant James Farley, 1st North Staffordshire Regiment

In the days that followed some 900 Dervish prisoners were taken, many of whom were offered – and accepted – the chance to serve in the Sudanese battalions.

The 1896 Dongola campaign was over. The North Staffordshires would soon be on their way back to Cairo, but the gunboats would prowl a further 200 miles up the Nile and soon bases had been set up for Egyptian Army battalions at Korti, El Debba and Merawi, all places well known from Wolseley's abortive campaign. But this was a very different kettle of fish. Kitchener had succeeded in establishing a proper firm base for any future operations and had cleared the Khalifa's forces from the whole of the Dongola province. It was a remarkable achievement for which Kitchener would be feted and promoted to major general. The doughty Hunter was also promoted to major general, the youngest it was said since Wellington, and appointed to be the governor of the newly recaptured Dongola province.

★★★

WHAT WERE THEY GOING TO DO NEXT? That was the obvious question. Kitchener wanted to advance as far as Berber as the next stage of the battle to smash the power of the Khalifa. To the military mind it was obvious.

> There is a pretence and halo of mystery always kept about future intentions. It is as plain as a pikestaff that we cannot sit still here: if we do it is tantamount to a confession to the enemy that we are afraid to go on. We must go on or go back, and we must go at least as far as Berber and open the Suakin road, the road to Korosko, and join hands with the Italians at Kassala along the rivers Atbara and Gash. My plan is already made out, and cut and dried. We can't sit crouched like two cats. We are the intruders, and they know we have come to stay – and they must begin to spit and scratch, or else the people behind them will come over to us.[20]
>
> Major General Archibald Hunter, Governor Dongola Province

Kitchener secured the support of Lord Cromer but had yet to convince Lord Salisbury. To the Conservative prime minister and his chancellor of the exchequer there was one obvious objection – the cost that would be incurred. Kitchener could point to the intelligence Wingate had gathered of French movements towards Fashoda in the Equatorial Sudan, but he still had to make a solid financial case that – in the long run – an advance to Berber would be cheaper. He pointed to the merits of the next stage of the Sudan Military Railway, which he intended to push forward straight across the Nubian Desert from Wadi Halfa to Abu Hamed and ultimately Berber in support of the advance and to allow a firm grip to be taken over the northern

Sudan. Once built the railway would reduce the need for the 500 miles of transportation along the Nile, which in itself offered further savings. Once Berber was taken, he pointed out, the focus would shift from Suakin, and that garrison could then be reduced – saving money. His arguments worked and a loan was granted to the Egyptian government for the Sirdar to prosecute his campaign.

Once the line along or near the Nile to Kerma had been completed by May 1897, work could begin in earnest on the 235-mile direct route to Abu Hamed. The problems thrown up for Percy Girouard in constructing a railway across the arid wastes of the Nubian Desert dwarfed the previous difficulties. The labourers and the steam engines both needed thousands of gallons of water a day if they were to continue working, so a hundred special 1,500-gallon waggons were built to be brought in on a regular basis by the trains. Still there was a need for local wells, so the desert was surveyed by Royal Engineer officers using their geological knowledge to locate likely spots. Two wells were successfully dug, although they had to get down some 90 feet before a decent supply was tapped. The new line would have been vulnerable to Dervish attacks, but they seemed at first unaware of its approach. When they noticed, raiding parties were despatched, but they were not strong enough to disturb the inexorable progress. Overall, the Khalifa seemed unaware of the encroaching risk from the north; indeed Berber only had a garrison of some 800 men, with only 300 rifles among them. The local emir was ordered to defend if attacked by infantry alone, but retreat if they were accompanied by gunboats.

On 29 July 1897, Kitchener sent Hunter ahead from the Merowi base with a mixed 'flying' column of some 3,000 men, based round Brigadier General Hector Macdonald's 2nd Egyptian Brigade, with orders to seize control of the intended railhead at Abu Hamed. It was a tough series of marches following the banks of the Nile, covering some 133 miles, and conducted mainly at night to avoid the blazing heat of the sun.

Kitchener also ordered forward his gunboats to penetrate the

Fourth Cataract, without waiting for the town to be captured. On 4 August, they began the perilous journey assisted by local tribesmen. The *Tamai* tried first, but the sheer pressure of the water current was far too much, and she was forced back downstream. *El Teb*, under the command of Beatty, was the next to try.

Started with the *El Teb* at 2.30. Four hundred natives having turned up considerably strengthened our hauling power, but were unfortunately another source of danger, as they were entirely undisciplined [which] caused the boat to forge out into midstream where there was an exceedingly strong fall of water in very rough water. In less than 10 seconds she turned completely over and everybody and everything were thrown into the water and swept away in different directions. We lost three men drowned out of the fifteen on board, and it must have been a near thing for us all. Personally, clad as I was in heavy boots, tight trousers and belt, I was nearly waterlogged, and was sucked under six times by the undertow which was very strong. The last time I thought it was all up, but hit a pole under water, to which I clung like a limpet, and which pulled me up again, which I shortly after vacated in view of a box which was close and I thought would be better, but it took me 5 minutes to get that box, which were the longest 5 minutes I ever spent. Luckily the *Tamai* was all ready and came to the rescue and picked us all up. Then our attentions were turned to trying to pick up the *El Teb*, which was being whirled round and round bottom up in the large pool. Time after time we laid hold of her – she eventually disappeared down a small cataract surrounded by a regular litter of boxes of all descriptions, and eventually fetched up on a rock about 5 miles down in the middle of a lot of rough water where it was very hard to get at her. Of course, every mortal thing was lost with her, a terrible piece of luck, and left me stranded with only what I stood up in to commence a long and tedious campaign in, and no opportunity of being able

to replace it for many a long day, but I must be thankful I still remained above water myself.[21]
Lieutenant David Beatty, *El Teb*

Watching observers reckoned that Beatty had been sucked under no less than five times. It had been a narrow escape for the future commander in chief of the Grand Fleet in the Great War. The *El Teb* would be rescued but was out of action for a substantial time, and Beatty was given command of the *Fateh*.

Meanwhile on the night of 6/7 August, Hunter's column had arrived just 2 miles from Abu Hamed. After constructing the usual zeriba to act as a firm base, at dawn on 7 August they advanced on the town. The Dervish forces were in shallow shelter trenches, but after one largely ineffective volley, they fled back into the narrow streets of Abu Hamed. Present was Royal Engineer officer, Lieutenant George Gorringe, who had been attached to the 10th Sudanese Battalion.

Each house had only one entrance and from the inside, the Dervishes were able to cause many casualties among the 10th Sudanese until we evolved a plan to deal with them. Fortunately, all the doors faced in the same direction, and opposite each was a small hole, close under the roof, for ventilation. Fergusson kept his men back in a position from which they could cover the doors by rifle fire, while a party under my command collected straw, and rushing up on the other side, set it alight and pushed it through the ventilation holes so that the roofs caught fire. Some of the enemy ran out and were shot down; others perished in the houses. The method was drastic, but it saved many casualties among our own men. Afterwards, the most pressing work was to clear the place of Dervish corpses. Our own dead were buried; but I decided to make the Dervish prisoners throw their dead into the swift current of the river as the ground was rocky and hard, tools were scarce, and our men were exhausted.[22]
Lieutenant George Gorringe, Royal Engineers

These corpses acted as the first intimation Kitchener received of the battle when two days later they floated past his headquarters at Merowe. The Dervishes suffered losses of some 450 killed and 150 prisoners, most of whom were recruited to the Sudanese battalions. The British forces lost only twenty-three killed and some sixty-one wounded.

The capture of Abu Hamed secured the intended railhead but there was another prize in sight – just 130 miles further upriver was Berber which was reported to be all but undefended. It was evident to Kitchener that it would be better to seize the town while they could, rather than give the Khalifa time to move up his forces. The first requirement was to get the gunboats through the Fourth Cataract, and as the seasonal flow of the Nile deepened the flow of water over the rocks, this became a more manageable prospect. By the end of August, all the gunboats available had managed to get through, including the *Metemmeh*, *Tamai*, *Fateh*, *Nasir* and the repaired *Zafir*. They had got through, but it still wasn't easy as Major Edward Stuart Wortley recalled.

It is most difficult and anxious, but we have succeeded in passing six gunboats over the worst place we shall meet with. The river is extremely difficult here: studded with islands, very rocky and narrow channels with great rushes of water – and the river has turns at right-angles which render steering very difficult. Our procedure with the steamers is as follows: on arrival at a dangerous place the boat is tied up to the bank and everything taken out of her and carried overland to the top of the cataract. Then a wire hawser is bound all round the steamer, fenders placed at intervals, then a very long rope is attached to the bow, and one from the port and starboards side. Then with full steam ahead she starts off. The great difficulty is passing the ropes over the rocks and getting from one rock of island to another. Swimming is very dangerous, but the natives are very good at it. We are all quite naked with helmets on and so it is a very strange sight, but the ladies in these parts do not mind![23]

Major Edward Stuart Wortley, Gunboat Flotilla

On 24 August, Berber was evacuated as the Dervishes fell back up the Nile towards Shendi. Hunter decided to seize the moment.

We only remained at Abu Hamed a few hours and then General Hunter decided to proceed to Berber with four gunboats and half a battalion of Sudanese. We passed over two cataracts, the steamer I was on hit a sunken rock very hard – made an enormous hole in her starboard bow and we only just managed to get her to the bank. However, in two days we repaired her all right. It is just as well for us that the enemy had evacuated this place for it extends for about 5 miles, the houses being built of mud and very close together. It is very difficult to turn an enemy out of mud houses, for they go from one to another and shoot you from behind the walls. Artillery fire had very little effect on them.[24]

Major Edward Stuart Wortley, Gunboat Flotilla

On 13 September, Hunter entered Berber. The British now held both ends of the Suakin to Berber route. Fort Atbara, a small, advanced post with port and dockyard facilities was established a few miles further up-river where the Atbara River joined the Nile. What would happen next had not yet been decided, indeed it was a matter for the British government, rather than local commanders. For the moment they could all rest on their laurels and ponder the next step.

Now, beyond patrolling up the river, we have entered on a period of inactivity, for we must now await the decision of the government as to what we are going to do – and how far this expedition is to reach. The railway to Abu Hamid will be completed about the middle of November and there is no reason whatever against 4,000 British troops in support of the Egyptian Army being at Khartoum by the beginning of March. It will be most deplorable if the present situation of affairs is not taken advantage of by a vigorous pursuit of the enemy – ending with the complete breakup of the Khalifa's power. We have, and shall have, all the fun of the fair on the gunboats.[25]

Major Edward Stuart Wortley, Gunboat Flotilla

In a quite staggering achievement, the first train on the desert railway line reached Abu Hamed on 31 October.

That railway from Haifa to Abu Hamed is a monument of the skill and resources of the Sirdar. It is his idea and his only. The execution of the idea has been in the hands of very young men, some of them mere lads, all of them lieutenants. Girouard, a Canadian, Director of Army Railways, is a most able man. Macaulay, Traffic Manager, Pritchard and Hall, in charge of Survey, Stevenson in charge of workshops and repairs, and Blakeney, form a strong combination of powerful physique, technical knowledge and practical resource, with unlimited zeal and full of the determination and cheerfulness of youth. The railway is the all-important factor of this expedition.[26]

Major General Archibald Hunter, Governor Dongola Province

Kitchener was not done there and set them to work to push the line all the way to Berber. The logistical significance of this cannot be over-exaggerated, linking as it did Cairo with the front line at Berber.

There was still plenty of work for the Royal Navy gunboats, though. The Khalifa had despatched one of his emirs, Mahmud Ahmed, with a force of around 10,000 to occupy the Metemmeh forts. Here they stood, adopting a defensive posture. Kitchener despatched his gunboats to carry out a reconnaissance, which soon turned into a firefight on 16 October. With them was Beatty in the *Fateh*.

Sighted Metemmeh. Distinguished the forts, of which there were nine, but we soon found they only had one gun in each. The Dervish army collected on the top of the ridge to view the situation. Baggaras hovered round each fort; object I have no doubt was to keep the Egyptian gunners in the fort up to the mark, but we had the satisfaction of wiping out a couple of those sportsmen during the day's entertainment. As we approached, the fire became general with all the ships and forts, and soon the noise was terrific as we steamed slowly past. We made excellent shooting, hitting the forts every time, but they were very thick, and I do not think did them much harm. We steamed past all the forts and then turned round and steamed back, shelling the town and the ridge as well as the forts. The magnificent array on the top of the hill dwindled away rapidly before several well-placed shrapnel![27]

Lieutenant David Beatty, *Fateh*

Firing a mixture of high explosive and shrapnel shells, and lashing suitable targets with their Maxims, the gunboats must have created quite an impression. They returned the next day to repeat the dose.

We started again at 4 a.m. It was a very pretty sight to see the boats steaming past keeping up a strong fire which was answered by a much better fire than the previous day. Each flash showed up vividly against the fading darkness, while on the ridge behind the town the rising sun shone on the spears of the Dervish army, who were again watching the proceedings, but who again disappeared on receipt of a shrapnel shell. The fire of the forts became more vigorous as we retired, while the army again appeared, a great host waving many banners, led by a man on a white horse and wearing a white gibbah, who was surrounded by clouds of horsemen. I am sure they considered they had gained a great victory.[28]

Lieutenant David Beatty, *Fateh*

It was subsequently rumoured that the man on the white horse was Mahmud Ahmed himself.

The gunboats returned to keep an eye on Metemmeh on numerous occasions, making a thorough nuisance of themselves, and on 26 October, Beatty was even assigned war correspondents to accompany him on one raid.

> I was sent up with the correspondents to give them a run. Wortley came, and very thankful I was, as he fairly held the floor. I am sure they ought to look upon Metemmeh reconnaissance as second only to Trafalgar! I gave them a very heavy lunch and stuffed them as full as they would hold of stories.[29]
>
> Lieutenant David Beatty, *Fateh*

Beatty would always be adept at handling the gentlemen of the press.

In December the whole campaign was hanging in the balance. Berber was important, but to remain there was to invite a confrontation with the combined strength of the whole of the Khalifa's vast army, coupled with Osman Digna's forces from the Red Sea littoral. What were they to do? Consolidate at Berber as the new border of Egypt? Fall back to Abu Hamed, or even Wadi Halfa? Or obtain the British reinforcements which would be needed to allow Kitchener to smash his way home to break the Khalifa's power for good – and finally avenge Gordon? But that decision lay in London.

13

FORWARD TO ATBARA, 1898

For the next three days the whole force marched out into
the desert, and whilst continually practising square formations, prayed for the enemy to appear and come on; but the
wily Dervish 'was not for it', and finally, as Mahmud would
not come to the mountain, the mountain, represented by
the Anglo-Egyptian Army, had to go to seek him.[1]
Captain Granville Egerton, 1st Seaforth Highlanders, British Brigade

KITCHENER WAS WORRIED. He had achieved so much, but the main
Dervish armies had not been beaten and his forces at Berber
were vulnerable to a concerted attack. In December 1897, Reginald Wingate passed on intelligence reports that suggested that
the Khalifa was amassing around 40,000 soldiers at Omdurman,
with a further 20,000 further forward under Mahmud Ahmed
and Osman Digna. It was increasingly evident that the Egyptian Army was not large enough to meet the full strength of
the Khalifa. The demands for garrison forces at each stepping
stone on the way up the Nile had reduced the frontline strength
at Berber to just five battalions. The falling waters of the Nile
had also made the Fifth Cataract impassable, marooning their
gunboats on the far side, leaving them cut off from Abu Hamed,
and reliant on Fort Atbara as a naval base. But Atbara was clearly
vulnerable to a Dervish attack, something of which Major Ivor
Maxse was aware on a visit to the fort.

I believe I am the first Englishman who has crossed the
Atbara River for many a long year. It was very easily done

for that 400 yards wide stream is already so reduced that I rode across on a polo pony without seriously wetting my feet – at a point about half a mile from the junction with the Nile. This was on Xmas Eve. There is something in the wind, but I cannot make up my mind what it may turn out to be. All I know is that many reports have reached us from the south to the effect that the Khalifa boasts that, 'He will march north with all his forces and smite the unbeliever and the Turk and drive all Egyptians into the sea!' He has been saying this for many years, but on this occasion the Sirdar seems to attach more probability to the words than heretofore. For he is concentrating all the available strength of the Egyptian Army at or within reach of Berber and the various posts are being moderately fortified.[2]

Major Ivor Maxse, 13th Sudanese Battalion, 2nd Egyptian Brigade

Even when the railway reached Berber, Kitchener would still be reliant on the river or camels to get supplies up to Atbara. There was also an underlying threat to Kitchener's own position in that he desperately needed British battalions to add to his forces, but with them might come a new commander, just as Wolseley had been ceded control back in 1884–5. Perhaps someone like General Francis Grenfell, Kitchener's predecessor as Sirdar, and the newly appointed commander of the British Army of Occupation in Egypt, might be appointed to take over the expedition command? This idea should not have unduly bothered him, but he was after all, only human. Added to this fearsome cocktail of stress were the relentless activities of the 'bean counters' in Cairo and London pressurising him over every penny of the cost of the operations.

You have no idea what continued anxiety, worry, and strain I have through it all – I do not think I can stand much more, and feel sometimes so completely done up that I can hardly go on and wish I was dead.[3]

Major General Herbert Kitchener

A half-hearted resignation was the result, but Lord Cromer had the good sense to reject it, recognising the strain Kitchener was under. Then at last came positive news. On 23 December, Lord Salisbury accepted the representations of Kitchener and Cromer and authorised the release of British troops to sort out the Sudan once and for all. Finally on 4 January 1898, Kitchener's other nagging fear was allayed when he was confirmed as commander of the combined British and Egyptian expeditionary force.

The Khalifa was also suffering from problems which meant that the threatened advance by his main army based around Omdurman failed to materialise. Disputes among his commanders, coupled with confusion over a coherent strategy, caused delays and in the end they remained static. They therefore missed the opportunity to strike at Atbara and Berber before these could be properly reinforced.

In January 1898 the British battalions began to arrive. Even by rail the journey was still an amazing experience, as related by journalist George Steevens.

> The scenery, it must be owned, was monotonous, and yet not without haunting beauty. Mile on mile, hour on hour, we glided through sheer desert. Yellow sand to right and left – now stretching away endlessly, now a valley between small broken hills. Sometimes the hills sloped away from us, then they closed in again. Now they were diaphanous blue on the horizon, now soft purple as we ran under their flanks. But always they were steeped through and through with sun – hazy, immobile, silent. It looked like a part of the world quite new, with none of the bloom rubbed off. Straight, firm, and purposeful ran the rails. Now they split into a double line: here was another train waiting – a string of empty trucks – and also a tent, a little hut made of sleeper baulks, a tank, points, and a board with the inscription, 'No. 5.' This was a station – a wayside station. But 'No. 6' is a Swindon of the desert. Every train stops there half-an-hour

or more to fill up with water, for there is a great trifoliate well there. Also, the train changes drivers. And here, 100 miles into the heart of the Nubian desert, two years ago a sanctuary of inviolate silence, where no blade of green ever sprang, where, possibly, no foot trod since the birth of the world, here is a little colony of British engine-drivers. They have a little rest-house shanty of board and galvanised iron; there are pictures from the illustrated papers on the walls, and a pup at the door. There they swelter and smoke and spit and look out at the winking rails and the red-hot sand – and wait till their turn comes to take the train. They don't love the life (who would?) but they stick to it like Britons, and take the trains out and home. They, too, are not the meanest of the conquerors of the Sudan.[4]

George Steevens, *Daily Mail*

A camp was established at Guheish, about 17 miles south of Abu Hamed. Then Major General William Gatacre arrived, the man designated to command the British Brigade. His British battalions were armed with a new bolt action rifle – the Lee-Metford, which had a magazine capacity of ten rounds and could achieve a rate of fire that was roughly twice that of the old Martini-Henry rifle, the rifle still issued across the Egyptian Army. However, the stopping power of the Lee-Metford bullet was under question – the ability to drop a charging warrior in his tracks. Gatacre decided something had to be done.

The present-shaped bullet .303 Lee-Metford rifle has little stopping power. Well, we have only this class of ammunition, so I am altering the shape of the bullet to that of the Dum-Dum bullet, which has a rounded point. I do this by filing the point off. Before I left Cairo, I provided 400 files and small gauges to test the length of the altered bullet, and daily here we have 2,800 men engaged on this work. I borrowed fifty railway rails and mounted them flat side uppermost, to form anvils on which to file. We have a

portion of men unpacking, and another portion packing, so that the same men are always at the same work. The men are getting very sharp at it; it would make a capital picture.[5]
Major General William Gatacre, Headquarters, British Brigade

They were called 'Dum-Dum' bullets after early variations produced by the Dum-Dum Arsenal in India.

Gatacre was also very concerned at the poor quality of the boots issued to his men. The journalist George Steevens was also appalled and did not mince his words.

The boots our British boys were expected to march in had not even a toe-cap. So that when the three battalions and a battery arrived in Berber hundreds of men were all but barefoot: the soles peeled off, and instead of a solid double sole, revealed a layer of shoddy packing sandwiched between two thin slices of leather. It is always the same story – knavery and slackness clogging and strangling the best efforts of the British soldier. To save some contractor a few pence on a boot, or to save some War Office clerk a few hours of the work he is paid for not doing, you stand to lose a good rifle and bayonet in a decisive battle, and to break a good man's heart into the bargain. Is it worth it? But it is always happening; the history of the Army is a string of such disgraces. And each time we arise and bawl, 'Somebody ought to be hanged!' So says everybody. But nobody ever is hanged![6]
George Steevens, *Daily Mail*

Gatacre worked his men hard, exercising them out in the desert as often as possible. On 25 February his brigade had been out on yet another tactical exercise when the alarm was raised. Kitchener sent orders that the whole brigade was to march off to ensure they reached Berber within five days to prevent the Egyptian troops there being overrun by the advance of Mahmud.

We only got about 2½ hours sleep. Then we started off again at 9 p.m. Gatacre again telling us that our arriving in time was a life-or-death matter for the people at Berber, and that we must be there in four days. Halted at 2 a.m. for 1½ hours and got a little food and a snatch of sleep. Then off again. Marched till 6 a.m. and then halted. Officers and men fell down flat at once and went to sleep, as some of us had been dozing on the march and waking to find ourselves falling. Halted an hour, then on again till past 11 a.m. A scorching hot day: very heavy going in patches of deep sand; boots wearing out on the flinty desert; no water and everybody suffering from thirst. All very exhausted and the men falling out in scores. These were brought on by camel. When at last we sighted the Nile again about 11 a.m., there was a regular stampede for the water and we all waded in and drank, not caring whether it was pure or not.[7]

2nd Lieutenant Ronald Meiklejohn, 1st Royal Warwickshire Regiment, British Brigade

After this tough march, trudging mile after mile through the heavy shifting sands, the Nile was as good as a crystal fountain. When they finally got to Berber, they found to their chagrin that the emergency was perhaps not quite as had been imagined.

We hear that our 'forced march' and all the talk of saving Berber was mainly Gatacre's imagination. We were not expected to arrive for another week at least, and our confidence in him is shaken. He has the reputation of wearing out his troops unnecessarily. Rather done up after the long march, but Gatacre still keeps us all on the move. Rumours – possibly Gatacre's – that the Dervish cavalry were near our camp last night, so we had to build a strong zeriba of mimosa – camel thorn – all-round the camp and had orders to fire on anyone trying to break through or remove it.[8]

2nd Lieutenant Ronald Meiklejohn, 1st Royal Warwickshire Regiment, British Brigade

***

AS THE BRITISH BATTALIONS MOVED UP THE NILE, the Egyptian Army was being concentrated in the Berber area, with a brigade despatched forward to Atbara. Meanwhile, instead of his whole massed army, the Khalifa had ordered forward just Mahmud Ahmed and Osman Digna, with a combined force of some 16,000 infantry and 4,000 horsemen, hoping to catch Kitchener unprepared for a thrust on Berber. For the Dervishes it was too little too late. On 10 February, Mahmud began crossing the Nile from Metemmeh to concentrate his forces at Shendi on the east bank, but the shortage of river transport meant this was not completed until 25 February. They then marched north, before cutting across 40 miles of bleak desert towards the fording point at Hudi on the Atbara River, with the intention of swinging round and outflanking Atbara Fort to strike direct at Berber. However, the delays cost them, giving Kitchener time to receive and assess the intelligence reports from his gunboats and spies. Having learnt that Mahmud was heading for Hudi, he decided to forestall him. On 20 March, Kitchener ordered the whole of his Anglo-Egyptian Army forward to the Hudi crossing point. By this time, he had one British brigade, three Egyptian brigades, several Egyptian cavalry squadrons, four artillery batteries and ten Maxim machine guns – in all totalling about 12,000 men.

On arrival at Hudi, the whole army set about building a strong overnight zeriba. By this time many of the men in the British Brigade were chafing under what they considered to be Gatacre's over-fussy precautions. One consequence was a mad moment during a false alarm of a Dervish attack on the night of 20/21 March.

Gatacre had impressed on us that we might now be attacked at any moment, with lurid descriptions of hordes of dervishes suddenly rushing us with sword and spear – and had succeeded in making the men thoroughly jumpy. We all had to sleep EXACTLY in the centre of our command

– company or section – with our feet to the zeriba, the great idea being that we should then automatically spring up facing the enemy. The men, as usual, had to sleep with their arms through the slings of their rifles, while officers had to have their sword knots round their right wrist, and their revolver at their left hand. Half the men had to be awake all night while subalterns had to take an hour's duty patrolling all sentries. My tour was from 1 till 2 a.m. so I rolled up in my blanket and went to sleep. About 10.30 p.m. I woke suddenly hearing the sentry shout, 'Stand to everyone! They're on us!'.[9]

2nd Lieutenant Ronald Meiklejohn, 1st Royal Warwickshire Regiment, British Brigade

He found a situation of utter chaos, triggered by a jittery sentry and culminating in the roar of musketry all along the side of the camp facing the desert.

I jumped up hastily, drawing my sword and revolver, and my company fixed bayonets, the men behaving most coolly, though there was a good deal of noise and shouting going on in other parts. The river showed up indistinctly below the steep banks and we waited rather breathlessly. Some bird flew off with a raucous cry and, later, a crocodile plunged heavily into a pool. The company wit remarking in a stage whisper, 'Blimey, old Mahmud's fallen in. 'ope he gets a good wetting!' Then, later, 'Pass the word to Mahmud to 'urry up. We're getting tired! Tell him to put it off till tomorrow!' The whole thing was a false alarm. Apparently, a donkey which had strayed outside the zeriba tried to make its way back, and brayed opposite a young sentry of the Lincolns, who promptly opened magazine fire. The picquets joined in, and the Seaforth Highlanders charged a small group of Lincolns, bayoneting two men. We got well chaffed by the officers of the Egyptian and Sudanese armies, who, incidentally, as usual, had all turned in in pyjamas, and Gatacre was very angry. Yet the whole affair was entirely due to his continual talk of our being attacked at any moment, and the unnecessary strain he puts on all of us.[10]

2nd Lieutenant Ronald Meiklejohn, 1st Royal Warwickshire Regiment, British Brigade

Generals were condemned for inadequate precautions; but also condemned for too many. One does have some sympathy here for Gatacre!

Once Mahmud Ahmed and Osman Digna realised the strength of the forces amassed against them they avoided Hudi and moved a further 30 miles up the Atbara to an alternative fording point at the small village of Nakhula. Here Osman Digna and the inexperienced Emir were in a quandary. Already at loggerheads, they had to review their options, which had been greatly limited by Kitchener's forward defensive blocking move: should they risk everything by a death or glory attack on the well defended Anglo-Egyptian zeriba; retreat back across the desert in ignominy to Metemmeh; or create their own zeriba fortress and hope to defeat any attack launched by Kitchener? It was this last option they chose, digging trenches and erecting a well-hidden strong zeriba a mile downstream of Nakhula, with its back to the north bank of the Atbara River, which was by this time of year almost dried up. Kitchener was not quite sure of his opponents' exact location and on 22 March edged further up the Atbara to the small village of Ras el Hudi, some 20 miles from Nakhula. From here he ordered his Egyptian cavalry on a series of forward reconnaissance patrols.

***

THE LURE OF ACTIVE SERVICE IN THE SUDAN was a beacon to every thrusting young officer in the British Army. If they had an ounce of ambition, they used all their influence to get themselves sent to the front. As a result, it is no surprise to find some of the

very best of this generation of officers were attached to the
expedition, seeking berths wherever they could find them. It is
fascinating to read the impressions of Kitchener as a commander
in chief from men who would themselves be army commanders
in the Great War just a few years later. One such was Douglas
Haig who had been posted out to the Egyptian cavalry. He soon
noticed that the Sirdar was not a natural delegator; Kitchener
liked to operate the levers of command himself. He was also
taciturn to the point of silence; something Haig himself would
be accused of in later days.

> He is a man that does everything himself and, in fact, has
> no headquarters staff at all! Indeed, General Hunter who
> has come to command the troops in the field cannot get
> the Sirdar to tell him what his position in the army is! In
> addition, the Sirdar is most silent, and no one has ever the
> slightest notion what is going to be done until he gives his
> orders! He has two aides-de-camp who have a hardish time,
> but beyond them he employs no staff at all. Sometimes it
> might be better for the comfort of the troops if he had a
> staff, but on the whole things get along very well and we
> cavalry get a pretty free hand.[11]
> Captain Douglas Haig, Egyptian Cavalry

Haig was not quite right, as Kitchener did have a small staff,
among which was another future army commander, Captain
Henry Rawlinson, who had been appointed as deputy assistant
adjutant general to Kitchener's forces.

> I think that I get on all right with Kitchener ['K']. I was
> told that he was a queer customer, but I have never failed
> to hit it off with anyone who means business, as he cer-
> tainly does. His is a curious and very strong character. I
> both like and admire him, but on some minor points he is
> as obstinate as a commissariat mule. He is a long-headed,
> clear-minded man of business, with a wonderful memory.

His apparent hardness of nature is a good deal put on, and is, I think, due to a sort of shyness. It made him unpopular at first, but, since those under him in the Egyptian Army have come to realise what a thoroughly capable man he is, there is a great deal less growling than there used to be. I heard a great deal, before I came up here, about the sketchy way in which the Egyptian Army managed their affairs, and their shilly-shally arrangements for supply. I am certain that, as far as management goes, they are very much maligned. Perhaps they err a little on the side of having too small a staff, just as the British Army errs on the side of having too many cooks. K is keeping down expenses all he can and won't pay for a staff officer until he can't do without him.[12]

Captain Henry Rawlinson, Headquarters

Rawlinson points to both the amazing administrative abilities of Kitchener as a 'one-man-show' at the centre of everything that was happening, but also to the risks of this dependence on just one man.

If anything were to happen to the Sirdar there would be chaos, as no one but he knows the state of preparedness in which the various departments are. He keeps all informa-tion regarding the details of railways, transport, steamers, supply and intelligence in his own hands, and shows won-derful skill in working the various strings. Everything works smoothly and well, as he is at the head of affairs, but he does too much and may break down if he is not hit. I am trying to work out plans to relieve him of much of the detail which he does himself, and so far with some success. He is full of brains and, if he can be induced to see that a certain amount of method and regularity are abso-lutely essential in a large army, he will one day be a very big man. Here he is an absolute autocrat, does exactly what he pleases, and won't pay any attention to red-tape regulations, or to the keeping of records of telegrams and letters. He rarely keeps a copy of any telegram or letter that he writes, and tries to prevent me from doing so, but he never, by any chance, forgets what he said or his motive in saying it. Despite, or perhaps in consequence of, the absence of red tape, things run smoothly. There is little or no correspondence, except by wire, and in the field almost every order is given verbally. Personally, I think this is carrying things too far and may, someday, lead to some bad misunderstanding in a crisis, but I admit that we in the British service go to the other extreme and, as a rule, write far too many orders. The system works because of K's wonderful memory and because they are all good men in the Egyptian Army. He has got the pick of the service, and they understand him, and he them.[13]

Captain Henry Rawlinson, Headquarters

One characteristic of the Sirdar was his hatred of the gentlemen of the press. He had made efforts to ban them, then having had that overturned he sought to restrict their opportunities as much as possible.

We correspondents are not allowed out on reconnaissances and have to conform to very strict rules from the Sirdar. Quite right, for we are in the heart of an enemy's country, and spies are all round. In fact, one of my servants is an ex-Dervish, and none of us know who may not be a spy of the Khalifa. The correspondent of the *Daily News* and he of the London *Daily Mail* have joined together in a mess. In a sense we are not deadly competitors, and it is the only way we can get on with some measure of comfort. We have a couple of horses each, a riding camel each, and about a dozen baggage camels. Of course, a little army of camel-men, horsemen, and personal servants. We had to bring up from Cairo, 2,000 miles away, large supplies, but unhappily these are getting scarce, and today Scudamore, the mess president, reported with tears in his eyes that our titbits in the way of tinned delicacies are exhausted, and we have fallen back on bully beef and army rations. If only Mahmud would come out and get smashed, we might get back to the Nile and into communication with Greek and English settlers, who would renew our supplies. The weather is hot – only 115 degrees in the shade! It is trying. I have been ill two or three times with 'liver' but I trust to pull through.[14]

William Kinnaird Rose, *Reuters*

There was also a story of the greatest journalist of them all, that slightly undermines faith in his exciting despatches from the front.

Old Bennet Burleigh of the *Daily Telegraph* who likes his liquor greatly, discovered he had no more whisky, so decided to go to Dakheila to get some, giving as an excuse the sending off of important despatches. He started off early on his 30-mile journey with his servant, on donkeys. Two hours later a wild and shaking figure arrived breathless at the outpost line. He said he had been chased 10 miles by Dervish cavalry who had fired volleys at him. He feared his servant had been killed. Later on, however, his servant rode calmly in on his donkey. It seems that the Egyptian cavalry saw two individuals on donkeys and sent a patrol to find out who they were, but, on their retiring rapidly, abandoned the chase. The firing was pure imagination, the results of too much whisky.[15]

2nd Lieutenant Ronald Meiklejohn, 1st Royal Warwickshire Regiment, British Brigade

A story that reveals almost too much.

***

THE IMPORTANCE OF CAVALRY SEEMS CONTROVERSIAL to the modern mind. But in 1898 there were few other ways of finding out what the enemy were doing or even where they, were. Aircraft were some years in the future and balloons and desert thorn bushes did not mix as they had found at Suakin. On 30 March, Major General Archibald Hunter went forward with a strong cavalry force to probe the exact position and nature of Mahmud's zeriba fortress.

> From observation, their camp is an oblong with right corner rounded off and slightly projecting, entrenched along its right and front faces, stockaded at intervals and covered in front with a strong zeriba, the zeriba of the front face lay at the foot of a slope whose crest had an elevation of about 20 feet, and distant from the crest line varying from 200 to 30 yards. Crest line of slope was intersected by two distant depressions. Two suitable positions for artillery to bombard this camp were noted. The exact length of the front face and the position of the left face were not accurately observed. I rode with Watson to nearer than 300 yards of the right and tried to provoke them to fire in order to judge of the line of the trenches inside, but they kept close down and only showed their heads and evidently waited for us to come on. The interior of camp thickly grown with bush: a bell of dom palms prevented forming any idea of rear face. By the dust, I put front face to be 1,200 yards long, and camp 1,000 yards deep.[16]
>
> Major General Archibald Hunter, Headquarters, Egyptian Division

Strangely, Kitchener chose this moment to have a crisis of confidence in his own leadership abilities. Faced with the prospect of launching a frontal assault on a well-fortified zeriba, he wavered, not able to decide whether to take the plunge and accept the inevitable heavy casualties. He consulted Hunter and Gatacre, and as might be expected, the latter was all 'gung ho', while Hunter was more cautious. Kitchener then appealed to a civilian

– Lord Cromer – back in Cairo for advice. This was frankly ridiculous and that experienced civil servant, recognising his limits, passed on the appeal to both the Egypt commander in chief, Grenfell, and the prime minister Lord Salisbury back in far off London. How they were meant to judge the efficacy of an attack on a zeriba they had never seen is puzzling. The answers received were splendid: the politician dodged the issue saying Kitchener should follow his instincts, in other words he was no help at all, while the professional soldier backed the much-respected Hunter's caution. Having received this advice Cromer duly passed it along, only to find Hunter had changed his mind and now had joined Gatacre in urging an attack. Doubtless cursing, Cromer then changed his advice and at long last Kitchener steeled himself for the fray. It had been a curious affair.

While Kitchener was wavering, the battalions did not neglect last-minute training for an assault on the Dervish zeriba.

> During these days the British Brigade assiduously practised advancing in line and firing on the move, a form of attack which General Gatacre had decided to adopt. Further, every expedient and idea that could be thought of was discussed and practised for making our way through the enemy's zeriba. Some extraordinary wild-cat schemes were evolved by enterprising individuals; ropes and grapnels to pull it down with; improvised ladders with which to cross it; blankets and hides to throw on the top of it – two or three camel loads of freshly skinned hides very nearly poisoned the whole brigade one hot day – and so on. One unfortunate Sudanese battalion was sent by its commanding officer at our own zeriba, and went through it, I believe, as through a paper hoop; but at a cost![17]
> Captain Granville Egerton, 1st Seaforth Highlanders, British Brigade

On Sunday 3 April, they lined up for church parade and to hear what had become the traditional bloodthirsty exhortation from Gatacre.

We had the hymn 'Soldiers of Christ Arise'; which was sung enthusiastically, and after the sermon General Gatacre made a speech in which he surpassed all previous efforts. He described the zeriba as 8 to 10 feet high and enormously thick and strong, held by thousands of terrible warriors, who, we gathered, were certain to get in among us. He ended by saying that some of us might think we had an easy task; others might picture wading ankle deep in blood; actually, we were more likely to find ourselves knee-deep in it before next Sunday. To anyone who did not know Gatacre it might have had a most depressing effect, and not calculated to cheer the spirits of troops or improve their morale. Actually, nobody took it very seriously, and we were all rather amused.[18]

2nd Lieutenant Ronald Meiklejohn, 1st Royal Warwickshire Regiment, British Brigade

On 5 April, the still cautious Kitchener ordered Hunter to make a second recce of the zeriba, this time accompanied by the whole of Lieutenant Colonel Robert Broadwood's Egyptian Cavalry Brigade, accompanied by horse artillery and two Maxim batteries.

Moved by lower line nearer to Atbara than before. Observed much more dust and movement than last time – enemy's cavalry 700 strong came out from upstream side of camp at 8.30 – gave them Maxims, forced them back to the bush by 9 a.m. Same time 500 cavalry came on at the gallop from downstream of their camp and looked as if they meant business but halted within 300 yards of us. Previous 700 cavalry again advanced and their infantry from front face of camp, and at least 1,500 strong came out and closed to 600 yards and opened fire. By edging round the two forces of hostile cavalry had got quite round us.[19]

Major General Archibald Hunter, Headquarters, Egyptian Division

Haig was there acting as a liaison officer, linking together the squadrons as they retired from the trap that had been sprung on them.

The horsemen which we had already repulsed advanced up a sort of dip in the ground and came round our flank from upstream. The Dervish infantry left their trenches and came at top speed towards us. And the cavalry which had gone down stream came directly across our line of retreat. Broad-wood gave me the order to see to the safety of the guns which meantime were trotting gaily on to the rear. I went direct to the Maxims and told them they must come into action against the most threatening of the enemy (which I indicated) as soon as the cavalry cleared their field of fire. I then went off to Broadwood (who was still in front) to get him to lead the cavalry to a flank. I met him coming back with Mahon's squadrons which were now pretty unsteady – as well they might be for the infantry was round their flank and only 500 yards off and firing like blazes. Broadwood at once led off the cavalry to the flank and the Maxims were able to open fire. This saved us for the moment, and the squadron again being steadied, we were able to fight our way out of the reach of infantry fire. Had the Dervish horsemen been all the papers say of them, we would never have got away. Fortunately, they ran away the moment we showed a bold front and only came on when we turned our backs. Our casualties were pretty severe thirty and ten killed. We had over twenty horses shot and many wounded.[20]
Captain Douglas Haig, Egyptian Cavalry

One very minor incident occurring during the brisk skirmish was later blown up out of all proportion, although Haig himself made light of it.

When the squadrons were returning just before the Maxims came into action, I was able to pick up a poor devil of an

Egyptian who was wounded in the shoulder and had given himself up for lost and put him in front of my saddle and carried him to the guns where we had some spare horses and the doctor. This is quite the gymkhana style of things which you used to see in India! In doing this I did not incur the slightest danger tho' there is no doubt that had I not taken this man the Dervishes would have got him.[21]

Captain Douglas Haig, Egyptian Cavalry

Back at the zeriba, the battalions were taking it in turns to have a bath in the river. The alarm as the cavalry returned resulted in a surrealistic 'call to arms' ready for action.

We suddenly heard heavy firing a mile or two away. Then the, 'Retire!' 'Fall-in!' and 'Double!' were sounded in rapid succession. Snow, the brigade major, galloped up and shouted out, 'Line the opposite bank at once!' Everybody dashed hastily out of the water, seized belts and rifles, and made for the high ground. We were a quaint crowd when we threw ourselves down on the crest of the rise! I person-ally had my sword and revolver, boots, helmet and trousers. Some were in a state of nature, save for a helmet, and there was every type of variation. Most of the Camerons had only kilts, in which they maintained they always 'fought'. The sun was blazing hot, and mimosa thorns most unpleas-ant in our scanty attire. Gradually the firing died down, and we could go back and retrieve the rest of our kit.[22]

2nd Lieutenant Ronald Meiklejohn, 1st Royal Warwickshire Regiment, British Brigade

After the dust had died down, the splendidly choleric Hunter was not happy when he considered what had happened, which left him teetering at the end of his tether with Kitchener.

This 5th April business was within an ace at one time of being disastrous. There was no purpose to be gained by sending me second time to reconnoitre. It was a certainty I could learn no more than I had already discovered on 30 March. The force sent with me was neither one nor the other. A reconnaissance is meant to acquire information and should be carried out by a few picked men on picked horses, moving by night if possible, observing by day, and galloping away if discovered trusting to their legs. The only other way to gain news is to go strong enough to get it in spite of the enemy, strong enough to fight him if needs be, which means to be backed up by infantry. Then you can withdraw in decency and carry off your wounded without trouble. On the 5th I was too strong to run away and not strong enough to drive his infantry back. The Sirdar wanted to know if the enemy were still *in situ*. I could tell him that, by not going nearer than 2 miles off by the dust.[23]

Major General Archibald Hunter, Headquarters, Egyptian Division

On 6 April, the Anglo-British forces edged further forward to Umdabiya, just 8 miles from Mahmud's position.

At 10 a.m., we got orders that we were to parade at 5 p.m. and attack Mahmud at dawn tomorrow. The Sirdar ended his order with the words 'The Sirdar feels absolutely certain that every man will do his duty. He has only these words to say, "Remember Gordon. The men before you are his murderers!"' We also got verbal orders to be careful of passing any enemy wounded, as their trick was to feign death and then stab from behind. Even the genuinely wounded might do this. If a man held up his hands he was to be spared.[24]

2nd Lieutenant Ronald Meiklejohn, 1st Royal Warwickshire Regiment, British Brigade

Then a couple of unintended comic moments as the British Brigade officers coped with their bombastic leader.

General Gatacre came round and spoke to each battalion. The conversation was typical and ran something as follows: General Gatacre, 'Now they all understand that they have to go straight through everything?' Major Quayle-Jones, 'Oh yes. Sir!' General G, 'If they come to a stone wall 10 feet high, the first company will go through it and the others follow!' Major Q-J, 'Yes, sir. We'll do it!' General G, 'There must be no firing in the zeriba. Only bayonets!' Major Q-J, 'Yes, sir!' General G, 'And they are not to stop for anything till they reach the river!' Major Q-J, 'All right, Sir, I'll stop them there!' It struck us as curiously reminiscent of a 'Punch and Judy' show.[25]

2nd Lieutenant Ronald Meiklejohn, 1st Royal Warwickshire Regiment, British Brigade

But the Battle of Atbara would be no laughing matter.

14

THE BATTLE OF ATBARA, 8 APRIL 1898

I overheard the observation from Egyptian, Soudanese, and English, that on 8th April 1898, Khartoum, the wrongs and massacre of 1884–5, and Gordon's death would be avenged. Nay, without exaggeration or stating anything outside of what was thought and said by officers and men, the whole army's watchword was: 'Remember Gordon and Khartoum!'[1]

Bennett Burleigh, *Daily Telegraph*

KITCHENER HAD DILLIED AND DALLIED, but the time had come for action. His resolve had been stiffened and he was now resolved to launch an attack on the Dervish zeriba. After two days of intensive preparations the army set off at around 19.00 on 7 April, leaving just the baggage to be guarded by some Egyptian infantry. They marched out in an echelon formation of squares, led by Gatacre's British Brigade, followed by the three Egyptian Brigades.

At 9 p.m., a halt was called, water was served out from camel-tanks and the men lay down to rest on the open desert, protected by vigilant sentries. A bitterly cold wind drove clouds of fine sand across the landscape and any soldier who strayed from his post would have had a difficulty in finding it again. The moon rose early and illumined the weird scene of thousands of uneasy sleepers lying in curious attitudes beside their rifles, in death-like silence, rank by rank. The reserve ammunition-mules and

artillery pack-mules received special attention to prevent them braying when the moon appeared. At one o'clock the march was resumed, and those who saw it will not forget the strange sight and stranger sound of thousands of soldiers rising from the ground and stealthily moving forward in ordered array – with no word uttered above a whisper. Only the grating and monotonous crunch of shoe-leather on dry sand could be heard and it had a sinister sound, though none could foretell the event. At four there was another halt, but the bitter cold prevented sleep and only the glow of the enemy's fires visible above some distant palms afforded a point of interest to the waiting soldiery.[2]
Major Ivor Maxse, 13th Sudanese Battalion, 2nd Egyptian Brigade

As ever, Bennett Burleigh just happened to be listening when two of the men made the perfect remarks to sum up the mood for the readers back home. You couldn't make it up, though perhaps Burleigh did!

It was whilst walking softly, so as not to disturb light sleepers, that I overheard a sentimental Seaforth Highlander say to a comrade, 'Ah, Tam, how many thousands there are at home across the sea thinking o' us the night!' 'Right, Sandy,' replied his chum. 'And how many millions there are that don't care a damn! Go to sleep, you fool!' And silence again fell.[3]
Bennett Burleigh, *Daily Telegraph*

At 01.00, the soldiers were roused and the advance recommenced, to cover the remaining 3 miles to the Dervish zeriba.

We moved on slowly. In places there was a wonderful aromatic scent from some desert vegetation. The night was brilliantly star-lit, and one could distinguish the masses of men moving slowly through the darkness. We speculated on what was before us. Some feared Mahmud might retire without fighting; others maintained we had a very stiff job to carry out. About 5 a.m. we halted for an hour about 1 mile from the enemy. Day and I lay down together to keep warm and tried to sleep. But we soon woke feeling very cold, and walked up and down to get warm. Gradually dawn came, and the order to rise was whispered along. No lights were allowed and words of command had to be given in a whisper. Then we moved off, getting our fighting formation. Soon we saw large fires appear in the valley beneath and realised that the enemy were still there! A huge flock of vultures, about 200, rose just on our left. They had doubtless gathered for the offal from the Dervish camp, but it looked as if they realised they would soon have a feast.[4]

2nd Lieutenant Ronald Meiklejohn, 1st Royal Warwickshire Regiment, British Brigade

They formed up with Broadwood's Egyptian cavalry taking station guarding the left flank, then the British Brigade, two batteries of artillery, with 1st Egyptian Brigade (Lieutenant Colonel Hector MacDonald) in the middle, and on the right, the 2nd Egyptian Brigade (Lieutenant Colonel John Maxwell), while the 3rd Egyptian Brigade (Lieutenant Colonel David Lewis) would follow up and act as a reserve. By this time, they were only about 600 yards from the zeriba. The defences were quite formidable, consisting of a 1½ mile bush zeriba behind which was a palm tree palisade and a series of layered rifle pits each holding two or three men. The area was some 600 yards deep with the rear given some protection by a thickly wooded area of palm trees and the dry riverbed.

At around 06.15 the artillery opened up a bombardment designed to 'soften up' the Dervish resistance.

The infantry sat down to watch the opening of the battle by the artillery. Three mule-batteries and the horse-artillery took part, twenty-four guns in all. 'Thud! Phutt!' went the first discharge, and we all looked hard as the shell burst well above the entrenchments in the middle of the enemy's camp. A pale-yellow flash in the midst of a ball of white smoke marked the exact spot, and then the 'Crack!' of the explosion came faintly back, like an echo, from the smoky-grey mist which hung over the place. That first gun resembled a toy explosion in a toy battle, but when report followed report in quick succession and the air above the trenches became dotted with white puffs dealing out shrapnel bullets, and the cannonade grew ever louder as the projectiles were multiplied, one realised that serious business was on hand. Then gradually, the strange scene became almost monotonous, and many a weary infantry-man dozed into sleep, while the Egyptian gunners plied their trade and searched with the precision of their arm the whole interior of the circular encampment.[5]

Major Ivor Maxse, 13th Sudanese Battalion, 2nd Egyptian Brigade

The firebrand, Lieutenant David Beatty, was keen to get his naval rocket troop into action but was at first thwarted.

The artillery moved out to the front of the line and com-menced a tremendous fire on their position and enveloped the whole place in a shower of shot and shell. Every single part of the camp seemed to be under fire at the same time. I with the rocket tube first occupied a position on the left of the artillery, but the distance was too great and the ground unsuitable, so I moved off to the right of the line, where I was able to get within 300 yards, but was ordered back to 400 yards. Here we did a certain amount of execution, firing the village in four places.[6]

Lieutenant David Beatty, HMS *Fateh*

Early on the Dervish horsemen made a demonstration but were soon dissuaded from approaching too close.

Enemy's cavalry came out of bush upstream, probably

2,000 strong, advanced towards our cavalry, received heavy Maxim fire and were driven back into bush, and took no more part in operations, confirming what I said of them, that they were 'perfectly cowed by the superiority of our cavalry and the effect of Maxims' fire.'[7]

Major General Archibald Hunter, Headquarters, Egyptian Division

When Kitchener judged the moment was right, he ordered the advance.

At 7.15 a.m., the infantry were ordered to form in column for assault; the British were disposed in three columns, covered by a battalion in line with the Maxims on the left, whilst the Egyptian force had in each brigade two battalions, covering a central assaulting column in double companies, with extreme right flank well protected. One battalion of the reserve brigade formed square in a central position round the transport and water, leaving two battalions in rear of the extreme left flank. At 7.40 a.m., I sounded the general advance.[8]

Major General Herbert Kitchener, Headquarters

The Cameron Highlanders advanced in line in front of the other three battalions. At their head was Major General William Gatacre.

Between you and me, a general officer should not get up into the firing line of his brigade without good reason; this I know, but I had good reasons for going there. When your whole brigade only covers a space of 200 yards by 200 yards, it is immaterial where you are, so far as the penetration of bullets is concerned, but what is important is that the GOC should be where he can watch any important point.[9]

Major General William Gatacre, Headquarters, British Brigade

To the left of the British Brigade, in column, were the Warwickshires acting as a flank guard. Although a subaltern, 2nd

Lieutenant Ronald Meiklejohn had been charged with protect-
ing the vital Maxims during the advance.

> Silently and slowly we moved forward, wondering when
> the enemy would open fire, but still ominous silence
> reigned. Then we moved up a gentle rise, at the top of
> which we found ourselves looking down on the zeriba
> some 300 yards from us. Still no sound. The Union Jack
> was flying gaily in the centre of the Camerons. Then, on
> the top of the rise the 'Halt!' sounded, and we opened fire,
> the front-rank kneeling and the rear standing. There was a
> terrific roar of musketry, as 12,000 rifles and twelve Maxims
> swept the enemy position, and almost immediately the
> Dervishes replied.[10]
>
> 2nd Lieutenant Ronald Meiklejohn, 1st Royal Warwickshire Regiment,
> British Brigade

They were braced for casualties but the Dervish return fire did
not have a crushing impact. That is not to say there were no
casualties. And for most of them it was the first time under fire.

> I suddenly heard shrill notes which for a couple of seconds
> I imagined might be birds calling; then an angry buzz past
> me rather like some huge infuriated bee. Yet I was so taken
> up directing the fire of my company that I did not grasp its
> significance. But a few seconds later there was a clatter, and
> I saw one of my company roll over on the ground, while
> shouts for stretcher bearers came from different parts of
> the line. Then, in a flash I realised that the sounds were
> Dervish bullets, and it was not too pleasant! One or two
> more men collapsed suddenly. I heard another grim clatter
> behind me and saw Private Power lying on his face. I halted
> my men at the guns and gave the order for section volleys,
> then went for a second to Power and told him a stretcher
> was coming and he would be all right. A red patch was
> slowly spreading on the front of his tunic and his face was

dead white. He only said, 'They've done for me, sir!'[11]
2nd Lieutenant Ronald Meiklejohn, 1st Royal Warwickshire Regiment,
British Brigade

The British would not be first into the zeriba. Some accounts attempt to obfuscate this, but it would be the Sudanese battalions of Hunter's Egyptian Division that hit home first. Lieutenant Colonel Charles Townshend was at the forefront of the battle with his battalion.

> We advanced with bayonets fixed, drums beating and colours flying – it was a grand sight! I dashed through the ranks, leading the battalion about 30 yards ahead, the men following excellently. General Hunter was riding along in the front rank of the battalion, for he accompanied the 12th Sudanese in the assault, cheering them on. A lot of men were firing as I called on the 12th to charge, waving them on. They broke into a rush with cheers, and we swept into the position through the zeriba. How I wasn't hit I don't know, for the Dervishes must have been firing at me. I was well ahead, and the bullets were cutting the ground all about me. They did not run till we were about 30 yards from them. It was a splendid charge. We were in first by a long way. The day before I had determined in my own mind to be first in and to show everyone that the 12th were second to none. I had the chance (as I had had at Chitral) and I took advantage of it.[12]
> Lieutenant Colonel Charles Townshend, 12th Sudanese Battalion, 2nd Egyptian Brigade

His men tore their way through the thorns.

> The disorder was great when we had got through the zeriba, a bickering fire was being kept up on us from the interior trenches. All companies were mixed up except the two reserve companies. I now collected a crowd and rushed the second line of trenches, after keeping up a short hot fire on

them. Two or three mines exploded on us: one of our men had the top of his head blown off: this makes me think that they must have been a sort of fougasse loaded with stones. We kept on surging through the crowd, carrying two or three lines of trenches by rushes and arrived on the riverbank.[13]
Lieutenant Colonel Charles Townshend, 12th Sudanese Battalion, 2nd Egyptian Brigade

Whatever one's opinion of Townshend, he is preferable to the appalling sentiments of another British officer who clearly espouses the sort of underlying racism which underpinned many Victorians' attitude to Africans, whichever side they were fighting on.

Inside, there was no stopping the blacks, who rushed about, and looted and shot their rifles off in the air, danced and behaved as the monkey, which they really are, they are certainly not men.[14]
Lieutenant Felix Ready, 2nd Egyptian Battalion, 1st Egyptian Brigade

It was only shortly afterwards that the Cameron Highlanders reached the zeriba to the left of the Sudanese battalions.

For the arduous task of pulling the thorns away we were served with skin gloves and sacks and blankets. We were dismissed with the request by the Sirdar to 'Remember Gordon', and as the sequel proved he was remembered. When we reached the zeriba it was torn away like straw, the men didn't bother about the skin gloves and such like but went at it with bare hands. Our gallant Captain Finlay was killed at the first trench. He leaped into the trench and killed two with his claymore – and was then speared and shot. The pipers were playing 'The Cameron Men' just behind us, and Piper Stewart was shot dead and the piper-major got a bullet through his helmet, while a bullet went through another piper's helmet and parted his hair. It cost us dear, seventeen

of our regiment being killed. I got a bullet through my kilt
and another through the sleeve of my jacket.[15]

Private J. W. Smith, 1st Cameron Highlanders, British Brigade

Meiklejohn was one of the first in his company to reach the
zeriba and was relieved to find it did not match prior descriptions.

The much-vaunted zeriba, which Gatacre had led us to
esteem such a terrible obstacle, was a miserable affair. A
few branches of camel thorns tangled together only 4 foot
high and a few feet thick. I had my sword in my right hand
and my revolver in my left and had stuck my sword scabbard through my Sam Browne belt to keep it from dangling
about my legs. I took a flying leap at the zeriba, but something caught at the top and I fell sprawling inside. I heard
a voice from my company just behind say, 'Blimey, he's
copped it!' A bullet whacked into the ground unpleasantly
close to my head and I was up in a moment. I saw two
Camerons bending over an officer just on my left. Close by
me was a Dervish gun, with several dead gunners beside it.
About 6 yards beyond the zeriba was a ditch and straggling
stockade – and here we met some of the enemy. My men
gave a cheer, and somebody shouted, 'Now you're into
them Warwickshire lads! Stick every mother's son!' There
was some angry work with bayonets and rifles.[16]

2nd Lieutenant Ronald Meiklejohn, 1st Royal Warwickshire Regiment,
British Brigade

Once they were in the zeriba, it was a brutal business. Whether
they had been told to take no prisoners seems a moot point, but
many of the men certainly professed to believe they had been
given licence to kill.

Wounded or no, bayonets were shoved through anything
human in the most brutal and cold-blooded fashion.
Instance – a man (Dervish) dropped his weapons and

threw up his arms for mercy in front of one of the 79th [Cameron Highlanders] who turned round and appealed to a sergeant who said, 'Put him out of misery, Sandy. We don't want none of these buggers 'ere!' The private turned round and bayoneted him through the neck and again through the back as he fell. However, there is only one thing to be said that one must remember what perfect devils these Dervishes are – their frightful cruel habits – Gordon's murder.[17]

Lieutenant Samuel Cox, 1st Lincolnshire Regiment, British Brigade

Fear also played a part in it, for showing mercy could endanger one's own life. Soldiers would take no chances, even when facing helpless camp followers.

They lashed out right and left, they were sticking spears into our men and cutting away at our men with swords, and our men were shooting them down like dogs, and pinning them to the ground with bayonets. Just where I was standing there came a big black woman flinging a great sword about smothered with blood, and I was going to bayonet her, but a fellow standing by me said, 'Don't do that to a woman!' So, I let her by, but the next moment I looked around just in time to see her cut an officer's head straight off, and then one of our fellows shot her down. After that I showed no mercy. I bayoneted every man, woman, and child that came near – for even the children were throwing spears. Oh dear, it was a sight I shall never forget. There were dead and dying all over the place, and the trenches were piled up to the top with blacks, and even our boots and clothes were saturated with blood and brains.[18]

Anon. Private 'D' Company, Royal Warwickshire Regiment, British Brigade

The fighting broke up into countless little individual duels; life or death for one or the other. It all happened so quickly.

I glimpsed one man in the ditch raise his rifle at me. I spun round and fired at him with my revolver at about 10 yards – and saw a spurt of dust fly up just beside his shoulder. Simultaneously a flash came from his rifle which seemed to pass just by my head with a loud, 'Whizz!' I was just going to fire again when two of my men were on him! Their bayonets flashed and went in up to the hilt, and he sank down in the ditch. Then one of my men and a Dervish had an exciting struggle. The latter was grasping the bayonet in one hand, while trying to draw his knife, and the two were going round in a circle. I was going to the rescue, but the Tommy recollected that his rifle was loaded and managed to pull the trigger, with the result that the Dervish was blown away a foot or so. Another of my men and a Dervish got too close to use their weapons, so grappled at each other's throats and fell to the ground. Another of my men ended the struggle by bayoneting the enemy. I came on a Dervish with a huge, long spear. He saw me and his spear flushed upward, but I was just in time. The point of my sword caught him full in the chest, and I felt nothing till the hilt came against his ribs. Letting my revolver loose, I caught his hand, for he made one supreme effort which nearly brought us both to the ground, then he crumpled up. I took his spear as a trophy, but the point was almost off it, and as it had fresh blood on the blade, he had evidently used it.[19]

2nd Lieutenant Ronald Meiklejohn, 1st Royal Warwickshire Regiment, British Brigade

Soon the zeriba was a slaughterhouse.

The sight inside the zeriba was really appalling. The trenches were piled up in places with dead or dying, while men, camels, donkeys, and horses, dead or badly wounded, lay thick on the ground, or struggled to get up. To make things more ghastly, several of the straw tukkles were on fire, and dense clouds of black smoke made a pall over parts of the

ground. Many bodies were burning, and there was a horrible smell of roasting flesh. Unfortunately, some women
and children had been involved in the carnage. One poor
wretch lay dying on the ground with a very young baby
beside her. But, as they fought also, it was very difficult to
distinguish them from the men in the dust and smoke. One
Amazon, stripped to the waist, came for me, and realising it
was a woman, I gave ground, keeping her off from knifing
me with my sword, which she tried to grasp. Luckily two
of my men managed to pinion her from behind, but she
fought and bit like a wild cat. They found her young baby
just behind, and that evening I saw her sitting very happily
with our lads, eating some of their rations, while she had
her baby on her lap.[20]

2nd Lieutenant Ronald Meiklejohn, 1st Royal Warwickshire Regiment,
British Brigade

As the Dervishes broke, many tried to escape out of the back
of the zeriba and across the almost dry bed of the Atbara River.

The Lee-Metfords rang fiercely as ever, and hundreds never
gained the Atbara's precipitous bank and shelter. Under
cover of the bank, a very brief stand was made by a few of
the enemy's riflemen, but the 'Tommies' forged through the
thick mimosa and palms with a shout, and the position was
won, and with it the victory of the Atbara. Firing, however,
still went on a little longer, for there were Dervishes in
hiding down the 30-foot bank, and to right and left, who
had to be dealt with. Bands of them also were running the
gauntlet of the men's fire across the 400 yards of white sand
that formed the river's bed. The crack shots crowded to the
banks and potted the runaways. A private of the Lincolns,
with unerring aim, hit four of the fugitives in succession.
There were others who ran with the fleetness of deer to the
south, but not so fast as the Lee-Metford bullets.[21]

Bennett Burleigh, *Daily Telegraph*

The killing went on long after the real issue was settled, but it was all over in little over an hour by 08.25. Over 2,000 Dervish dead were found in the zeriba, with another 1,000 dying of their wounds. The Anglo-Egyptian force suffered 80 killed and 479 wounded.

Initially, there was a widespread acceptance of the enormous contribution the Sudanese battalions had made to the successful outcome of the battle. Certainly, their officers were delighted with their performance in action.

> The jubilant Sudanese who crowded round their officers with joyous beaming faces and insisted on shaking hands all round – first a short shake, then a salute, another shake and another salute, accompanied by proud grins. These are the men who deliberately run ahead of their officers to try and stop the bullets where the fire is hottest, so how can anyone be surprised that their officers believe in them and place them among the best fighting troops in existence? They have dash and pluck and endurance, and plenty of steadiness when carefully officered and strictly disciplined; but above all they are intensely human and should never be treated like machines.[22]
>
> Major Ivor Maxse, 13th Sudanese Battalion, 2nd Egyptian Brigade

But afterwards their contribution was marginalised in press reports to the chagrin of many of the Egyptian Army commanders.

> I hear the reports of the newspaper people make out that the British did it all, which is rather rough on us who lost a great deal heavier than they did, and as far as our work went, we had practically done before Gatacre had begun! We had quite enough bullets flying about to satisfy every-one, and it was a very pretty fight.[23]
>
> Lieutenant Colonel John Maxwell, Headquarters, 2nd Egyptian Brigade

The British battalions were certainly celebrating the victory and counting the cost in the aftermath. And what a reception they gave to Kitchener. Hunter may have worked out most of the tactical details of the attack, but it was nevertheless the Sirdar's triumph.

It was then, I think, that the realisation of victory came to us, and cheer after cheer went up. We were not a pretty sight, officers and men begrimed and covered with dust and blood. Then the Sirdar came riding up, and we all formed round him cheering wildly, for some 5 minutes. He looked deeply affected. Then we began to fall in by companies and battalions, and it was a great relief seeing various pals once again and finding they were safe, while it seemed strange to realise one had come safely through oneself.[24]

2nd Lieutenant Ronald Meiklejohn, 1st Royal Warwickshire Regiment, British Brigade

In the fighting, one NCO reported a series of close shaves that were so far out of the ordinary as to draw the attention of even the Sirdar himself,

After that day I became an object of curiosity to officers and men, who unanimously dubbed me the 'invulnerable' and appear to fancy I can undergo the fire of a whole regiment without any bad effect. As a matter of fact, I went through the battle with my clothes riddled by bullets, and yet, notwithstanding the official account, without a wound. When attacking the entrenchments, I had to congratulate myself on my habit of wearing boots a size too big, as both my shoes were torn to pieces by bullets. Almost at the same moment a bullet smashed the wooden stock of my gun, which I threw away to grasp my sword. I then noticed that the thongs of my bag had been cut in two; that my water gourd, containing my tea, had been drilled; that my sleeves were in holes, and I heard on my helmet something like a hailstorm. Sword in hand, I followed my comrades, and was quickly engaged with two hideous [Dervishes], who finished my undressing by slicing my jacket with their lances. A bullet tickled the top of my right hand enough to bruise it, and I believe it is to this wound, though I dare not swear it, that the official despatch alludes. In short, when we reformed companies, it was discovered that my uniform, including shoes, helmet and accoutrements, had received 162 wounds, each more deadly than the other. I was naked and marched along dragging my tatters with me. I looked so funny that my colonel took me to show me to the general though rarely had I been less presentable. Sir Herbert Kitchener could hardly credit his eyes.[25]

Corporal Laurie, 1st Seaforth Highlanders, British Brigade

The wounded had to be cared for and this proved to be a real problem. There was a terrible shortage of doctors and medical staff, while even basics like chloroform were in short supply.

Kitchener is a rum 'un, and a ripper. He is as hard as nails and as cool as a cucumber. He had a pretty anxious time from the beginning of the night march until the end of the battle, but the only thing I saw him disturbed about was the treatment of the British wounded, who, from lack of proper arrangements, suffered unnecessarily from the heat and from thirst. The medical arrangements in the British Brigade were not nearly as good as those of the Egyptian Army, and 'K' was furious.[26]

Captain Henry Rawlinson, Headquarters

To be fair, the British medical personnel tried their best, as Corporal George Skinner relates.

Our party consisted of one staff sergeant, one sergeant,

two corporals and thirteen men, with five medical officers. We had plenty of work now, dressing the wounded
as fast as they were brought in, which of course in the
worst cases had been temporarily dressed. We had a very
rough day of it. The wounds in most cases being serious,
the enemy's bullets being such large ones made a big hole
and in many cases fracturing the bone. There were only
two spear wounds in all, the remainder being gunshots and
sword cuts. Five of our wounded died during the day. At 7
p.m., the same evening, we had to pack up and, with the
wounded carried on litters and stretchers, with the lesser
cases on camels, make our journey back to the camp we
had left the day before, which we reached at 2 a.m. the
following morning. It was a very trying journey as we had
to travel very steady on account of the wounded. As soon
as we reached camp, we prepared hot milk (tinned) and
Bovril for them after which we were able to get a little rest
– which we were very thankful for.[27]
Corporal George Skinner, Medical Staff Corps

However, even this account conceals a point of grievance, as the
Egyptian troops were ordered to carry back the British wounded.

At 4.30 we were told to carry the English wounded on
stretchers. Of course, I don't mind carrying a wounded
dog, but at the same there is no doubt the English brigade
ought to have carried their own wounded; the wounded
had no one who could understand them if they wanted
anything, besides it rather gives the Egyptian a very poor
idea of the Englishman.[28]
Lieutenant Felix Ready, 2nd Egyptian Battalion, 1st Egyptian Brigade

★★★

AFTER THE BATTLE WAS THE TIME for criticism of the generals, especially by those who felt their contribution was not sufficiently

recognised. One bitter officer was Lieutenant Felix Ready, who had no time for any of his generals and their staff.

> There is no doubt the whole of the staff here is absolutely rotten; they know nothing whatever of regimental work and there is no one to tell them what a laughing-stock they are to the whole army. The only man anyone has any confidence in is the Sirdar, he is excellent as an organiser, but not a regimental soldier. General 'H' is absolutely incapable of anything but commanding in the field. If people at home knew how this army was maintained simply by a slavery of the regimental officers, they wouldn't be so keen on coming out here. Of course, all the rewards go to the staff; hardly any to the regimental officers. But I should fill a book if I went on about the extraordinary proceedings of this army.[29]
> Lieutenant Felix Ready, 2nd Egyptian Battalion, 1st Egyptian Brigade

There was also some legitimate criticism of the tactics employed by Gatacre in his approach to the zeriba.

> General Gatacre was a man one of whose fancies was that he delighted in improvising new methods and new formations, and he decided for this battle on an entirely novel form of attack. The Cameron Highlanders were to advance in line, firing on the move, the Seaforths and Lincolns were to follow behind and close up to the Camerons in column. When the Camerons reached the zareba they were to halt and let the Seaforths and Lincolns pass through their line and into the zareba. These two battalions were then to deploy into line and carry on. Every sort of objection was raised to this method by commanding officers, and it is not difficult to see that it was a movement most difficult to carry out properly in the face of anything like a determined enemy. I have previously expressed my regard and admiration for our general as a man and a soldier, but in

this particular instance there is little doubt he was in error.
The attack did not work out well, nor did it work out as it
was intended.[30]
Captain Granville Egerton, 1st Seaforth Highlanders, British Brigade

Captain Granville Egerton relished telling the amusing tale of
his somewhat bombastic superior.

General Gatacre's flag, a small Union Jack, was carried by
his chief clerk, Staff Sergeant Wyeth, of the Army Service
Corps, who, poor fellow, was mortally wounded early in the
engagement. Some months afterwards, when the general
was inspecting the ordnance workshops at our camp on the
Nile, a NCO was brought to his notice as having done very
good work. Gatacre complimented him highly, and said,
'Now, what can I do for you? I'll tell you what, you shall carry
my flag when we advance to Omdurman!' I believe the man's
face was a picture, and he did not see it at all in the same light.[31]
Captain Granville Egerton, 1st Seaforth Highlanders, British Brigade

However, despite the quibbling, the Battle of Atbara was
accepted as a significant victory and a major stepping stone to
the overthrow of the Khalifa.

★★★

ONE REAL SURPRISE WAS THE CAPTURE of the Dervish Emir
Mahmud Ahmed by the men of the 10th Sudanese Battalion.
This was an uncommon event as the Dervish leaders usually
died alongside their men.

The crowning mercy of our victory was the capture alive
of Mahmud, the defeated general. When he saw that all
was over, he disdained to fly, and seated in his 'dem', or
inner stronghold, awaited the death that for his ruthless
crimes he so thoroughly deserved. His bodyguard formed

up in front of the 'dem', and sold their lives in defence of their master very dearly. Mahmud was taken alive – considerable money rewards had previously been promised to the native troops for his capture, which accounts probably for this arch-ruffian's life being spared.[32]

Captain Granville Egerton, 1st Seaforth Highlanders, British Brigade

Bennett Burleigh claimed to have seen the interview between Mahmud and Kitchener.

A guard of half-a-dozen men and a sergeant of the 10th Battalion Sudanese came up with a stalwart, bare-headed, Dervish prisoner, who was wearing an emir's ornate jibbah. An officer galloped up with the news that the captive was none other than Mahmud himself. He approached, slightly limping, his short baggy cotton drawers smeared with blood from a bayonet prod. A tall native, standing some 6-foot, as much negroid as Arab in feature, with a thin tuft of hair on his chin, a man of about thirty years of age – this was the Taaisha Baggara, and nephew of the Khalifa, the supposed truculent Dervish General. He held his head up and scowled at his guard. The Sirdar and General Hunter wheeled round, and Mahmud was brought before them. I was an onlooker. 'This is the Sirdar!' said General Hunter, indicating Sir Herbert Kitchener. General Hunter spoke quite angrily, for he was vexed at the Baggara leader's assumed indifference; besides, he held in fine contempt the brutal and cruel Taaisha chief. Mahmud paid no special attention. 'Sit down', quietly said the Sirdar to him, which, in Eastern parlance, was rather an ominous beginning for Mahmud – an omen of death. 'Why have you come into my country, to burn and to kill?' said the Sirdar. 'I have to obey the Khalifa's orders, as a soldier, without question, as so must you the Khedive's!' replied Mahmud, speaking for the first time.[33]

Bennett Burleigh, *Daily Telegraph*

Subsequently Burleigh secured an interview with Mahmud. It reveals a simmering tension between the young ambitious Emir and Osman Digna, who once again had managed to escape, probably as he had early on seen that the defence of the zeriba was doomed against such a display of firepower.

> Mahmud's manners can be described as pleasant: he was chatty in talk and displayed an overweening conceit in his tribe. Osman Digna, he said, in answer to my question, had gone with the cavalry. It was that officer who had induced him to leave the Nile, promising to show a route whereby he might fall upon Berber unawares. He had, previous to his capture, written to the Khalifa, complaining in strong language of Osman's misdirection, and his general luke-warmness in the cause. Mahmud's faith in his followers was extravagant enough. He believed that if his cavalry had been present and had fallen upon our infantry, whilst he attacked us in front, they would have routed us. Mahmud declined to believe that the British Brigade alone, as so many held, could have carried the zeriba; for although he thought the English soldiers good, he declared that he had better men in his 'dem' to serve as his bodyguard. Our artillery, he added, did little harm, and killed nobody. This was another absolute untruth. I never saw a higher percentage of losses inflicted by cannon; it was probably as much as 20 per cent.[34]
> Bennett Burleigh, *Daily Telegraph*

But above all Mahmud was serenely confident that the Khalifa would triumph in the final battle to decide the campaign.

> Of course, had I known that you possessed so many soldiers, I should have brought more. I had, as a matter of fact, sent for reinforcements, but they did not arrive in time from Omdurman. The war, I assure you, is by no means ended. The Khalifa has men like the sands of the sea. They will meet you at Shabluka and Omdurman, and you cannot

conquer, for my master has 60,000 soldiers, many guns, and holds strongly fortified positions, utterly unlike my poor zeriba.[35]

Emir Mahmud Achmed

The Khalifa and Kitchener would both have to wait for that final reckoning.

15

ONE LAST HEAVE

> The Guards were very funny when they saw the camp; every officer seemed to want a tent to himself. Their colonel wanted to put the men's kitchen right in front of Lyttelton's tent but was told he had better put them elsewhere. Really the way they are pampered is disgraceful.[1]
>
> Lieutenant John Gough, 2nd Rifle Brigade, 2nd Brigade

THE BATTLE OF ATBARA had been a considerable victory, but the main forces of the Khalifa, held back at Omdurman, still had to be overcome. Kitchener withdrew his forces back to the Atbara Fort and Berber, to be rested and reinforced ready for the final challenge. A vital part of this process was the extension of the desert railway which reached Berber on 29 May, and the Atbara Fort on 14 July, facilitating the flow of men, stores and munitions into the advanced bases. The most important reinforcement was the 2nd British Brigade, under the command of Brigadier General Neville Lyttelton, and consisting of the 1st Grenadier Guards, 2nd Lancashire Fusiliers, 1st Northumberland Fusiliers and 2nd Rifle Brigade. There was much amusement and envy among the campaign veterans at the belated arrival in early August of these 'pampered' battalions in contrast to the tough life they had been leading. But at least the break in the fighting had given everyone a chance to rest.

> After many days wandering in the desert with the clothes we stood up in, and literally nothing more, we at length retrieved our scanty kits and got back to comforts if not

luxury. When the bare sand has been your bed for weeks on end, and one scanty blanket your only covering by night, a frowsy towel, a tooth brush, and a piece of soap your only articles of toilet, to find oneself within the four walls of a native mud hut with a camp stool to sit upon and a pillow of sorts on which to rest your head, is, for the moment, luxury indeed. The four battalions of the British Brigade were located in two villages on the riverbank. Here we went into what the newspaper correspondents termed 'summer quarters on the Nile' and prepared to spend 4 months of weary waiting for the advance upon Khartoum.[2]

Captain Granville Egerton, 1st Seaforth Highlanders, British Brigade

After the reinforcements arrived, the original 1st British Brigade was placed under Brigadier General Andrew Wauchope, while Major General William Gatacre took command of the newly formed British Infantry Division. In addition, the 4th Egyptian Brigade (Lieutenant Colonel John Collinson) was added to Major General Archibald Hunter's Egyptian Division. Three new gunboats augmented Kitchener's naval flotilla, which gave him yet more firepower. Nothing was left to chance as they prepared for the climax of the advance on Khartoum. Some 8,200 British, 17,600 Egyptian/Sudanese troops, 44 guns, 20 Maxims, and 10 Nile gunboats had been amassed and began to move forward to the next concentration area around Wad Hamed.

One unwelcome arrival to the assembled host was the warrior cum journalist, Winston Churchill, who had earned quite a reputation with his reports from the front while serving in the Malakand campaign in 1897. Kitchener was one of those who looked askance at Churchill's journalistic activities and had politely declined the opportunity to have him serve in the Sudan. However, by mobilising all the advantages of his elevated position in society, Churchill had managed to secure an attachment as a supernumerary officer to the 21st Lancers, the only British cavalry regiment sent out to join the final stages of the campaign. However, just to show that his critics may have had a point, he also secured a contract to write a column as a journalist for the *Morning Post*. His long journey to the front was fraught with fears that Kitchener or his staff might send him packing, but he made it undetected. One of Churchill's contemporaries in the officers' mess of the 21st Lancers left a sharp, but affectionate, word picture of the 'great man' on his arrival.

> He was in the pink flush of his youth. He was then about twenty-three and it is useless to say that he was universally popular with his brother officers. He was not. He did not seek popularity. In fact, it almost seemed that sometimes he went out of his way to rub people up the wrong way. Then as now, he could not tolerate fools easily, but fools apart, he certainly gave one the impression that he felt he knew more than most of us. It has been said by an unkind cynic that, 'The Churchills have a divine right to be rude!' but certainly if Winston was a little too quick-witted and sharp tongued for some of his brother officers, he got as good as he gave for – since he combined soldiering with the job of war correspondent for the *Morning Post* – he was not allowed to forget it. Some of his despatches did not spare adjectives. So, the invariable greeting was: 'Well, Churchill, how are the blazing yellow sands and purple sunsets today?' He also had his leg pulled unmercifully about drawing civilian pay as well as his army pay. As a soldier, Winston was full of dash, as brave as a lion and always looking for trouble. It must be remembered that he was then a very young, unformed character, with immense vitality, bubbling with brains and impatient of restraint.[3]
> Lieutenant John Vaughan, 'C' Squadron, 21st Lancers

Churchill would prove himself a competent officer.

The defeated Mahmud Ahmed may have remained confident in the Khalifa's ultimate victory, but in Omdurman, doubts were beginning to surface. Contrary to the image of extremist religious fanatics rushing into battle, not everyone was enamoured with the prospect of martyrdom. One such refusenik was Babikr Bedri, who lived in Omdurman.

> When the Khalifa of the Mahdi determined on resistance, people began to wonder – and I among them – what would become of them if Omdurman were besieged, or if the Khalifa were defeated by the government army and abandoned the town, taking the people and their families with them. I had searched my thoughts till I was weary for some plan that might save me from the siege or from the campaign.[4]
> Babikr Bedri

But the Khalifa was also preparing his defences in and around Omdurman. This would not be an easy place for the Anglo-Egyptian Army to storm.

> The Khalifa of the Mahdi was sure that the invading army would soon reach Omdurman, and he made preparations to meet it. A rumour for a time gained credence that he and his brother Ya'qūb and their followers had decided to fly to Kordofan or Darfur, but it was falsified when the Khalifa ordered the building of eleven forts in Omdurman and six on the east bank, and two each in Khartoum and Tuti Island, and put machine guns and artillery and garrisons in all of them.[5]
> Babikr Bedri

And so, both sides got ready for the battle to come. There was time for one great parade of Anglo-Egyptian strength.

> This morning the whole army paraded for inspection in the desert. We arose from our slumbers at 3.45 a.m. and got back to breakfast about 9 a.m., fairly weary in mind and body. When all the brigades were in line, I believe, they covered about 3 miles of ground. We sat about in the desert

for most of our time out, as a force so large takes some little time to put in motion.[6]

Captain Alfred Hubbard, 1st Lincolnshire Regiment, 1st Brigade

By 24 August, the concentration of the Kitcheners army was complete and the advance up the Nile could begin. This time there would be no mistake; this time Gordon *would* be avenged.

★★★

FEELING THEIR WAY AHEAD and on the flanks of the infantry were the cavalry. The first real problem was to determine whether the Shabluka hills and Sixth Cataracts were defended. Among the cavalry patrols sent out was Winston Churchill.

The Shabluka position was considered to be formidable. It was impossible to ascend the cataract in boats and steamers in any force that would be effective, unless the whole range of hills had first been turned from the desert flank. Such an operation would have presented a fine tactical opportunity to a Dervish army crouched behind the Shabluka hills ready to strike at the flank of any army making the indispensable turning movement. It was therefore no doubt with great relief that Sir Herbert Kitchener received from his cavalry, his scouts and his spies, the assurance that this strong position was left undefended by the enemy. Nevertheless, all the precautions of war were observed in making the critical march through the desert round the end of the hills. All the mounted forces made a wide circling movement. For us, although we were only on the inner flank, the distance was perhaps 25 miles from our morning watering-place on the Nile bank north of the Shabluka to where we reached the river again at the evening bivouac on the southern and Omdurman side of the barrier. Those of us who, like my troop, composed the advance patrols, expected as we filtered through the thorn scrub to find enemies behind every

bush, and we strained our ears and eyes and awaited at every instant the first clatter of musketry. But except for a few fleeting horsemen, no hostile sight or sound disturbed or even diversified our march, and when the vast plain reddened in the sunset, we followed our lengthening shadows peacefully but thirstily again to the sweet waters of the river.[7]
2nd Lieutenant Winston Churchill, 'A' Squadron, 21st Lancers

The Khalifa had surrendered the Shabluka position without a fight. The Anglo-Egyptian Army marched west into the desert, diverting all the way round the hills to get back to the Nile.

In the absence of fighting, the journalists sought out amusing stories and colourful incidents to entertain their readers back home in Britian.

During the earlier part of the day's march Mr. Scudamore's 'drink camel' *i.e.* the animal which carried his stores of alcohol and soda water, occasionally came to a sudden halt and toyed with the branches of a nebek or mimosa thorn. At such times his master showed great kindness and forbearance; he did not urge on the hesitating beast with gibes and blows, but calling several of us round him, quietly dismounted and relieved the camel's load by 'drinks all round'. How touching an example of humanity towards poor dumb animals![8]
Ernest Bennett, *Westminster Gazette*

During overnight camps, the soldiers took a keen interest in the local wildlife, setting the different species in a battle to the death for the amusement of the watchers.

Scorpions proved most troublesome in all our camps. In some places they simply swarmed, and both officers and men, and, still more, native servants, suffered from their painful stings. Another insect pest was a huge yellow spider of loathsome aspect and malignant disposition, called by

the natives 'Abu Shebek' (Father of Spiders). This creature
was frequently captured and conveyed to some regimental
mess, where it was forced to engage in single combat with
a scorpion. These adversaries were, as a rule, pretty evenly
matched, and the 'Warwickshire Pet' a monstrous spider,
appeared to be invincible until it was matched against
the 'Cameron Slogger' a redoubtable scorpion, who vanquished his opponent after a desperate struggle amid loud
cheers from the victorious mess.[9]

Ernest Bennett, *Westminster Gazette*

It was a tough series of marches through the infernal scrublands, with the sun blazing down, great clouds of dust, and the
all-embracing thirst. Illness caused many to drop out. On 28
August, the sweating columns arrived at Wad el Abid. Initially,
they did not build a zeriba overnight and as a result suffered a
bit of a scare.

We were encamped on the edge of the bush in line of
quarter columns of half battalion. We were not to build a
zeriba as the Dervishes were still supposed to be far distant,
but instead a section of the company on guard under an
officer were to remain awake and under arms all night.
About an hour after getting in there was an alarm from the
left and word was passed down 'Stand to your arms!' The
men stood to arms in the coolest and quietest way possible,
not a sign of fluster or hurry. Very soon afterwards it was
found out that one Dervish horseman had ridden up to the
20th [Lancashire Fusiliers] who were on the left and had
thrown a spear in amongst them. He got off without even
a shot being fired at him, which fairly raised the Sirdar's ire.
Well after this episode it was thought that the Dervishes
might be closer than had been imagined so we had to turn
to and build a zeriba. Nothing further however was heard.[10]

Lieutenant Douglas Loch, Grenadier Guards, 2nd Brigade

One can sense that the Lancashire Fusiliers were rather excited by this incident, which certainly broke the monotony.

> About a quarter to ten a mounted Dervish came up to the corner of our zeriba at full speed, knocked a sentry flat and hurled a spear at a knot of men – no one hit. Wolley Dod got the spear which had a barbed head about 1½ feet long. The sentries were unloaded according to orders – so as it was very hazy, the man got away. I was about 10 yards off at the time but could not get my revolver out in time. The whole thing was over in half a minute, and at first it was thought that it was a runaway mule, so no alarm was given.[11]
>
> 2nd Lieutenant Hugh Farmer, 2nd Lancashire Fusiliers, 2nd Brigade

On 30 August, they were making their final approach across the plain riven by khors, heading towards the Kerreri Hills which they knew lay just in front of Omdurman.

***

AS THE HUGE COLUMNS OF KITCHENER'S ARMY grew ever closer the Khalifa appeared to have three options: he could abandon Omdurman and run; he could move forward to fight where the Kerreri Hills and Jebel Sergham stretched across Kitchener's approach route; or he could defend to the last the city itself. Reginald Wingate had redoubled his efforts, calling in his various spies to report on the strength and intentions of the Khalifa's forces. Kitchener was desperate to avoid the painful street fighting if at all possible, so on 1 September, took action to demonstrate the power of modern artillery against built up areas. On the Nile east bank, an irregular Camel Corps of some 2,500 tribesmen who had abandoned the Khalifa, were deployed under the command of Major Edward Stuart-Wortley, to which had been added a howitzer battery. These were to operate in conjunction with six gunboats under the command of Commander

Colin Keppel. Together they would shell Omdurman, flaying
the Khalifa's palace and even – symbolically – the Mahdi's tomb.

> The Sirdar ordered me to clear the east bank as far as the
> Blue Nile the day before he engaged the enemy, in order
> to place the howitzer battery there to shell Omdurman.
> I found the villages occupied and cleared them one after
> another. The Jaalins behaved very well, but the other tribes
> stood still in front of any opposition, and confined their
> action to shouting, and firing their rifles in the air, or any-
> where except in the direction of the enemy. Sir Evelyn
> Wood's son, who was my staff officer, and I had a very
> narrow escape. I had dismounted in front of a village, with
> fifty men, and was crossing over the river to speak to Colin
> Keppel, when twenty-five horsemen came out, and charged
> amongst us. I rallied about ten men, and we killed about
> fifteen of the cavalry. I don't wish again to have a similar
> experience. However, we cleared the villages, and landed
> the battery from the gunboats, which immediately com-
> menced shelling the Mahdi's tomb. By dusk it was knocked
> to pieces, and frightful havoc played with the principal parts
> of the town. Meanwhile I embarked on Keppel's gunboat,
> and with his fleet we engaged all the forts of Omdurman,
> Tuti Island, and Khartoum – a most exciting and beautiful
> sight. Their forts were very strong, but we put shell after
> shell into their embrasures.[12]
>
> Major Edward Stuart-Wortley

One observer was Ernest Bennett, who as a correspondent took
the opportunity to run ahead of the main column when he
heard the distant roar of the guns.

> I ran as hard as I could up the rough slopes and reached
> the crest of the ridge. Little could be seen from the lower
> slopes, but from the summit a splendid spectacle presented
> itself. The terrible 50-pounder shells had found the range

and were playing havoc with the walls and public buildings of Omdurman. Nothing can resist Lyddite. Thick walls were pierced like brown paper, and the stones hurled high in the air amid clouds of dust and flame. A shell had torn a vast hole through the lofty domelike structure which covered the Mahdi's sepulchre, the gilded top of which had been carried clean away. The effect of the shells upon the wretched people who chanced to be near to the Mahdi's tomb at the time of the bombardment was truly awful, as I saw with my own eyes two days afterwards.[13]

Ernest Bennett, *Westminster Gazette*

By this time the Khalifa's forces had already moved out of the city and were gathering in the Khor Shambât valley behind the Jebel Surgham hills. Among them was Babikr Bedri, who had been called up along with most of the able-bodied men in Omdurman. When they heard the sound of gunfire behind them, they were given a very different account as to what was happening.

We heard the noise of firing in our own army, and on inquiring the reason understood that one steamer had been sunk and another captured, and that its steering-wheel had been brought to the Khalifa, who had ordered a volley to be fired as a victory salute. There was in our company a man named Majdhûb Abü Bakr – he had a long spear with which he began to strike the earth, then he stuck the shaft upright in the rain-wet sand of the watercourse, and shouted at us, 'Hey! You recusants! See the sign of victory!' We said nothing, and after a little the sound of the steamers firing on the forts ceased, and the veins in the man's throat swelled enormously as he assured us doubters that all the steamers were captured. There were ten of us whom he was thus insulting. In the afternoon, the steamers started firing again, and our friend Majdhüb's triumphing rather faded away. I said to him, 'Those damned unbelievers have been raised from the dead before the Day of Resurrection, God's curse on them!' And he hung his head in miserable disappointment.[14]

Babikr Bedri, Black Flag

As the Khalifa's army gathered, they were watched in their approach by a young cavalry subaltern.

> After skirting a hill called Surgham, I made for a sand hillock on the top of the next rise. Dismounting I got out my glasses and telescope. I could see the mosque and buildings of Omdurman clearly enough and had also marked the tracks of two natives running at speed from my observation post which they must have used for the same purpose. What I could not make out was a kind of white and black coloured wall running for 3 or 4 miles from east to west just north of the city. The wretched mirage was beginning to make my view more uncertain when I realised that my wall was moving towards me and was in fact the whole Dervish army advancing! So I was able to report accordingly. I think that I estimated them as 30,000. As my sand hill was also a good firing position, I remained where I was and presently the regiment picketed the whole ridge to my right and left. Preceded by weak mounted patrols the Dervishes continued to advance throughout the day. These mounted Dervishes were very bold and rode up to within 200 yards of our pickets when they were shot more often than not.[15]

Lieutenant John Vaughan, 'C' Squadron, 21st Lancers

Also nearby was Winston Churchill.

> A friendly subaltern who had been on patrol came along with what to us was momentous and decisive news, 'Enemy in sight!' he said, beaming. 'Where?' we asked! 'There, can't you see? Look at that long brown smear! That's them. They

haven't bolted!' and he went on his way. We had all noticed
this dark discoloration of the distant horizon but had taken
it to be a forest of thorn bushes. The best field-glasses failed
to disclose any other impression from the point where we
were halted.[16]

2nd Lieutenant Winston Churchill, 'A' Squadron, 21st Lancers

Churchill's horse was relatively fresh, so he was despatched back
to report to Lieutenant Colonel Rowland Martin at the outpost
line. His orders caused Churchill a great deal of anxiety!

'Go back as quickly as you can without knocking up your
horse, and report personally to the Sirdar. You will find him
marching with the infantry!' So, I was to meet Kitchener
after all! Would he be surprised to see me? Would he be
angry? Would he say, 'What the devil are you doing here? I
thought I told you not to come?' Would he be disdainfully
indifferent? Or would he merely receive the report without
troubling to inquire the name of the officer who brought
it? Anyhow, one could not have a better reason of service
for accosting the great man than the news that a hostile
army was advancing against him.[17]

2nd Lieutenant Winston Churchill, 'A' Squadron, 21st Lancers

He was not unnaturally nervous as he approached the Sirdar.

Kitchener was riding alone two or three horses' lengths in
front of his headquarters staff. I approached at an angle,
made a half circle, drew my horse alongside and slightly
in rear of him, and saluted. He turned his grave face upon
me. The heavy moustaches, the queer rolling look of the
eyes, the sunburnt and almost purple cheeks and jowl
made a vivid manifestation upon the senses. 'Sir,' I said, 'I
have come from the 21st Lancers with a report!' He made a
slight nod as a signal for me to continue. I described the situation in terms which I had studied on my ride to make as

compendious as possible. The enemy were in sight, apparently in large numbers their main body lay about 7 miles away and almost directly between our present position and the city of Omdurman. Up to 11 o'clock they had remained stationary, but at 5 minutes past 11 they were seen to be in motion, and when I left 40 minutes before they were still advancing rapidly. He listened in absolute silence to every word, our horses crunching the sand as we rode forward side by side. Then, after a considerable pause, he said, 'You say the Dervish army is advancing. How long do you think I have got?' My answer came out in a flash, 'You have got at least an hour – probably an hour and a half, Sir, even if they come on at their present rate!' He tossed his head in a way that left me in doubt whether he accepted or rejected this estimate, and then with a slight bow signified that my mission was discharged. I saluted, reined my horse in, and let his retinue flow past.[18]

2nd Lieutenant Winston Churchill, 'A' Squadron, 21st Lancers

Churchill later discovered that Kitchener had merely shrugged to learn of his presence – he had more pressing matters to concern himself with.

Kitchener then rode up to the top of Jebel Surgham (also called Signal Hill by the British) to see for himself. Also up on the ridge was Lieutenant Douglas Loch in his capacity as the signal officer of 2nd Brigade.

I galloped on to the hill, Jebel Surgham. I found I could communicate with the cavalry so opened communication at once with camp. What a thrill I had when I got to the top of that hill. Looking south, Omdurman could be clearly seen with the Mahdi's tomb sticking up in the middle. In front of the town seemed to be numbers of palm trees. Houses seemed to be scattered for miles and along the riverbank nearly to our camp. There was another sight, far more interesting and far more exciting. The whole Dervish army advancing across the plain and only about 7 or 8 miles off. Up to this moment I own to having been rather sceptical as to the size and strength of the Dervishes, but I had no doubt now. There they were in three great long lines with batches of what looked like cavalry in between. As I was looking up came the Sirdar, Wingate, Slatin and Lawrence Drummond. They consulted together as to the position etc. It was awfully interesting standing there and hearing them talk about the whole thing. They put the number down at about 40,000 but at that distance it was impossible to distinguish much. It was altogether a glorious sight. Blue sky and a burning sun, with the red sand in the foreground, Omdurman in the distance, the Nile looking blue on the left with the gunboats steaming up and down shelling the Omdurman forts, the howitzers also on the east bank adding their booming. On the right, the great Dervish host. The Dervishes continued to advance until they were about 4½ miles off. The Sirdar then said, 'I think I will just go back and see that everything is ready for them!' As he said it a real satisfied smile came over his face – you could see the man was delighted at what he had seen.[19]

Lieutenant Douglas Loch, Grenadier Guards, 2nd Brigade

Kitchener and his staff rode back, encountering Hunter who then took the leading role in organising a defensive position round the tiny Arab village of El Egiega with the Nile to its back.

The whole army accordingly strung out into line, making a huge semi-circle with each flank down on the river. The British division made a small and rather useless zeriba, and the Egyptians dug trenches. The ground in front for at least 2,000 yards appeared as flat as a billiard table, and one felt that anyone advancing across this was going to have a very poor time of it. In front of us, in the background of this flat expanse of plain rose Djebel Surgham, and the

ridges running to each side of it, shutting out our view of Omdurman and of the approaching Dervish army. We waited and waited, and still they did not come, until late in the afternoon word arrived that the Khalifa had halted his array on the other side of the ridges about 3 miles away, and we were warned and prepared for a night attack.[20]
Captain Granville Egerton, 1st Seaforth Highlanders, 1st Brigade

The prospect of a night attack rattled even such a cool warrior as Hunter. Darkness would negate much of the advantage granted by their superior weaponry.

So long as [the] enemy came on in daylight, I had no fear. But my conviction till I die will be that if he had attacked us in the dark before dawn, with the same bravery he attacked us next day by daylight, we should have been pierced, divided, broken, and rolled into the river. Few people can realize and still less know from practical knowledge what happened when an enemy gets inside your formation. Friend kills friend, contrary orders are given, bugles are sounded to everyone's confusion, all is dark and dusk, and [the] roar of animals and shrieks of dying and wounded, and clamour of natives, and shrill yells of enemy, and curses and prayers and a babble of confusion and horror.[21]
Major General Archibald Hunter, Headquarters, Egyptian Division

Kitchener ordered his gunboats to use their searchlights to monitor any possible movement and to keep the Dervish host on tenterhooks. Wingate and Rudolf Slatin also played their part by despatching local Arab villagers and other agents to spread rumours that it was the Sirdar who planned a night attack.

That night Churchill was strolling by the river when he encountered David Beatty, someone he would get to know very well in later life.

As I strolled in company with a brother officer along the

riverbank, we were hailed from the gunboats which lay 20 or 30 feet from the shore. The vessel was commanded by a junior naval lieutenant named Beatty who had long served in the Nile flotillas and was destined to fame on blue water. The gunboat officers, spotlessly attired in white uniforms, were eager to learn what the cavalry had seen, and we were by no means unwilling to tell. We had a jolly talk across the stretch of water while the sun sank. They were particularly pleased to learn of the orders against the use of firearms inside the zeriba and made many lugubrious jokes at our expense. This included offering us hospitality on the gunboat if the worst came to the worst. We put the suggestion aside with dignity and expressed our confidence in the plan of using cavalry swords and lances on foot amid the sand dunes against a Dervish mob in pitch darkness. After a good deal of chaff came the piece of good fortune. 'How are you off for drinks? We have got everything in the world on board here. Can you catch?' And almost immediately a large bottle of champagne was thrown from the gunboat to the shore. It fell in the waters of the Nile, but happily where a gracious Providence decreed them to be shallow and the bottom soft. I nipped into the water up to my knees, and reaching down seized the precious gift which we bore in triumph back to our mess.[22]

2nd Lieutenant Winston Churchill, 'A' Squadron, 21st Lancers

Small groups of officers gathered all around to discuss their prospects.

Captains Caldecott, Grenfell and Etches came and we all had a chat. The two former declared we should not have a fight at all, but a naval officer from one of the gunboats, who joined us, said, 'If you fellows had seen what I saw this afternoon you'd think a bit differently!' Caldecott laughed and remarked that the 'black swine' would all bolt during the night, to which the reply was, 'Well, if you are alive this time tomorrow, you will have a very different opinion of these Dervishes!' Both Caldecott and Grenfell were killed and Etches wounded, though only slightly. Then Winston Churchill strolled up and we had a long talk. He was far less argumentative and self-assertive than usual. He said the enemy had a huge force and, if they attacked during the night, he thought it would be 'touch and go' about the result.[23]

2nd Lieutenant Ronald Meiklejohn, 1st Royal Warwickshire Regiment, 1st Brigade

Never was a dawn more eagerly awaited than on Friday 2 September 1898.

16

THE BATTLE OF OMDURMAN,
2 SEPTEMBER 1898

When one saw his almost countless host advancing over
that skyline with absolute confidence, at a steady jog, with
no attempt at taking cover, and heard the roar from thousands and thousands of throats, it certainly did look as if
nothing could stop them. I don't think any of us realised in
the least what numbers he could turn out, or what amount
of fanatical blind courage was still left in his army. Nor, I
think, did many of us realise what a terrible power of 'stopping' we possessed.[1]
Captain James Watson, Headquarters

COME THE DAWN ON FRIDAY 2 SEPTEMBER 1898, Kitchener's men
shook themselves awake to face a world of uncertainty as the
army stood to at 03.30. They had expected to be attacked the
day before, they had feared an attack during the night – what
would the new day bring? They would not have been human
if they did not harbour fears, both of what might happen,
but of how they would respond to the trials that lay ahead of
them. Many were aware of their ghastly fate if the Dervishes
should somehow break through the 'wall of death' that the
Anglo-Egyptian Army could create in front of them by means
of their artillery, rifles and Maxims. It did not seem likely, but
it was still a possibility that could not be discounted. And who
among them did not remember the reports of previous battles
and the fate of soldiers once their formation was breached and
the stabbing spears made a mockery of bayonet drills practised

on the barrack square. But most put such doubts aside – at least for the moment. And despite it all, many had managed to doze off for a little while.

> We slept of course on our posts. One English officer, a battalion and one member of each brigade staff being up all night. I slept just 2½ hours, but at last day broke – we had been standing to our arms since 3.30 a.m. – and nothing had happened. I am glad to say three out of four of my battalions had a solid hot breakfast between 3.30 a.m. and dawn.[2]
> Lieutenant Colonel David Lewis, Headquarters, 3rd Egyptian Brigade

All over the camp men were attending to their breakfast, often considered the most important meal of the day – after all this time it might be their last.

> We rose from our broken slumbers in the dull grey light of daybreak, and by the time the first sunlight had flushed the surface of the Nile everybody was hard at work over his breakfast. When one knows that within an hour or two the normal routine of regular meals may be rudely interrupted by the exigencies of a whole day's fighting, it behoves one to eat at least as substantial a breakfast if it can be got, as one does in London before catching a morning express to Edinburgh.[3]
> Ernest Bennett, *Westminster Gazette*

For most of the soldiers it might be plainer fare than that consumed by the gentlemen of the press, but at least most had the necessities to staunch their hunger, while the Nile provided an unlimited source of water.

> The men had their breakfasts at once, which consisted of coffee and biscuits and half the company only remained at the zeriba. I went down and got my water bottles filled, the officers had some cocoa and biscuits. The morning opened

fair with every prospect of a hot day. As soon as it was light, we proceeded to make holes in the zeriba ready for an advance.[4]

Major W. L. Bagot, 1st Grenadier Guards, 2nd Brigade

In the background there was the hustle and bustle of preparations. Lieutenant George Gorringe reported to Kitchener that he had completed the task of getting the boats carrying ammunition and supplies for the troops into the correct position. The Sirdar's pithy response, long remembered by Gorringe, showed that he too had his mind full.

So that is now in order. We have done our work. If they cannot win the fight, God help them![5]

Major General Herbert Kitchener, Headquarters

Kitchener had issued orders that they were to commence a general advance at 06.00, but first they would await the reports from his cavalry patrols: the 21st Lancers, commanded by Lieutenant Colonel Rowland Martin, were probing to the south, while the Egyptian cavalry and the Camel Corps under the command of Lieutenant Colonel Robert Broadwood moved out to the south-west. Among the Lancer patrols was one led by Winston Churchill. He was beside himself with an inner excitement.

I was now called out from my troop to advance with a patrol and reconnoitre the ridge between the rocky peak of Jebel Surgham and the river. Other patrols from our squadron and from the Egyptian cavalry were also sent hurrying forward in the darkness. I took six men and a corporal. We trotted fast over the plain and soon began to breast the unknown slopes of the ridge. There is nothing like the dawn. The quarter of an hour before the curtain is lifted upon an unknowable situation is an intense experience of war. Was the ridge held by the enemy or not?

Were we riding through the gloom into thousands of ferocious savages? Every step might be deadly; yet there was no time for over-much precaution. The regiment was coming on behind us, and dawn was breaking. It was already half-light as we climbed the slope. What should we find at the summit? For cool, tense excitement I commend such moments. Now we are near the top of the ridge. I make one man follow 100 yards behind, so that whatever happens, he may tell the tale. There is no sound but our own clatter. We have reached the crest line. We rein in our horses. Every minute the horizon extends – we can already see 200 yards. Now we can see perhaps.[6]

2nd Lieutenant Winston Churchill, 'A' Squadron, 21st Lancers

At first, to his disappointment, he could see no sign of the Dervish army. Where were they? Were they really coming? Or had they fallen back overnight? He would soon know.

But wait! The dawn is growing fast. Veil after veil is lifted from the landscape. What is this shimmering in the distant plain? Nay – it is lighter now – what are those dark markings beneath the shimmer? *They are there!* These enormous black smears are thousands of men; the shimmering is the glinting of their weapons. It is now daylight. I slip off my horse; I write in my field service notebook 'The Dervish army is still in position a mile and a half south-west of Jebel Sorghum'. I send this message by the corporal direct as ordered to the Commander in Chief. I mark it 'XXX'. In the words of the drill book 'with all despatch', or as one would say 'Hell for leather!'[7]

2nd Lieutenant Winston Churchill, 'A' Squadron, 21st Lancers

'With all despatch' could never be quick enough for the anxious Kitchener, who was chafing with impatience awaiting the reports from his cavalry patrols that would decide his next movements and the shape of the battle. Just like Kitchener's predecessor

Wellington, at the Battle of Waterloo, he had a heavy reliance on staff 'gallopers' to disseminate his orders and collect intelligence as to the enemy movements. Churchill was still pressing forward, as he moved off the ridge down to the sandhills, observing all the while the advance of the Dervish host, trying to gain as much intelligence as possible. In his preoccupation with his task, he almost went too far.

> The enemy come on like the sea. A crackle of musketry breaks out on our front and to our left. Dust spurts rise among the sandhills. This is no place for Christians. We scamper off; and luckily no man nor horse is hurt. We climb back on to the ridge, and almost at this moment there returns the corporal on a panting horse. He comes direct from Kitchener with an order signed by the Chief of Staff. 'Remain as long as possible, and report how the masses of attack are moving.' Talk of Fun! Where will you beat this! On horseback, at daybreak, within shot of an advancing army, seeing everything, and corresponding direct with headquarters.[8]
>
> 2nd Lieutenant Winston Churchill, 'A' Squadron, 21st Lancers

Churchill would stay up on the ridge until he was directly ordered to return. Gradually the cavalry fell back, the 21st Lancers returned to the southern end of the zeriba, while the Egyptian cavalry and Camel Corps drew back to the Kerreri Hills to the north of the plain. Kitchener had directed Broadwood there to try and draw the Dervishes across the face of his defensive positions. As the cavalry fell back, they were followed by some 20,000 Dervishes distinguished by the green flags of their commanders Emirs Wad el Sheih and Ali Wad Helu – this would prove important in the battle to come.

Back in the camp, the Anglo-Egyptian Army had been getting ready to advance. One way or another there would surely be a battle that day. The question was: would the Dervishes attack across the open plain in front of them or would they withdraw and trigger a desperate bout of street fighting in Omdurman?

> Just as we were beginning to move forward, back came the
> message, 'The Dervishes are moving to attack us!' and we
> were ordered to remain in our entrenchments. We could
> hardly believe the news! We could not have selected a
> better place to be attacked in. Here was a huge open plain
> without an inch of cover for an attacking enemy within
> 2,000 yards of our position.[9]
> Major Horace Smith-Dorrien, 13th Sudanese Battalion, 2nd Egyptian
> Brigade

Now there was a frenzy of last-minute preparations.

> So, they were really coming! Unload the ammunition
> mules, open the boxes and put ready behind the troops,
> better have a couple of Maxims here, and get that battery
> up to that corner. Sirdar up and down the line to see if any-
> thing more can be done to improve position. The blacks
> tapping down their earth parapets, forming rough sorts of
> head cover, stretchers ready, doctors ready. There was a lot
> done in those few minutes.[10]
> Captain James Watson, Headquarters

Ernest Bennett was trolling round the zeriba gathering information and 'colour' for the vivid newspaper reports destined to
enthral his readers back in England.

> By the time I reached the British portion of the zeriba the
> men were all in their places, with reserve companies in
> position a little to the rear. Every officer had seen to the
> working of his revolver, and all the Tommies had opened
> the breech of their Lee-Metfords and tested the magazine
> action – a very necessary precaution amongst the sand and
> dust of Egypt. The two batteries on the extreme left were
> drawn up, with the grim muzzles of the 15-pounders and

the Maxim-Nordenfeldts pointing towards Jebel Surgham. Case upon case of shells lay ready to hand, and a number of these missiles were spread out on the sand close beside the gun-carriages.[11]

Ernest Bennett, *Westminster Gazette*

Among the infantry he noticed a certain tenseness – and who could blame them?

A large number of the Tommies had never been under fire before, e.g., the Guards and the Lancashire Fusiliers, and there was a curious look of suppressed excitement in some of the faces, as they stared over the desert to catch a glimpse of the enemy they were at last destined to behold, after many long marches by day and false alarms by night.[12]

Ernest Bennett, *Westminster Gazette*

By now they knew the Dervish host was on its way. Before they saw them there was a muffled roar of a huge crowd, reminiscent of a football crowd. They were chanting, 'La Illah illa'allah wa Muhammed rasul Allah' which translates as 'There is but one God, and Muhammad is his Prophet'.

Soon we could hear in the distance a loud murmur – the enthusiastic shouting of many thousand voices – a curious weird sound. We had to wait for some time in expectation, watching our squadrons of cavalry as they retired at a walk across our front towards Kerreri Ridges and over the very ground on which 10,000 Dervishes were soon to die. Then we saw the tops of numerous flags, then the heads of swarms of men marching in regular formations and without hesitation. Not a sign of any confusion in their ranks.[13]

Major Ivor Maxse, Headquarters, 2nd Egyptian Brigade

Captain Granville Egerton watched the vast host swirl into view

from the zeriba. He could not help but be impressed by the
awesome spectacle unfolding in front of his eyes.

> Just about 6.10 a.m., gazing intently through my glasses, I
> saw just topping the ridge in front a little white speck – it
> was the first of the enemy's banners to appear. In another
> minute the whole of the immense array came in sight –
> one long dense line of some 50,000 men, in perfect order,
> with intervals between the different armies or divisions.
> Innumerable flags and banners waved from all parts of this
> multitude, and near the centre could be seen the gigantic
> black banner of the Khalifa, which we were to meet later in
> the day under very dramatic circumstances. On they came
> with cavalry on either flank, and many Emirs pacing their
> horses slowly in front. It was a sight to be remembered as
> long as life lasts – a pageant that I imagine can never recur,
> and however much the Khalifa and his Arab hordes deserved
> their fate, the end of Mahdism was indeed majestic.[14]
> Captain Granville Egerton, 1st Seaforth Highlanders, 1st Brigade

There were many different reactions to such an awesome repre-
sentation of armed might marching inexorably towards them.
There were just so many of them; could even modern weapons
shoot them all down?

> Caldecott exclaimed, 'That's the best sight I've ever seen!'
> I remarked that it looked like being a big fight, and he said
> he did not suppose all of us would get through it. He then
> said that he was owed some money for a pony, and would
> I see about it if he got a bullet in him. Was surprised as
> this seemed so unlike Caldecott, the least 'nervy' indi-
> vidual in the world. General Gatacre came riding round,
> and remarked, 'You look very fierce, Captain Caldecott!'
> He then pointed to a huge black flag in the middle of the
> Dervish line and said, 'I mean to have that flag before long!'[15]
> Lieutenant Ronald Meiklejohn, 1st Royal Warwickshire Regiment, 1st Brigade

It seems Gatacre had not modified his egregious personality under the stress of battle.

At 06.45, the guns of the 32nd Field Battery had opened fire at a range of some 2,800 yards, followed shortly afterwards by the Nile gunboats. It was an almost unmissable target before them – and they did not miss. Shells crashed home into the Dervish ranks.

> The British 15-pounders and the short Maxim-Nordenfeldts of the Egyptian gunners were admirably worked, and the precision of the shell fire was marvellous. Scores of shrapnel burst just over the advancing line, and other shells struck the ground under their feet, tearing huge gaps in the ranks and throwing up clouds of earth and stones. The division of the enemy nearest to the zeriba was advancing over the ridge between Surgham and the river, and with a good field glass I could see the fearful havoc played by the fire, of our guns. Beneath the descending shower of bullets from a well-placed shrapnel, a little crowd of men would fall torn and bleeding upon the sand, and sometimes a shell splinter would crash into a horse and hurl the animal with its rider to the ground. Despite this awful fire, the brave Dervishes came steadily on down the slope, though the line of their march was thickly strewn with dead and wounded.[16]
>
> Ernest Bennett, *Westminster Gazette*

The Khalifa's warriors pressed on regardless – some observers noticed there was perhaps a slight quickening in the pace, but that was all. On they came.

> Watching through glasses, one almost felt that nothing could stem his onslaught. Suddenly they seemed to halt for a moment or two. A cloud of smoke came from them and an enormous rattle of musketry. I personally, and I think most of us, held my breath for a moment, expecting to

hear a hail of bullets, as at the Atbara, but nearly all fell short, causing dust spurts well in front of the zeriba, or passing over very high.[17]

Lieutenant Ronald Meiklejohn, 1st Royal Warwickshire Regiment, 1st Brigade

The Dervish artillery also attempted a response but that proved equally ineffective.

A battery which they had placed on the western slope of Surgham fired at the portion of our line held by the Camerons and Seaforths. More than forty rounds were fired from these Dervish field guns, but the shells did little, if any, damage, as, although the fuses were beautifully timed and the projectiles burst at an excellent height above the ground, the range was too long, and they all fell short. They burst like maroons at the Crystal Palace, with a loud report and little else.[18]

Ernest Bennett, *Westminster Gazette*

As they drew closer the soldiers could make out more detail of their approaching foes.

It was pitiful for the Dervishes that their armament and ammunition was of such bad quality that projectiles of all kinds were of no more danger than stones, thrown from a distance. It would have been a different matter if they with their splendid spears had got to close quarters. The spectacle was wonderful. The advancing hosts were in formed masses, each formation wearing a uniform 'Jibbah', a long tunic with large patches of coloured cloth. Each formation had its flags and standards and was led by its Emir mounted on a horse caparisoned and carrying armour and plumes. Each Emir had with him other mounted Arabs. All were accoutred in steel chain armour and tunics. They wore steel casques on their heads. Much of this was found to be the original armour taken from the Crusaders.[19]

2nd Lieutenant Hugh Farmer, 2nd Lancashire Fusiliers, 2nd Brigade

Some 8,000 Dervishes under the command of Emir Osman Azrak charged across the wide-open flat plain between the Kerreri and Jebel Surgham hills, while a further 6,000 led by Khalifa Sherif and the redoubtable Osman Digna pushed over the ridge lying between the Jebel Surgham and the Nile.

Facing them, on the left of the Anglo-Egyptian line, were the Infantry Division commanded by Major General William Gatacre. The left flank was held by Colonel Neville Lyttleton's 2nd Brigade, covering the gap between Jebel Surgham and the Nile, with Brigadier General Andrew Wauchope's 1st Brigade next in line behind a zeriba hedge. Then the three Egyptian brigades of the Egyptian Division commanded by Major General Archibald Hunter, First Lieutenant Colonel John Maxwell's 2nd Brigade, in the middle Lieutenant Colonel Hector Macdonald's 1st Brigade and finally on the right, Lieutenant Colonel David Lewis's 3rd Brigade. In reserve was Lieutenant Colonel John Collinson's 4th Brigade, which was held back at the centre of the defence works alongside the baggage and hospital. In the absence of the raw materials for a zeriba they had dug shallow trenches, which would prove a wise move. Gatacre's men were drawn up behind the thorny zeriba in a tight close-order formation, with the front rank kneeling and the rear rank standing behind them. All along the British line the Lee-Metfords were trained on their enemies as the range shortened. The Grenadier Guards on the left opened fire first, at what might be considered a rather excessive range of some 2,400 yards.

We had a beautiful field of fire. As the Dervishes came over the ridge, one of the men was heard to say, 'I don't care how far I march to see a sight like this!' The sights were continuously lowered as the Dervishes got nearer, and I never heard better volleys at field firing. The effect was

great and streams of bodies marked their advance, which
came to a standstill east of Surgham Hill. The damage
done by both artillery and infantry fire enormous. Standards which were grouped in large squares, rocked and fell
like sinking ships.[20]

Colonel Villiers Hatton, 1st Grenadier Guards, 2nd Brigade

One by one the battalions opened fire, each one delivering shat-
tering repeated blows with every volley fired into the host body
of the Dervishes.

With my glasses I could see great gaps being torn through
the Dervish ranks. Still on they pressed with fierce courage
and a savage spluttering fire, their horsemen riding about,
redressing the shattered ranks, and ever advancing. To
the thunder of the field battery of 12-pounders was now
added the rattle of the Maxims. Then we of the infantry,
who had been quietly sitting down behind the zeriba, the
men laughing when the bullets struck the sand in front or
whistled over their heads, received the order to fire long
range volleys. Eagerly we jumped up to take our share in
the work. The plain in front of us was swept by a veritable
storm of lead.[21]

Lieutenant Louis Burrowes, 1st Lincolnshire Regiment, 1st Brigade

In return for their part in the slaughter the Lincolnshires suffered only a smattering of casualties. This was not a fair fight,
but then war is not a game played with any concept of fairness.

Fortunately for us, the Dervishes were wretched shots, and
though their fire was heavy and continuous, and they were
well-armed with Remingtons, and had [an] abundance of
ammunition, they did little damage. We could see the flash
of their Krupp guns on Signal Hill – guns taken by them
at the destruction of Hicks Pasha's army and at the fall
of Khartoum, but their fire seemed to be quite innocuous.

Some of our people had narrow escapes. My soldier-servant was kneeling with four other men of the company in rear and was not able to get into the firing line at first, as we were cramped for room. I was standing in front of him, directing the men where to aim, when I heard a bang, and a bayonet was pushed against my back. I turned to ask what the devil was up, when one of the men said, 'Your servant is done for, Sir!' I was just going to have a stretcher for him, when he pulled his head out of his helmet and said, 'I am all right, Sir!' The bullet – a spent one – had hit him right in the centre of his helmet, knocking it inside out. The force stunned him, but otherwise he was not hurt. The bullet must have come from the hill on our left. He was afterwards hit in the arm. As he passed me, holding his arm, he said, 'I am pipped at last, Sir!' but he had a smile on his face, as if he was rather glad.[22]

Lieutenant Louis Burrowes, 1st Lincolnshire Regiment, 1st Brigade

As if the artillery and massed rifle fire was not enough, the British had another 'ace' up their sleeve. The unreliable Gatling guns had been replaced with the deadly Maxim machine guns. Captain Douglas Churcher of the Royal Irish Fusiliers was in charge of one detachment wielding this new Excalibur.

We opened fire and I never heard such a fiendish row in all my life. I got the Maxims men to the left and as far as I could tell they didn't come any further, then I turned them on the right and kept on firing away at any body of men I could see. After about an hour of this all the Dervish army retired. We had lots of bullets round us, but none of my men were hit. Everyone seems to be delighted with our Maxims as we did not have a hitch with them all day long.[23]

Captain Douglas Churcher, Maxim Detachment

Ernest Bennett took a close interest in the work of the Maxims.

The Maxims poured forth an unceasing stream of bullets. A belt of cartridges was fixed, and instantly began to glide through the breech mechanism; then 'Ta-Ta-Ta-Ta-Ta!' the belt was empty and thrown aside to make way for another. It was not difficult to see how the gun was doing its terrible work, for if the aim became unduly depressed, a screen of dust and sand was thrown up in front of the enemy's line, and the only thing needed was a trifling elevation of the barrel. There is a sort of fascination about a Maxim in full swing. Water is placed round the barrel in a metal casing, in order to keep the steel from becoming red hot. As it is, in 3 minutes after the water is poured in it boils furiously, and steam rushes out of the valves. Still, as long as the barrel is in contact with water of any kind, all goes well. In the midst of the Dervish attack the water suddenly gave out in Captain Smeaton's battery, and the machinery would speedily have ceased work from overheating but for the ready help of the men who stood by, and immediately emptied their water-bottles into the empty tubing. The Maxims, thus refreshed, continued their work, and up to 8.30 a.m. no less than 90,000 rounds of ammunition had been fired from these weapons alone.[24]

Ernest Bennett, *Westminster Gazette*

This was part of a grim future of warfare he could not have envisioned.

The British firepower scythed away at the front ranks of the advancing Dervishes. This was a mechanical slaughter, with nothing of the so-called romance of war.

My company fired sixty-five volleys in about three-quarters of an hour, at a range after the first few rounds of 800 yards. The curtain or sheet of lead formed by this infantry fire, coupled with that of the Maxim guns, was one that no Dervish was able to pass, and I am convinced that not a single man got nearer than 700 yards to the British infantry, though many of them in front of the Egyptian troops reached a much closer distance. Foiled in their endeavour to close with the hated infidel, hundreds of brave men threw themselves into folds and depressions of the plain and planting their banners in the sand kept up a hot but ill-directed fire on our lines.[25]

Captain Granville Egerton, 1st Seaforth Highlanders, 1st Brigade

Ill-directed the fire might have been, but the sheer volume of bullets fired at the British zeriba was bound to cause some casualties.

The din of battle was terrific. The roar of the artillery, the shriek of shells, the crisp volleys of the Lee-Metfords, and the unceasing rat-tat-tat of the deadly Maxims were so deafening that it was only occasionally in brief intervals that one realised that bullets by hundreds were flying around us. Other proofs, however, of this were soon in evidence. In every direction the medical service men were to be seen carrying the dead and wounded on stretchers to the rear. As I walked across the zeriba with the Rifle Brigade, who were ordered to reinforce the line facing west, three men were hit by Dervish bullets, and immediately afterwards I saw a corporal of the Camerons shot clean through the head. As I said above, comparatively few bullets were heard, but every now and then a man fell to the ground. Colonel Money's horse was shot under him; he secured another mount, and in a few minutes his second horse rolled over, pierced by another Dervish bullet. Shortly afterwards, as I was watching the Maxim fire, a Highlander suddenly fell over 2 yards to my left. He was, I think, shot through the upper part of the arm; but what amused me was the self-conscious, shamefaced look which came over his face when the stretcher arrived. He looked sheepishly round to see if anybody noticed it and was evidently quite ashamed of being carried off![26]

Ernest Bennett, *Westminster Gazette*

Among the medical staff was George Skinner, who was further back in the zeriba.

> The shots from the enemy were rather high and falling more in the middle of the square, making it very danger-ous for the stretcher bearers crossing the square. As I was accompanying a stretcher party across with the first man wounded of the Cameron Highlanders, we had hardly got more than half the distance to the dressing station when one of the bearers who was changing positions with another man was shot in the head, and a lance corporal who was assisting another wounded man was shot in the right shoulder. Several very narrow escapes were had – a bullet passing through my helmet made me dodge![27]
>
> Corporal George Skinner, Medical Staff Corps

Captain Caldecott, who had had some ominous qualms before the battle, was one of those hit among the Warwickshires. The Dervish firing was essentially unaimed and random in its effects. Some were lucky; some were not.

> Poor Caldecott, who commanded 'G' Company the next to mine and who was not 10 yards from me, was hit in the head by a rifle bullet. The doctor came up at once, but it was no good, the bullet penetrated either the brain or spinal cord. Some of the men had marvellous escapes. One bullet went clean through a man's helmet, without hurting him, took the good-conduct stripe off another man's arm, and then hit a sergeant in the leg. A rifle bullet buried itself in the ground not 2 inches to the right of my right foot. One of my sergeants stepped forward and dug it out with his bayonet and gave it to me saying, 'Perhaps you'd like to have this, Sir, as it was such a close shave!'[28]
>
> Captain Dennis Granville, Royal Warwickshire Regiment, 1st Brigade

Yet there has to be sense of proportion. There were British and

Egyptian casualties, but they were as nothing compared to the wholesale slaughter inflicted on the men advancing across the open plain against modern weapons. In desperation the Dervishes launched a cavalry charge – a forlorn hope – every man who took part was a hero, rushing onward to near certain death or maiming. Yet still they charged.

> A small party of Dervishes, headed by a white banner – I suppose that banner had, at one time, led an army – but when I particularly noticed it, there were about a dozen men round it only and they came slowly and deliberately on straight for us. As one man dropped another took on the banner – until only three were left – still on they came and then only one man was left – and he staggered slowly on, spear in one hand and banner in the other – no one could hit him though thousands of bullets were directed at him.[29]
>
> Captain Alfred Hubbard, 1st Lincolnshire Regiment, 1st Brigade

Lieutenant Hamilton Hodgson was watching this tragic scene through his binoculars.

> I never could have imagined anything so cool and brave as these men were, especially one, the last but one to fall. He had his arm wounded and limped too, yet his ambition was to get the flag and he got it and carried some 50 feet at a sort of slow trot when he was shot. As he fell his companion took it and came on a few yards only when he fell – and with him the flag. I was so sorry for those men – they were simply wiped out.[30]
>
> Lieutenant Hamilton Hodgson, 1st Lincolnshire Regiment, 1st Brigade

Even hard-bitten journalists could not but admire the raw courage of these men in a fight without hope.

> The honour of the fight must still go with the men who died. Our men were perfect, but the Dervishes were superb

– beyond perfection. It was their largest, best, and bravest
army that ever fought against us for Mahdism, and it died
worthily of the huge empire that Mahdism won and kept so
long. Their riflemen, mangled by every kind of death and
torment that man can devise, clung round the black flag
and the green, emptying their poor, rotten, home-made
cartridges dauntlessly. Their spearmen charged death at
every minute hopelessly. Their horsemen led each attack,
riding into the bullets till nothing was left but three horses
trotting up to our line, heads down, saying, 'For goodness'
sake, let us in out of this!'[31]

George Steevens, *Daily Mail*

The first attacks on the left and the centre were melting away
before their eyes all along the line. No human being could pass
unscathed through such a storm of fire.

Now they are getting closer, and the Martinis of Blacks and
Egyptians speak. Guns, Maxims, rifles – a terrible concert.
Our men's black powder stopped the view, but you could
hear the shouts, and occasionally through a rift in the smoke
catch sight of a banner and black face. This part of the fight
was at its height. Modern weapons versus numbers. The
din was terrific, and the stretchers were plying. Then their
fire slackened, and great cheers began to go up. They were
stopped. Ceasefire sounded. We got the first clear view of
what we had done, and it was sufficiently appalling. They
were retiring, but many of them, especially some 2,000 in
a depression in front of our centre, were still keeping up a
hot fire, and none of them had had enough yet.[32]

Captain James Watson, Headquarters

Such a shallow hollow in the ground could not protect them
from the shrapnel shells of the British artillery.

By now the Dervishes were retiring everywhere, and the

firing slackened. The artillery began shelling the small number who were in the hollow in front of us and the Lincolns, and after a bit they too began to retire, firing as they went. We got out the best company marksmen – including myself – and picked off most of them. One man refused to retire but kept on firing at us till three of us gave him a kind of volley, when he fell.[33]

Lieutenant Ronald Meiklejohn, 1st Royal Warwickshire Regiment, 1st Brigade

Accounts tend to concentrate on the heroic resistance of the eight British battalions, but to their right, Maxwell's 2nd Egyptian Brigade (8th Egyptian, 12th Sudanese, 13th Sudanese and 14th Sudanese Battalions) came under the most concentrated and powerful assault on their line. Inevitably there are less witness accounts, but we must not minimise the crucial part they played in defeating the initial attack. Major Ivor Maxse, at the brigade headquarters, reviewed the situation they faced.

Sitting on our horses or cantering along the rear of the line of our men in a shallow trench, waiting, ready for the order to fire, the appearance of this first part of the Dervish attack was of supremest interest. Looking at them advancing straight on our two Sudanese (Maxwell's and Macdonald's) brigades and on Wauchope's brigade through field glasses, at a distance of 800 yards, with all our field guns belching shrapnel and our Maxims pumping lead into that vast mass of men, the question arose in our minds: shall we, or shall we not, kill sufficient numbers of them to render the attack of the survivors, at close quarters, ineffectual? You see we were in a thin line to enable every possible rifle to bear. If this line were pierced at any one point – it would be more than uncomfortable for us all! Personally, I felt no doubt at any time that as soon as our infantry fire was opened at 500 to 600 yards, we should break up the attack.[34]

Major Ivor Maxse, Headquarters, 2nd Egyptian Brigade

Lieutenant Colonel Charles Townshend was right in the thick of it as the commanding officer of the 12th Sudanese, and he briskly describes the collapse of the attack in front of his men who stood up well to the threat.

> Clouds of men appeared over the high ridge and hill to the south-west and opened a heavy musketry fusillade on us. The bullets began to sing overhead as these new forces of the enemy got nearer. I saw one or two men of ours hit and carried away in stretchers, one poor fellow dead. I got the men to lie close down in the trench with which I had strengthened our front, and I felt glad that we had done so. I turned my glasses to the mass of enemy coming straight down on my front. On they came, running now and firing from the hip as they came. I was walking up and down behind the regiment, the men all lay in their trench, the rifles all ready to fire, only waiting for my order, but I determined that not a trigger should be pulled until they were 400 yards from us. Many of the men kept looking round to me as much as to say, 'Let us fire now!' The masses of the enemy; began rushing and cheering, the Emirs leading them with flags just as one sees with the Pathans on the North-West Frontier of India. I now began to think that it would not do to wait until this mass got much closer, so I sang out the order for sights to be put at 600 yards, and then opened with a heavy independent fire, and in a short while our line was all smoke and a ceaseless rattle of Martini rifles. The enemy came on till they reached about 400 yards, and then they seemed to enter a rain of bullets. Struck by a leaden tempest, they bundled over in heaps, and soon they stood huddled in groups under the retaining power of the Martini Henry. I saw a brave man leading them on with a large flag – I have his flag – I have never seen a braver! Alone he came on and on, until about 150 yards from us, and then he and his flag fell like a piece of crumpled white paper on the ground and lay motionless.

The Dervishes were now retiring, not running, but skulking away. Some of them walked off as if they were the victors. Our men were cheering now, and I got them up in the trench and we kept up our close and searching fire. No troops in the world could have lived under that fire; no Europeans would have faced it. The valour of those poor half-starved Dervishes in their patched jibbas would have graced Thermopylae.[35]

Lieutenant Colonel Charles Townshend, 12th Sudanese Battalion, 2nd Egyptian Brigade

The Dervishes were able to get much closer to his trenches as his Sudanese soldiers were only armed with single-shot Martini-Henry rifles which had a much slower rate of fire than the bolt-action Lee-Metfords. However, to partially compensate, the bullet they fired was heavier, which gave it an incredible 'stopping' power. Ivor Maxse also witnessed the capture of the Dervish banner.

That banner was picked up by a man of the 12th Sudanese who paced the distance, after 'cease fire' had sounded, and was shot at for his pains. In fact, there was still a good deal of promiscuous shooting from wounded Dervishes lying in small depressions – one lot of fifty men being so persistent that the Maxims had to be kept on them till they desisted. Thus, the attack of these thousands of misguided, brave men died away from sheer loss in killed and wounded: and there they lay before us in thousands.[36]

Major Ivor Maxse, Headquarters, 2nd Egyptian Brigade

The first great attacks of the battle were over.

★★★

DURING THE MAIN ATTACK ACROSS THE PLAIN there had been a separate drama as a further mass, estimated at the time as some

20,000 Dervishes commanded by Wad el Sheih and Ali Wad
Helu, advanced under their green flags straight for the Kerreri
Hills on to which Broadwood's Egyptian Cavalry and Camel
Corps had withdrawn. Here the situation soon seemed to be
spinning out of control.

> The Dervishes were climbing the hill at a great pace. The
> fire of the horse battery was of not the slightest effect in
> checking them, and by the Sirdar's orders the Maxims were
> now sent to the infantry, who had taken up a defensive
> position at the camp. The horse battery took up a second
> position on the second ridge of the Kerreri Hill. The cavalry
> still stood supporting the camel corps still in action on the
> southmost ridge. By this time, the Dervishes had crossed
> the westerly part of the southerly ridge, and a hot fire
> now fell upon the squadrons. The camel-men mounted,
> and together with the squadrons fell back over the stony
> ground behind the second or more northerly ridge. Our
> losses were severe during this short retirement. The cavalry
> was halted behind the guns which were in action. I said I
> thought the position unsuitable for us. I had scarcely made
> the remark, before my trumpeter was shot above the right
> temple, the bullet remaining embedded at the back of
> his head (he was still quite cheerful); his horse was also
> wounded. My leading troop leader standing next to me was
> hit, and the guide behind him was hit on the thigh. Two
> other horses were also hit – all in less time than it takes
> to write. The cavalry retired northwards with the artillery
> battalions, two guns of which had to be abandoned.[37]
> Captain Douglas Haig, Egyptian Cavalry

Broadwood pulled the cavalry back to the north, and in doing so
used them as a tempting 'bait' to draw off the Green Flag forces
and thereby separate them from the main battle. They fell back
some 3 miles, moving in a controlled manner to break contact
with their pursuers who were mainly on foot. After halting at

around 08.00 they then rode round in a wide loop, heading back south to take up their allotted station to the right of the infantry in the main defensive positions which they reached at 09.00. The men of the Camel Corps were far more at risk as they were slower over rough ground than the nimble cavalry. They were ordered straight back to the main camp, covered by the intensive fire from the gunboats *Melik* and *Abu Klea*, both armed with two quick-firing 12-pounder guns, a 4-inch howitzer and four Maxim machine guns. This intervention saw the Camel Corps safely back to the cover of the 3rd Egyptian Brigade. Overall, Broadwood's force had performed an invaluable role in diluting the strength of the Khalifa's forces during the first stage of the battle.

★★★

THE FIRST GREAT ATTACKS OF THE KHALIFA'S ARMY had been defeated. Modern weapons had vanquished numbers and quenched seemingly unquenchable élan by dint of mass slaughter. The plain in front of the Anglo-Egyptian Army seemed covered with corpses and the wounded. The day seemed won. But where were the main Mahdist army retreating to? Were they in fact retreating or perhaps preparing a second onslaught? Kitchener did not anticipate another assault on the zeriba, but he wanted to know what his enemy was doing before he abandoned that sanctuary. At 07.30, the 21st Lancers were ordered out to perform a reconnaissance to discover what was happening behind the Jebel Surgham Hills and all along the route to Omdurman. As the Lancers mounted the ridge, Egerton recounts what happened next.

> At length the order came to cease fire and fill up pouches, and I remember saying to a brother officer, 'Well, thank God, that job's over!' but it wasn't, not by any manner of means. Very soon after this I saw the 21st Lancers ride out straight to the front, following up the enemy over the ridges of Surgham Hill, and a very few minutes later one of our

regimental signallers brought me a heliograph message from Colonel Martin, commanding the 21st, to the Sirdar, which ran, 'About 400 enemy on hill to our front, where we saw them yesterday. What are your orders?' There seemed to be no orderlies about, and so I got my horse and went to seek the Sirdar. I discovered him after some little search on the right centre of the zeriba, surrounded by his staff, and gazing intently at the Kerreri Hills to our right front. I said, 'A heliograph message for the Sirdar!' He replied, 'Read it!' which I did, and he then said, 'Wait!' In about half a minute he said: 'Tell him to worry them on their flank, and head them off from Omdurman!' I galloped away with this message and sent it off at once.[38]

Captain Granville Egerton, 1st Seaforth Highlanders, 1st Brigade

The scrap of paper still exists in the magnificent collections of the National Army Museum. Timed at 08.30, it actually reads, 'Annoy them as far as possible on their flank and head them off if possible from Omdurman.'[39] It is not a precise order, that is true, but Kitchener is preoccupied with avoiding street fighting in Omdurman. He had worked out that some third of the force he had seen with his own eyes the day before was still not accounted for. Where were they? If they were behind Jebel Surgham then they might reach Omdurman before he could. He considered there was no time for delay, and this concern would inform his order for the Anglo-Egyptian brigades to begin the march south. As for the 21st Lancers, his cautious intent is evident in the repetition of 'as far as possible' and 'if possible'; this was not a *carte blanche*, they had been assigned a limited role. But this was not how it appeared to Rowland Martin. He commanded a relatively newly formed regiment who had not yet seen action and who had been cruelly teased for their lack of battle honours by the sarcastic assertion that their motto was, 'Thou shalt not kill'. This seemingly harmless 'banter' would have a major impact on the tragic events that followed.

As the 21st Lancers moved out their morale was high. Most of all they seemed confident as to what was going to happen.

> Everyone expected that we were going to make a charge. That was the one idea that had been in all minds since we had started from Cairo. Of course, there would be a charge! In those days, before the Boer War, British cavalry had been taught little else. Here was clearly the occasion for a charge. But against what body of enemy, over what ground, in which direction or with what purpose, were matters hidden from the rank and file![40]
>
> 2nd Lieutenant Winston Churchill, 'A' Squadron, 21st Lancers

Martin sent out two patrols ahead, while the main body of the 21st Lancers sheltered under the lee of the Jebel Surgham hill. The first, under the command of Lieutenant Robert Grenfell, was probing round the south-west face of the hill, when it was forced back after coming under heavy rifle fire from the summit – they did not get far enough to have any chance of locating the Black Flag force. The second, under Lieutenant Arthur Pirie, pushed forward to the south, moving parallel to a stream of Dervish wounded and checking for any signs of serious opposition. Here they encountered a force, which Pirie estimated to have been some 1,000 strong (more likely around 700–800) in open ground, which he considered was attempting to block the Omdurman Road at the point where it crossed a low sandy ridge. What he could not – or did not – see at around 09.00 when he turned back to report his findings to Martin was the Khor Abu Sunt, a dry watercourse that lay behind it. This was a shallow gully – about 5–6 feet deep and 10–20 feet wide – that ran across their path of advance down to the Nile. Here there were a further 2,000 spearmen that had been despatched from the main Black Flag body still hidden behind Jebel Surgham. This Dervish reinforcement used the concealed approach provided by the khor which ran down from the hill. Having received these reports, Martin moved his regiment in the formation 'column of troops', at the 'walk', taking a line of approach parallel to the khor. They could now see a line of about 150–200 Dervishes on the slight ridge, and Martin may have assumed that Pirie had exaggerated their numbers in his estimate. Among them were several riflemen who opened a vigorous fire, something that certainly attracted the attention of Lieutenant Raymond de Montmorency.

> I could see over my right shoulder, about 300 yards away, a dense mass of Dervish footmen pouring a hail of bullets into us. Luckily, as usual, most of them were too high. But it was not comfortable to be riding along slowly in column of troops with the enemy blazing into our right flank, and I found myself calling out, 'Why the blazes don't we charge before they shoot us down?'[41]
> Lieutenant Raymond de Montmorency, 'B' Squadron, 21st Lancers

Then, casting caution to the winds, Martin ordered the troops to wheel right into a single line – and launched a charge by his whole regiment of some 440 men towards the slight ridge and the Dervish riflemen.

> Two minutes before we charged, I was smoking and chatting and passing remarks about the enemy, little knowing that some of us would soon be counted with the slain. One of our men – a very witty fellow – passed the remark as we were advancing in line 'Here goes my £36 and my ticket for my grave!' And it came true, for, poor fellow, he was the first to fall, shot through the neck. We then got the order, 'Right wheel into line – gallop!'' Then the dreadful sound went, 'Charge!' Wild with excitement, we galloped for all we were worth, lances down at the 'Engage!'[42]
> Private Thomas Abbott, 'C' Squadron, 21st Lancers

This was what they had been waiting for – the much-longed-for chance to 'prove' themselves as 'real' cavalrymen.

Now here are 400 cavalry men, facing an enemy shooting to kill, there is nothing that will stop them from digging their spurs in and urging the horses into a gallop. The die is cast and down go the lances into the 'engage infantry' position. The galloping horses, beating hooves and the flying bullets produced an increased awareness of the action, a mixture of excitement and fear as we raced on towards the enemy.[43]

Private W. Rix, 'A' Squadron, 21st Lancers

There weren't that many riflemen among the Dervishes, but they were firing as fast as they could at the onrushing line of charging horsemen.

As we closed on them, I noticed that my squadron leader and second-in-command were riding with heads down as if against a hailstorm, and I found myself doing the same. It was very much like a hailstorm, as the bullets made a continuous 'Whiz!' 'Whiz!' 'Whiz!' with an occasional clink as one hit a sword, or a lance point.[44]

Lieutenant Raymond de Montmorency, 'B' Squadron, 21st Lancers

During the first few yards of the charge, Churchill made a snap decision. He was very aware of an earlier shoulder injury and did not fancy exposing it to the tremendous impact inevitable in using the '*arme blanche*'.

I had always decided that if I were involved in hand-to-hand fighting, I must use a pistol and not a sword. I had purchased in London a Mauser automatic pistol, then the newest and the latest design. I had practised carefully with this during our march and journey up the river. This then was the weapon with which I determined to fight. I had first of all to return my sword into its scabbard, which is not the easiest thing to do at a gallop. I had then to draw my pistol from its wooden holster and bring it to full cock. This dual operation took an appreciable time, and until it was finished, apart from a few glances to my left to see what effect the fire was producing, I did not look up at the general scene.[45]

2nd Lieutenant Winston Churchill, 'A' Squadron, 21st Lancers

As they grew near to the line of Dervishes, Churchill became aware of what lay just behind these skirmishers.

There now came into view a depression like a shallow sunken road. This was crowded and crammed with men rising up from the ground where they had hidden. Bright flags appeared as if by magic, and I saw arriving from nowhere Emirs on horseback among and around the mass of the enemy. The Dervishes appeared to be ten or twelve deep at the thickest, a great grey mass gleaming with steel, filling the dry watercourse.[46]

2nd Lieutenant Winston Churchill, 'A' Squadron, 21st Lancers

In a moment, the whole situation had changed – they were charging pell-mell into an ambush laid by Osman Digna. They had been completely fooled.

Just before we struck them, I saw straight in front of me a khor with rocks on either side filled with a dense mass of Dervishes packed round three flags, yelling defiance, waving their spears and swords, and firing their Remingtons. Amid the smoke and waving arms I could see their upturned faces grinning hate. My charger attempted to incline to his left, but I managed to keep him straight and the next moment he jumped the rocks and I was in the khor and among them. They were as thick as bees and hundreds must have been knocked over by our horses. My charger – a polo pony – behaved magnificently, literally trampling straight through them.[47]

Lieutenant Raymond de Montmorency, 'B' Squadron, 21st Lancers

The cavalry may have been outnumbered but they had one tremendous advantage as they struck home – the vast kinetic force of a horse and rider ridden at speed. But once in the khor it was every man for himself in a few seconds that seemed like minutes, a blur of wild impressions and the sense of life-or-death decisions triggering instantaneous actions – if not, death would surely be the result. Lieutenant Robert Smyth, who commanded the left-hand troop of 'A' Squadron, gives a breathless picture conveying the frenzied nature of the fighting.

> Am met by swordsman on foot. Cuts at my right front. I guard it with sword. Next, man with fat face, all in white having fired, missed me, throws up both hands. I cut him across the face. He drops. Large, bearded man in blue, with two-edged sword and two hands cuts at me. Think this time I must be done for, but pace tells, and my guard carries it off. Duck my head to spear thrown which just misses me. Another cut at my horse, miss guard, but luckily cut is too far away and only cuts through my breastplate and gives my horse a small flesh wound on neck and shoulder. Then I remember no more till I find myself outside with four or five of my troop.[48]
>
> Lieutenant Robert Smyth, 'A' Squadron, 21st Lancers

De Montmorency certainly had more than his fair share of close shaves as his squadron hit home where the Dervishes in the khor were thickest packed.

> The two Dervishes that gave me most trouble as I passed through the khor were one a fine clean-shaven, light skinned, well-bred looking swordsman who cut at me with a huge sword, right hand on hilt and left hand on right wrist. I can remember him well, the hissing yell of 'Allah!' and the ferocious look (of) hate with which he struck. I parried the blow, but the strength of his cut knocked me half off my horse and as I recovered my seat, a coal-black

fiend put his rifle straight at my chest. Before he had time
to fire I threw myself on to the other side of my horse's
neck, and he missed me. At this moment my horse and
Private Miller's cannoned at the bottom of the khor and we
passed out of it side by side – each of us having thus only
one side to defend.[49]
Lieutenant Raymond de Montmorency, 'B' Squadron, 21st Lancers

Churchill had managed to get through unscathed but once out
of the khor he soon realised that these Dervishes had fought
cavalry before – they knew exactly what to do once the initial
impetus of a charge had been dissipated.

I had the impression of scattered Dervishes running to
and fro in all directions. Straight before me a man threw
himself on the ground. The reader must remember that I
had been trained as a cavalry soldier to believe that if ever
cavalry broke into a mass of infantry, the latter would be at
their mercy. My first idea therefore was that the man was
terrified. But simultaneously I saw the gleam of his curved
sword as he drew it back for a ham-stringing cut. I had
room and time enough to turn my pony out of his reach,
and leaning over on the offside I fired two shots into him at
about 3 yards. As I straightened myself in the saddle, I saw
before me another figure with uplifted sword. I raised my
pistol and fired. So close were we that the pistol actually
struck him. Man and sword disappeared below and behind
me. On my left, 10 yards away, was an Arab horseman in
a bright-coloured tunic and steel helmet, with chain-mail
hangings. I fired at him. He turned aside. I pulled my horse
into a walk and looked round again. In one respect a cavalry
charge is very like ordinary life. So long as you are all right,
firmly in the saddle, your horse in hand, and well-armed,
lots of enemies will give you a wide berth. But as soon as
you have lost a stirrup, have a rein cut, have dropped your
weapons, are wounded, or your horse is wounded, then

is the moment when from all quarters your enemies rush upon you.[50]

2nd Lieutenant Winston Churchill, 'A' Squadron, 21st Lancers

As soon as possible the Lancers who had reached the other side sought to draw themselves away from the main body of the Dervishes and reform into some kind of formation. It was crucial that they rallied, as they were all aware of their vulnerability when isolated.

Where was my troop? Where were the other troops of the squadron? Within 100 yards of me I could not see a single officer or man. I looked back at the Dervish mass. I saw two or three riflemen crouching and aiming their rifles at me from the fringe of it. Then for the first time that morning I experienced a sudden sensation of fear. I felt myself absolutely alone. I thought these riflemen would hit me and the rest devour me like wolves. What a fool I was to loiter like this in the midst of the enemy! I crouched over the saddle, spurred my horse into a gallop and drew clear of the mêlée.[51]

2nd Lieutenant Winston Churchill, 'A' Squadron, 21st Lancers

Churchill located and joined the rest of his troop, who already formed up some 200–300 yards away. Here they began to count the cost.

I was still impressed with the idea that we had inflicted great slaughter on the enemy and had scarcely suffered at all ourselves. Three or four men were missing from my troop. Six men and nine or ten horses were bleeding from spear thrusts or sword cuts. We all expected to be ordered to charge back again. The men were ready, though they all looked serious. Several asked to be allowed to throw away their lances and draw their swords. I asked my second sergeant if he had enjoyed himself. His answer was, 'Well, I don't exactly say I enjoyed it, Sir; but I think I'll get more used to it next time!' At this the whole troop laughed![52]

2nd Lieutenant Winston Churchill, 'A' Squadron, 21st Lancers

His troop had been lucky to strike the weakest point of the Dervish line. In consequence they suffered far less than the rest of the regiment. Further along the khor, 'D' Squadron were hit hard.

I got through them with nothing worse than a blow on the head, which crushed my helmet, and a sword cut, slight, on my horse's quarters. Not so my poor squadron, which suffered more than any of the others. I had eleven killed and thirteen wounded out of the total casualties. When I got through, I saw Nesham being run away with, and smothered in blood, and so weak he could hardly sit on his horse. I gave my sword to my trumpeter and went after him, but he fell off from exhaustion and loss of blood before I could catch him, his left hand nearly severed and a bad gash on his leg. I sent him to the rear as soon as I could, and then rushed back to my squadron. I then met a man whom I could not recognize, as his nose was cut off and his face covered with blood. He was one of my sergeants, and having rallied his troop as far as he was able, rode up to me sitting at attention and asked if he might fall out and get his nose put on.[53]

Major Frank Eadon, 'D' Squadron, 21st Lancers

Men who had survived the worst of the cut and thrust in the khor were just thankful to be alive. They had seen at first hand the awful fate of some of their friends and comrades.

I felt myself all over to see if I was wounded, and then thanked God for bringing me through such an awful affair. The men that came down were cut to pieces – head and hands and feet cut clean off, and most of them had their insides hanging out. Oh! it was a shocking sight.[54]

Private Thomas Abbott, 'C' Squadron, 21st Lancers

Overall, the spirit of most of the survivors seemed to be undaunted, possibly because they had not yet realised what had happened.

> Directly we got through the khor and had gone about 100 yards, we halted and faced about, and then saw that the enemy had begun to retire westward, keeping up a heavy fire on us all the time. We could see their emirs rushing forward and trying to induce them to attack us while we were rallying. But their followers were not for it. They had already had enough of British cavalry! At this moment I noticed that Private Byrne of my troop was as pale as death and reeling in his saddle from loss of blood. So I told him he might fall out. But he answered, 'No, no, Sir, I'm all right! Fall in No. 2 Troop! Where are the Devils?'[55]

Lieutenant Raymond de Montmorency, 'B' Squadron, 21st Lancers

Thomas Byrne had just been involved in an act of great courage as he had rescued Lieutenant Richard Molyneux (an attached officer from the Royal Horse Guards) in amid the thick of the fighting. Molyneux's horse was down, which left him on foot, badly wounded in the right arm and surrounded by four Dervishes intent on finishing off. Byrne responded to his frantic call for help, despite already having been wounded himself. He launched a solo charge which scattered the Dervishes and allowed Molyneux to escape. Byrne would be awarded the VC for his heroic act.

The troop having reformed, there were several heroic officers and men who then voluntarily rode back into the khor to rescue their fallen comrades before it was too late. Among them was de Montmorency, despite having already received a slight spear wound and a heavy blow from a blunt weapon on this left

arm. He had every excuse not to go back, but he considered it
his duty.

> I went to see if I could find any of my men still alive in the
> khor. I particularly missed Sergeant Carter, my troop ser-
> geant, a magnificent soldier and a very skilful man-at-arms,
> I knew he would have been with me unless something
> had happened to him. Making for the khor I met Major
> Wyndham on foot running in magnificent style, with his
> revolver in his right hand up in the air. One Dervish horse-
> man 40 yards behind was galloping after him with a spear.
> Directly I rode at this horseman he turned and attempted
> to make off and so I had to shoot him in the back.[56]
> Lieutenant Raymond de Montmorency, 'B' Squadron, 21st Lancers

Both Lieutenant Smyth and Captain Paul Kenna went back to
complete the rescue of Major Walter Crole-Wyndham.

> See Major Wyndham running, gallop to help him. Am just
> too late, Kenna has seized him, and he takes him out not
> me. Rally my troop as well as I can. Horrible sights, every-
> one seems to be bleeding including my own horse. I don't
> know then if he is badly hurt or not. It seems to be blood,
> blood, blood everywhere, horses and men smothered,
> either their own or other people's.[57]
> Lieutenant Robert Smyth, 'A' Squadron, 21st Lancers

Meanwhile, de Montmorency had re-entered the khor itself – by
this time a valley of death for the 21st Lancers who had fallen or
been dragged off their horses.

> The sight of our mutilated dead made me 'see red' and go
> for every Dervish I met like a fury. It had the same effect
> afterwards on our men. I could not find Carter's body, but
> suddenly I came upon the body of an officer lying face down-
> wards. At first, I thought it was Smyth. At this moment I saw

Kenna and Corporal Swarbrick riding about near me, so I called them both to the body and dismounting found it to be Grenfell's – terribly mutilated. As the regiment was now 400 yards away and the enemy, who had begun to advance again firing heavily, were only 200 yards off, we determined to bring Grenfell's body away before it could be further mutilated. After a great effort – for a dead man is a terrible weight to lift – I managed to get him on to my horse, which took fright at the unusual burden and plunging forward, broke away from us and galloped off. Kenna and Corporal Swarbrick immediately went in pursuit of my horse and, though the enemy was firing furiously at us and every moment getting closer, they caught him and most gallantly brought him back to me. I made one more effort to get the body on to the horse, but found it impossible to lift quickly, and as we were only three and in a few more moments several hundred Dervishes would be round us there was nothing to do but to retire. So I mounted and we rode off together amid a hail of bullets. There is no doubt that the Dervishes are the worst shots in the world, and that not one of them in a hundred could hit a haystack at 50 yards.[58]

Lieutenant Raymond de Montmorency, 'B' Squadron, 21st Lancers

Both de Montmorency and Kenna would be awarded the Victoria Cross for their outstanding bravery.

It did not take long before the survivors correctly assessed their situation. Any optimism over a second charge was soon dissipated. What they did next showed the futility of the charge.

Once out of the shambles of the stream bed the scene was one of confusion. Many horses were dead, others were trotting around riderless, some were in a distressing state standing with their heads down, most of them streaming with blood from the many gashes received from the fearsome double-edged swords wielded by the Dervishes.

Mr Churchill wanted the men to charge the enemy again, but the Colonel wisely forbade it, instead we formed line, wheeled round to face the enemy's flank, dismounted and opened up a sustained rifle fire. This was more than they could stand, and they finally retreated.[59]

Private W. Rix, 'A' Squadron, 21st Lancers

Their rifle fire, firing from the flank of the khor, soon broke the resistance of the Dervishes. This was the real answer to the tactical situation that had faced them.

This fire checked the enemy and drove them back again. They retreated westward in confusion. The regiment mounted and advanced slowly after them. So we recovered all our dead and also three of their standards. They left some seventy-two dead. As they retired, they crossed the front of the 2nd British Brigade, which we could not see, just coming over the ridges west of Jebel Surgham, and almost at the same moment the 32nd Field Battery RA opened fire at about 2,000 yards range on the confused mass of the enemy. We could see the shrapnel bursting among them, much to our satisfaction, for we didn't bear any feeling of kindness to that black mass that had just mutilated so many of our gallant comrades.[60]

Lieutenant Raymond de Montmorency, 'B' Squadron, 21st Lancers

The mutilated state of the 21st Lancers lying scattered around the khor aroused much hatred for the perpetrators, but after reflection Ernest Bennett came up with a mature response, which was logical but would have had little traction on tired grieving men in the immediate aftermath of battle.

Indignation against the Dervishes for such mutilations may easily be exaggerated. Sickening as it is to gaze upon a comrade's features hacked out of all human semblance, one cannot forget that the men who did the deed had seen thousands of their brethren slain by our awful fire without a possibility of retaliation. It is worth remembering, too, that the mutilation of the human body is not the exclusive monopoly of barbaric peoples; anyone who has seen the effects of shellfire – bodies ripped open, jaws torn off, and kindred horrors – may find it difficult to differentiate very markedly between the accursed usages inseparable from every system of warfare – civilised and barbarous alike.[61]

Ernest Bennett, *Westminster Gazette*

Smyth saw at close hand the eviscerated bodies, but still managed to console himself that it had all been worthwhile.

I was told off to get six men of my troop to collect our dead. The less said or written about that the better. It was a ghastly sight. The tears streamed down my cheeks and I was physically sick. It was terrible. At this present moment I don't wish the morn' repeated, it cost too dear. I have always wanted to be in a charge and have got my desire and am satisfied. As far as cavalry goes it is the biggest thing since Balaklava and I am proud of belonging to the 21st Lancers. Wise or unwise, it was a brave deed nobly done.[62]

Lieutenant Robert Smyth, 'A' Squadron, 21st Lancers

And indeed, some of the men enjoyed the sheer atavistic joys of killing. The next brief quote certainly has a chilling nature.

I am ready for another man-killing job. It is nice to put a sword or a lance through a man; they are just like old hens, they just say, 'Quar!'[63]

Private Rawding, 21st Lancers

The 21st Lancers may have thought their fire dispersed the Dervishes in the khor, but that position could not have been held long given the later advance of the Lyttleton's 2nd Brigade towards Jebel Surgham.

> We had gone but a few hundred yards towards Omdur-man and were about opposite Surgham Hill, when from the ridge a lancer horse galloped towards us, riderless and dripping all over with blood. An ADC rode by saying, 'The 21st Lancers have caught it hot!' We immediately front formed and Gatacre said, 'Look out! The Khalifa is just in front of you!' I said, 'So much the better!'[64]
>
> Colonel Villiers Hatton, 1st Grenadier Guards, 2nd Brigade

From his perception as a senior, experienced infantryman, Lyttelton had little time for the 'bravado' of the charge of the 21st Lancers. To him it was all a waste of time.

> It was now that the Lancers got so sharply engaged. As we were following them, I saw a riderless grey horse galloping towards us, which my ADC caught. It was covered with blood, especially on the mane, and its rider had evidently been badly wounded, had bled over the mane and fallen off. On reaching the top of some rising ground I saw the 21st dismounted on the other side of a nullah, and I heard all about their charge. The nullah was full of Dervishes, and the ground not at all suitable for galloping; but the 21st, who had never been in action before, would not be denied and charged home. The Dervishes, used to cold steel, did not flinch, and though the Lancers went through them and cleared the nullah they suffered more loss than they inflicted. I do not altogether blame them, but they knew I was close behind them, and the affair was an infantry job, and it ought to have been left to me.[65]
>
> Brigadier General Neville Lyttelton, Headquarters, 2nd Brigade

Such perceptions were not confined to senior infantryman. As a professional cavalry officer, Captain Douglas Haig was appalled at what he considered was total incompetence when he heard of the charge.

> Away the regiment went, four squadrons in line, and came down in this nullah filled with rifle and spearmen. The result was scarcely as bad as might have been anticipated, for the two flank squadrons suffered little. Two troops of the centre squadrons were, however, practically wiped out. The loss inflicted on the enemy (judging by the corpses) was trifling, 14 or 15 at most. We onlookers in the Egyptian Cavalry have feared this all along, for the regiment was keen to do something and meant to charge something before the show was over. They got their charge, but at what a cost? I trust for the sake of the British Cavalry that more tactical knowledge exists in the higher ranks of the average regiment than we have seen displayed in this one.[66]
> Captain Douglas Haig, Egyptian Cavalry

Overall, it could be said that great gallantry does not excuse a blunder. Courage is not always enough in warfare. In the years since then, the participation of Winston Churchill in the charge has given a renown to what should have been notoriety. A more reasoned and much more detailed analysis was provided by Ismat Hasan Zulfo, an officer in the Sudanese Army, who long after the battle interviewed many of the Dervish survivors in researching his book *Karari* published in 1973. Rather than just call Osman Digna wily, or cunning, both terms that border on the insulting, Zulfo examines Digna's tactical skills properly. First, he presents an appreciation of the background to the 'trap' laid on along the Khor Abu Sunt.

> Osman Digna was aware of his own vulnerability. A direct confrontation with the enemy could result in the annihilation of his men. From his position he could see thousands of casualties being taken to Omdurman. He had long been aware that the enemy differed in kind from his former

enemies. Since the Battle of Atbara, he was mindful of
their clear superiority in modern weapons of destruction.
The only solution was to engage with the enemy as soon as
possible and to avoid exposing his men to their long-range
fire. For such exposure was to the enemy's advantage. With
his slight force his only chance of getting even with the
enemy was to prepare a tactical surprise. Surprise depends
on two factors. The first is putting the enemy in a completely unexpected situation in terms of arms, or timing,
or position, or concentration. The second factor is speed.
After achieving surprise, it is necessary to exploit it and to
deliver the decisive blow before the enemy can recover. It
is just like a quick stab; blood is seen before pain is felt.[67]
Ismat Hasan Zulfo

Osman Digna did not have enough men to cover the whole front
between the Jebel Surgham and the Nile. The distance was too
great, the ground for the most part too open.

He chose Khor Abu Sunt where it was widest and
was deep enough to conceal his men. All this aided an
ambush. But an ambush normally takes place on a road
or in a spot where the enemy is to pass. It is difficult to
carry out an ambush against an enemy who is mounted
and advancing on a wide front and has the freedom to
choose one of several routes to his destination. Had the
Lancers taken any other route, engagement would have
been impossible. Osman Digna managed to entice the
enemy to his chosen position. After making sure that he
had laid a trap for the enemy, Osman Digna prepared for
the first element of surprise – deception – by creating
a situation which was not what it seemed. Instead of a
single line of riflemen made up of only a few hundred
soldiers in an exposed position, the enemy found themselves facing more than 2,000 men. Thus, the element of
surprise turned primarily on their capacity to hide the

bulk of their actual numbers. As for the second factor – speed – this must depend mainly on the prompt delivery of the fatal blow.[68]

Ismat Hasan Zulfo

It was here that Osman Digna's plans had gone askew – literally. The reinforcements sent from the Black Flag were not yet properly in position *en masse* behind the tempting line of Dervishes visible on the low ridge in front of the khor.

> For when the Lancers plunged into the khor they landed among the thin lines of the Hadendowa, the early occupants, and not among the densely packed mass of reinforcements. Had it gone according to plan, the line of riflemen would have been immediately above the massed reinforcements, and the whole regiment, and not just Grenfell's troop, would have crashed headlong to their doom. Osman Digna was probably preoccupied with organizing the reinforcements and failed to notice the misalignment between the line of riflemen above, the bait, and the mass of men in the depression – the trap.[69]
>
> Ismat Hasan Zulfo

But from the British perspective, most telling of all was the fact that the 21st Lancers had entirely failed to perform their primary function in checking the ground behind Jebel Surgham – and Kitchener was therefore left in ignorance of the Khalifa's Black Flag force lurking there all unseen.

★★★

IT MAY HAVE SEEMED ALL OVER bar the shouting as Kitchener made his decision to abandon the safe harbour of his zeriba and trenches to march directly for Omdurman, but the most critical passage of the battle had yet to take place. At 09.15, Kitchener marched his infantry brigades out of the zeriba heading in a somewhat ramshackle order towards Jebel Surgham. The result was nearly catastrophe for the Anglo-Egyptian Army. For the Khalifa and his generals had by no means given up, and something like two-thirds of their force was still intact. Indeed, some have claimed that the first attack was a sacrifice designed to draw out the Anglo-Egyptian Army from behind its zeriba to its doom on the open plain, although this seems unlikely.

Not long after the Anglo-Egyptian brigades started to advance across the plain there was a somewhat farcical incident involving the gentlemen of the press.

> Two or three newspaper correspondents, eager for loot, rode out amongst the wounded, when up jumped a Dervish with a huge spear and put them all to rout, pursuing them back to the nearest troops amidst a discharge of revolvers dangerous to everyone except to the Dervish, for whom the shots were intended.[70]
>
> Major Horace Smith-Dorrien, 13th Sudanese Battalion,
> 2nd Egyptian Brigade

Major Hugh Fitton picks up the story.

> He had got within about 60 yards of our line when Lieutenant Smyth dashed up on horseback with his revolver and fired twice at him, hitting him the second time. The man closed however and aimed a blow at Smyth's midriff with his spear, which luckily caught Smyth on the elbow joint – instead of the ribs – making a nasty wound. Smyth then shot him dead at arm's length. A very gallant but rather unnecessary performance as no one's life was in danger and there was a line of 2,000 men, each ready to shoot him down within 60 yards.[71]
>
> Major Hugh Fitton, Headquarters, Egyptian Division

It is strange to record, amid so much slaughter, that this somewhat trivial and unnecessary incident led to the award of the

Victoria Cross to Captain Nevill Smyth who was serving with the Intelligence Section on detachment from the 2nd Dragoon Guards.

One of the many tragedies of Omdurman was the butchery of the wounded by the advancing troops. The rationale for this was the continued resistance of the Dervish warriors who were either wounded or feigning death. These men were still some-times lethally dangerous, especially to the unwary who strayed too close. This was the problem against a brave and determined enemy: when was it safe to accept surrender? It is a sad but understandable truism that troops rarely risk their own lives in order to take prisoners in the heat of battle. This explains some of the excess killing. In a perverse way it was a compliment to the indomitable nature of the men they killed.

> We moved directly across the advance of the enemy in the first phase of the battle and watched carefully for any wounded man anxious to kill an infidel before he died. It was well we did so, for within ten paces of where I was riding a seemingly dead man rose to his feet and began slashing with a large two-handed sword at the men nearest him. In a moment four or five of my men were round him like wasps, and he fell bayoneted to rise no more. On these occasions, I fancy the Sudanese soldier of the Egyptian Army takes no chances. He knows his countrymen too well and makes quite certain at once about getting in the first dig.[72]
>
> Captain Granville Egerton, 1st Seaforth Highlanders, 1st Brigade

This view that the Sudanese took pleasure in finishing off the wounded was widespread among the British observers.

> Our native battalions were soon busily engaged in killing the wounded. The Sudanese undertook this task with evident relish, and never spared a single Dervish along their path. On our left front, at the foot of the Surgham slope, where the opening shell fire of the batteries on the

left had covered the hillside with dead and wounded, a large number of servants and camp followers were also busy. These harpies, intent solely on loot, had armed themselves with various weapons. Some carried clubs or spears, others had managed to secure old rifles. They advanced with great caution, and I saw them fire repeatedly into bodies which were already quite dead, before they dared to rush in and strip the corpse of its arms and clothing.[73]

Ernest Bennett, *Westminster Gazette*

George Steevens was an appalled witness to events as they crossed the battlefield.

The wounded of a Dervish army ought not really to be counted at all, since the badly wounded die and the slightly wounded are just as dangerous as if they were whole. It is conceivable that some of the wounded may have been counted twice over, either as dead, when they were certain to perish of their wounds or of thirst, or else as prisoners when they gave themselves up. Yet, with all the deductions that moderation can suggest, it was a most appalling slaughter. The Dervish army was killed out as hardly an army has been killed out in the history of war. It will shock you, but it was simply unavoidable. Not a man was killed except resisting – very few except attacking. Many wounded were killed, it is true, but that again was absolutely unavoidable. It was impossible not to kill the Dervishes: they refused to go back alive.[74]

George Steevens, *Daily Mail*

There was even a close escape for Captain Douglas Churcher and some of the 'great and good' as his Maxims moved forward.

We had one narrow escape of being shot by a Sudanese battalion. It was during the first half of the pursuit, my

Maxims were on the right of our brigade which was in line, on my right was a Sudanese regiment, and we were advancing over the plain, being constantly potted at by wounded and hiding Dervishes. When one of the wounded made a rush at the Sudanese company nearest to us, they commenced firing at him – right in our direction! The Sirdar and General Gatacre, and all their staff were quite close to me, and for a minute the bullets were flying all round us. One went clean through the rifle of a sergeant of my detachment. The Sirdar was in an awful rage.[75]

Captain Douglas Churcher, Maxim Detachment

Perhaps it could be considered murder by both sides, but whatever it was, it was the ugly face of war.

As Kitchener's brigades wheeled round to the left to advance in echelon across the plain and then on to Omdurman, an element of chaos intruded on what should have been an orderly progression. The two British brigades were to occupy as soon as possible the ridge side by side between Jebel Surgham and the Nile. As Wauchope's 1st Brigade pressed on to pull up alongside with Lyttelton's 2nd Brigade, a gap began to open out between them and Maxwell's 2nd Egyptian Brigade. Then a further complication was introduced as Hunter was concerned with his open right flank of the Egyptian Division as they moved to the south. As a result, he decided to change the natural order of advance for his brigades to place Macdonald's highly regarded 1st Egyptian Brigade, reinforced by three batteries and Maxims, to act as a flank guard on the right, while Collinson's 4th Egyptian Brigade brought up the rear with the transport. All well enough intentioned, but the result was that as Wauchope hurried to catch up with Lyttelton, so Maxwell and Lewis, with the 3rd Egyptian Brigade, tried to close the opening gap while Macdonald moved out to the right flank. To reach his allotted position he had to march about a mile diagonally into the desert and Macdonald found himself isolated almost a mile from the 3rd Egyptian Brigade.

Stuck out in the open plain, MacDonald had a better – but still not clear – view of what lurked behind Jebel Surgham. He sighted an indeterminate number of Dervishes and adjusted the line of march to face them. As the situation became more and more threatening, he ordered a galloper, Harry Pritchard, to race across to Lewis to ask him to coordinate with his moves by clearing out the Dervishes who were on Jebel Surgham, and so take the ones behind it in flank while Macdonald attacked them head-on. Unfortunately, Lewis had just received a direct order from the Sirdar to make up the distance with Maxwell and the British brigades. MacDonald next tried a direct appeal to Kitchener, as Pritchard relates.

> I was to tell him of the mass of Dervishes behind the Jebel and to inquire whether Macdonald should attack them; and I was to ask also for the cooperation of Lewis's brigade. The Sirdar's reply was, 'Cannot he see that we are marching on Omdurman? Tell him to follow on!' I endeavoured to explain MacDonald's dangerous situation, but without effect, so I had to take this cold comfort back to MacDonald.[76]
> Lieutenant Harry Pritchard, Headquarters, 1st Egyptian Brigade

Then it happened. The Khalifa's brother, the Emir Ya'Qub, led into action the Black Flag force, estimated as around 12,000 warriors. They charged forward from their concealed location behind the Jebel Surgham to attack the 3,000 men of MacDonald's 1st Brigade (9th, 10th, and 11th Sudanese, and 2nd Egyptians).

Kitchener had left his force exposed to the possibility of defeat in detail, but to his credit he reacted swiftly when the Black Flag assault was launched. In essence, he altered the alignment of his army, issuing direct rapid-fire orders to his brigades for them to face west rather than south towards Omdurman. Wauchope's 1st Brigade was to rush back to render direct assistance to MacDonald. Meanwhile, all other brigades were to march to their right. Thus, Lewis's 3rd Egyptian Brigade was to drive into the right flank of the Black Flag; Maxwell's 2nd Egyptian

Brigade was to storm over the heights of Jebel Surgham, to come down threatening the rear of the Khalifa's force; Lyttelton's 2nd Brigade would swing round from their position on the ridge by the Nile to cut off any possible retreat to Omdurman; Collinson's 4th Egyptian Brigade would also swing right marching across the plain towards MacDonald; while the Camel Corps and Egyptian Cavalry would be responsible for keeping an eye on the Green Flag forces, which were believed to be still lurking behind the Kerreri Hills and therefore still posing a direct threat to MacDonald's rear. Nevertheless, although orders can – and were – quickly issued, this was not chess. It would take time to move whole brigades about the battlefield. And so, *everything* depended on the steely resolve of MacDonald's 1st Egyptian Brigade: they simply *had* to bear the brunt of the battle for approximately half an hour. If they were overwhelmed, then there was a very real chance that the 2nd and 4th Egyptian Brigades might also be caught remote from support and fall like dominos. This was the decisive moment of the battle. But Kitchener could have had no better man in command at the decisive point than Hector MacDonald. His one big advantage was that some element of surprise had been lost by the early sighting of the Dervishes gathering near the end of the Jebel Surgham which allowed him to get into line facing this first threat – and the fact that his brigade had been allotted strong artillery and Maxim support. Firepower would be crucial – they had to stop the Dervishes before they got to close quarters.

> The force in front of me was a very large one and I knew that the one on my right was a very large one and I determined to defeat, if possible, the nearer force before the other could join. At a range of 1,100 yards, I brought forward the artillery and opened fire, the infantry which were advancing in fours from the flanks of companies forming line. No sooner had we opened fire than up went innumerable standards, amongst them a prominent black one, the Khalifa's, and they opened a furious fusillade and

at once bore down upon us. Their advance was very rapid
and determined, and though they appeared to be mowed
down by the artillery and Maxims they still pressed on in
such numbers and so quickly that I brought up the infantry
into line with the guns, but in spite of the hail of lead now
poured at effective ranges into their dense masses they still
pressed forward in the most gallant manner.[77]

Lieutenant Colonel Hector Macdonald, Headquarters, 1st Egyptian
Brigade

He had pulled from column into line, with from the left the 11th
Sudanese, the 2nd Egyptians, the 10th Sudanese, a gun battery
and two Maxims and on the far right the 9th Sudanese. Each
battalion had four companies in line with two companies in
support.

The Dervish fire meanwhile was getting pretty hot, and
they had started to advance, whereupon the 9th Battalion became very excited, and could with difficulty be
restrained from charging forward. Without any orders
they opened independent firing. Each battalion as it came
up, hearing the firing on its right, thought the order had
been given to open independent fire, and did so. The 9th
Battalion were now almost out of hand. If they broke line
and rushed forward into the mass of Dervishes in front the
game would be up. Our game was to keep them at bay by
our fire until we had killed so many that we could charge
the remainder.[78]

Lieutenant Harry Pritchard, Headquarters, 1st Egyptian Brigade

Any indiscipline would have been fatal, but when Macdonald
detected poor fire discipline, he took immediate action.

Colonel MacDonald, seeing how the brigade was getting
out of hand, rode out in front, and riding down in front
of the line, knocked up their rifles and shouted to them

to cease fire. The battalion officers and non-commissioned officers did the same, and after a few minutes, in which Colonel MacDonald galloped up and down in front of the line, they all ceased fire and ordered arms. Colonel Mac-Donald kept them standing quite still while he harangued them for a couple of minutes in no measured terms. It was very unpleasant for them standing still in the open under a hot fire without being able to reply to it, but it had the effect of getting them thoroughly in hand, and from that time on they worked like a machine.[79]

Lieutenant Harry Pritchard, Headquarters, 1st Egyptian Brigade

One can picture the scene as Macdonald shouted at his men, accompanied by his brigade major, a trumpeter and Harry Pritchard himself, all the while under heavy fire and with onrushing Dervishes rapidly closing in. But undisciplined fire or a futile half-baked counterattack would have doomed them all. Whatever the risk, Macdonald had to reestablish control to ensure the controlled volleys that would slaughter their opponents.

The Dervishes took advantage of the cessation of fire, and pushed forward to within about 400 yards, from whence their riflemen poured in a heavy but frightfully ill-aimed fire. Colonel MacDonald now ordered firing to recommence by company volleys. After a few minutes the Dervishes launched their attack. With a great yelling they rose up and rushed forward, headed by about 200 mounted emirs, galloping as hard as their horses could lay legs to the ground. Colonel MacDonald ordered independent firing to commence. The guns fired case shot, and every rifle and Maxim fired as fast as they could load. It was a stirring moment. It must have been a terrific fire for the Dervishes to face. So rapid was our fire, that above the sound of the explosions could be heard the swish of our bullets going through the air just like the swish of water. It literally swept away the line of charging Dervishes. One or two horsemen got within 100 yards, and it really looked as if they would reach us. The leading emir was hit twice, one could see him reel in his saddle, but he still came on at full gallop, and was just lifting his spear when he fell within 40 yards of our line, exactly as if he had been knocked off by the branch of a tree.[80]

Lieutenant Harry Pritchard, Headquarters, 1st Egyptian Brigade

The Dervish warriors were cut down in swathes, among them Emir Ya'Qub who was reported to have been hit by Maxim fire, along with two of his men who attempted to retrieve his corpse. These men were heroes.

Then a new crisis burst on Macdonald and his embattled 1st Egyptian Brigade. Just as he was considering advancing toward Wauchope's and Lewis's brigades, some 10,000 of the Green Flag Dervishes under the command of Ali Wad Helu and Osman Wad made an unwelcome appearance from the direction of the Kerreri Hills. MacDonald reacted with a combination of speed, determination and sheer brilliance. He had gained a grip on his men, and he used it to great effect as he carried out a fearsomely complicated manoeuvre while under attack from both sides. One by one he withdrew his battalions from the line facing westwards and formed a new line behind them facing almost north.

MacDonald swung back half of the 9th Battalion, so that this battalion made an arrowhead. They were ordered to open independent firing, while Major Laurie's Battery came into action on the right of the 9th firing case. This slightly checked the Dervishes, who had begun a heavy fire, and the 11th Battalion, after having twenty-seven men hit while marching across, had time to form up with admirable steadiness and order; but when they opened fire the Dervishes were within 300 yards and still coming on, while the Khalifa's force were still attacking the other face of the brigade, so that it was under a heavy crossfire, fortunately very ill-directed. Captain Peak's Battery, which had just come up, came into action on the right of the 11th, and the Camel Corps, who had all along been watching and sparring with Ali Wad Helu's force, now dismounted and formed on the right of the brigade.[81]

Lieutenant Harry Pritchard, Headquarters, 1st Egyptian Brigade

Meanwhile the Black Flag force wilted away, coming under fire from their right flank from Lewis's 3rd Egyptian Brigade.

Macdonald had become engaged with the Dervishes under the Black Flag. We formed line to the right and crossed the ridge of Jebel Surgham in time to be of considerable support to the 1st Brigade who had become heavily engaged in front. We pressed on and the large Dervish force in the valley at our feet was soon annihilated. I do not claim that we helped much, but we were a great moral support.[82]

Lieutenant Colonel David Lewis, Headquarters, 3rd Egyptian Brigade

Aided by this intervention, MacDonald was able to move his 10th Battalion to join the northern facing line, while the 2nd Egyptian Battalion shuffled across to take their place.

The 3rd Battery (Captain De Rougemont's) came into action between the 10th Battalion and the camel corps, so that now there were one and a half battalions firing at the Khalifa's force, while two and a half battalions, Camel Corps, and three batteries were firing the other way at Ali Wad Helu's force. The infantry were on independent firing, the guns firing case. The noise was deafening and was added to by the bursting of the Dervish shells, which, however, were bursting too close to us to do any damage. MacDonald's trumpeter was shot at his side. The casualties of the brigade gradually rose to 168, while those of the Camel Corps on its right rose to 40. It was the last effort of the Dervishes, their last chance, and bravely they tried to push home, but the ground was open, and nothing could live in the open against our fire. MacDonald's brigade had now been heavily engaged for well over an hour, and the ammunition began to get very low. More had been sent for, but had not yet arrived. The Dervish attack, however, was weakening.[83]

Lieutenant Harry Pritchard, Headquarters, 1st Egyptian Brigade

As the Khalifa's Black Flag attack collapsed, the whole of the 1st Egyptian Brigade was swung round to face the Green Flag attack from the north. As they did there was an unfortunate accident.

Colonel MacDonald wheeled the 2nd Battalion and half of the 9th into line with the remainder of his force. As Colonel MacDonald rode up to the officer commanding the 9th Battalion to tell him to bring up the left half of his battalion in line with the right half, that officer's horse suddenly whipped round, and let fly a tremendous kick at Colonel MacDonald, catching him fair on the leg just below the knee. It was a wonder that it did not break his leg. As it was, the pain was so great that he nearly fainted. He succeeded, however, in recovering himself almost immediately, and continued directing his brigade.[84]

Lieutenant Harry Pritchard, Headquarters, 1st Egyptian Brigade

Around this time, Wauchope's 1st Brigade arrived on the scene, with the 1st Lincolnshire moving to prolong MacDonald's right, while the rest moved to his left. In many British accounts much is often made of the arrival of the 1st Lincolnshire Regiment 'just in time' to 'save' the Sudanese line by adding their firepower to the battle.

Our regiment was ordered to the right to reinforce the Sudanese and here we had to double across the Dervishes' firing line, which caused us to have a lot of casualties. We formed up on the right of the Sudanese and formed into line, when volley firing was again given. It was between 500 and 1,000 yards we were firing. We fixed bayonets and fired about thirty volleys and then we advanced again across the battlefield and several wounded. We passed them and we also got the order to destroy all arms by breaking them on the rocks and some of our men were breaking them on the heads of the Dervishes.[85]

Private George Teigh, 1st Lincolnshire Regiment, 1st Brigade

But Major Seymour Vandeleur had a different perspective.

If the Green Flags had co-operated with the former attack and caught us in rear when we were engaged in front, it would have been extremely unpleasant. But the earlier attack had exhausted itself before the second came on, so we beat them in detail. The 1st British Brigade (Wauchope's) could be seen hurrying to support us, but the Dervish attack was 'done for' before they came up.[86]

Major Seymour Vandeleur, 9th Sudanese Battalion, 1st Egyptian Brigade

It is important to grasp that not everything good achieved that day was down to British skill at arms. The Sudanese and Egyptian battalions had fought well early in the battle, but this was their real triumph. In exceptionally difficult and dangerous circumstances they had kept their discipline and nerve to win the day in the deciding phase of the battle. This was their triumph – and at the time this was realised.

The brunt of it fell on MacDonald's brigade, and the way he handled his men, and his men played up, was splendid. It was a very serious 10 minutes, and the charge the Dervishes made there, literally thousands right up to the bayonet point, was enough to try the best troops in the world. Wauchope's brigade was sent off to the right to assist, but the danger was over before they arrived. The Dervish dead in front of Mac's brigade were literally in banks.[87]

Captain James Watson, Headquarters, Egyptian Division

As the firing petered out, Vandeleur moved out in front of his men. It was nearly a fatal mistake.

> The thing was over, and the cease fire sounded, so I rode out in front of my men to stop the shooting – when a Baggara spearman lying down unhurt about sixty paces from us made for me. He ran at a great pace and my horse being nervous interfered with my aim. His first spear whizzed past my head. I hit him with two revolver bullets but still he closed with me. I then warded off his spear thrust with my right-hand and revolver, and he fell dead – finished off by one of the men's bullets. But in doing it his spear wounded me in the hand cutting the third finger and palm. Smyth[88] – who had a similar experience – and I both agree that the new 'man-stopping' bullet is not much use against a good Dervish.[89]
>
> Major Seymour Vandeleur, 9th Sudanese Battalion, 1st Egyptian Brigade

With the final threats overwhelmed on the plain, the Anglo-British battalions advanced onwards up and over Jebel Surgham driving into the flank of the Black Flag forces and threatening to cut them off from Omdurman.

Although the courage of most of the Black Flag Dervishes was unquestionable, there were tens of thousands of warriors. It would have been strange were there not some who found themselves trapped by circumstance. They did not want to be martyrs; but a combination of powerful peer group pressure and fear of the possibly fatal consequences of not following the 'true path' had dragged them to the battlefield. One such was Babikr Bedri, who made no bones about his lack of enthusiasm for the bloodthirsty fray – and he had come up with a cunning plan to escape with his life.

> At about seven in the morning, we heard the noise of fire-arms, both the enemy's and our own; and at about eight the wounded from Uthmân Diqna's regiment began to

pass by us to the rear. We noticed that for every wounded man there were four others carrying or supporting him; so, I said to our little group, 'Look here, if one of us gets wounded I shall get wounded too – with his blood; and the rest of you can carry us away, since that seems to be allowed!'[90]

Babikr Bedri, *Black Flag*

Now the moment of truth had arrived. The fight was coming ever closer, and it was obvious that they would soon be required to make the final sacrifice for the Khalifa.

After a little we were drawn up in one rank with the Black Flag before us, and we saw the arms of the enemy flashing in the sun as they advanced (a sight I knew); and when we saw them like moving yellow cliffs, the Khalifa of the Mahdi called to the officers of the Guard, 'Abja-kkal Up! Lead your comrades to repulse these enemies of God!' The Reinforcement Guard leapt up, and we saw them advance about 100 metres or a little more, firing at intervals, and the enemy fired on them with a sound like 'Runnnn!' They did not return. Some of them were killed, and some of them pretended to be killed. The enemy army did not pause in its advance upon us soldiers of the Black Flag, until it was quite near, and their bullets started to reach us, or went pouring and whizzing over our heads. Then Muhammad the Mahdi's son shouted, 'How long are we to stand here? Are we to wait here till they catch hold of us with their hands?' And he spurred his horse, and the Black Flag was snatched out of the ground. Before this I had noticed ahead of us a little hillock of sand with some bushes on its slope, and had said to my friends, 'If any of us can reach that sandhill, he will be safe home.' The flag advanced, and we ran with it till we reached the sandhill, where we flung ourselves down in one rank and watched the flag fall and rise again, fall and rise again, and at the

third fall the hail of bullets thickened about us. I ask you
to believe, that I who had never feared to meet the enemy
– today I nibbed my face into the sand trying to bury
my head in it, thoughtless of suffocation, so distracted
was I by the fear of death, which in dangers no less acute
than this I had sought so eagerly. Then Bâbikr Mustafa,
the man on my right, received a wound in the left hand,
and I came to my senses at last and remembered what
I had promised my comrades. I slipped off my turban,
smeared it in my neighbour's blood, and bound it on my
left arm; then I called to my companions, 'Now two of us
are wounded!' They jumped up from cover, and four of
them carried back each one of us, and we got away; and
when we got through the wadi each man of the ten ran
where he would.[91]

Babikr Bedri, Black Flag

He managed to make it to safety and would only die aged 94
years, long afterwards in 1954. Sensible caution can indeed be a
safer path than headstrong valour.

As Bedri fled, the British troops were approaching. Many of
the Dervishes fought to the last, embracing death as their bodies
littered the ground around the black symbol of the Khalifa's
power.

We had all along observed in front of us the Khalifa's great
black standard, planted firmly in the desert sand. Our directions led us close past the banner, and I do not think in all
my life I have ever seen anything more grand and dramatic
than the picture it presented. It stood upright, and round
it lay a mass of white clad bodies, in appearance forming
what might have been likened to a large white croquet
ground or lawn tennis court outlined on the yellow sand.
There must have been two or three hundred men of the
bodyguard, amongst them the famous Emir Osman Azrak,
who had thus done their duty according to their lights and

fallen fighting to the last round the emblem of their worth-
less ruler. A sight to stir the blood and rouse the admiration
of any soldier.[92]

Captain Granville Egerton, 1st Seaforth Highlanders, 1st Brigade

Captain James Watson was there when the great banner was
presented to Kitchener.

> After everything else had gone down, a band of his most
> faithful followers could be seen gathered round his enor-
> mous black silk flag. But in time, they, and the flag, like
> everything else, went down before our fire, and when our
> line reached the spot, the flag was brought in triumph to
> the Sirdar. For the rest of the day his orderly carried it about
> after him – no light job for the flag itself was fully 8 feet by
> 10 feet and the staff about 22 feet high.[93]

Captain James Watson, Headquarters

The iconic standard of the Khalifa was now the symbol of the
Sirdar's triumph.

By 11.30 the whole of the Khalifa's army was in full retreat.
Following the breakdown of the Green Flag attack on Mac-
Donald's 1st Egyptian Brigade, Colonel Broadwood saw his
opportunity and launched his cavalry, thereby turning the retreat
into a rout. Douglas Haig was with them. As they rode across
the killing fields, they were still plagued by wounded Dervishes
who refused to contemplate surrender.

> The Egyptian cavalry now galloped out in pursuit
> towards the round-topped hill. We crossed the front of
> the infantry. Many wounded men still rose up and fired
> at us as we approached, and spearmen tried to hurl a
> spear. As we proceeded westwards, many little groups
> of men dropped down on their knees in submission,
> though some firmly resisted till killed by our lances. I
> saw, too, men beg for pardon, and then, when we had

passed, treacherously assault some unsuspecting trooper from the rear.[94]

Captain Douglas Haig, Egyptian Cavalry

Then a charge proper began, this time in accordance with more professional practice, sweeping through an already broken force that was no longer capable of offering a serious collective resistance. Even so they came under some rifle fire.

We commenced our gallop; my squadron on the left, the centre one directing, and a third squadron on the right. The fire increased as we advanced, and men on my left who had flung down their arms in submission picked them up again – so that we were enveloped with a crossfire from all directions. The squadron on my right passed in rear of mine to my left, and the right one did likewise, its leader galloping right across my front. My men seemed to bend their heads to the right as one does to escape a storm of rain. I had seen eight horses go down in my front rank, and being unsupported on my right flank, I, too, brought up my right and moved now directly on Signal Hill. Our three squadrons had attacked some ten or more thousand resolute and armed men all scattered across the plain. I lost only five men wounded, but nineteen horses. Our horses were now dead beat, and we moved to the hill after dressing our wounded.[95]

Captain Douglas Haig, Egyptian Cavalry

It is undeniable that this long-forgotten cavalry charge was far more successful than the much-vaunted attempt by the 21st Lancers. As would so often be the case in the Great War, Haig had a far better grasp of military affairs than Churchill and his like. Certainly the Egyptian horsemen impressed the watching infantry.

The Egyptian cavalry now made a grand charge among the retiring enemy, and we had a splendid view of this. They galloped right through them, their swords flashing in the sun, then reformed and back through them, cutting them up.[96]

Lieutenant Ronald Meiklejohn, 1st Royal Warwickshire Regiment, 1st Brigade

The battle was won.

17

ON, ON TO OMDURMAN

I picked up Sirdar just as he was nearing the Khalifa's enclosure – I don't know what he felt but I know how I felt and how he looked – I told him he was Lord of Khartoum if he cared to be. The campaign was over, and we could now enjoy ourselves like boys rattling in a stockyard. And we did have an afternoon, poking into houses, in and out of narrow alleys, kicking down doors, forcing gateways, chasing devils all over the place, most surrendered, but we had to kill some 300 or 400.[1]

Major General Archibald Hunter, Headquarters, Egyptian Division

MURDER IS MURDER BUT BOTH 'SIDES' had plenty of excuses, perhaps even reasons, for going well beyond any 'rules of war' during the victorious Anglo-Egyptian advance across the battlefield and on to Omdurman. Individual Dervishes lying wounded, or feigning death on the ground, launched vicious surprise attacks on the approaching soldiers, sometimes even assaulting men attempting to help them. The response as we have already seen could be brutal and out of all proportion. Thus, on a battlefield carpeted with Dervish corpses, men took offence at the death of a single British officer. They would have their vengeance.

Grenfell, Lyttleton's ADC, as he rode said, 'They have killed my brother!' The men heard this, and I have no doubt it made them polish off the wounded and dangerous Dervishes with their bayonets in a very determined way. This had to be done and was done by order. The Queen's

Company and No. 3 Reserve Company being responsible that we were not shot from behind. The order was in going over the battlefield to be very careful of wounded, or apparently wounded, Dervishes who, if offered resistance and to finish them if necessary, otherwise loss would ensue.[2]
Colonel Villiers Hatton, 1st Grenadier Guards, 2nd Brigade

This is a theme that recurs time and time again in the surviving accounts. Yet there was a still more sinister implication that the slaughter of the Dervish wounded was either directly, or indirectly, sanctioned.

I rode over the battlefield about 20 minutes after the end of the fight, and it was a most painful and sickening sight, especially where shells had burst. All the wounded were shot or bayoneted immediately the fight was over. This was done by Egyptian troops, and seems hardly the thing, but it was absolutely necessary, and certainly the most merciful thing to do. The Dervish wounded were very dangerous, and quite a number of men were killed by them.[3]
Lieutenant Arthur White, 2nd Rifle Brigade, 2nd Brigade

The tender mercy of the bullet or bayonet has a dreadful ring to it. Notice that according to Lieutenant Arthur White, this was carried out by the 'Egyptian troops', despite the fact that there were numerous examples of the British 'taking no chances' as they crossed the battlefield. After all, to their mind the Dervishes had brought it on themselves. The vicious merciless killing that typified the fighting in the Mahdist wars surely reached its apogee in the aftermath of the Battle of Omdurman. Both sides dehumanised 'the enemy' – whether for religious reasons, simple racism, or a perception that their enemies were 'monsters'. As such their opponents were not 'really' human, but mere creatures to be dealt with, with no need for humanity. Thus, both sides fought with a vicious brutality, with scant consideration for any concepts of surrender, mercy or taking prisoners. Men fought to the death on both sides; and both sides were more than happy to oblige. 'Kill them all' has a long pedigree in warfare.

After a short halt to reorganise at about 11.30, the advance on Omdurman began. Ahead of them went the 21st Lancers to check for any formed opposition and thereby ensure no unwelcome surprises.

> I then got an order to take a patrol and locate the direction and numbers of the retreating enemy. I took six of the men with the best horses and rode south-west. The desert was covered with individuals making off as fast as they could on foot. It was alright so long as I was in sight of the regiment, the enemy threw down their weapons and threw up their hands. But when I made the second ridge, perhaps 2 miles on, it was not at all so alright. There was a bit of mirage, but not very bad and I was guessing the length of the dust column of the enemy through my glasses when one of my men shouted: 'Look out, Sir, there is a bloke shooting at you!' With that he dropped his lance and galloped at a bush in which the sniper was seated and ran him through. Of course, the enemy's firearms were very varied and not very accurate, but I thought that if I made another bound to the next ridge it might be more awkward and 'K' might get no report at all, so I wrote them down as 20,000 marching south-south-west and returned to the regiment.[4]
> Lieutenant John Vaughan, 'C' Squadron, 21st Lancers

Behind them the infantry slogged on in the burning heat and dust. After all, there was still an urgent requirement for all possible haste.

> It was all important to keep the enemy on the move, and not give any time for the organisation of a defence within the gigantic rabbit warren of mud houses that constituted the city of Omdurman. The whole force consequently

marched through the fierce noonday heat towards the south. The want of water by this time began to make itself severely felt, and the troops were suffering considerably from this cause and from exhaustion, when we at length reached a ravine running in from the Nile bank. This ravine was known as Khor Shambat, and was full of a yellow, muddy liquid, in which lay several dead animals, and further down more than one corpse. These facts in no way prevented practically every soldier and animal drinking copiously, and it is extremely probable that from this one source alone much of the subsequent dysentery and enteric that affected the returning troops may be traced.[5]
Captain Granville Egerton, 1st Seaforth Highlanders, 1st Brigade

Second Lieutenant Hugh Farmer watched his men gulp down water with little or no precautions.

Arrangements for water were very bad. I saw men drink from stagnant pools in which were the bodies of dead animals. At the best, water was drawn from the Nile in flood, thick with silt. The men took off their trousers, rinsed them, and filtered water through them to make it clear enough to drink. Fuel was too scarce to allow of boiling much water.[6]
2nd Lieutenant Hugh Farmer, 2nd Lancashire Fusiliers, 2nd Brigade

The Khor Shambat was about 2 miles from Omdurman. Conscious of the need for speed, Kitchener left the main body behind and pressed on with his headquarters, accompanied by First Lieutenant Colonel John Maxwell's 2nd Egyptian Brigade and the 32nd Field Battery.

We had covered half the distance perhaps to the Mahdi's tomb, the great dome of which stood out prominent above the mass of houses, when we met men with the news that the Khalifa was inside the by-wall with from 2,000 to 3,000

riflemen determined to fight to the end and to refuse all
quarter. Williams field battery was brought up, and the
brigade pushed on. About 5 p.m. we got to the north-west
angle of the by-wall. It's a stupendous structure, stone, and
from 15 to 18 feet high, but entirely without loopholes or
any kind of defence. Inside is a perfect mass of houses and
a labyrinth of narrow alleys. We took with us four guns of
the battery and the 13th Sudanese.[7]

Captain James Watson, Headquarters, Egyptian Division

They could still have been faced with a terrible battle, house-
by-house and street-by-street, against an unknown number of
Dervishes determined to fight to the last. It was the sort of situation that no army would ever want to face. The Khalifa must
not be given the time to organise resistance.

None of us, not even the Sirdar, knew how much or
how little resistance to expect; a spy had reported that
the Khalifa – and some 2,000 riflemen – was praying in
the Mosque square and that he was exhorting his men to
make a last stand. We entered the outskirts of the place
immediately on leaving Khor Shambat and the difficulties of keeping communication up between the different
units of the brigade in the intricate alleys and when crossing various khors full of water was a most difficult task,
which fell chiefly on my shoulders and those of Maxwell's
ADC.[8]

Major Ivor Maxse, Headquarters, 2nd Egyptian Brigade

Omdurman was defended by a great defensive wall – the
Sur. The 13th Sudanese, under the redoubtable Major Horace
Smith-Dorrien were the most advanced battalion, charged with
moving eastwards along the north face of the Sur until they
reached the Nile. They would then turn south and attack the
forts in turn, assisted by the fire from the gunboats.

The enemy made a poor fight of it, and, firing a few shots, bolted from each fort in turn. Then a deep and forbidding-looking khor was reached running from under the walls of the Sur into the river, and many yards wide. It was nothing more nor less than a main drain, rendered more obnoxious by the bodies of several dead animals. However, it had to be crossed, and the fort, from which they were firing on the opposite side of it, taken. So into it we plunged, and, after a struggle with mud and water, were safely landed on the other bank, and a few minutes later were in possession of the fort. Here also was the first big gate into the Sur, which soon yielded to battering, and the troops rushed in, met by a mild discharge of rifles, the firers of which made a hasty retirement behind the houses, throwing down their arms. After proceeding some 200 yards into the Sur through the gate, it was ascertained that the main gate leading to the Khalifa's house was some 500 yards farther on, so back came the leading companies of the 13th outside the Sur, and again moving south, came opposite the main gate.[9]

Major Horace Smith-Dorrien, 13th Sudanese Battalion,
2nd Egyptian Brigade

Major Ivor Maxse was full of suppressed excitement as he watched the gates being smashed open.

They heard voices within, and a half company was drawn up ready to shoot, whilst the gate was being smashed open with a beam. It was all very interesting and very exciting for those who took a share in the adventure, for no one could guess what might occur at any moment. At last half the gate was forced open, we squeezed into the enclosure and beheld numbers of the Khalifa's riflemen bolting up the streets and alleys. Only one body of Dervishes and some stray individuals showed signs of fight and were promptly shot. The majority had had enough of slaughter, like ourselves, and threw down their arms when ordered. At first slowly, then quicker and quicker, the piles of Remingtons and bandoliers grew in the street – till they amounted to thousands, guarded by a few sentries. Undoubtedly our air of confident assurance and habit of commanding blacks imposed on the enemy and prevented them from realising that only one battalion and some guns had entered the enclosure.[10]

Major Ivor Maxse, Headquarters, 2nd Egyptian Brigade

If the Dervishes surrendered their weapons immediately without resistance, then they would be allowed to live; anything else, any hesitation, and they were shot out of hand. The 2nd Egyptian Brigade's over-riding priority at this point was to capture the Khalifa. They pressed through the narrow streets heading for his house close by the mosque, the arsenal and the Mahdi's tomb.

A low wall surrounded the Mosque Square into which the faithful flocked daily for prayer through several wide entrances – one of which was near the back door of the Khalifa's house. When we approached this entrance from the mosque side, six horsemen were observed galloping across it from behind the Khalifa's house, and their long spears remained visible just above the wall as they rode on. They saw us making for the entrance and only 30 yards from it, whereupon two of their number stopped and waited behind the wall. One dismounted and could no longer be seen, the other sat on his horse and poised his spear above his head – ready for action; their four companions galloped away as fast as they could. Evidently something was up, so a section of the leading company of the 13th Sudanese was drawn across the entrance with bayonets fixed and rifles loaded. A pause ensued, during which we all watched the spear poised above the wall in the Baggara's hand. Then suddenly like a flash of lightning the two desperate men charged home, one on foot the other mounted. The man on foot threw one spear before he started from behind the wall, then closed with another in his hand and wounded one of our blacks. The horseman made good his point and transfixed a Sudanese corporal through the skull with his spear, pinning him against the mosque wall and instantly killing him. Both the Baggaras then fell dead, at the feet of our men riddled with bullets, as was also the horse. It was a gallant act gallantly performed in order to gain a few moments time for the Khalifa to escape us.[11]

Major Ivor Maxse, Headquarters, 2nd Egyptian Brigade

It was widely believed that the Khalifa was one of the four horsemen that had managed to escape, although this is by no means certain.

Then there was a terrible shock as they came under fire from an unexpected source.

Then suddenly the battalion and staff assembled round the Khalifa's house felt shells bursting above their heads and shrapnel bullets whizzing about them. These were most accurately aimed and very unpleasant. Obviously, we had come under the fire of the two British guns which had been posted outside the great enclosure, and our musketry had attracted their attention. They knew not that they were shooting at their friends. Hunter at once ordered the Khalifa's house to be evacuated.[12]

Major Ivor Maxse, Headquarters, 2nd Egyptian Brigade

There was at least one casualty as the shrapnel bullets smashed down around the Khalifa's house.

I saw a terrible sight – Hubert Howard lying gasping on his back, his horse standing over him and his head in a pool of blood! The wound was right through his brain, and he never recovered consciousness. We buried him next day out in the open and a cross is being erected over his grave.[13]

Major Ivor Maxse, Headquarters, 2nd Egyptian Brigade

The town was by this time secured and all resistance had collapsed. Indeed, as the British units marched in, they received quite a reception. Despite their fatigue, the Guards put on a show as they entered.

We got up the drums and played 'The British Grenadiers' and then marched through. Thousands of women, 'U-U-U-U'd their evident joy and many Dervishes who had no doubt recently been fighting us. Some of these kissed my hands and then raised them to their foreheads.[14]

Colonel Villiers Hatton, 1st Grenadier Guards, 2nd Brigade

Many of the men noticed the place smelt awful.

The town stunk absolutely abominably, the narrow streets being filled with every sort of refuse and every few yards pools of filthy water. The buildings were of mud bricks and seemed pretty clean. The square in the middle of the town had twelve gallows with accommodation for fifty at a time. I've never smelt such a smell as there was – as the graves were only a few inches deep, dead cattle putrefying in corners and the natives had contributed their best. The Mahdi's tomb in the centre of the town had been stoved in by a shell and many houses were in ruins.[15]

2nd Lieutenant Hugh Farmer, 2nd Lancashire Fusiliers, 2nd Brigade

The prisoners of the Khalifa were released from their fetters, some Abyssinians, others European.

It had been a long and tiring day. After some initial confusion the regiments were assigned to their billeting areas.

That night most of the troops bivouacked out on the big parade ground to the west of the town, but it was a devil of a business getting there – streets blocked with transport camels, whole regiments who had lost their way! Omdurman was a veritable pandemonium during the earlier hours of the night. But later when the moon rose the various units were able to get to their bivouacs. We got our dinner about 10 p.m. and the best part of a bottle of champagne each. I had been nursing it carefully for that particular night. I seldom recall being so tired and I think everyone else was much the same.[16]

Captain James Watson, Headquarters, Egyptian Division

This kind of informal celebration was not unique, indeed, the staff were not the only officers to celebrate in some style that night.

The Royal Warwickshires bivouacked in a street near the Mahdi's tomb. We had saved a dozen bottles of champagne for this occasion so had about half a pint each, and it made me, and others, almost drunk. I think we all realised that we had taken part in one of the most-spectacular – and perhaps 'safest' – battles ever fought![17]

Lieutenant Ronald Meiklejohn, 1st Royal Warwickshire Regiment, 1st Brigade

Such instances were however not typical of the experiences in Omdurman on the night of 2 September. Most had no wine, no champagne and no cigars. And they had a disturbed sleep, as various elements within the Anglo-Egyptian Army ran riot. The Omdurman civilians were treated abominably in the aftermath of victory.

Everyone except a few necessary picquets threw themselves down where they stood and slept the sleep of the just. But in the tortuous, sweltering lanes and enclosures of the wicked city there was no rest or sleep, internecine war and sharp fighting went on throughout the night, murder, rapine, and every devilment stalked through the streets, and I imagine there is little doubt that therein some of the soldiers of the Sudanese troops took a very free hand. There was little to be wondered at in this, for it must be remembered that a large number of the men in the ranks of the Sudanese regiments of the Egyptian Army had formerly served the Khalifa in Khartoum and Omdurman, and had, when captured in former engagements, been at once incorporated in the battalions of His Highness the Khedive. I happened to be field officer of the day of my brigade, and it was my duty to visit throughout the night our various picquets, sentries, and posts. The noises, the screams of agony and terror, the shouting and the constant discharge of rifles and whistling of bullets in the city purlieus on either side of our bivouacs were somewhat disconcerting, but came no nearer, and apparently meant no harm to us. For a time, however, they made me rather anxious, in case of a sudden attack or alarm, for a brigade which was practically drunk with sleep and exhaustion. This apprehension was evidently not shared by two sentries of the Cameron Highlanders, whom I cautioned against firing unless it was absolutely necessary, for one of them replied to me. 'Oh, no, Sir, a'wm thinkin' it's only the people rejoicin' at the victory!' It seemed quite obvious to me that a great number, at any rate, were doing anything at the moment but rejoicing![18]

Captain Granville Egerton, 1st Seaforth Highlanders, 1st Brigade

Major General Archibald Hunter realised what was happening, but he was not overly concerned.

Macdonald's Brigade was tired and preferred to rest in the main street. The cunning beggars – the blacks did nothing but loot the prettiest slave girls and best trophies to be had.

It was past 1 a.m. when we went to bed. I slept till dawn like a top, after one of the best days I ever passed.[19]

Major General Archibald Hunter, Headquarters, Egyptian Division

The Egyptian and Sudanese troops were not the only ones engaging in looting – something which is to many soldiers reprehensible when done by someone else, but just the collection of souvenirs when they indulge in it themselves.

I have got about a dozen spears, two or three swords, some daggers, a gibbah – sort of coat – which was taken off one of the Khalifa's bodyguard. I will send them all home from Cairo. You might get some expert to look at the swords as there are a lot of the old crusaders' swords about here, and I believe the oldest of the ones I send is rather a good one.[20]

Lieutenant Edward George Boyle, 2nd Rifle Brigade, 2nd Brigade

Most controversially, the tomb of the Mahdi was not only penetrated by the British shells, but his body was also rudely disturbed.

The Mahdi's tomb, a high white-washed dome landmark for miles round, it stands right above everything in the place and was consequently made a mark for our artillery who battered it a good deal from the other side of the river, and it is to be blown up tonight as unsafe. The bones of the Mahdi have been chucked into the river, which I think rather bad form, I believe 'Monkey' Gordon[21] has his skull. The rest of the place consists of an enormous collection of wretched mud brick-built hovels, and it seems a sin to have wasted blood and treasure and immense hard labour over the likes of it. Climate too is vile, very hot and very damp and the air reeks with the awful smell of dead men and animals.[22]

Major William Sparkes, 4th Egyptian Battalion, 3rd Egyptian Brigade

Next day the army moved into healthier billets well outside the town.

18

AFTERMATH

> Kitchener deserves all he gets. He has run the show himself.
> His has been the responsibility, some of us have helped too.
> And none has reasons other than to be proud. We have
> done what we said we would and thank goodness the loss
> of life has been extraordinarily small.[1]
>
> Major General Archibald Hunter, Headquarters, Egyptian Division

THE SYMBOLIC END OF THE CAMPAIGN took place at Khartoum, the
scene of the death of Major General Charles Gordon. His heroic
demise had become the stuff of legend and now – at last – he was
avenged. There was an urgent desire to mark their victory with an
imposing ritual and to hammer home the message that the British
Empire was once again in control of the Sudan. At the heart of this
was Major General Herbert Kitchener, the architect of victory.

> The Sirdar arrived in the gunboat *Melik* which made fast
> at the steps immediately opposite the flag staffs. When all
> was ready the Sirdar disembarked and with the headquar-
> ter staff immediately behind him, took up his position in
> front of the centre of, and facing the palace. On his right
> the British troops, on his left the Egyptian Army. Troops
> were called to attention. Then came a short funeral service
> for Gordon in which all the chaplains: Church of England,
> Roman Catholic and Presbyterian took part.[2]
>
> Captain James Watson, Headquarters, Egyptian Division

Few of the men watching were unmoved by this stage and even

Kitchener was clearly upset.

> The service was simple and most impressive and, when
> dear old Father Brindle[3] gave the benediction at the end, I
> have never, except in family trouble felt so like bursting into
> tears. The Sirdar, who is, as a rule, absolutely unmoved,
> had great round tears on his cheeks. Then we hoisted both
> the Egyptian flag and the Union Jack over the palace.[4]
>
> Captain Henry Rawlinson, Headquarters

George Steevens watched as Kitchener gave the signal for James
Watson to have the honour of hauling up the British flag.

> The Sirdar raised his hand. A pull on the halliards: up ran,
> out flew, the Union Jack, tugging eagerly at his reins, daz-
> zling gloriously in the sun, rejoicing in his strength and his
> freedom. 'BANG!' went the *Melik's* 12-pounder, and the
> boat quivered to her backbone. 'God Save our Gracious
> Queen' hymned the Guards' band. 'BANG!' from the *Melik*
> – and Sirdar and private stood stiff – 'BANG!' – to attention,
> every hand at the helmet peak in 'BANG!' – salute. The
> Egyptian flag had gone up at the same instant; and now,
> the same ear-smashing, soul-uplifting, 'BANGs!' marking
> time, the band of the 11th Sudanese was playing the Khedi-
> vial hymn. 'Three cheers for the Queen!' cried the Sirdar:
> helmets leaped in the air, and the melancholy ruins woke to
> the first wholesome shout of all these years. Then the same
> for the Khedive. The comrade flags stretched themselves
> lustily, enjoying their own again; the bands pealed forth the
> pride of country; the twenty-one guns banged forth the
> strength of war. Thus, white men and black, Christian and
> Moslem, Anglo-Egypt set her seal once more, for ever, on
> Khartoum.[5]
>
> George Steevens, *Daily Mail*

'For ever' may seem optimistic from our perspective in the

twenty-first century. However, the symbolism was deliberate and entirely endorsed the determination of the watching
officers.

> The gunboats on the river crashed out a salute with a live
> shell – they had no blank and the moan of the shell hurtling
> through the still air added a weird and unusual note to the
> ceremony, which marked it, in my mind, as being not an
> occasion for triumph but for solemn resolve. This hoisting
> of the Jack, which we had definite orders to put up, was,
> of course, an event of deep political significance. Where
> our flag goes up, it does not quickly come down. But what
> it meant to me, and I think to most of us, was not that we
> had added so many thousand square miles to the British
> Empire, but that we had pledged ourselves to complete the
> work for which Gordon died thirteen years ago, and to free
> this land from brutality and tyranny.[6]
>
> Captain Henry Rawlinson, Headquarters

Afterwards, they were free to look round what remained of the
governor's palace, with several being shown by Rudolf Slatin
the place where he believed Gordon met his end. Major General
Archibald Hunter, the old warrior, was unrepentant as he considered the remnants of Khartoum and the damage wreaked on
the Mahdi's chosen capital at Omdurman.

> Khartoum is a complete ruin. It will be rebuilt. Omdurman
> will be strongly garrisoned and otherwise it will be grad-
> ually obliterated. The Mahdi's tomb was a splendid target
> and was hit plumb in the centre of the dome at the third
> round. It is beautifully built of red brick and lime and took
> some demolition. You are at liberty to assign any cause
> you please to its removal. We may say that so long as it
> stood it was a menace to our rule and an inducement to
> a removal of fanaticism. We may say that in its semi-de-
> molished state it was a danger to life and living, anyhow so

long as it stood it was a conspicuous memorial to celebrate
the victory of the Savage over us, and now that it ceases
to exist our disgrace may be forgotten and atoned for. The
poor devil's bones are gone too and quite right. Many folk
wonder where they are, so just let them wonder. I wonder
what happens when you can't find your complete set at the
'Last Parade'.[7]

Major General Archibald Hunter, Headquarters, Egyptian Division

His gleeful remarks did him little credit, but such sentiments
were shared by many among Kitchener's forces.

★★★

GORDON HAD BEEN AVENGED at an enormous cost to human life.
Although the Anglo-Egyptian Army had only lost 48 killed and
434 wounded, the Khalifa's Dervishes had suffered anything
up to 10,000 dead and thousands more wounded. Afterwards,
serious questions were raised back home as to the merciless
despatching of the wounded. This was referenced in several
journalists' reports, but also in letters home from soldiers that
were printed in the press.

The British were desperate to refute these charges, despite
the evidence within the accounts of their own soldiers. Even
Churchill was embarrassed when his reports from the battle
were deployed by the editor of the pacifist *Concord* magazine in
a letter published in the *Westminster Gazette* on 19 October. The
pacifist quoted from Churchill's reports detailing the horrors of
the battlefield, including that the Dervishes were 'destroyed, not
conquered by machinery'. Churchill replied with considerable
vigour.

Had the editor of *Concord* been present in the zeriba on the
morning of September 2, and had he seen 40,000 savages
advancing with hostile intent, he would not have protested
against the soldiers opening fire. He would as a reasonable

man have perceived that if the spearmen came to close
quarters with the troops, a far greater slaughter would
take place than actually occurred – a slaughter in which
he himself might have been unfortunately included. Once
fire was opened the loss of the Dervishes was mechanical. There was a hail of bullets. The Dervish advance
continued, and, in the interests of the Peace Preservation
Society, it was necessary that the hail of bullets should also
continue. The courage of the enemy was their destruction. When they had had enough, they withdrew. I submit,
that it is unfair as well as irrational to attribute cruelty
and bloodthirstiness to soldiers who, placed in a position
where they have to defend their lives, use the weapons
with which they are armed with skill, judgement, and
effect.[8]
2nd Lieutenant Winston Churchill, 'A' Squadron, 21st Lancers

Nevertheless, despite this special pleading, the balance of evidence is very clear that many of the wounded were butchered as
they lay on the battlefield, whether they resisted or not. After the
battle, two medical aid posts were established, one at the Khor
Shambat and one in Omdurman itself, to assist any Dervishes
who could get there. As can be imagined, this was a long way to
crawl for the badly wounded. The Dervish wounded who were
not murdered were often abandoned to their fate.

A day or two later I rode over the battlefield, a grisly sight.
I saw two wounded Arabs who had been shot through both
thighs and unable to walk. They were propelling themselves
along the ground in a sitting posture with short sticks and
left a conspicuous track in the sand. A day or two after, I
came across these two just arriving in our lines, I should say
nearly 3 miles from where I had first seen them.[9]
Brigadier General Neville Lyttelton, Headquarters, 2nd Brigade

The dreadful nature of the wounds inflicted on the bodies of the Dervishes were also a matter of some controversy. The desire for a bullet that would stop a charging warrior dead in his tracks had led to the introduction of 'dum-dum' bullets. These were both officially issued and – as we have seen – created by the soldiers by making a cross-shaped incision or filing off the tip of the normal bullet. Ernest Bennett explains the thinking behind it and decried what he considered to be sentimentality from those who objected.

> A new bullet, by the way, was used in the recent campaign. Its title is sufficiently significant. It is called the 'man-stopping bullet' and simply means that an ordinary .303 Lee-Metford bullet is scooped out at the end to the depth of about half an inch. When this missile strikes an object, the hollow nose instantly expands like an umbrella, inflicting a tremendous shock, which was frequently not secured when the ordinary solid bullet, with its enormous velocity (2,000 feet a second at the muzzle), passed clean through an enemy's body, but failed to administer a sufficiently crushing blow. *Apropos* of dum-dum bullets, man-stopping bullets, a good deal of false sentiment has been evoked in England and France. The main object of a soldier in battle is to put his opponent out of action, and it is found by experience that the ordinary bullet does not adequately secure this result when employed against barbarous or semi-barbarous enemies. A civilised combatant, when he is struck by a bullet – even if the wound be a comparatively slight one, say through the shoulder – almost invariably sits down on the ground; but the nervous system of the savage is a far less delicate organism, and nothing short of a crushing blow will check his wild onset.[10]
>
> Ernest Bennett, *Westminster Gazette*

On this point the rest of the world emphatically disagreed. All forms of dum-dum bullet would be banned after protests from the German government at the Hague Convention in 1899.

Ironically, the British would often accuse the Boers, Germans, or Turks of using them in subsequent conflicts.

Another unsavoury controversy arose from the disrespectful treatment meted out to the body of the Mahdi. The British were determined there should not be a physical rallying site to his memory. The magnificent tomb was destroyed, and his bones were cast into the Nile, less his head which Kitchener intended to send to the Royal College of Surgeons in London. He was only dissuaded by the shocked reaction of Queen Victoria to the very idea, and the skull was hurriedly buried in an unmarked grave at Wadi Halfa. Kitchener was also required to write a somewhat chastening letter of apology to his affronted sovereign.

The Anglo-Egyptian wounded were treated far better than their Dervish opponents, but the medical arrangements were far from perfect. And after all they were a long way from a modern, clean hospital.

> During the evening the sick were put on board the barges to go down the river. I went on board to see Frankie Rhodes, who had been shot in the shoulder, there were also Boniton and Molyneux, both wounded in shoulder and arm. They seemed very cheery and looked all right, but they had absolutely nothing, no clothes, food or filtered water. We all did what we could, and found them soups, beef tea, pyjamas, flannel shirts, handkerchiefs etc. This was disgraceful and no provision seems to have been made to deal with the British wounded. There were also, I believe, practically no medicines or medical appliances – in a word it was as bad as could be and what would have happened had there been a large number goodness only knows. There must have been some blunder, as far as one knows this is the only blot of the whole business.[11]
> Major W. L. Bagot, 1st Grenadier Guards, 2nd Brigade

★★★

AFTER THE BATTLE IT IS IMPORTANT TO ANALYSE the performance of generals on both sides. In the case of the Battle of Omdurman, there was little doubt that neither side had distinguished themselves in the art of tactics. The Dervish force had failed to take advantage of any theoretical opportunities and had launched a series of uncoordinated attacks which had been defeated in detail. Against modern weapons, their only real chance of victory lay in a requirement to secure surprise and in securing circumstances that would limit the field of fire open to the Anglo-British forces. The best chance for this was surely a night attack.

> If we had had the laying out of the Khalifa's plan of attack, we could not have done it better for ourselves than he did. The enemy made every kind of tactical mistake possible. They ought to have attacked us in our lines the night before, when they might perhaps have broken through the Egyptians who had no proper zeriba. If bent on attacking in daylight they should have started an hour or two before, so that if they kept quiet, they might have reached to within 800 yards of our line before being detected and decimated by gun and rifle fire.[12]
>
> Brigadier General Neville Lyttelton, Headquarters, 2nd Brigade

This then had been their big chance. Once it had been missed then they were doomed. Even when they secured an opportunity against Lieutenant Colonel Hector Macdonald's 1st Egyptian Brigade, the attacks by the Black and Green Flag forces were not coordinated and were destroyed in succession. They had secured a degree of surprise, but the Dervishes still had too much open ground to cross. The only example of success was the ambush at close range of the 21st Lancers, but that was an isolated circumstance.

As for Kitchener, his tactics and control of the battle came in for some criticism. This tended to concentrate on the uncontrolled advance on Jebel Surgham following the defeat of the first great Dervish attack. There is no doubt that this was incompetent, born of a combination of Kitchener's over confidence that the Dervishes would not risk another attack, coupled with his overall priority to prevent street fighting in Omdurman. Whatever the reasoning, it did not look good, as Douglas Haig reported in a letter to his 'mentor' General Evelyn Wood.

> Although in possession of full information, and able to see with his own eyes the whole field, he spreads out his force, thereby risking the destruction of a brigade. He seems to have had no plan, or tactical idea, for beating the enemy beyond allowing the latter to attack the camp. This the Dervishes would not do in force, having a wholesome fear of gunboat fire. Having six brigades, is it tactics to fight a very superior enemy with one of them and to keep the others beyond supporting distance? To me it seems truly fortunate that the flower of the Dervish army exhausted itself first in an attack and pursuit of the cavalry. Indeed, the prisoners say, 'You would never have defeated us had you not deceived us.'[13]
> Captain Douglas Haig, Egyptian Cavalry

It is worth noticing that Haig attributes far too much credit to the role of the Egyptian cavalry. Their performance under Lieutenant Colonel Robert Broadwood had been good, but it was just one of several factors that led to victory. And after all, for all the carping of his critics, Kitchener had won the day.

> When Kitchener headed for Omdurman with two unbeaten contingents of Dervishes hovering still on his flank, he was merely taking the road which would lead to the most decisive result – confident, after the experiences of the morning, that he could beat off the enemy's attacks. The sequel justified his opinion and refuted that of the critics, who perhaps forgot what has been proved a thousand times

over – the impossibility of bringing off a victory without running some risk.[14]

Major Ivor Maxse, Headquarters, 2nd Egyptian Brigade

The Anglo-Egyptian victory was a brutal demonstration of European firepower, but things could have gone wrong, and Captain James Watson paid tribute to the steadiness of the troops, and particularly of the Egyptian and Sudanese soldiers who had held their post and kept their discipline – although his thinking reflects the prejudices of his time.

A layman's inference would be that it was a gigantic butchery with very little danger or trial to our troops, but when you are dealing with overwhelming numbers of savage troops, versus smaller numbers armed with modern weapons, it must be one of two things: either you succeed in keeping them off, in which case if they are brave and fanatical you must inflict enormous losses, with comparative slight loss to yourselves; or else they get in and you are wiped out. But the layman is apt to forget that unless your fire is steady – and your men are steady too – you won't keep them at a distance! In a fight like that it's not the bullets that will upset your men, there aren't enough of them for that, it's the sight of overwhelming numbers coming steadily on all round apparently cocksure and without a waver. It's inclined to make the officer catch his breath, and he an educated man who knows the power of modern firearms and realises that one's only strength is in steadiness and keeping together, but when the black and Egyptian men who can't reason much stand and face the music as if they were field firing, I say it's a high trial and they deserve credit. What I wish to point out is that the fight may appear to have been a walkover for if any battalion of Macdonald's brigade had loosened back, and fired unsteadily, those dervishes would have been in them in 3 minutes. And once a small stream had trickled through our line the flood would have followed and the Khalifa might have had his luncheon party in Omdurman after all.[15]

Captain James Watson, Headquarters, Egyptian Division

In truth, the battle was not perhaps Kitchener's finest hour, but Omdurman was the culmination of a two-year campaign, during which the Sirdar demonstrated an exceptional range of military skills, particularly with regard to logistics. Although things went wrong, they often do in battles – as many of his officers would discover for themselves.

★★★

GENERALS AND ADMIRALS WEREN'T BORN as old men. The young officers who fought in the Sudan would face action in both the Boer War of 1899–1902 and the Great War, 1914–18. Then it would be their turn to send young men into battle. Kitchener himself would go on to ever greater acclaim, as governor of the Sudan, commander in chief during the later stages of the Boer War, commander in chief of the Indian Army, consul general of Egypt, and finally Secretary of State for War during the Great War. He died on his way to visit Russia when HMS *Hampshire* was sunk by a German mine in rough seas just west of Orkney on 5 June 1916. Winston Churchill surely need not detain us as his rise to become the most famous British prime minister is well documented. The dashing young cavalry officer Douglas Haig, would excel in staff and command roles in the Boer War, before rising to the peak of commander in chief of the British Army on the Western Front, 1916–18. On 29 January 1928, he died of a heart condition, probably exacerbated by the long years of wartime stress. Henry Rawlinson, Horace Smith Dorrien, Ivor Maxse, Lord Gleichen, Granville Egerton and Charles Townshend all rose to high rank as generals in 1914–18. At sea, Charles Beresford rose to be an admiral, but his career was hampered by frequent forays into politics as a member of parliament, and further dogged by a virulent quarrel with the First Sea Lord

John Fisher. David Beatty rose to the very top becoming commander in chief of the Grand Fleet from 1916–18, and First Sea Lord. Arthur Wilson also rose to be First Sea Lord from 1910 but found himself somewhat out of his depth in the modern navy. Some deserved better than the cards dealt by fate. Although Archibald Hunter performed brilliantly against the Boers, he was considered too old for a field command in the Great War and was forced to languish on the sidelines which frustrated the old warhorse! Neville Lyttelton suffered a similar fate. They were fortunate compared to the two heroes of the 21st Lancers charge at Omdurman. Raymond de Montmorency was killed fighting the Boers at the Battle of Stormberg on 23 February 1900, while Paul Kenna died commanding a brigade at Gallipoli on 21 August 1915. Perhaps most tragically of all, Hector Macdonald rose to be a major general, fighting with great distinction in the Boer War, but he was caught up in a distressing scandal over allegations of homosexuality and shot himself on 25 March 1903.

***

THE WHEEL OF HISTORY KEEPS ON TURNING and for the British Empire there was always some flashpoint, some theatre of concern, somewhere in the world. It was only a matter of days before the growing concern at the French manoeuvring in the Equatorial Province of Sudan triggered renewed action from Kitchener. Perhaps there was 'no rest for the wicked', but on 7 September Kitchener received a report from this new front.

> Dervish steamer arrived from Fashoda today, a good deal surprised to find us here. They report white men at Fashoda who fired on them. This has created great excitement – probably French. Sirdar is off [the] day after tomorrow to Fashoda with three gunboats, two battalions and a battery, and we must show whoever's there, their best and shortest way home.[16]
>
> Captain James Watson, Headquarters, Egyptian Division

The scare that rocked empires was caused by a small French expedition of just over 130 men under Captain Jean-Baptiste Marchand to the old Fashoda fort located on the upper reaches of the White Nile. This was part of the 'Scramble for Africa' that so enthused the colonial powers in the late nineteenth century. The French were trying to lay claim to a belt of territory stretching right across Africa, while the British had their eyes on a north to south domination, linking right through to South Africa. These two ambitions were not compatible and Fashoda for a while looked like being a flashpoint to war, especially as France was still nursing a grievance over the British assertion of domination over Egypt since 1882. The British response was certainly emphatic, leaving Marchand totally outnumbered. Fortunately, Kitchener had the good sense to behave with restraint and the meeting was amicable as both sides remained calm.

Is not the whole situation too absurd? Here is this little expedition of 120 men and eight Europeans shut up in a position hundreds of miles distant from their nearest support and with which it will take them months to communicate, with scarcely any ammunition and supplies and in sorry plight; whilst we have taken over the protection and administration of the whole country under their very eyes – and have treated them with considerable kindness as well. They fully realize the futility of all their efforts and will be as glad to be recalled as we shall be to get rid of them. They – and we – fully expect that when the French government knows the situation, they will not hesitate to recall them. Personally, one cannot help having a regard for the pluck of these men who in face of fearful natural obstacles have gone to the place where their insane government told them to go. Of course, we gave them formal protests against their occupation of Fashoda and the presence of the French in any part of the Nile valley, and we made regulations prohibiting the transport of all war material in the Nile. When all

our official work was over, we went and paid them a visit
and drank their health in sweet champagne![17]
Major Reginald Wingate

However, back in London and Paris the affair created a huge
diplomatic crisis, which was inflamed by the respective national
newspapers, with both sides accusing the other of naked greed
and unnecessary aggression. In the end, calmer heads prevailed,
and the French backed down, still bruised by their comprehen-
sive defeat in the Franco-Prussian War of 1870. Instead of seeking
new enemies and a war they probably couldn't win, they 'turned
the other cheek' and commenced a long-term strategy of securing a protective alliance with the British. On 3 November 1898
the French ordered Marchand to withdraw, and although some
saw it as a humiliation, it led to a rapprochement with the
signing in March 1899 of the Anglo-French Convention, which
settled the respective spheres of influence in the region. Within
another five years the *entente cordiale* had been signed. For once,
diplomacy had triumphed over war; at least in the short-term.

And of course, although the campaign to destroy the power
of the Khalifa Abdullaj al-Taishi was over, the search for vengeance continued. He still had control of around 7,000 warriors,
and for over a year he managed to evade the columns sent to
pursue him. In January 1899, Major Reginald Wingate was
appointed as the new Sirdar. He led a strong column of some
8,000 Egyptian Army servicemen in pursuit of the Khalifa, following intelligence leads to close in on his prey. On 25 November
1899, he finally cornered the Khalifa at Umm Diwaikarat in the
Kordofan Province. The Dervishes launched one last hopeless
charge and were duly shot to pieces. When members of the 8th
Sudanese Battalion picked their way across the battlefield, they
found the corpses of the Khalifa and his chiefs.

Seeing his followers retiring, he made an ineffectual attempt
to rally them, but recognizing that the day was lost he had
called on his emirs to dismount from their horses and

seating himself on *his firwa* or sheepskin – as is the custom of Arab chiefs who disdain surrender – he had placed Ali Wad Helu on his right and Ahmed Fadel on his left, whilst the remaining Emirs seated themselves round him and in this position they had unflinchingly met their death.[18]
Major Reginald Wingate

The Khalifa was clearly a brave man, accepting his death in a manner reminiscent of Charles Gordon. To the British he was the epitome of evil, but his native countrymen seem to have been more ambivalent. He could be seen as a devout adherent to his religion, a reasonable administrator in the face of extraordinary pressures, and courageous in combat. Yet there were also reports of a regime of extraordinary brutality. Was it all British propaganda? A proper examination of his rule, untrammelled by over-arching concerns of nationalism and religion, might prove interesting.

When the British took over, they were scathing as to the state of the country, possibly forgetting their own role in financing rebellion wherever possible and in forcing a near total mobilisation of manpower to withstand repeated invasions over the last twenty years. What they promised in victory was sound government to wash away the pain – and crimes – of the past.

All vestige of responsibility among the people is dead. They are mere serfs, dirt under the feet of their masters. Hence there is nobody and nothing to appeal to as an assistance towards establishing a system of law and order. However, all will come in time, patience and given money and fair play. Some people imagine Khartoum will be rebuilt, trade will revive, peace and plenty be established and reverenced, all by a wave of a wand or by the raising of a flag here and there. They have had fourteen years of Dervish rule, after sixty years of the Turk. And it will take ten years to put things straight.[19]
Major General Archibald Hunter

But it was not happy ever after. There were still religious differences, a wrecked economy, great swathes of desert, communication problems and just the sheer intimidating size of the Sudan. Many of the British colonial administrators meant well, bringing a public-school educated sensibility to service for the general good, but that general good was only so far as it satisfied British interests. The administrative structure they created was weak, dominated by a small coterie of officials and their advisors – any real democratic input was minimal. The British were also seen to have overly favoured the northern provinces of Sudan to the detriment of the south, and this certainly stored up more trouble for the future. In 1955, the Sudanese declared their independence, which was formally accepted by both the British and Egyptian governments on 1 January 1956. Within a year the Sudanese were demanding that the British remove the statues of Kitchener and Gordon erected in all their triumphal glory in Khartoum. Now the tomb of the Mahdi has been rebuilt and is a place of reverence and worship. The British final solution to Mahdism can in retrospect be seen to have been nothing more than just another passing phase.

The Sudanese have not, however, enjoyed their freedom. The region is afflicted by a potent mixture of factionalism, corruption, religious intolerance and an overall political instability. Civil war broke out with the southern provinces, there have been wars with Eritrea, military dictatorships that came and went, mass population displacements and endemic starvation. Casualties have been numbered in the hundreds of thousands in a human catastrophe that no one seems able to resolve. Today it is one of the most dangerous countries in the world. Perhaps Gladstone had been right to try and stay out of it? Could the result be any worse had the British never set foot in the Sudan?

NOTES

1. The Reason Why

1. G. W. Steevens, *With Kitchener to Khartoum* (New York: Dodd, Mead & Company, 1898), p. 325.
2. A. B. Tulloch, *Recollections of Forty Years Service* (Edinburgh and London: William Blackwood and Sons Limited, 1903), p. 250.
3. A. B. Tulloch, *Recollections of Forty Years Service*, pp. 264–5.
4. A. B. Tulloch, *Recollections of Forty Years Service*, p. 266.
5. A. B. Tulloch, *Recollections of Forty Years Service*, p. 267–9.
6. F. B. P. Seymour, quoted by C. Royle, *The Egyptian Campaigns 1882–1885 Vol. 1* (London: Hurst and Blackett, 1886), p. 120.

2. The Bombardment of Alexandria

1. H. K. Wilson, quoted by E. E. Bradford, *Life of Admiral of the Fleet Sir Arthur Knyvet Wilson* (London: John Murray, 1923), pp. 66–7.
2. A. B. Tulloch, *Recollections of Forty Years Service* (Edinburgh and London: William Blackwood and Sons Limited, 1903), p. 373.
3. A. B. Tulloch, *Recollections of Forty Years Service*, pp. 275–6.
4. C. W. de la Poer Beresford, *The Memoirs of Admiral Lord Beresford* (Good Press: Kindle edition), pp. 236–8.
5. A. B. Tulloch, *Recollections of Forty Years Service*, pp. 280–81.
6. C. W. de la Poer Beresford, *The Memoirs of Admiral Lord Beresford*, pp. 230–31.
7. C. W. de la Poer Beresford, *The Memoirs of Admiral Lord Beresford*, p. 233.
8. P. Marling, *Rifleman and Hussar* (London: John Murray, 1931), p. 72.
9. A. B. Tulloch, *Recollections of Forty Years Service*, p. 286.
10. H. K. Wilson, quoted by E. E. Bradford, *Life of Admiral of the Fleet Sir Arthur Knyvet Wilson*, p. 68.
11. J. Philip, *Gibraltar and the Egyptian War* (Aberdeen: D. Wyllie & Son, 1893), pp. 36–7.

12. J. Philip, *Gibraltar and the Egyptian War*, pp. 37–8.
13. H. K. Wilson, quoted by E. E. Bradford, *Life of Admiral of the Fleet Sir Arthur Knyvet Wilson*, pp. 70–71.
14. H. K. Wilson, quoted by E. E. Bradford, *Life of Admiral of the Fleet Sir Arthur Knyvet Wilson*, p. 71.
15. G. Wolseley, quoted by G. Arthur, *The Letters of Lord and Lady Wolseley 1870–1911* (London: William Heinemann, 1922), p. 73
16. E. B. Hamley, quoted by A. I. Shand, *The Life of General Sir Edward Bruce Hamley Vol. 2* (Edinburgh and London: William Blackwood and Sons Limited, 1895), p. 90.
17. A. Male, *Scenes through the Battle Smoke* (London: C. H. Kelly, 1901), pp. 317–18.

3. The Advance to Qassasin

1. C. B. Balfour, quoted by A. Leask, *Putty from Tel-el-Kebir to Cambrai: The Life and Letters of Lieutenant General Sir William Pulteney 1861–1941* (Solihull, Helion & Company Limited, 2015), p. 63.
2. J. Grierson, quoted by D. S. Macdiarmid, *The Life of Lieut. General Sir James Moncrieff Grierson* (London: Constable and Company Ltd, 1923), p. 37.
3. W. F. Butler, *Sir William Butler: An Autobiography* (London: Constable and Company, 1911), p. 222.
4. W. F. Butler, *Sir William Butler: An Autobiography*, p. 223.
5. G. Wolseley, quoted by C. Royle, *The Egyptian Campaigns 1882–1885 Vol. 1* (London: Hurst and Blackett, 1886), p. 283.
6. G. Wolseley, quoted by C. Royle, *The Egyptian Campaigns 1882–1885 Vol. 1*, p. 284.
7. J. Philip, *Gibraltar and the Egyptian War* (Aberdeen: D. Wyllie & Son, 1893), pp. 53–4.
8. J. Philip, *Gibraltar and the Egyptian War*, p. 56.
9. J. Philip, *Gibraltar and the Egyptian War*, pp. 56–7.
10. J. Philip, *Gibraltar and the Egyptian War*, pp. 59–60.
11. C. B. Balfour, quoted by A. Leask, *Putty from Tel-el-Kebir to Cambrai: The Life and Letters of Lieutenant General Sir William Pulteney 1861–1941*, p. 63.
12. C. B. Balfour, quoted by A. Leask, *Putty from Tel-el-Kebir to Cambrai: The Life and Letters of Lieutenant General Sir William Pulteney 1861–1941*, p. 63.
13. E. B. Hamley, quoted by A. I. Shand, *The Life of General Sir Edward*

Bruce Hamley Vol. 2 (Edinburgh and London: William Blackwood and Sons Limited, 1895), p. 97.

14. J. Philip, *Gibraltar and the Egyptian War*, pp. 68–9.
15. J. Philip, *Gibraltar and the Egyptian War*, pp. 68–9.
16. J. Philip, *Gibraltar and the Egyptian War*, p. 71.
17. J. Philip, *Gibraltar and the Egyptian War*, p. 75.
18. Lieutenant Colonel Henry Ewart was commander of the Household Cavalry Composite Regiment.
19. R. A. J. Talbot, The Moonlight Charge, *Newark Advertiser*, 4 October 1882, p. 6.
20. J. Philip, *Gibraltar and the Egyptian War*, p. 76.
21. A. B. Tulloch, *Recollections of Forty Years Service* (Edinburgh and London: William Blackwood and Sons Limited, 1903), pp. 309–10.
22. G. Graham, quoted by R. H. Vetch, *Life, Letters and Diaries of Lieut. General Sir Gerald Graham* (Edinburgh and London: William Blackwood and Sons, 1901), p. 243.
23. C. M. Watson, quoted by S. Lane-Poole, *Watson Pasha: A Record of the Lifework of Sir Charles Moore Watson* (London: John Murray, 1919), p. 113.
24. C. M. Watson, quoted by S. Lane-Poole, *Watson Pasha: A Record of the Lifework of Sir Charles Moore Watson*, p. 113.
25. G. Graham, quoted by R. H. Vetch, *Life, Letters and Diaries of Lieut. General Sir Gerald Graham*, pp. 244–5.

4. The Battle of Tel El Kebir
1. G. Wolseley, quoted by G. Arthur, *The Letters of Lord and Lady Wolseley 1870–1911* (London: William Heinemann, 1922), p. 76.
2. Wolseley, Despatch, 16/9/1892.
3. E. B. Hamley, quoted by A. I. Shand, *The Life of General Sir Edward Bruce Hamley, Vol. 2* (Edinburgh and London: William Blackwood and Sons Limited, 1895), pp. 106, 108–9.
4. N. Lyttelton, *Eighty Years: Soldiering, Politics, Games* (Borodino Books. Kindle edition), pp. 107–8.
5. E. B. Hamley, quoted by A. I. Shand, *The Life of General Sir Edward Bruce Hamley, Vol. 2*, pp. 116–17.
6. J. Gordon, *My Six Years with the Black Watch* (Boston: The Fort Hill Press, 1929), p. 49.
7. J. Philip, *Gibraltar and the Egyptian War* (Aberdeen: D. Wyllie & Son, 1893), pp. 84–5.

8. E. B. Hamley, quoted by A. I. Shand, *The Life of General Sir Edward Bruce Hamley, Vol. 2*, p. 130.

9. W. F. Butler, *Sir William Butler: An Autobiography* (London: Constable and Company, 1911), pp. 228–9.

10. W. F. Butler, *Sir William Butler: An Autobiography*, p. 231.

11. The man killed was Private James Pollock of the Cameron Highlanders.

12. E. B. Hamley, quoted by A. I. Shand, *The Life of General Sir Edward Bruce Hamley, Vol. 2*, pp. 132–3.

13. J. Philip, *Gibraltar and the Egyptian War*, pp. 86–7.

14. J. Gordon, *My Six Years with the Black Watch*, p. 52.

15. A. Alison, quoted by A. I. Shand, *The Life of General Sir Edward Bruce Hamley, Vol. 2*, p. 160

16. P. Marling, *Rifleman and Hussar* (London: John Murray, 1931), p. 83.

17. W. F. Butler, *Sir William Butler: An Autobiography*, p. 237.

18. T. Littlejohn, quoted by J. M. Brereton, *A History of the 4th/7th Dragoon Guards, 1685–1980* (Catterick: The Regiment, 1982).

19. J. Philip, *Gibraltar and the Egyptian War*, pp. 89–90.

20. A. Male, *Scenes through the Battle Smoke* (London: C. H. Kelly, 1901), p. 457.

21. C. M. Watson, quoted by S. Lane-Poole, *Watson Pasha: A Record of the Lifework of Sir Charles Moore Watson* (London: John Murray, 1919), p. 117.

22. C. M. Watson, quoted by S. Lane-Poole, *Watson Pasha: A Record of the Lifework of Sir Charles Moore Watson*, p. 119.

23. C. M. Watson, quoted by S. Lane-Poole, *Watson Pasha: A Record of the Lifework of Sir Charles Moore Watson*, pp. 123–4.

24. R. C. B. Lawrence, quoted by S. Lane-Poole, *Watson Pasha: A Record of the Lifework of Sir Charles Moore Watson*, pp. 127–8.

25. C. B. Balfour, quoted by A. Leask, *Putty from Tel-el-Kebir to Cambrai: The Life and Letters of Lieutenant General Sir William Pulteney 1861–1941* (Solihull, Helion & Company Limited, 2015), p. 64.

26. J. Grierson, quoted by D. S. Macdiarmid, *The Life of Lieut. General Sir James Moncrieff Grierson* (London: Constable and Company Ltd, 1923), pp. 44–5.

27. A. Male, *Scenes through the Battle Smoke*, pp. 476–8.

28. W. F. Butler, *Sir William Butler: An Autobiography*, p. 221.

5. The Rise of the Mahdi

1. W. S. Blunt, *Gordon at Khartoum* (London: Stephen Swift and Company, 1911), p. 82.
2. C. M. Watson, quoted by S. Lane-Poole, *Watson Pasha: A Record of the Lifework of Sir Charles Moore Watson* (London: John Murray, 1919), p. 137.
3. A. C. P. Haggard, *Under Crescent and Star* (William Blackwood and Sons, Edinburgh & London, 1899), pp. 40–41.
4. F. Power, *Letters from Khartoum: Written during the Siege by the late F. Power* (London: Sampson Low, Marston, Searle and Rivington, 1885), p. 24.
5. E. O'Donovan, quoted by J. E. Bowen, *The Conflict of East and West in Egypt* (New York: G. P. Putnam's Sons, 1887), p. 145.
6. Anon., quoted by T. Archer, *The War in Egypt and the Sudan Vol. II* (London: Blackie and Son, 1886), 249–50.
7. F. Power, *Letters from Khartoum: Written during the Siege by the late F. Power*, pp. 69–70.
8. F. Power, *Letters from Khartoum: Written during the Siege by the late F. Power*, pp. 67–8.
9. C. Gordon, 'Chinese Gordon on the Soudan', *Pall Mall Gazette*, 9 January 1884, p. 11.
10. E. Baring *Modern Egypt: Vol. 1* (New York: The Macmillan Company, 1916), p. 426.
11. F. Grenfell, *Memoirs of Field Marshal Lord Grenfell* (London: Hodder and Stoughton Limited, 1925), p. 79.
12. G. Graham, quoted by R. H. Vetch, *Life, Letters and Diaries of Lieut. General Sir Gerald Graham*, (Edinburgh and London: William Blackwood and Sons, 1901), p. 256.
13. G. Graham, quoted by R. H. Vetch, *Life, Letters and Diaries of Lieut. General Sir Gerald Graham*, p. 261.

6. Battles of Suakin, 1884

1. H. K. Wilson, quoted by E. E. Bradford, *Life of Admiral of the Fleet Sir Arthur Knyvet Wilson* (London: John Murray, 1923), p. 87.
2. F. Scudamore, quoted by J. W. Hawkins, *Fred: The Collected Letters and Speeches, Vol. 2: 1878–1885* (Solihull: Helion & Company, 2014), p. 88.
3. F. Burnaby, quoted by J. W. Hawkins, *Fred: The Collected Letters and Speeches, Vol. 2: 1878–1885*, p. 182.

4. J. Macdonald, quoted by B. Burleigh, *Desert Warfare being the Chronicle of the Eastern Soudan Campaign* (London: Chapman and Hall Limited, 1884), p. 14.

5. F. Burnaby, quoted by J. W. Hawkins, *Fred: The Collected Letters and Speeches, Vol. 2: 1878–1885*, p. 183.

6. J. Macdonald, quoted by B. Burleigh, *Desert Warfare being the Chronicle of the Eastern Soudan Campaign*, p. 15.

7. J. Macdonald, quoted by B. Burleigh, *Desert Warfare being the Chronicle of the Eastern Soudan Campaign*, p. 16.

8. E. Baring *Modern Egypt: Vol. 1* (New York: The Macmillan Company, 1916), p. 409–10.

9. National Army Museum: J. A. Starr, Typescript Account.

10. National Army Museum: J. A. Starr, Typescript Account.

11. H. K. Wilson, quoted by E. E. Bradford, *Life of Admiral of the Fleet Sir Arthur Knyvet Wilson* (London: John Murray, 1923), p. 86.

12. H. K. Wilson, quoted by E. E. Bradford, *Life of Admiral of the Fleet Sir Arthur Knyvet Wilson*, pp. 89–90.

13. B. Burleigh, *Desert Warfare being the Chronicle of the Eastern Soudan Campaign*, p. 49.

14. F. Villiers, quoted by J. W. Hawkins, *Fred: The Collected Letters and Speeches, Vol. 2: 1878–1885*, p. 89.

15. National Army Museum: J. A. Starr, Typescript Account.

16. P. H. S. Barrow, quoted by B. Burleigh, *Desert Warfare being the Chronicle of the Eastern Soudan Campaign*, p. 165.

17. National Army Museum: J. A. Starr, Typescript Account.

18. National Army Museum: J. A. Starr, Typescript Account.

19. P. Marling, *Rifleman and Hussar* (London: John Murray, 1931), p. 83.

20. P. Marling, *Rifleman and Hussar*, p. 83.

21. A. Scott-Stevenson, quoted by V. Schofield, *The Highland Furies: The Black Watch, 1739–1899* (London: Quercus, 2012), p. 523–4.

22. National Army Museum: J. A. Starr, Typescript Account.

23. G. Graham, quoted by R. H. Vetch, *Life, Letters and Diaries of Lieut. General Sir Gerald Graham*, (Edinburgh and London: William Blackwood and Sons, 1901), p. 275.

7. The Siege of Khartoum

1. C. Gordon, *The Journals of Maj-General C. G. Gordon, C.B., at Khartoum* (London: Kegan, Paul and Trench, 1885), p. 90.

2. F. Power, *Letters from Khartoum: Written during the Siege by the late*

F. Power (London: Sampson Low, Marston, Searle and Rivington, 1885), pp. 96–8.

3. C. Gordon, quoted by B. M. Allen, *Gordon and the Sudan* (London: Macmillan and Co, Limited, 1931), p. 275.

4. C. Gordon, quoted by E. W. C. Sandes, *The Royal Engineers in Egypt and the Sudan* (Chatham: The Institution of Royal Engineers, 1937) p. 132.

5. F. Power, *Letters from Khartoum: Written during the Siege by the late F. Power*, pp. 104–5.

6. F. Power, *Letters from Khartoum: Written during the Siege by the late F. Power*, pp. 112–13.

7. C. Gordon, quoted by B. M. Allen, *Gordon and the Sudan*, p. 365.

8. C. Gordon, *The Journals of Maj-General C. G. Gordon, C.B., at Khartoum*, pp. 197–8.

9. Anon. stoker, quoted in F. Power, *Letters from Khartoum: Written during the Siege by the late Frank Power*, pp. 117–9.

10. C. Gordon, *The Journals of Maj-General C. G. Gordon, C.B., at Khartoum*, p. 70.

11. C. Gordon, *The Journals of Maj-General C. G. Gordon, C.B., at Khartoum*, pp. 134–5.

12. C. Gordon, *The Journals of Maj-General C. G. Gordon, C.B., at Khartoum*, pp. 215–16.

13. C. Gordon, *The Journals of Maj-General C. G. Gordon, C.B., at Khartoum*, pp. 252–3.

14. C. Gordon, *The Journals of Maj-General C. G. Gordon, C.B., at Khartoum*, p. 275.

8. The Starting Gate

1. C. Townshend, quoted by E. Sherson, *Townshend of Chitral and Kut* (London: William Heinemann Ltd, 1928), p. 21.

2. G. Wolseley, quoted by H. E. Colville, *History of the Sudan Campaign, Part 1* (London: HMSO, 1889), p. 29–30.

3. Quoted by H. E. Colville, *History of the Sudan Campaign, Part 1*, p. 30.

4. W. F. Butler, *Sir William Butler: An Autobiography* (London: Constable and Company, 1911), p. 272.

5. W. F. Butler, *Sir William Butler: An Autobiography*, p. 273.

6. W. F. Butler, *Sir William Butler: An Autobiography*, pp. 273–4.

7. C. W. de la Poer Beresford, *The Memoirs of Admiral Lord Beresford* (Good Press. Kindle edition), pp. 268–70.
8. W. F. Butler, *Sir William Butler: An Autobiography*, pp. 276–7.
9. C. W. de la Poer Beresford, *The Memoirs of Admiral Lord Beresford*, pp. 274 & 278.
10. J. A. Sherlock, quoted by T. A. Haultain, *The War in the Sudan* (Toronto: The Grip Printing, 1885) pp. 76–7.
11. C. W. de la Poer Beresford, *The Memoirs of Admiral Lord Beresford*, pp. 284–5.
12. A. E. Gleichen, *With the Camel Corps up the Nile* (Uckfield: Naval & Military Press, 2004), pp. 28–9.
13. A. E. Gleichen, *With the Camel Corps up the Nile*, pp. 32–3.
14. A. E. Gleichen, *With the Camel Corps up the Nile*, p. 38.
15. A. E. Gleichen, *With the Camel Corps up the Nile*, p. 41.
16. Anon. officer, quoted by G. le M. Gretton, *The Campaigns and History of the Royal Irish Regiment from 1662 to 1902* (Edinburgh & London: William Blackwood and Sons, 1911), pp. 265–6.
17. Anon. officer, quoted by G. le M. Gretton, *The Campaigns and History of the Royal Irish Regiment from 1662 to 1902*, p. 266.
18. Anon. officer, quoted by G. le M. Gretton, *The Campaigns and History of the Royal Irish Regiment from 1662 to 1902*, p. 268.
19. Anon. officer, quoted by G. le M. Gretton, *The Campaigns and History of the Royal Irish Regiment from 1662 to 1902*, p. 267.
20. Anon. officer, quoted by G. le M. Gretton, *The Campaigns and History of the Royal Irish Regiment from 1662 to 1902*, pp. 267–8.
21. Anon. officer, quoted by G. le M. Gretton, *The Campaigns and History of the Royal Irish Regiment from 1662 to 1902*, pp. 266–7.

9. The Desert Column

1. W. W. C. Verner (edited by J. Whittaker), *The Military Diary of Colonel W. W. C. Verner* (Leeds: Peregrine Books, 2003), p. xviii.
2. National Army Museum: H. Kitchener, Letter, 26/12/1884.
3. C. Townshend, quoted by E. Sherson, *Townshend of Chitral and Kut* (London: William Heinemann Ltd, 1928), p. 29.
4. A. E. Gleichen, *With the Camel Corps up the Nile* (Uckfield: Naval & Military Press, 2004), pp. 93–5.
5. C. W. de la Poer Beresford, *The Memoirs of Admiral Lord Beresford* (Good Press. Kindle edition), pp. 295–6.

6. C. W. de la Poer Beresford, *The Memoirs of Admiral Lord Beresford*, p. 299.
7. W. W. C. Verner (edited by J. Whittaker), *The Military Diary of Colonel W. W. C. Verner*, p. 27.
8. A. E. Gleichen, *With the Camel Corps up the Nile*, pp. 102–3.
9. A. E. Gleichen, *With the Camel Corps up the Nile*, p. 109.
10. C. W. de la Poer Beresford, *The Memoirs of Admiral Lord Beresford*, pp. 301–2.
11. C. Townshend, quoted by E. Sherson, *Townshend of Chitral and Kut*, p. 32.
12. G. Baillie-Hamilton Binning, quoted by T. Machin, *Colonel Frederick Burnaby 1842–85: A Great Victorian Eccentric* (Publish Nation: Kindle edition).
13. C. W. de la Poer Beresford, *The Memoirs of Admiral Lord Beresford*, p. 303.
14. W. W. C. Verner (edited by J. Whittaker) *The Military Diary of Colonel W. W. C. Verner*, pp. 40–1.
15. C. Townshend, quoted by E. Sherson, *Townshend of Chitral and Kut*, p. 33.
16. C. W. de la Poer Beresford, *The Memoirs of Admiral Lord Beresford*, p. 304.
17. G. Baillie-Hamilton Binning, quoted by T. Machin, *Colonel Frederick Burnaby 1842–85: A Great Victorian Eccentric*, pp. 151–2.
18. C. W. de la Poer Beresford, *The Memoirs of Admiral Lord Beresford*, pp. 305–6.
19. C. W. de la Poer Beresford, *The Memoirs of Admiral Lord Beresford*, p. 306.
20. W. W. C. Verner (edited by J. Whittaker), *The Military Diary of Colonel W. W. C. Verner*, pp. 42–3.
21. C. W. de la Poer Beresford, *The Memoirs of Admiral Lord Beresford*, pp. 306–7.
22. C. W. de la Poer Beresford, *The Memoirs of Admiral Lord Beresford*, p. 307.
23. G. Baillie-Hamilton Binning, quoted by T. Machin, *Colonel Frederick Burnaby 1842–85: A Great Victorian Eccentric*, pp. 152–4.
24. C. Townshend, quoted by E. Sherson, *Townshend of Chitral and Kut*, p. 34.
25. C. W. Wilson, *From Korti to Khartoum* (Uckfield: Naval & Military Press Ltd), pp. 29–30.

26. A. E. Gleichen, *With the Camel Corps up the Nile*, pp. 131–2.

27. C. W. Wilson, *From Korti to Khartoum*, pp. 28–9.

28. C. W. de la Poer Beresford, *The Memoirs of Admiral Lord Beresford*, pp. 308–9.

29. W. W. C. Verner (edited by J. Whittaker), *The Military Diary of Colonel W. W. C. Verner*, pp. xix–xx.

30. W. W. C. Verner (edited by J. Whittaker), *The Military Diary of Colonel W. W. C. Verner*, p. 44.

31. W. S. Blunt, *Gordon at Khartoum* (London: Stephen Swift and Company, 1911), pp. 262–

32. C. W. de la Poer Beresford, *The Memoirs of Admiral Lord Beresford*, pp. 314–15.

33. A. E. Gleichen, *With the Camel Corps up the Nile*, pp. 140–41.

34. C. W. Wilson, *From Korti to Khartoum*, pp. 33–6.

35. C. W. de la Poer Beresford, *The Memoirs of Admiral Lord Beresford*, pp. 310–11.

36. C. Townshend, quoted by E. Sherson, *Townshend of Chitral and Kut*, p. 36.

37. W. W. C. Verner (edited by J. Whittaker) *The Military Diary of Colonel W. W. C. Verner*, pp. xx–xxi.

38. W. W. C. Verner (edited by J. Whittaker) *The Military Diary of Colonel W. W. C. Verner*, p. xxi.

39. W. W. C. Verner (edited by J. Whittaker) *The Military Diary of Colonel W. W. C. Verner*, pp. xix–xx.

40. W. W. C. Verner (edited by J. Whittaker) *The Military Diary of Colonel W. W. C. Verner*, p. xxii.

41. C. W. Wilson, *From Korti to Khartoum*, pp. 63–4.

42. C. Townshend, quoted by E. Sherson, *Townshend of Chitral and Kut*, pp. 37–8.

43. A. E. Gleichen, *With the Camel Corps up the Nile*, pp. 151–3.

44. A. E. Gleichen, *With the Camel Corps up the Nile*, pp. 153–4.

45. W. W. C. Verner (edited by J. Whittaker), *The Military Diary of Colonel W. W. C. Verner*, pp. xii–xxiii.

46. C. W. Wilson, *From Korti to Khartoum*, pp. 73–4.

47. C. W. Wilson, *From Korti to Khartoum*, pp. 75–6.

48. C. W. Wilson, *From Korti to Khartoum*, pp. 76–8.

49. C. Townshend, quoted by E. Sherson, *Townshend of Chitral and Kut*, pp. 38–9.

50. W. W. C. Verner (edited by J. Whittaker), *The Military Diary of Colonel W. W. C. Verner*, p. 55.
51. P. Marling, *Rifleman and Hussar* (London: John Murray, 1931), p. 131.
52. C. W. Wilson, *From Korti to Khartoum*, p. 112–13.
53. C. W. de la Poer Beresford, *The Memoirs of Admiral Lord Beresford*, pp. 329–30.
54. C. W. de la Poer Beresford, *The Memoirs of Admiral Lord Beresford*, pp. 331–2.
55. C. W. Wilson, *From Korti to Khartoum*, p. 129.
56. C. W. Wilson, *From Korti to Khartoum*, pp. 151–2.
57. C. W. Wilson, *From Korti to Khartoum*, pp. 167.
58. C. W. Wilson, *From Korti to Khartoum*, p. 170.
59. C. W. Wilson, *From Korti to Khartoum*, pp. 171–2.
60. C. W. Wilson, *From Korti to Khartoum*, pp. 173–4.
61. R. Slatin, quoted by G. Brooke-Shepherd, *Between Two Flags: The Life of Baron Sir Rudolf von Slatin Pasha* (London: Weidenfeld and Nicholson, 1972), p. 73.
62. C. W. Wilson, *From Korti to Khartoum*, p. 179.
63. C. W. Wilson, *From Korti to Khartoum*, pp. 176–7.
64. C. W. Wilson, *From Korti to Khartoum*, p. 203.
65. C. W. de la Poer Beresford, *The Memoirs of Admiral Lord Beresford*, p. 337.
66. C. W. de la Poer Beresford, *The Memoirs of Admiral Lord Beresford*, pp. 343–4.
67. C. W. de la Poer Beresford, *The Memoirs of Admiral Lord Beresford*, pp. 344–5.
68. C. W. de la Poer Beresford, *The Memoirs of Admiral Lord Beresford*, pp. 346–7.
69. C. W. Wilson, *From Korti to Khartoum*, pp. 240–42.
70. C. W. Wilson, *From Korti to Khartoum*, p. 249–50.
71. C. W. de la Poer Beresford, *The Memoirs of Admiral Lord Beresford*, pp. 349–50.
72. C. W. de la Poer Beresford, *The Memoirs of Admiral Lord Beresford*, pp. 350–51.
73. C. W. de la Poer Beresford, *The Memoirs of Admiral Lord Beresford*, pp. 351–2.
74. C. W. de la Poer Beresford, *The Memoirs of Admiral Lord Beresford*, pp. 352–3.
75. C. W. Wilson, *From Korti to Khartoum*, pp. vi–vii.

10. All Hopes Fade Away

1. I. Hamilton, *Listening for the Drums* (Faber and Faber Ltd, 1944), pp. 177–8.
2. W. F. Butler, *Sir William Butler: An Autobiography* (London: Constable and Company, 1911), p. 304
3. H. Brackenbury, *The River Column* (Edinburgh and London: William Blackwood and Sons Limited, 1885), pp. 161–2.
4. I. Hamilton, *Listening for the Drums*, pp. 179–80.
5. W. F. Butler, *Sir William Butler: An Autobiography*, pp. 304–5.
6. H. Brackenbury, *The River Column*, pp. 182–4.
7. H. Brackenbury, *The River Column*, pp. 242–5.
8. I. Hamilton, *Listening for the Drums*, p. 181.
9. C. Townshend, quoted by E. Sherson, *Townshend of Chitral and Kut* (London: William Heinemann Ltd, 1928), p. 41.
10. W. W. C. Verner (Edited by J. Whittaker), *The Military Diary of Colonel W. W. C. Verner* (Leeds: Peregrine Books, 2003), p. xxvii.
11. C. W. de la Poer Beresford, *The Memoirs of Admiral Lord Beresford* (Good Press. Kindle edition), pp. 364–5.
12. C. W. de la Poer Beresford, *The Memoirs of Admiral Lord Beresford*, p. 370.
13. W. W. C. Verner (edited by J. Whittaker), *The Military Diary of Colonel W. W. C. Verner*, p. xxviii–xxix.
14. W. W. C. Verner (edited by J. Whittaker), *The Military Diary of Colonel W. W. C. Verner*, pp. xxix.
15. P. Marling, *Rifleman and Hussar* (London: John Murray, 1931), p. 131.
16. W. W. C. Verner (edited by J. Whittaker), *The Military Diary of Colonel W. W. C. Verner*, pp. xxix–xxx.
17. C. W. de la Poer Beresford, *The Memoirs of Admiral Lord Beresford*, pp. 373–4.
18. B. J. C. Doran, quoted by G. le M. Gretton, *The Campaigns and History of the Royal Irish Regiment from 1662 to 1902* (Edinburgh & London: William Blackwood and Sons, 1911), pp. 283–4.
19. W. W. C. Verner (edited by J. Whittaker), *The Military Diary of Colonel W. W. C. Verner*, p. xxx.
20. A. E. Gleichen, *With the Camel Corps up the Nile* (Uckfield: Naval & Military Press, 2004), pp. 254–5.
21. Despatch from Wolseley, quoted by H. Brackenbury, *The River Column*, pp. 248–51.
22. H. Brackenbury, *The River Column*, pp. 248–51.

23. I. Hamilton, *Listening for the Drums*, pp. 181–2.
24. W. E. Gladstone, quoted by J. Morley, *The Life of William Ewart Gladstone, Vol. II* (London: Edward Lloyd Limited, 1908), p. 365.
25. Hansard: Egypt and the Sudan Vote of Censure, 26/2/1885.
26. E. Baring *Modern Egypt: Vol. 1.* (Kindle edition).
27. National Army Museum: G. Wolseley, Letter, 23/3/1885.
28. I. Hamilton, *Listening for the Drums*, p. 181.

11. Battles of Suakin, 1885

1. E. Gambier Parry, *Suakin, 1885, Being a Sketch of the Campaign of this Year* (London: Kegan Paul, Trench & Co, 1886), pp. 55–6.
2. E. Gambier Parry, *Suakin, 1885, Being a Sketch of the Campaign of this Year*, pp. 81–3.
3. E. A. De Cosson, *Fighting the Fuzzy-Wuzzy* (London: Greenhill Books, 1990), pp. 86–7.
4. E. Gambier Parry, *Suakin, 1885, Being a Sketch of the Campaign of this Year*, pp. 47–8.
5. E. A. De Cosson, *Fighting the Fuzzy-Wuzzy*, pp. 64–5.
6. E. A. De Cosson, *Fighting the Fuzzy-Wuzzy*, pp. 99–100.
7. E. A. De Cosson, *Fighting the Fuzzy-Wuzzy*, pp. 142 & 147.
8. N. Stewart, *My Service Days India, Afghanistan, Suakin '85, and China* (London: John Ousley, Ltd, 1908), p. 121.
9. E. Gambier Parry, *Suakin, 1885, Being a Sketch of the Campaign of this Year*, pp. 172–3.
10. N. Stewart, *My Service Days India, Afghanistan, Suakin '85, and China*, pp. 121–2.
11. E. Gambier Parry, *Suakin, 1885, Being a Sketch of the Campaign of this Year*, p. 173 & 180.
12. E. A. De Cosson, *Fighting the Fuzzy-Wuzzy*, pp. 151–3.
13. Southey, quoted by F. Loraine Petre, *The Royal Berkshire Regiment, Vol. I, 1743–1914* (Reading: Royal Berkshire Regiment, 1925), pp. 329–30.
14. N. Stewart, *My Service Days India, Afghanistan, Suakin '85, and China*, pp. 124–5.
15. N. Stewart, *My Service Days India, Afghanistan, Suakin '85, and China*, pp. 125–6.
16. E. Gambier Parry, *Suakin, 1885, Being a Sketch of the Campaign of this Year*, pp. 187–190.
17. E. A. De Cosson, *Fighting the Fuzzy-Wuzzy*, p. 170.

18. Knight Commander of the Bath.

19. National Army Museum: H. M. Paget, Letter, 3/1885.

20. National Army Museum: F. Ferguson, Letter, 9/4/1885.

21. E. Gambier Parry, *Suakin, 1885, Being a Sketch of the Campaign of this Year*, pp. 214–7.

22. J. H. Thornton, *Memories of Seven Campaigns* (Westminster: Archibald Constable and Co, 1895), p. 235.

23. J. H. Thornton, *Memories of Seven Campaigns*, p. 235.

24. E. Gambier Parry, *Suakin, 1885, Being a Sketch of the Campaign of this Year*, pp. 100–101.

25. N. Stewart, *My Service Days India, Afghanistan, Suakin '85, and China*, p. 139.

26. G. J. Wolseley, quoted by A. Preston, *In Relief of Gordon Lord Wolseley's Campaign Journal of the Khartoum Relief Expedition, 1884–1885* (London: Hutchinson & Co, 1967), pp. 192–3.

27. E. A. De Cosson, *Fighting the Fuzzy–Wuzzy*, p. 278.

28. J. Grierson, quoted by D. S. Macdiarmid, *The Life of Lieut. General Sir James Moncrieff Grierson* (London: Constable and Company Ltd, 1923), p. 60.

12. Softly Softly: The Dongola Campaign of 1896–7

1. A. Hunter, quoted by D. H. Doolittle, *A Soldier's Hero: General Sir Archibald Hunter* (Rhode Island: Anaean Publishing Company, 1991), p. 80.

2. F. I. Maxse, *Seymour Vandeleur: The Story of a British Officer* (London: William Heinemann, 1906), pp. 137–8.

3. F. I. Maxse, *Seymour Vandeleur: The Story of a British Officer*, pp. 135–6.

4. A. Hunter, quoted by D. H. Doolittle, *A Soldier's Hero: General Sir Archibald Hunter*, pp. 20–22.

5. A. Hunter, quoted by D. H. Doolittle, *A Soldier's Hero: General Sir Archibald Hunter*, pp. 33–4.

6. A. Hunter, quoted by D. H. Doolittle, *A Soldier's Hero: General Sir Archibald Hunter*, p. 80.

7. National Army Museum: J. F. Burn-Murdoch, Diary, 7/6/1896.

8. C. Townshend, quoted by E. Sherson, *Townshend of Chitral and Kut* (London: William Heinemann Ltd, 1928), pp. 132–3.

9. C. Townshend, quoted by E. Sherson, *Townshend of Chitral and Kut*, p. 133.

10. A. Hunter, quoted by D. H. Doolittle, *A Soldier's Hero: General Sir Archibald Hunter*, p. 80.
11. A. Hunter-Weston, quoted by E. W. C. Sandes, *The Royal Engineers in Egypt and the Sudan* (Chatham: The Institution of Royal Engineers, 1937) p. 159–60.
12. E. F. Knight, *Letters from the Sudan* (London: Macmillan and Co., 1897), pp. 239–40.
13. National Army Museum: J. J. B. Farley, *Some Recollections of the Dongola Expedition*, p. 13.
14. National Army Museum: J. J. B. Farley, *Some Recollections of the Dongola Expedition*, p. 16.
15. National Army Museum: J. J. B. Farley, *Some Recollections of the Dongola Expedition*, p. 19.
16. National Army Museum: J. J. B. Farley, *Some Recollections of the Dongola Expedition*, pp. 20–21.
17. National Army Museum: J. J. B. Farley, *Some Recollections of the Dongola Expedition*, pp. 20–21.
18. National Army Museum: J. J. B. Farley, *Some Recollections of the Dongola Expedition*, p. 23.
19. National Army Museum: J. J. B. Farley, *Some Recollections of the Dongola Expedition*, p. 24.
20. A. Hunter, quoted by D. H. Doolittle, *A Soldier's Hero: General Sir Archibald Hunter*, p. 101.
21. D. Beatty, quoted by W. S. Chalmers, *The Life and Letters of David, Earl Beatty* (London: Hodder and Stoughton, 1951), pp. 25–6.
22. G. F. Gorringe, quoted by E. W. C. Sandes, *The Royal Engineers in Egypt and the Sudan*, p. 197.
23. National Army Museum: H. R. Mends Collection, E. J. M. Stuart Wortley, Letter, 24/8/1897.
24. National Army Museum: H. R. Mends Collection, E. J. M. Stuart Wortley, Letter, 18/9/1897.
25. National Army Museum: H. R. Mends Collection, E. J. M. Stuart Wortley, Letter, 18/9/1897.
26. A. Hunter, quoted by D. H. Doolittle, *A Soldier's Hero: General Sir Archibald Hunter*, p. 125.
27. D. Beatty, quoted by W. S. Chalmers, *The Life and Letters of David, Earl Beatty*, pp. 28–9.
28. D. Beatty, quoted by W. S. Chalmers, *The Life and Letters of David, Earl Beatty*, p. 29.

29. D. Beatty, quoted by W. S. Chalmers, *The Life and Letters of David, Earl Beatty*, p. 29.

13. Forward to Atbara, 1898

1. G. Egerton, *With the 72nd Highlanders in the Sudan Campaign* (London: Eden Fisher and Co Ltd, 1909), p. 7.
2. F. I. Maxse, quoted by J. Baynes, *Far From a Donkey: The Life of Sir Ivor Maxse* (London: Brasseys, 1995), p. 52.
3. H. Kitchener, quoted by G. H. Cassar, *Kitchener: Architect of Victory* (London: William Kimber, 1977), p. 76.
4. G. W. Steevens, *With Kitchener to Khartoum* (New York: Dodd, Mead & Company, 1898), pp. 28–30.
5. W. F. Gatacre, quoted by B. Gatacre, *General Gatacre: The story of the Life and Services of Sir William Forbes Gatacre, 1843–1906* (London: John Murray, 1910) p. 228.
6. G. W. Steevens, *With Kitchener to Khartoum*, pp. 69–70.
7. National Army Museum: R. Meiklejohn, Diary, 26/2–2/3/1898.
8. National Army Museum: R. Meiklejohn, Diary, 3–4/3/1898.
9. National Army Museum: R. Meiklejohn, Diary, 20–21/3/1898.
10. National Army Museum: R. Meiklejohn, Diary, 20–21/3/1898.
11. D. Haig, quoted by Dorothy Haig, *Douglas Haig before the Great War: His Letters and Diaries* (Advance Proof Copy, The Moray Press, 1934), p. 90.
12. H. Rawlinson, quoted by Frederick Maurice, *The Life of General Lord Rawlinson of Trent* (London: Cassell and Co, Ltd, 1928), p 31–2 & 34.
13. H. Rawlinson, quoted by Frederick Maurice, *The Life of General Lord Rawlinson of Trent*, pp. 31–2, 34.
14. W. Kinnaird Rose, Letter, 28/3/1898, quoted by *The Brisbane Courier* (Queensland), 25/5/1898.
15. National Army Museum: R. Meiklejohn, Diary, 7/4/1898.
16. A. Hunter, quoted by D. H. Doolittle, *A Soldier's Hero: General Sir Archibald Hunter* (Rhode Island: Anaean Publishing Company, 1991), p. 154.
17. G. Egerton, *With the 72nd Highlanders in the Sudan Campaign*, p. 10.
18. National Army Museum: R. Meiklejohn, Diary, 3/3/1898.
19. A. Hunter, quoted by D. H. Doolittle, *A Soldier's Hero: General Sir Archibald Hunter*, p. 155.

20. H. Rawlinson, quoted by Frederick Maurice, *The Life of General Lord Rawlinson of Trent*, p. 92–4.
21. D. Haig, quoted by Dorothy Haig, *Douglas Haig before the Great War: His Letters and Diaries*, p. 95.
22. National Army Museum: R. Meiklejohn, Diary, 7/4/1898. However, this clearly refers to the incident on 5/4/1898.
23. A. Hunter, quoted by D. Doolittle, *A Soldier's Hero: General Sir Archibald Hunter*, p. 160.
24. National Army Museum: R. Meiklejohn, Diary, 7/4/1898.
25. National Army Museum: R. Meiklejohn, Diary, 7/4/1898.

14. The Battle of Atbara, 8 April 1898

1. B. Burleigh, *Sirdar and Khalifa on the Reconquest of the Sudan* (London: Chapman and Hall Ltd, 1898), pp. 223–4.
2. F. I. Maxse, *Seymour Vandeleur: The Story of a British Officer* (London: William Heinemann, 1906), p. 205.
3. B. Burleigh, *Sirdar and Khalifa on the Reconquest of the Sudan*, p. 222. I have removed the fake Scottish accents!
4. National Army Museum: R. Meiklejohn ,, 8/4/1898.
5. F. I. Maxse, *Seymour Vandeleur: The Story of a British Officer*, p. 206.
6. D. Beatty, quoted by W. S. Chalmers, *The Life and Letters of David, Earl Beatty* (London: Hodder and Stoughton, 1951), p. 33.
7. A. Hunter, quoted by D. H. Doolittle, *A Soldier's Hero: General Sir Archibald Hunter* (Rhode Island: Anaean Publishing Company, 1991), p. 158.
8. H. Kitchener, Official Despatch, 22/4/1898.
9. W. F. Gatacre, quoted by B. Gatacre, *General Gatacre: The story of the Life and Services of Sir William Forbes Gatacre, 1843–1906* (London: John Murray, 1910), p. 203.
10. National Army Museum: R. Meiklejohn, Diary, 8/4/1898.
11. National Army Museum: R. Meiklejohn, Diary, 8/4/1898.
12. C. Townshend, quoted by E. Sherson, *Townshend of Chitral and Kut* (London: William Heinemann Ltd, 1928), pp. 150–51.
13. C. Townshend, quoted by E. Sherson, *Townshend of Chitral and Kut*, p. 151.
14. National Army Museum: F. Ready, Letter, 18/4/1898.
15. British Newspaper Library: J. W. Smith, Letter, quoted in *Sunderland Daily Echo and Shipping Gazette*, 14/5/1898, p. 3.
16. National Army Museum: R. Meiklejohn, Diary, 8/4/1898.

17. Samuel Cox, quoted by John Meredith, *Omdurman Diaries, 1898* (Barnsley: Pen and Sword, 1998), p. 87–8.
18. British Newspaper Library: Anon., quoted in *Leamington Spa Courier*, 28/5/1898, p. 5.
19. National Army Museum: R. Meiklejohn, Diary, 8/4/1898.
20. National Army Museum: R. Meiklejohn, Diary, 8/4/1898.
21. B. Burleigh, *Sirdar and Khalifa on the Reconquest of the Sudan*, pp. 242–3.
22. F. I. Maxse, *Seymour Vandeleur: The Story of a Briitsh Officer*, p. 209.
23. J. Maxwell, quoted by G. Arthur, *General Sir John Maxwell* (London: John Murray, 1932), p. 57–8.
24. National Army Museum: R. Meiklejohn, Diary, 8/4/1898.
25. British Newspaper Library: Corporal Laurie, Letters to the Editor, *Aberdeen Press and Journal*, 25/8/1898, p. 7.
26. H. Rawlinson, quoted by Frederick Maurice, *The Life of General Lord Rawlinson of Trent* (London: Cassell and Co, Ltd, 1928), p. 34.
27. National Army Museum: G. Skinner, Diary, 8/4/1898.
28. National Army Museum: F. Ready, Letter, 14/4/1898.
29. National Army Museum: F. Ready, Letter, 15/4/1898.
30. G. Egerton, *With the 72nd Highlanders in the Sudan Campaign* (London: Eden Fisher and Co Ltd, 1909), pp. 13–4.
31. G. Egerton, *With the 72nd Highlanders in the Sudan Campaign*, pp. 21–2.
32. G. Egerton, *With the 72nd Highlanders in the Sudan Campaign*, pp. 19–20.
33. B. Burleigh, *Sirdar and Khalifa on the Reconquest of the Sudan*, p. 255–6.
34. B. Burleigh, *Sirdar and Khalifa on the Reconquest of the Sudan*, p. 275–6.
35. M. A. Ahmad, quoted by B. Burleigh, *Sirdar and Khalifa on the Reconquest of the Sudan*, p. 277.

15. One Last Heave

1. J. E. Gough, quoted by I. F. W. Beckett, *Johnnie Gough, V.C. A Biography of Brigadier General Sir John Edmond Gough* (London: Tom Donovan Publishing Ltd, 1989), p. 39.
2. G. Egerton, *With the 72nd Highlanders in the Sudan Campaign* (London: Eden Fisher and Co Ltd, 1909), p. 22.

3. J. Vaughan, *Cavalry and Sporting Memories* (Bala: The Bala Press, 1954), pp. 54–5.

4. B. Bedri, *The Memoirs of Babikr Bedri* (London: Oxford University Press, 1969), p. 229.

5. B. Bedri, *The Memoirs of Babikr Bedri*, pp. 227–8.

6. A. Hubbard, quoted by P. Harrington and F. Sharp, *Omdurman 1898: The Eyewitnesses Speak* (London: Greenhill Books, 1998), p. 52.

7. W. S. L. Churchill, *My Early Life: A Roving Commission* (London: Macmillan & Co. Ltd., 1944), p. 187.

8. E. Bennett, *Downfall of the Dervishes* (London: Methuen & Co., 1899), pp. 115–16.

9. E. Bennett, *Downfall of the Dervishes*, pp. 121–3.

10. National Army Museum: E. Loch, Diary, 28/8/1898.

11. H. M. Farmer, quoted by K. S. Eady, *Cornerstones: The Life of H. M. Farmer from Omdurman to the Western Front* (Warwick: Helion & Company, 2019), p. 41.

12. E. M. Stuart–Wortley, Letter, quoted in *Eckington, Woodhouse and Staveley Express*, 23/9/1898.

13. E. Bennett, *Downfall of the Dervishes*, pp. 145–6.

14. B. Bedri, *The Memoirs of Babikr Bedri*, p. 233–4.

15. J. Vaughan, *Cavalry and Sporting Memories*, pp. 53–4.

16. W. S. L. Churchill, *My Early Life: A Roving Commission* (London: Macmillan & Co. Ltd., 1944), p. 189.

17. W. S. L. Churchill, *My Early Life: A Roving Commission*, p. 190.

18. W. S. L. Churchill, *My Early Life: A Roving Commission*, pp. 191–2.

19. National Army Museum: E. Loch, Diary, 1/9/1898.

20. G. Egerton, *With the 72nd Highlanders in the Sudan Campaign*, pp. 30–31.

21. A. Hunter, quoted by A. Hunter, *Kitchener's Sword Arm: The Life and Campaigns of General Sir Archibald Hunter* (Staplehurst: Spellmount, 1996), pp. 154–5.

22. W. S. L. Churchill, *My Early Life: A Roving Commission*, pp. 194–5.

23. National Army Museum: R. Meiklejohn, Diary, 1/9/1898.

16. The Battle of Omdurman, 2 September 1898

1. National Army Museum: J. J. Watson, Letter, 11/9/1898.

2. National Army Museum: D. F. Lewis, Typescript account, Sudan Campaign 1898, p. 11.

3. E. Bennett, *Downfall of the Dervishes* (London: Methuen & Co., 1899), pp. 156–7.

4. National Army Museum: W. L. Bagot, Diary, 2/9/1898.

5. H. Kitchener, quoted by E. W. C. Sandes, *The Royal Engineers in Egypt and the Sudan* (Chatham: The Institution of Royal Engineers, 1937), p. 262.

6. W. S. L. Churchill, *My Early Life: A Roving Commission* (London: Macmillan & Co. Ltd., 1944), p. 197.

7. W. S. L. Churchill, *My Early Life: A Roving Commission*, p. 198.

8. W. S. L. Churchill, *My Early Life: A Roving Commission*, p. 199.

9. H. Smith Dorrien, *Smith-Dorrien: Isandlwana to the Great War* (Leonaur, 2009), p. 53.

10. National Army Museum: J. J. Watson, Letter, 7/9/1898.

11. E. Bennett, *Downfall of the Dervishes*, pp. 14–15.

12. E. Bennett, *Downfall of the Dervishes*, p. 161.

13. F. I. Maxse, quoted by J. Baynes, *Far From a Donkey: The Life of Sir Ivor Maxse* (London: Brasseys, 1995), p. 56.

14. G. Egerton, *With the 72nd Highlanders in the Sudan Campaign* (London: Eden Fisher and Co Ltd, 1909), p. 32.

15. National Army Museum: R. Meiklejohn, Diary, 2/9/1898.

16. E. Bennett, *Downfall of the Dervishes*, pp. 166–7.

17. National Army Museum: R. Meiklejohn, Diary, 2/9/1898.

18. E. Bennett, *Downfall of the Dervishes*, pp. 165–6.

19. H. M. Farmer, quoted by K. S. Eady, *Cornerstones: The Life of H. M. Farmer from Omdurman to the Western Front* (Warwick: Helion & Company, 2019), pp. 44–5.

20. National Army Museum: Villiers Hatton, Diary, 2/9/1898.

21. L. A. Burrowes, Letter, quoted in *Launceston Examiner* (Tasmania), 29/10/1898.

22. L. A. Burrowes, Letter, quoted in *Launceston Examiner* (Tasmania), 29/10/1898.

23. National Army Museum: D. W. Churcher, Omdurman Diary, 2/9/1898.

24. E. Bennett, *Downfall of the Dervishes*, pp. 170–1

25. G. Egerton, *With the 72nd Highlanders in the Sudan Campaign*, pp. 34.

26. E. Bennett, *Downfall of the Dervishes*, pp. 167–8.

27. National Army Museum: G. Skinner, Diary, 2/9/1898.

28. National Army Museum: D. Granville, Letter, 15/9/1898.

29. A. Hubbard, quoted by P. Harrington and F. Sharp, *Omdurman 1898: The Eyewitnesses Speak* (London: Greenhill Books, 1998), pp. 68–9.
30. National Army Museum: H. Hodgson, Letter, 9/9/1898
31. G. W. Steevens, *With Kitchener to Khartoum* (New York: Dodd, Mead & Company, 1898), p. 282.
32. National Army Museum: J. J. Watson, Letter, 7/9/1898.
33. National Army Museum: R. Meiklejohn, Diary, 2/9/1898.
34. F. I. Maxse, quoted by J. Baynes, *Far from a Donkey: The Life of Sir Ivor Maxse*, p. 56.
35. C. Townshend, quoted by E. Sherson, *Townshend of Chitral and Kut* (London: William Heinemann Ltd, 1928), pp. 161–2.
36. F. I. Maxse, quoted by J. Baynes, *Far From a Donkey: The Life of Sir Ivor Maxse*, pp. 56–7.
37. D. Haig, quoted by Dorothy Haig, *Douglas Haig before the Great War: His Letters and Diaries* (Advance Proof Copy, The Moray Press, 1934), p. 118–9.
38. G. Egerton, *With the 72nd Highlanders in the Sudan Campaign*, pp. 35–6.
39. National Army Museum: H. Kitchener, order to 21st Lancers, 2 September 1898.
40. W. S. L. Churchill, *My Early Life: A Roving Commission*, p. 203.
41. R. H. de Montmorency, quoted by J. R. Rodd, *Social and Diplomatic Memories, 1894–1901* (London: Edward Arnold & Co, 1923), p. 216.
42. *The Daily News* (Perth, Western Australia), 10 December 1898.
43. W. Rix, quoted by T. Brighton, *The Last Charge: The 21st Lancers and the Battle of Omdurman, 2 September 1898* (Marlborough: The Crowood Press, 1998), pp. 97–8.
44. R. H. de Montmorency, quoted by J. R. Rodd, *Social and Diplomatic Memories, 1894–1901*, p. .216.
45. W. S. L. Churchill, *My Early Life: A Roving Commission*, pp. 204.
46. W. S. L. Churchill, *My Early Life: A Roving Commission*, p. 205.
47. R. H. de Montmorency, quoted by J. R. Rodd, *Social and Diplomatic Memories, 1894–1901*, pp. 216–17.
48. R. Smyth, quoted by P. Harrington and F. Sharp, *Omdurman 1898: The Eyewitnesses Speak* (London: Greenhill Books, 1998), p. 128.
49. R. H. de Montmorency, quoted by J. R. Rodd, *Social and Diplomatic Memories, 1894–1901*, p. 217.
50. W. S. L. Churchill, *My Early Life: A Roving Commission*, pp. 206–7.
51. W. S. L. Churchill, *My Early Life: A Roving Commission*, p. 207.

52. W. S. L. Churchill, *My Early Life: A Roving Commission*, p. 228.
53. F. H. Eadon, quoted by T. Brighton, *The Last Charge: The 21st Lancers and the Battle of Omdurman, 2 September 1898* (Marlborough: The Crowood Press, 1998), p. 90.
54. *The Daily News* (Perth, Western Australia), 10 December 1898.
55. R. H. de Montmorency, quoted by J. R. Rodd, *Social and Diplomatic Memories, 1894–1901*, pp. 217–18.
56. R. H. de Montmorency, quoted by J. R. Rodd, *Social and Diplomatic Memories, 1894–1901*, p. 218.
57. R. N. Smyth, quoted by P. Harrington and F. Sharp, *Omdurman 1898: The Eyewitnesses Speak*, p. 128.
58. R. H. de Montmorency, quoted by J. R. Rodd, *Social and Diplomatic Memories, 1894–1901*, pp. 218–19.
59. W. Rix, quoted by T. Brighton, *The Last Charge: The 21st Lancers and the Battle of Omdurman, 2 September 1898* (Marlborough: The Crowood Press, 1998), p. 98.
60. R. H. de Montmorency, quoted by T. Brighton, *The Last Charge: The 21st Lancers and the Battle of Omdurman, 2 September 1898*, pp. 92–3.
61. E. Bennett, *Downfall of the Dervishes*, pp. 180.
62. R. N. Smyth, quoted P. Harrington and F. Sharp, *Omdurman 1898: The Eyewitnesses Speak*, p. 128–30.
63. Private Rawding, quoted by F. Emery, *Marching over Africa: Letters from Victorian Soldiers* (London: Hodder and Stoughton, 1986), p. 172.
64. National Army Museum: Villiers Hatton, Diary, 2/9/1898.
65. N. Lyttelton, *Eighty Years: Soldiering, Politics, Games* (Borodino Books. Kindle edition), p. 147.
66. D. Haig, quoted by Douglas Scott, *The Preparatory Prologue: Douglas Haig Diaries and Letters* (Barnsley: Pen and Sword Military, 2006), p. 102.
67. I. H. H. Zulfo, *Karari: The Sudanese Account of the Battle of Omdurman* (London: Frederick Warne, 1980), pp. 200–202.
68. I. H. H. Zulfo, *Karari: The Sudanese Account of the Battle of Omdurman*, pp. 200–202.
69. I. H. H. Zulfo, *Karari: The Sudanese Account of the Battle of Omdurman*, pp. 200–202.
70. H. Smith Dorrien, *Smith-Dorrien: Isandlwana to the Great War*, p. 133.
71. National Army Museum: H. G. Fitton, Letter, 5/9/1898.

72. G. Egerton, *With the 72nd Highlanders in the Sudan Campaign*, pp. 37–8.

73. E. Bennett, *Downfall of the Dervishes*, p. 182.

74. G. W. Steevens, *With Kitchener to Khartoum*, pp. 284–5.

75. National Army Museum: D. W. Churcher, Omdurman Diary, 2/9/1898.

76. H. L Pritchard, quoted by E. W. C. Sandes, *The Royal Engineers in Egypt and the Sudan*, p. 269.

77. H. Macdonald, quoted by J. Pollock, *Kitchener: The Road to Omdurman* (London: Constable and Company Ltd, 1998), p. 133.

78. H. L Pritchard, *The Sudan Campaign, 1896–1899* (London: Chapman and Hall Ltd, 1899), pp. 205–6.

79. H. L Pritchard, *The Sudan Campaign, 1896–1899*, p. 206.

80. H. L Pritchard, *The Sudan Campaign, 1896–1899*, pp. 206–8.

81. H. L Pritchard, *The Sudan Campaign, 1896–1899*, p. 210.

82. National Army Museum: D. F. Lewis, Typescript account, Sudan Campaign 1898, pp. 13–14.

83. H. L Pritchard, *The Sudan Campaign, 1896–1899*, p. 212.

84. H. L Pritchard, *The Sudan Campaign, 1896–1899*, p. 213.

85. G. Teigh, quoted by J. Meredith, *Omdurman Diaries, 1898* (Barnsley: Pen and Sword, 1998), p. 182.

86. S. Vandeleur, quoted by F. I. Maxse, *Seymour Vandeleur: The Story of a British Officer*, pp. 231–2.

87. National Army Museum: J. J. Watson, Letter, 7/9/1898.

88. Captain Nevill Smyth, VC, Intelligence Section. See pp. 381–2.

89. S. Vandeleur, quoted by F. I. Maxse, *Seymour Vandeleur: The Story of a British Officer*, pp. 231–2.

90. B. Bedri, *The Memoirs of Babikr Bedri* (London: Oxford University Press, 1969), p. 236.

91. B. Bedri, *The Memoirs of Babikr Bedri*, pp. 236–7.

92. G. Egerton, *With the 72nd Highlanders in the Sudan Campaign*, pp. 40–41.

93. National Army Museum: J. J. Watson, Letter, 11/9/1898.

94. D. Haig, quoted by Dorothy Haig, *Douglas Haig before the Great War: His Letters and Diaries*, p. 120–21.

95. D. Haig, quoted by Dorothy Haig, *Douglas Haig before the Great War: His Letters and Diaries*, p. 121.

96. R. Meikeljohn, quoted by J. Meredith, *Omdurman Diaries, 1898* (Barnsley: Pen and Sword, 1998), p. 87–8.

17. On, On to Omdurman

1. A. Hunter, quoted by D. H. Doolittle, *A Soldier's Hero: General Sir Archibald Hunter* (Rhode Island: Anaean Publishing Company, 1991), p. 173.
2. National Army Museum: Villiers Hatton, Diary, 2/9/1898.
3. A. White, Letter, 3/9/1898, quoted in *Evening News* (Sydney, New South Wales), 28/10/1898.
4. J. Vaughan, *Cavalry and Sporting Memories* (Bala: The Bala Press, 1954), pp. 57–8.
5. G. Egerton, *With the 72nd Highlanders in the Sudan Campaign* (London: Eden Fisher and Co Ltd, 1909), pp. 41–2.
6. H. M. Farmer, quoted by K. S. Eady, *Cornerstones: The Life of H. M. Farmer from Omdurman to the Western Front* (Warwick: Helion & Company, 2019), p. 46.
7. National Army Museum: J. J. Watson, Letter, 11/9/1898.
8. F. I. Maxse, quoted by J. Baynes, *Far From a Donkey: The Life of Sir Ivor Maxse* (London: Brasseys, 1995), p. 61.
9. H. Smith Dorrien, *Smith-Dorrien: Isandlwana to the Great War* (Leonaur, 2009), pp. 139–40.
10. F. I. Maxse, *Seymour Vandeleur: The Story of a British Officer* (London: William Heinemann, 1906), p. 235.
11. F. I. Maxse, *Seymour Vandeleur: The Story of a British Officer*, pp. 237–8.
12. F. I. Maxse, *Seymour Vandeleur: The Story of a British Officer*, pp. 237–8.
13. F. I. Maxse, quoted by J. Baynes, *Far From a Donkey: The Life of Sir Ivor Maxse*, p. 62.
14. National Army Museum: Villiers Hatton, Diary, 2/9/1898.
15. H. M. Farmer, quoted by K. S. Eady, *Cornerstones: The Life of H. M. Farmer from Omdurman to the Western Front*, p. 46.
16. National Army Museum: J. J. Watson, Letter, 11/9/1898.
17. National Army Museum: R. Meiklejohn, Diary, 2/9/1898.
18. G. Egerton, *With the 72nd Highlanders in the Sudan Campaign*, pp. 44–6.
19. A. Hunter, quoted by D. H. Doolittle, *A Soldier's Hero: General Sir Archibald Hunter*, p. 173.
20. E. G. Boyle, Letter, 5/9/1898, quoted in the *Daily Telegraph* (New Zealand), 18/11/1898.
21. The nickname of Major William Gordon, of the Royal Engineers,

the officer commanding the gunboat Melik and a relation of General Gordon.

22. National Army Museum: W. S. Sparkes, Letter, 13/9/1898.

18. Aftermath

1. A. Hunter, quoted by D. Doolittle, *A Soldier's Hero: General Sir Archibald Hunter* (Narragansett: Anawan Publishing Company, 1991), p. 173.

2. National Army Museum: J. J. Watson, Letter, 11/9/1898.

3. The Reverend Robert Brindle of the Royal Army Chaplains' Department. He later became the Bishop of Nottingham.

4. H. Rawlinson, quoted by Frederick Maurice, *The Life of General Lord Rawlinson of Trent* (London: Cassell and Co, Ltd, 1928), p. 42.

5. G. W. Steevens, *With Kitchener to Khartoum* (New York: Dodd, Mead & Company, 1898), p. 313.

6. H. Rawlinson, quoted by Frederick Maurice, *The Life of General Lord Rawlinson of Trent*, p. 42.

7. A. Hunter, quoted by D. Doolittle, *A Soldier's Hero: General Sir Archibald Hunter*, pp. 174–5.

8. W. S. L. Churchill, quoted by R. S. Churchill, *Winston S. Churchill: Youth, 1874–1900 (Volume I)* (Rosetta Books. Kindle edition), pp. 423–4.

9. N. Lyttelton, *Eighty Years: Soldiering, Politics, Games* (Borodino Books. Kindle edition), p. 150.

10. E. Bennett, *Downfall of the Dervishes* (London: Methuen & Co., 1899), pp. 227–9.

11. National Army Museum: W. L. Bagot, Diary, 3/9/1898.

12. N. Lyttelton, *Eighty Years: Soldiering, Politics, Games*, pp. 148–9.

13. D. Haig, quoted by Douglas Scott, *The Preparatory Prologue: Douglas Haig Diaries and Letters* (Barnsley: Pen and Sword Military, 2006), p. 103.

14. F. I. Maxse, *Seymour Vandeleur: The Story of a British Officer* (London: William Heinemann, 1906), p. 227.

15. National Army Museum: J. J. Watson, Letter, 11/9/1898.

16. National Army Museum: J. J. Watson, Letter, 7/9/1898.

17. R. Wingate, quoted by Ronald Wingate, *Wingate of the Sudan: The life and Times of General Sir Reginald Wingate* (London: John Murray, 1955), p. 119–20.

18. R. Wingate, quoted by R. Puch, *Wingate Pasha: The life of General*

Sir Francis Reginald Wingate, 1861–1953 (Barnsley: Pen & Sword Military, 2011), p. 81.

19. A. Hunter, quoted by D. H. Doolittle, *A Soldier's Hero: General Sir Archibald Hunter*, p. 174.

ACKNOWLEDGEMENTS

First, thanks to the National Army Museum who administer a wonderful collection of documents, not forgotten, but carefully catalogued and preserved for historians to use. Second, to all those authors whose brilliant books I have listed in the footnotes. They have provided the personal experience quotes that are at the heart of this book. For obvious reasons, for once there is no oral history! Grateful thanks to Jim Grundy who sent me many suggested quotes and who has set up an excellent Facebook page on *Egypt, Sudan, and Somaliland, 1882–1922*. My chums Gary Bain, John Paylor, Warren Smith and Philip Wood read an early draft with a cheerfulness that belied the amount of moaning they did – sorry, observing – when I sent Gary and Warren chapters over the Christmas break! Thanks to all the team at Profile Books who have shown an amazing degree of tolerance over the years: my editor, Georgia Poplett; the production supremo, Penny Daniel; the wonderful copy editor, Penny Gardiner. As ever thanks to my agent Ian Drury, a man who would bring a touch of class to any Guards Regiment – even riding a camel. Thank you all.

LIST OF ILLUSTRATIONS

Picture Credits

INDEX